WELFARE ECONOMICS

Ten Introductory Essays

SECOND EDITION

CONSULTING EDITOR | **WILLIAM LETWIN**
London School of Economics

WELFARE ECONOMICS

Ten Introductory Essays

Second Edition

by

E. J. Mishan

LONDON SCHOOL OF ECONOMICS

RANDOM HOUSE | NEW YORK |

First Printing

Published in the United States by Random House, Inc., New York, and simultaneously in Canada by Random House of Canada Limited, Toronto.
Library of Congress Catalog Card Number: 69–12894
Manufactured in the United States of America by
The Colonial Press Inc., Clinton, Mass.
Designed by Leon Bolognese

TO MY PARENTS

PREFACE

The practical importance of an understanding of welfare economics can be questioned today only by those unfamiliar with its subject matter. Whether the United Kingdom should finance the building of the supersonic Concord airliner, whether a channel tunnel should be built, whether Britain should enter the Common Market, whether to invest in a road or a railway, or whether to conserve natural beauty and how much, are all political questions which, in so far as they are influenced by economic considerations, must ultimately be referred to the propositions of welfare economics. True, the informed public has recently become aware of such things as public investment criteria, allocation rules, and cost-benefit studies. It is not, however, expected to know that these "new" devices derive their rationale from theories of welfare economics. The student with any claim to formal training in economics, on the other hand, is expected to know not only that welfare economics is central to all discussions of economic policy, but also to have fairly clear notions of the methods and the limitations of that branch of the subject.

The essays in this volume have been selected with such a purpose in mind—to convey to the student of economics, and also to teachers who have not been following developments in this field very closely, a distinct and common sense impression of the chief ideas used in welfare economics together with an account of their limitations. The essays are regarded as introductory in the sense that their subject matter is accessible to anyone who has worked through one of the many excellent economics textbooks for the undergraduate that are now on the market. Except for some occasional and elementary notation no mathematics is used in the text of these papers, and none is required to follow the exposition.

Part 1 contains "A Survey of Welfare Economics, 1939–1959," reprinted here by the kind permission of the editors of the *Economic Journal*. I am immodest enough to believe that, despite the passage of almost a decade, it will still offer to the beginner a useful conspectus of the main areas of the subject. Two modifications of the account provided in the "Survey," one on welfare criteria and the other on the significance of Pareto optimality, are both important enough to be developed later in two papers contained in Part 3, "The Recent Debate on Welfare Criteria," and "Pareto Optimality and the Law," respectively.

Part 2 on concepts of economic surplus contains two short papers; the first, "Realism and Relevance in Consumer's Surplus," was published while I was a student at the London School of Economics. Its aim was to make simple sense of a concept over which there was a good deal of controversy and misunderstanding at the time of writing, despite excellent papers by Henderson and Hicks also published in the same journal, *Review of Economic Studies,* during the early 1940s. The other paper, "Rent as a Measure of Welfare Change," *American Economic Review* (1959), is obviously complementary to the consumer's surplus paper and, indeed, comprehends it. That rent ought to be treated symmetrically with consumer's surplus is something which economists have long comprehended even though, in deference perhaps to Ricardo and Marshall, they continued to define it in the traditional way with minor modifications. Setting the definition of rent on all fours with consumer's surplus was, therefore, an inevitable step, and the general reader who has not by now thought it out for himself should have no difficulty in assimilating the definition and, also, the greater generality of the budget constraint that accompanies it. I did take the opportunity in the paper to indicate the flexibility of the economic surplus concept and the manner in which, conceptually at least, the surpluses arising from simultaneous changes in factor and product prices may be added together.

Part 3 on some crucial aspects of welfare economics begins with the "Reappraisal of the Principles of Resource Allocation," *Economica* (1957), and was written specifically to correct the unwarranted conclusion I had reached in the paper "The Principle of Compensation Reconsidered," published five years earlier as a graduate student at the University of Chicago. The more useful parts of that paper, in particular the geometric construction of community indifference curves are, however, reproduced in the "Reappraisal" in order that the new paper be self-contained. Though the treatment in the "Reappraisal" has the earmarks of a possibility theorem, one that prevents us drawing any of the familiar conclusions about taxes, subsidies, tariffs, and optimal positions, I prefer to regard the main contribution of the paper as specifying the kinds of empirical information we must have before we can affirm such conclusions.

The "Second Thoughts on Second Best" paper, *Oxford Economic Papers* (1962), is not to be construed as an attack on the Lipsey-Lancaster paper of 1957, which is to be counted as one of the landmarks in the economist's progress toward increased sophistication. All that was said in their seminal paper needed to be said, and it is to the credit of the authors that they stated their case cogently and, indeed, elegantly. There was, however, a danger at that time of its implications being misconstrued by impatient and incautious students as amounting to a sweeping condemnation of any attempt to apply allocative rules to an economy. My paper was no more than a response to the need to place their contribution in better perspective. Other contributions, in particular that of H. A. John Green in 1963 and by Davis and Whinston in 1965 (both in the *Review of Economic Studies*), cover some of the same ground as I do, but their results are derived mathematically as distinct from the intuitive approach employed by me.

The third paper, "The Recent Debate on Welfare Criteria," *Oxford Economic Papers* (1965), summarizes the famous "Exchange of Notes" which was started in the 1962 *Economic Journal* by the late Sir Dennis Robertson and in which Professors J. E. Meade and I. M. D. Little also participated, as well as the exchanges between C. M. Kennedy, A. K. Sen, and myself in the following year. Tests of hypothetical compensation are among the slipperiest concepts invented by economists and without the use of such constructs as the community indifference curve and the Samuelson utility possibility curve, initially elusive differences of interpretation could not have been mapped out so plainly, and made intelligible to the nonspecialist. What finally emerges from the debate is that apparently acceptable dual welfare criteria may favor an economic change that has in fact very little to commend it.

In the "Reflections on Recent Developments in the Concept of External Effects," *Canadian Journal of Economic and Political Science,* the attempt is made to sift the chaff from the grain provided by some of the better-known contributions to one of the most useful concepts in welfare economics.

The final paper in Part 3, "Pareto Optimality and the Law," *Oxford Economic Papers* (1967), is a formalization of a theme contained in Chapters 5 and 6 of my antigrowth book, *The Costs of Economic Growth.* The comfortable view that, "ideally" at least, an optimal output would be obtained irrespectively of which of the conflicting parties attempts to bribe the other may well have stood in the way of economists lending weight to a reform of the law in favor of the victims of the growing incidence of "spillover effects." The paper constitutes an attempt to convince economists that the legal issue of who is to compensate whom is not "merely" a distributional one. It has significant allocational implications also.

Part 4 contains two recent essays. The first, "Interpretation of the Benefits of Private Transport," *Journal of Transport Economics and Policy* (1967), sounds a warning against the sloppy use of measures of consumers' surplus. Unless precautions are taken one may conclude that social benefits of private motoring are growing when in fact they are shrinking. More positively it reminds us that certain stringent conditions have to be met before the ostensible measure of wealth, or cost-saving, has the significance commonly attached to it.

The final essay, "A Proposed Normalization Procedure for Public Investment Criteria," *Economic Journal* (1967), was inspired by what seemed to me to be some unnecessarily complex investment criteria put forward by competent writers who were unanimous in rejecting the internal rate-of-return method. However, all rejections of the internal rate-of-return method appeared to arise from illustrations purporting to reveal its inferiority to the present discounted-value method. No general theoretical argument against its use was put forward. It was in trying to discover whether such a a general case could be made that it occurred to me that, when "properly" interpreted—that is, when the investment streams were normalized in the manner proposed—both the present discounted-value criteria and internal rate-of-return criteria necessarily gave identical results. One cannot vouch for the significance of the discovery but it is always gratifying to a theoretical mind to be able to remove anomolies of this kind.

A final word concerns the references to bibliographic entries. Numbers in type matching the text, appearing in brackets, refer to the Bibliography section at the back of the book. Numbers in boldface type—these are also in brackets—refer to entries in the References sections that follow chapters 6, 7, 8, and 9.

Permission to reprint these papers has been given by the editors of the *American Economic Review*, the *Canadian Journal of Economic and Political Science*, the *Economic Journal, Economica*, the *Journal of Transport Economics and Policy, Oxford Economic Papers*, and the *Review of Economic Studies*. I appreciate their kind and immediate response to my requests.

E. J. M.
London

CONTENTS

Introduction 3

Part 1 **Survey** 9

CHAPTER 1 *Survey of Welfare Economics—1939–1959* 11

Part 2 **Concepts of Economic Surplus** 87

Surplus 89
CHAPTER 2 *Realism and Relevance in Consumer's*
CHAPTER 3 *Rent as a Measure of Welfare Change* 102

Part 3 **Crucial Aspects of Welfare Economics** 115

CHAPTER 4 *A Reappraisal of the Principles of Resource Allocation* 117
CHAPTER 5 *Second Thoughts on Second Best* 141
CHAPTER 6 *The Recent Debate on Welfare Criteria* 157
CHAPTER 7 *Reflections on Recent Developments in the Concept of External Effects* 180
CHAPTER 8 *Pareto Optimality and the Law* 225

Part 4 **Applications of Welfare Economics** 273

CHAPTER 9 *Interpretation of the Benefits of Private Transport* 275

CHAPTER 10 *A Proposed Normalization Procedure for Public Investment Criteria* 284

Bibliography 311

Index 323

WELFARE ECONOMICS

Ten Introductory Essays

SECOND EDITION

Introduction

Academic economists appear to suffer no qualms from the fact that, at this moment in history, welfare economics is in rather a bedraggled state and, as an organized study, much neglected. This is unfortunate, for never since the early nineteenth century has the prestige of economics been so high. If economic advice has been eagerly sought in the postwar period, it has no less eagerly been proffered. Armed with the latest ideas on monetary and fiscal policy, with powerful statistical techniques, and with such fashionable contraptions as input-output models and mathematical programming, the professional economist is now to be found in every corner of the world vigorously plying his trade. He is a popular medicine man both in the richer countries which can afford his occasional follies and in the poorer countries which cannot. Much of the advice he offers is, of course, little more than common sense: if there is general unemployment he will propose stimulating effective demand; if there is inflation he will propose monetary and fiscal measures to reduce effective demand; if there are areas of dire poverty he will recommend that governments take more initiative in redistributive policies; if there is widespread inefficiency in productive methods he will want to call in foreign experts; if there is a crucial shortage of capital he will propose measures for tapping domestic and foreign sources. There will always be differences of opinion about timing, magnitudes, and the precise measures to be employed, but there will nonetheless be broad agreement about the policies inasmuch as there is broad agreement about the ends to be realized. On the other hand, a good deal of the advice the economist offers is about allocation proper. In so far as it increases the outputs of some products without diminishing the supplies of other products, there can be general agreement that such advice is useful. However, allocation economics invariably goes farther than this: it seeks to determine which outputs are to be expanded and which are to be curtailed. To put the matter in another light, the economist, whether employing informal methods of analysis or whether distilling his inspiration from a linear programming model, directly or implicitly has recourse to a set of product prices for the economy, or area, in question. And he carries this off despite the fact that there is, as yet, no established theory of welfare economics to justify his procedure.

This is a fact which we economists seem loath to face up to. Our continual evasion of it can be attributed partly to ignorance of the full implications of the methods employed. Sometimes we are dazzled by the apparent elegance of the new techniques, for it is, perhaps, hard to believe that such conspicuous virtues as they manifest—balance, precision, symmetry—do not issue in propositions of great truth and generality. But more often we seem to be in too great a hurry to "get on with the job," and to demonstrate the wondrous flexibility of our new gadgets, to pause and to acknowledge, even to ourselves, that unless specific ends are entrusted to us—and they seldom are—specific recommendations of what has to be done presuppose social ends or definitions of the social good which the economist—glib though he is about allocation rules, about increasing "social value," or about maximizing *the* objective function—does not make explicit.

Indeed, he cannot do so, for the question of social ends or of welfare criteria is the one crucial question to which welfare economists have frequently addressed themselves in the last few years, though without coming close to any common conclusion. Moreover, if the recent exchange of notes in the *Economic Journal* is anything to go by, what agreement there might have been seems to be in a state of rapid dissolution. Out of the current chaos we can but hope that some new synthesis of reconstruction will shortly emerge.

Turning to the subject at large, economics is in one respect like the physical sciences. The rapid development of techniques continues unabated though basic philosophical uncertainties remain with us. In this respect, however, economics has a unique responsibility, for it is more than just another discipline devoted to shaping tools of analysis or, as we should now put it, to evolving fruitful hypotheses. The world we live in is being transformed ever more swiftly by "built-in" technological progress, and economics finds itself in a position of authority inasmuch as it is believed, rightly or wrongly, to sanction this sustained social upheaval resulting therefrom and to sanction also the economic system which generates it. And many economists do sanction it, though sometimes inadvertently, by frequent indulgence in facile and misleading phrases such as "the expansion of the horizon of choices," though reserving for themselves a right of stricture in relatively minor matters: in problems involving the balance of payments, the extent of existing monopoly power, the structure of the tax system, government spending, price supports, subsidies, and the like. By avoiding the more searching questions suggested by the study of welfare criteria, by their broad acceptance of the existing system, still directed largely by private enterprise, and by their apparent acceptance of the sort of technology that is emerging therefrom, value judgments are implied which ought to be made explicit. The current attitude of all too many economists then, their concentration on familiar points of controversy while unwilling to reassess the rationale of the existing social structure, in particular the adequacy of the market mechanisms in the face of unprecedented technological advance, does have far-reaching consequences. For their sanction of the market cannot be confined to its function as a "neutral mechanism" reliably responding to changing patterns of demand. The sanction must also extend to the private sector aspect of the market, in which guise it is seen as an active agency for promoting innovation, for selecting the types of gadgets it offers to the public and, above all, as an agent of ruthless persuasion in molding the material and psychological climate in which we are caught. Though the economist today might wish to deny responsibility and take refuge in the dicta of positive economics, his image in the eyes of the public leaves him no choice. He may argue, albeit unconvincingly, that he is as much an ordinary John Citizen as victim of his environment, and that *qua* economist he has nothing to say about what ought to be done. Yet a future generation may see him as having conspired by his very passivity to impart a direction to events the consequences of which, could they be foreseen today, would be universally condemned.

True, we cannot be expected to foresee all the many consequences of current economic activity. But this is no reason for not directing more of our intellectual resources into probing further into the basic questions. In view of the current population explosion, the swelling cataracts of motorized traffic, the growing avalanche of organized tourism, the technological striving for yet faster speeds that only results in increased travel time and jams us one into the other, creating confusion and frustration, the endless noise, vibration, and psychological pressure to keep up, the collapse of organized faith, and the apparent disintegration of mores and morals—in view of all this, one must be well under thirty, or else recklessly optimistic, to feel any confidence in the economic growth that has resulted from private enterprise as a factor contributing to the future happiness of mankind.

One word of warning, however. Although welfare economics is in a quandary right now, it does not follow that we do nothing until we have found a way out of the current impasse. For one thing, we can be more honest with ourselves and confess openly that we do not seem to know quite what we are doing when we are "maximizing welfare." For another, welfare economics, even in its present shaken state, can perform a modest role. For instance, in certain limited circumstances, which ought to be spelled out in detail, it may suggest a better economic organization than the existing one. In underdeveloped countries, it may be possible to prescribe policies designed to ensure that more of some goods are produced without any reduction of other goods, and without any other unwanted consequences. Again, in certain situations, the welfare economist may reveal the nature, and even guess at the magnitude, of conspicuous external economies or diseconomies, making it apparent that—second-best theory notwithstanding—current production determined by commercial considerations is too small or too large.

The world today is in a frightful hurry, and with people too busy selling the future to one another, one cannot expect such staid suggestions that we pause, look around us, and ponder a great deal more, to be recognized as sterling advice. I should, therefore, be pleasantly surprised to know if anything in this volume has led to some occasional head-scratching on some fundamental questions about the nature of current economic prescription, about the value of economic growth, or perhaps, in more cynical moods, about what it is after all that the world economy is maximizing right now—other than gross productive power, or human population on this planet.

PART 1

SURVEY

CHAPTER 1

A Survey of Welfare Economics, 1939–1959*[1]

I. Introduction

While it continues to fascinate many, welfare economics does not appear at any time to have wholly engaged the labors of any one economist. It is a subject which, apparently, one dabbles in for a while, leaves and, perhaps, returns to later in response to a troubled conscience—which goes some way to explain why, more than other branches of economics, it suffers from an unevenness in its development, a lack of homogeneity in its treatment, and until very recently, a distressing disconnectedness between its parts.[2]

A survey of the literature, therefore, which sought to do no more than elucidate in rough chronological order the ideas of the

* From *Economic Journal,* Vol. 70 (1960), pp. 197–256.

[1] I wish to acknowledge, with gratitude, the services of Dr. S. A. Ozga, who gave freely of his time in discussing a first draft with me. The paper has benefited greatly from his many suggestions and criticisms. I am indebted also to Mr. Klappholz for some useful criticism on my excursion into methodology, and to Mrs. Diana Oldershaw for thoroughness and care in the cheerless task of compiling a bibliography. (See pp. 311–322.)

[2] Little's *Critique,* in my opinion, has gone far to remedy this particular defect.

chief writers, while it might whet the appetite of some, would almost certainly leave the mind of the general reader in a dazed and dissatisfied condition. An alternative procedure, and that adopted here, is the bolder one of occasionally tightening up loose connections and, especially in the later sections, suggesting, if not adopting, a particular perspective. While such a method imparts a more coherent picture than could possibly emerge from a noncommittal account of the principal ideas, some degree of personal predilection is obviously unavoidable. It is a matter of prudence that the reader at all times bear this in mind.

On the question of coverage, since welfare economics is here understood as analysis—theoretical welfare economics, as it is sometimes called—and not the application of welfare propositions to economic situations, everything in the larger literature on economic policy has been disregarded. Index numbers, as indicators of welfare changes, are given only footnote treatment, since in all essentials the problems associated with them are the same as those uncovered in the controversy over hypothetical compensation, a matter discussed at some length in Section III. Excluded also is the controversial field of socialist economics except in so far as theoretical innovations are thrown up by the disputants. Again, the accent being on the formal development of welfare economics, the nonstatic aspects inevitably receive less attention.[3] Thus, until Section V, the framework of our exposition remains a static one. No growth or innovation takes place, no uncertainty exists, and individual tastes remain unaltered. In addition, the working population is fixed and is, in some sense, fully employed. Within this framework it is further assumed that individual behavior is consistent, and—unless otherwise proposed—that the individual is the best judge of his own wants.

To avoid tedious qualification at every stage of the analysis, we shall assume henceforth, unless otherwise indicated, that each individual consumes some of each of the goods and supplies some of each of the factors in the economy; that all goods and factors are sufficiently divisible to warrant the concept of marginal adjust-

[3] A great deal of welfare economics, in the broader meanings of the term, is spoken by the elder-statesman type of economist, and much of it rings wise and true. But while it warns us, rightly, of the limitations of our analysis, it does not contribute directly to the formal development of the subject. Some of these broader considerations, however, are touched upon in the final section.

ment; that each class of goods or factors is a homogeneous group, any unit in that group being a perfect substitute for any other; and, lastly, that all relevant functions are differentiable and have sufficient curvature to yield tangency solutions.[4] Nothing unexpected or fundamental emerges from the removal of any of these simplifications, with the exception of divisibility. The consequence of removing this simplification is, however, dealt with in Section IV and an occasional footnote. Finally, in order to purge the text of continual amplification, illustration, and comment, which would otherwise impede the flow of the argument, footnotes have been freely resorted to. The general reader is advised to omit them on a first reading.

Since we have affirmed that the subject matter of this survey is theoretical welfare economics, we may begin by hazarding a definition of the term. Theoretical welfare economics is, then, that branch of study which endeavors to formulate propositions by which we may rank, on the scale of better or worse, alternative economic situations open to society. The words "better" and "worse" obviously call for clarification, and to this end we first consider the situation of the individual. His indifference map may be regarded as a picture of his chosen ranking of the conceivable combinations of goods and services. If we say that when he moves to a higher indifference curve (or that when he expands the effective area of his choice[5]) he is better off, or he increases his welfare, we are giving expression to an ethical judgment; namely (*a*) that the individual—and no one else—is the best judge of his own well-being. In the Crusoe economy no more than this is required for welfare economics. But it is required. Without it, we may re-

[4] If the functions are not differentiable we get kinks and corner solutions. If they have insufficient curvature we have corner solutions in the choice of output possibilities, and boundary optima in exchange situations. In such cases, though the optimal solution in terms of outputs is unambiguous, relative prices may be indeterminate within a wide range. Treatment of these things is popular in the literature on linear programming.

[5] An interesting suggestion for welfare economics in terms of expanded choice rather than indifference curves has been made by Lancaster [142]. (See Bibliography, p. 317). Though it transpired that the definitions he adopted were not consistent (see [183], [64], and [191]), it should not be hard to think of some consistent set of definitions which would enable us to determine changes in welfare by reference only to budget data, like index numbers. However, one cannot envisage any great advantage for welfare economics from this innovation.

Since the above note was written, Lancaster has submitted a new set of definitions and a general proof in the *Economic Journal* (December 1959).

mark that Crusoe moves to a higher indifference curve, but we are then only describing how Crusoe acts: we are not judging his welfare. We can agree that under the utility hypothesis the individual believes himself to be better off in choosing a goods combination II rather than I. But since it is we, as welfare economists, who are to decide how to rank the alternatives facing him, unless we are agreed to accept his own ranking as final, his preference field is irrelevant as an index of his welfare.

Since welfare economics is, however, concerned chiefly with community welfare, we shall require additional ethical judgments. The most widely accepted of these is (*b*) that the welfare of the community depends on the welfare of the individuals comprising it, and on nothing else. The mathematical expression of this statement is, of course, Bergson's social-welfare function in its general form, discussed in Section II. We can make this function a little more specific by attributing to it an ethical property which, it is believed, most people will accept—(*c*) that if at least one person is better off, no one being worse off, the community as a whole is better off.[6]

Turning to the more likely case, in which changes in economic organization make some people better off and others worse off, several avenues are open to us: (d_1) we can defer final judgment on the alternative patterns of welfare open to the community until we have completely specified the social-welfare function—that is, until we have ranked all possible combinations of individual welfares—which, in practice, means that we shall defer it indefinitely;[7] (d_2) we can exercise our judgment about resulting welfare distributions whenever we have to rank alternative situations. And, we may go further, and indicate the guiding aim of our policy on distribution, such as to equalize real incomes in some sense. Finally, (d_3) we might try to evade this judgment on welfare distribution by the conservative principle of compensated adjustment. We must suppose, as in (d_1), that any degree of welfare redistribution is feasible, and, on this principle, redistribute in

[6] In such cases Graaff [84] would say that the social-welfare function was of the "Paretian type."

[7] It may be noted in passing that the view that a prior mapping of a boundary encompassing all possible welfare combinations open to the community may proceed without ethical presuppositions reckons without ethical judgments (*a*) and (*b*) above.

order that no one is left worse off, though some are better off, in effect meeting the criterion (*c*) above.

There remains the question of methodology, which is touched upon only in the slightest manner in the formal treatment of this subject.[8] The question to be answered is whether welfare propositions, like positive propositions in economics, are capable of being tested. In the latter we postulate a set of propositions, or axioms, *A*, and test the implications, *B*. In effect, hypotheses about welfare can be cast into the form, if *W* then *R*; by which we mean that if we accept certain assumptions about the nature of the economic universe, and if we accept some particular definition of an improvement in social welfare, then we can draw an inference, *R*—namely, that when certain conditions are met social welfare is increased. This inference, *R*, a welfare proposition, can, conceptually, at least, be subjected to a test, inasmuch as we can inquire of each person whether or not he is better off, or else compare the ranges of goods available to him in two alternative situations.

Formally, then, propositions in welfare economics may be subjected to tests in the same way as those of positive economics. But there are far greater difficulties involved in testing an implication "fulfilling these conditions will make everyone better off" than in testing, say, the implication "if the price rises he will consume less." Generally, in positive economics any of the implications we seek to observe are simpler than direct tests of the set of axioms from which it is deduced—if these axioms can be tested at all. In welfare economics, however, if anything it seems the other way about: a test of the implications is more difficult than a direct test of the assumptions. Indeed, so remote is the likelihood of testing welfare implications that one is tempted to relinquish

[8] An exception to this opinion is a recent and highly stimulating paper by G. C. Archibald [6], to which I am extremely indebted. It is difficult, however, to accept his suggestion that welfare economics can be studied without committing ourselves to welfare judgments by the simple expedient of sewing them on to a definition of welfare. This, of course, is possible, but no worthwhile advantage seems to follow from this ruse. The definition, he concedes, if it is to wear, must be "interesting." But an "interesting" definition, in the context of welfare, is surely one that has broad ethical appeal. A definition which embodies no acceptable ethical proposition and yet is interesting to someone, is interesting only as a weird exercise. In order to decide whether a definition of an improvement in social welfare is to be adopted as the base on which to erect welfare propositions, we are impelled to ponder on its ethical implications.

the orthodox methodology and have recourse to an admittedly inferior method—some might say an inadmissible method—of attempting to ascertain the validity of the premises, W. After all, if (a) the assumptions about consistency and the shapes of the technological and behavior functions are correct, and (b) if no other considerations are relevant, then good logic ensures that the implication, R, follows—that if the rules deduced are met, welfare, as defined, is increased.

Both these are, of course, very big ifs. In regard to (b), since our attention may be drawn to additional considerations as the subject progresses, we can never be sure we have not overlooked some factor which bears on the individual's welfare. As for (a), some of the assumptions have so far entered into positive theorizing that their undeniable usefulness as assumptions has come to be associated with a belief in their validity. We may decide, after all, that people are in fact sufficiently consistent, and that tastes are sufficiently constant for the period in question, to make little difference to the result. As for the others: the nature of the production functions involved, the relationship between income distribution and relative prices, the interdependence of individual welfares, may gradually yield to patient investigation, so that any assumption about these things can be more than mere guesses. But it is a slow business. In the meantime, the practice has been to allow for our ignorance about such functional relations by requiring that our welfare propositions hold for all conceivable properties of such functions—a procedure which is, perhaps, too severe a test of the applicability of welfare propositions, and is, apparently, in large measure responsible for the indiscriminate pessimism now in vogue,[9] a matter which will receive further attention in the final part of this survey.

The above remarks are to be understood as an attempt to explicate the kind of methodology which appears consistent with the writings of the better-known economists, and to elaborate the sense of the frequent statement that welfare propositions rest on both factual and ethical assumptions. Unless both are granted, the first

[9] The word to be underlined here is *indiscriminate*. There may well be grounds for pessimism concerning the scope for applications of welfare economics, but, as is contended in the final section, most of the pessimism generated is for the wrong reasons.

as being "realistic," the second as being "widely acceptable," the welfare propositions deduced from them are of no practical importance.

II. The Optimum Conditions

Looking back over the last two decades at developments in welfare economics, the names that most readily spring to mind are those of Bergson, Kaldor, Hicks, Scitovsky, Samuelson, Little, Arrow, and Graaff. The temptation is to plunge at once into a discussion of the welfare criteria proposed by Kaldor, Hicks, Scitovsky, and others, and of the social-welfare function introduced by Bergson, and later explored by Arrow and others, for these are the things which excited the most controversy at the time and still pique the curiosity by their elusiveness. For the purpose of exposition, however, this temptation is to be resisted. During the period in which these welfare criteria were being subjected to close scrutiny, treatment of the optimum conditions was one of the staple materials in textbooks on welfare economics, and examples of their application continued to pour into the journals. A survey of this more pedestrian activity, which can usefully be regarded as a search for the necessary conditions of a position of maximum social welfare, is logically anterior in that the range of welfare possibilities open to society should be unfolded prior to the engagement of an apparatus of social choice involving ethical judgments. The next few pages, therefore, will be taken up with the examination of the optimum conditions of social welfare, leaving social-welfare functions and welfare criteria (which may be thought of as properties of a social-welfare function) to be dealt with in Section III.

THE THIRTIES

Although several noteworthy contributions appeared in the thirties, no common mode of treatment emerged. For one thing, while the welfare import of a Crusoe economy seemed plain enough, the significance for the community as a whole of meeting the so-called optimum conditions was not always clearly understood. For another, there were a variety of ways in which an optimum position might be expressed and discrepancies among authors as to the proper number of conditions necessary to identify it. A comparison in these respects of the various contributions, in order of appearance, would be a fascinating if exhausting game. The intellectual reward, however, would be slight. We therefore omit in the text further reference to the pre-1939 literature on this aspect[10] except for a few paragraphs on Pigou and Bergson, a brief appraisal of the main features of whose works provide the necessary background to the developments of the period that concerns us.

The standard work of reference in the interwar period was, of

[10] The somewhat disconnected nature of earlier developments in this field can be illustrated by outlining some of the principal features of three well-known contributions in the thirties; in chronological order, Lerner, Kahn, and Hotelling.

In his article on monopoly (A. P. Lerner, "The Concept of Monopoly and the Measurement of Monopoly Power," *Review of Economic Studies* [1934]), Lerner adopts as a definition of optimum a situation in which no individual can improve his welfare without making another worse off. It is met when the rates of substitution between pairs of goods for all individuals are equal to the technical rate of substitution. According to Lerner, this translates into the condition that product price ratios be proportional to marginal displacement costs, which condition is satisfied if price equals marginal cost. Any divergence between price and marginal cost is a measure of loss entailed by monopoly power.

In his later paper on Socialism ("Economic Theory and Socialist Economy," *Review of Economic Studies* [1934]), without saying more about optimum, he introduces the condition that all factors have the same ratio of marginal physical products, failing which a net increase of output is possible. Though Kahn (R. F. Kahn, "Some Notes on Ideal Output," *Economic Journal* [1935]) objects to Lerner's calling this condition an objective test on the grounds that it may be fulfilled while at the same time the "wrong" amounts of goods are produced, a rereading of Lerner reveals that its objectivity consists in its being recognizable by a government bureaucrat producing goods in accordance with some arbitrary scale of values. Significantly, Lerner adds that a pricing system eliminates not only this source of waste but also that from producing the "wrong" goods when measured against people's demands, the latter source of waste being the more important.

Since the apparent purpose of Kahn's paper on ideal output was to put a sharper edge on some of the Pigovian tools, he adopted Pigou's welfare objective of maximizing the national dividend. To do this without reference to distribution is, according to Kahn, to suppose we are maximizing the satisfaction which would obtain if differences in the marginal utility of money to different people did not exist. So as not to become involved in distributional problems he assumes this to be the case, and is able, therefore, to take the price of a commodity, or factor, as denoting its marginal utility, or disutility, respectively, for the community. These latter assumptions, it may be observed in passing, are not those adopted by Pigou in his *Economics of Welfare*.

Kahn's paper is remembered chiefly for its amendment of two corollaries of the Pigovian system. First, whereas Pigou would have expanded industries with external economies and contracted those with external diseconomies in the belief that these effects were the exception rather than the rule, Kahn proposed that, in the event of such effects being common, the rule should be such as to shift recourse, Pigou's *Economics of Welfare*.[11] In scope, in erudition, in systematic and lucid exposition, the work is a classic which no interested student can read without pleasure and, indeed, without occasional wonder. Mention of issues which are at the hub of current controversy may be discovered ensconced in the middle of an innocent-looking paragraph or tucked away modestly in some passing footnote. Aware of the obstacles to any generalization in this field, Pigou moves cautiously. Only welfare which can be brought into relationship with the measuring rod of money falls within his province. For the most part he declines the services of the partial consumer's surplus technique initially favored by Marshall, preferring a more general approach, and adopts a dual criterion for the detection of improvements in social welfare: an increase in the national dividend without any increase in the supply of factors, and a transfer of wealth from rich to poor. In regard to the first, while there are insuperable difficulties in measuring the national dividend as a total figure, an increase in its value—brought about either by increasing some goods without diminishing others or by transferring factors to activities in which their social value is higher

---

sources from industries whose external economies were below the average to those industries where they were above the average. Second, and more of a departure from tradition, in the absence of external effects, the industries to expand are those whose ratios of price to marginal cost are above the average, and the industries to contract are those whose ratios are below the average. Ideal output requires no more than an equal degree of monopoly in all sectors of the economy. Criticism of this latter proposition seems to have ignored his "provisional" assumption that all factors were perfectly inelastic in supply.

Hotelling's famous paper (H. Hotelling, "The General Welfare in Relation to the Problems of Taxation and of Railway and Utility Rates," *Econometrica* [1938]) was one of the first attempts to vindicate the partial welfare approach of consumers' and producers' surplus in the light of a general welfare analysis. His fundamental theorem attempted to demonstrate that any excise tax which replaced an income tax yielding the same revenue placed the individual in a less-preferred position. A bridge, or other public utility, in which price was set above marginal cost (in order that total receipts cover total costs in decreasing-cost projects) was an example of an excise tax on a product or service in contrast to the alternative of raising the requisite revenue by an income tax, leaving price to equal marginal cost in the public utility.

A rather different argument is used later in the paper to uphold the consumer's surplus notion, which anticipates by a few months the Kaldor formula: if, in introducing an investment, some distribution of the burden is possible such that everyone concerned is better off than without it, there is a prima facie case for introducing it. This, he admits, leaves aside the question of whether the necessary distribution is practical. Provided, however, the benefits are great and widespread, it should be introduced even if some are actually made worse off. Extreme hardship, however, would warrant compensation.

[11] A. C. Pigou, *The Economics of Welfare*, 4th ed. (London; Macmillan, 1932).

—is deemed an improvement in welfare provided that the share of the poor is not thereby reduced. As for the second, any reorganization of the economy which increases the share of the poor without injuring the national dividend is to be accepted as a gain in social welfare. Any other consequence of economic reorganization is ambiguous.

In order that output be truly ideal we must measure in terms of social, and not private, value; hence, his clear distinction between (i) the value of the marginal *private* net product, which is no more than the marginal physical product of the factor, as appropriated by the producer, times the market price of that product, and (ii) the value of the marginal *social* net product, which is the total of the products and services arising from the employment of the additional factor, no matter to whom they may accrue, each product or service being multiplied by the relevant market price. A large part of the book is devoted to pointing up situations in which (i) and (ii) diverge. In the event that (ii) exceeds (i) in any industry, that industry is to be expanded. If the reverse is true, the industry is to be contracted.

The Economics of Welfare is frequently associated with the controversies of the thirties over interpersonal comparisons of utility. But its enduring contribution is to be found in the continued emphasis on the vital distinction between social and private valuations of economic activities, a distinction evoked nowadays more by reference to "external effects" or "external economies and diseconomies of production and consumption."

Though Bergson's seminal paper appeared in 1938,[12] his influence on several of the later writers was marked. In particular, Lange, Samuelson, Arrow, and Graaff[13] drew inspiration from his approach and technique. The approach used was the time-honored one of constructing a more general model under which the contributions of the previous writers could conveniently be grouped. In essence, social welfare was to be thought of as some function of the goods bought, and the factors supplied, by each of the individuals in the community plus, for completeness, any other relevant variables. Without giving it any specific form, this

[12] A. Bergson, "A Reformulation of Certain Aspects of Welfare Economics," *Quarterly Journal of Economics* (1938).

[13] See bibliography, items 144, 222, 14, and 24.

social-welfare function can be maximized subject to the constraints of the production functions. Of the variety of expressions which can be concocted of the first-order conditions for this maximum, Bergson selects four which lend themselves to the following interpretation:

1. The marginal social welfare "per dollar" of each commodity be the same for all individuals.
2. The marginal social diswelfare "per dollar" of each kind of work be the same for all individuals.
3. The marginal-value productivity of each type of labor be equal to the wage of that type of labor.
4. The increment in value from shifting a marginal unit of any nonlabor factor from a good *X* to a good *Y* be equal to the costs involved in this shift. This condition is more familiar in the special case in which the costs of shifting the factor are nil. The condition then requires that the value of the marginal product be the same in all uses.[14]

Conditions (1) and (2) are but formal corollaries of a maximum welfare position for society: in the jargon, they have no more "operational significance" than the equal marginal utilities per penny at which the "discerning" consumer aims. If by unanimous consent the distribution of the work and of the product are ideal, these two conditions are deemed to be fulfilled: no other test is possible.

Bergson's method had the virtue of recognizing that the latter two conditions containing the rules for ideal output were separable from any prepossessions about the distribution of welfare which would be reflected in the first two conditions, an inference which was in contradistinction to the impressions conveyed by certain of the Cambridge writers, that they could be accepted only in conjunction with a particular distribution of welfare, equality.[15]

[14] As may be gathered from a further reading of the text, condition (3) may be viewed as a special case of a more general interpretation of condition (4), extended: (*a*) to cover all factors and not merely nonhuman ones, and to apply to all occupations including leisure, and (*b*) to include, in the differences in welfare referred to, the preferences of resource-owners as between occupations in addition to external economies and diseconomies.

[15] On the other hand, Bergson states that only the Cambridge School (which he associates with Marshall, Edgeworth, Pigou, and Kahn) have a clear-cut social-welfare function. If social welfare is the sum of the individual utilities, di-

DEVELOPMENT AFTER 1939

Though continually displayed at slightly different angles by the various writers, the optimum conditions after 1939 began to look distinctly shopworn. A chronological reading imparts more of a sense of repetition than of evolution. Our purpose will be served with least tedium if, therefore, we proceed at once to an exposition of the logic of the optimum as it appears today, illustrating in footnotes the practice of some of the chief writers.

In their various formulations all of the optimum conditions are derivable from what is commonly called a Pareto optimum,[16] defined as a position from which it is not possible, by any reallocation of factors, to make anyone better off without making at least one person worse off (or, more briefly henceforth; to make "everyone" better off).[17] Since, at this level of abstraction, no institutional restrictions are placed on the degree of factor movement, large or small, a true summit position is implied. In general, there are many such summit positions, each characterized by a different distribution of welfare.[18] Only a particular form of the

---

minishing marginal utility implies that the maximum social welfare is consistent only with equality of the marginal utility of money income among all individuals. If all have equal capacity for enjoyment, this first-order condition for a maximum is fulfilled when all incomes are the same. Francis Ysidro Edgeworth, the first editor of the *Economic Journal,* was not, of course, a Cambridge economist. At seventeen he entered Trinity College, Dublin, and then went on to Magdalene Hall, and Balliol, Oxford. Later he became Tooke Professor of Political Economy at King's College, London, after which he was Drummond Professor of Political Economy at Oxford. Sir Roy Harrod, in correspondence with me, has made it plain from his fairly intimate acquaintance with the man, that Edgeworth's approach and style of thought were very much in contrast with those of the Cambridge School. He was catholic in his views, extremely widely read, and had a high regard for certain continental writers, such as Auspitz, and Lieben and Pierson. Though he shared in some of the views of the Cambridge School, he laid a special stress on the *inequality* of capacities for enjoyment and, therefore, on the desirability of an unequal distribution of income.

[16] See V. Pareto, *Cours d'Economie Politique,* 2 (Lausanne, 1897), 90 ff., and also E. Barone, "The Ministry of Production in the Collectivist State," in F. A. von Hayek (ed.), *Collectivist Economic Planning* (London: Routledge, 1935).

[17] When used as an abbreviation of the relevant expression, "everyone" will be placed in quotation marks, otherwise it carries its normal meaning. If the goods were sufficiently divisible, then a situation in which at least one could be better off and no one worse off would also be a situation in which, literally, everyone could be made better off.

[18] To choose as between such positions we must therefore be prepared to make ethical judgments.

social-welfare function enables us to select among all summit positions that yielding the highest social welfare. The Cambridge concept of ideal output, or ideal allocation of factors, a position from which no reshuffling of factors can add to the social value of the total product, expresses essentially the same idea as a summit or Paretian optimum position.[19] However, its attainment is contingent upon the fulfillment of a single rule, which we shall designate the *allocative rule,* requiring that the value, at the margin, of any class of factor be the same in all occupations in which it is used.

In consequence, as we should expect, the allocative rule is equivalent to any one of the alternative statements of the optimum conditions. Ignoring for the present the distinction between private and social valuation, and assuming for the moment, as does Pigou, that factor supplies are perfectly inelastic, we can decompose the allocative rule into three popular optimum conditions.[20] (1) *The Exchange optimum,* which requires that for each individual, the rate of substitution be the same for all pairs of goods in the economy.[21] It is simple to demonstrate with the aid of the familiar box diagram[22] that no movement from a tangency position can make both individuals better off. (2) *The Production optimum,* which requires that for each product the rate of substitution between any pair of factors be the same.[23] Once this condi-

[19] Lerner's "Rule" for the Controlled Economy [148, Chapter 16]—six conditions linked by equality signs—amounts to the Pigou condition that the value of the marginal social net product be the same in all uses *plus* those conditions under which, in a decentralized economy, firms will in fact realize the Pigou conditions, assuming a coincidence of private and social net products.

Though tested in the increasing complexity of successive chapters, the Rule emerges triumphant. Even indivisibilities leave it unscathed, provided that the value of the product of the indivisible block of factors be estimated with reference to the area under the relevant demand curve—this area representing approximately the revenue of a perfectly discriminating monopolist.

[20] These three do not give the most compact form of the optimum conditions. As we shall see later, the first could be easily made part of the third. But in this limited form they appear frequently in welfare analysis, and will generally suffice when the results of the analysis in question are negative.

[21] The reader is reminded of our simplification: that all goods be highly divisible; that each individual buys some of all the goods; that all factors enter into each of the goods—unless modified in the text.

[22] The lengths of the two axes measure the given quantities of the two goods to be divided between the two individuals, the origins of whose indifference maps lie in opposite corners. The locus of mutual tangencies is commonly referred to as the contract curve, after Edgeworth.

[23] The geometric representation is similar to that of the exchange optimum, except that the amounts of the factors are measured along the two axes, and that

tion is fulfilled, it is not possible to produce any more of a good without producing less of some other good (for brevity, henceforth; to produce more of "every" good). (3) Building on these two "lower-level" optima, each of which is the locus of "efficient points," is the *Top-Level Optimum.*[24] It requires that the subjective rate of substitution, common to all individuals, be equal to the rate of transformation (or, rate of objective substitution) for all pairs of goods in the economy.[25] Once top-level optimum is achieved, it is not possible to describe a higher level of welfare for "everyone" given the production possibilities of the existing supply of factors.[26]

It is commonly alleged that a sufficient condition for the allocative rule, and therefore for the optimum conditions also, is that

---

in principle the isoproduct curves may be numbered. The locus of mutual tangencies is frequently referred to as the locus of efficient points, or, sometimes, as the production contract curve.

[24] Myint [189, Chapter 8] talks of (i) the subjective optimum, (ii) the physical optimum, and (iii) the general optimum of production and exchange, respectively.

[25] The standard diagram here is of the transformation curve, or production possibility curve, between two goods being tangent at some point to a community indifference curve. The data necessary to the transformation curve are taken directly from the locus of efficient points in the isoproduct diagram. The concept of the community indifference curve will be discussed later.

[26] To show that these three conditions can be derived from the allocative rule, express the equality of the value of the marginal product in all lines of output as

$$p_x \frac{\partial X}{\partial A} = p_y \frac{\partial Y}{\partial A} = \qquad (a)$$

$$p_x \frac{\partial X}{\partial B} = p_y \frac{\partial Y}{\partial B} = \qquad (b)$$

where X and Y are products, A and B are factor units, p_x, p_y, are prices of the products X and Y, $\partial X/\partial A$ is the marginal physical product of factor A in the production of X, and so on.

Then: (1) Exchange optimum follows from there being but a single set of product prices facing each individual. Without this provision, the *value* of the marginal product would be ambiguous. (2) The production optimum follows from dividing (a) by (b) to give $\partial B/\partial A$ in X equal to $\partial B/\partial A$ in Y. (3) Top-level optimum follows if we divide (a) through by p_y and $\partial X/\partial A$, and (b) through by p_y and $\partial X/\partial B$, to obtain

$$\frac{p_x}{p_y} = \left[\frac{\dfrac{\partial Y}{\partial A}}{\dfrac{\partial X}{\partial A}} = \frac{\dfrac{\partial Y}{\partial B}}{\dfrac{\partial X}{\partial B}} = \cdots \right] = \frac{\partial Y}{\partial X}$$

p_x/p_y faces each individual, so that to each the rate of substitution is $\partial Y/\partial X$, and this is equal to the rate of transformation $\partial Y/\partial X$ (on the right-hand side of the equation) between the products, using any of the factors at the margin.

(It may be observed that this last equation reveals, in brackets, that the ratio of the marginal physical products for all pairs of goods is the same for each of the factors—an alternative statement of the production optimum.)

in all markets the price of the product is equal to its marginal cost. For multiplying each side of the equality by the marginal physical product of any of the factors yields the equality between the value of the marginal product and the factor price. And since—granted factor markets competitive and, provisionally, ignoring nonpecuniary considerations—the price of any class of factor is the same everywhere, so also is the value of the marginal product.

But is this condition *necessary* to the allocative rule? According to Kahn,[27] the rule is not violated if product prices are not equal to their corresponding marginal costs, provided that they are proportional to them. This "proportionality" thesis, however, requires not only a zero elasticity of all factor supplies, explicitly assumed by Kahn, but also that no good be both a final product and an intermediate good.[28]

If we now remove the assumption of a zero elasticity in the supply of factors, a summit position is not consistent with the proportionality thesis. If, for instance, product prices everywhere exceed their corresponding marginal costs by a given proportion, the value of the marginal product of each factor exceeds its supply price by the same proportion, granted the above proviso about intermediate goods. Factor owners may benefit by extending their supplies at prices less than the values of their corresponding marginal products, while consumers may gain from lower prices on additional purchases of the various products. The allocative rule should therefore be interpreted to include nonpecuniary activities, in particular leisure, among the alternative occupations open, without constraint, to the factor owner. Put otherwise, to the set of optimum conditions mentioned above, we must add a lower-level optimum condition requiring that the rate of transformation between factor and product be the same as the subjec-

[27] Kahn, *op. cit.*

[28] In this connection, Little [161, p. 163] gives the following example. Coal, though a finished good, is priced as an intermediate good at its marginal cost. Electricity is priced as a finished good above its marginal cost. The rate of substitution of these two goods is therefore not equal to their rate of transformation. What this seems to show, however, is that, since the prices of all finished goods are required to be a given proportion of the value added at the margin by any (or, in the long run, all) of the factors, if an intermediate good is used as a finished good, in its latter use the price should be the appropriate proportion of its marginal cost, whereas when sold as an intermediate good its price should be set equal to its marginal cost. Whether it is possible always to maintain two different prices for the one product is a different matter.

tive rate of substitution between factor and product for every individual. We shall refer to this condition briefly as the factor-product condition.

What about occupational preference? If occupations X and Y pay the same rate but the individual prefers Y, he will place more of his factors there. In the limiting case he places all of his factors in Y. He may do this—though others may not—even though X pays a higher rate than Y, and therefore the market value of his marginal factor is higher in X than in Y. But if the individual voluntarily forgoes extra payments in X, it is obviously because the loss in market value he sustains by reason of his choice is, at least, made up by the value that the individual places on his preference for Y (the words *at least* are inserted to allow for the individual who has placed none of his factors in X and whose premium for Y exceeds the current difference in pay between X and Y). The allocative rule should, in consequence, be amended to require that factors be so allocated that, to each individual factor owner, the value of any remaining preference for Y over X is equal, at least, to the additional market value of his marginal factor in X. An alternative statement is that a Pareto optimum has not been achieved if a worker can improve his welfare by moving to a lower-paid occupation. These opportunities for individual betterment are, however, exhausted by the factor-product condition mentioned above. For, given the rates of transformation between factor and product in the two occupations, a worker who prefers occupation Y to X will place more of his factors in Y than one who does not, in the limiting case placing none of his factors in X.

In passing, it may be mentioned that another, more compact, scheme of optimum conditions can be adopted which encompasses the formulations of several well-known writers. Summarized in a single rule that the rate of substitution between each pair of goods —goods to include, now, both products and factors—for every individual be equal to their corresponding rate of transformation, this statement comprehends six conditions: (1) that the rates of substitution be equal for all individuals as between (*a*) pairs of products, (*b*) pairs of factors, and (*c*) any product and any factor; and (2) that the common rate of substitution be equal to the technical rate of transformation in each of the pairs (*a*), (*b*), and (*c*).[29] It may be observed, first, that in fact (1) is implied by (2), for if each individual equates his rate of substitution to the rate of transformation a common rate of substitution as between the individuals emerges for each pair of goods. Second, that intertemporal substitution can be allowed for in (1) and (2) by regarding products and factors at different dates as different goods. Something like the conditions in this form will be found in Hicks[30] and in Chapter 8 of Little's *Critique*.[31]

Having amended our allocative rule to take account of factor-product adjustment and occupational preference or, alternatively, having completed one or the other scheme of optimum conditions, we must recognize, first, that perfect competition is neither a necessary nor a sufficient condition for meeting the allocative rule, or the optimum conditions, even under the provisional assumption

[29] These conditions can be summarized in the following example of an optimum position, where *A* and *B* are different factors, and *X*, *Y*, and *Z* their marginal physical products in three alternative uses.

	X	*Y*	*Z*	.	.
A	1	5	8	.	.
B	2	10	16	.	.
.	.	.	.	.	.

Since each of these figures is a marginal physical product, or rate of transformation of factor into product, if we assume that, through prices, each individual equates his rate of substitution to each of these figures, then we fulfill (*c*) for (2), and therefore also for (1). Reading horizontally, we see that, at the margin, a unit of factor *A* can be transformed into 1 unit of *X*, 5 of *Y*, or 8 of *Z*. This ratio of 1:5:8 is true also for the second line, and represents the product rate of transformation (using any of the factors at the margin) to which the individuals must equate their rates of substitution, thus fulfilling (*a*) for both (2) and (1). Finally, if we glance down the columns we remark that the rate of technical substitution of *A* for *B* is 2:1 in each of the products *X*, *Y*, *Z*. If each individual equates his factor rate of substitution to this technical rate of transformation between factors, (*b*) is fulfilled for both (2) and (1). Obviously, in such a table, for any number of rows and columns the ratios, row-wise, are all the same, which give another ratio which holds for all of the columns. A failure at any point in these ratios indicates a failure at some point in the optimum conditions.

[30] See bibliography, item 96.

[31] See bibliography, item 161. Dealing with the intertemporal conditions, Little mentions the condition that the rate of substitution over time between goods be the same for each individual and equal to the rate of transformation over time. This is treated as one condition, not two. For the rest he ignores transformation and substitution as between factors themselves, and as between factors and products; instead he has two conditions requiring a common rate of substitution as between goods and money and as between bonds (or shares) and money.

In a simple riskless economy one would suppose Irving Fisher's concept of the rate of interest which equates the marginal time preference of all individuals with the rate of return over cost would satisfy the intertemporal requirements of an optimum position. We shall, however, touch on this point again in Section V.

of coincidence of private and social valuation.[32] It is not necessary, since, without perfect competition, the allocative rule could be employed to guide the controlled economy into equating prices to marginal costs. It is not sufficient[33] simply because a situation in which price-equals-marginal costs in all lines—a corollary of perfectly discriminating monopoly as well as of perfect competition—does not necessarily entail proper adjustment to the factor-product condition. True, all factors are paid the full value of their marginal product, but—to introduce an inevitable indivisibility at this stage—since universal perfect competition is consistent with fixed hours of work in production,[34] each worker is subjected to a constraint which, in general, prevents his adjusting the supply of his labor to the going wage-rate. Consequently, his own valuation of his marginal factor may fall short of, or exceed, that of the market.[35]

Furthermore, even if perfect competition did meet the optimum conditions laid down, these conditions themselves are only necessary conditions for a Pareto optimum. Since they are all in fact first-order conditions, they are consistent with a constrained minimum position (*a* in Figure 1). Second-order conditions are required which, as it happens, are no other than the stability conditions for equilibrium positions.[36] Nevertheless, even if the second-

[32] This is true despite continued allegations to the contrary. For recent examples see Dorfman, Samuelson, and Solow [59, p. 410], and Henderson and Quandt [95, p. 211].

[33] In industries subject to decreasing returns to scale, owing to some scarce factor being unpriced and left out of the firm's production functions, marginal cost to the industry exceeds the inclusive average cost to the firms (since, in these circumstances, average costs do not include rent payments to this scarce factor). In perfect competition firms would then expand output to the point where the marginal cost to the industry exceeded the price of the product, the latter being equaled by the average costs of firms (excluding, of course, rent to the unpriced factor). A common example of such a case is deep-sea fishing. If someone appropriated the fishing area and charged a rent, based on the catch, so as to maximize his receipts (given the price of fish), perfect competition would result in an output for which price equaled average costs for the firms (including rent) and marginal cost to the industry.

[34] When we allow for this constraint, or indivisibility in the supply of factors required of the individual, the supply curve of labor to the industry is no longer the horizontal addition of the supply curves of the individual laborers, but a schedule of the number of positive responses to an all-or-nothing offer over a range of such offers.

[35] Even though his marginal valuation exceeds the market price of his labor unit, by accepting the all-or-nothing offer he may still make a surplus, or rent, in the occupation.

[36] See Hicks [96, p. 704]. Reder [207, p. 45] adds that the attainment of stable

order conditions are fulfilled, or we have good reason to believe that the position in question is one of maximum, since only marginal conditions are involved we are assured only of a local maximum (*b* in Figure 1), which may not, of course, be the largest

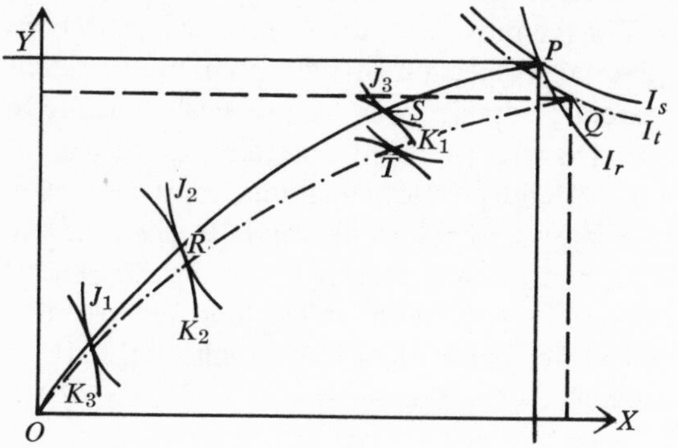

Figure 1

maximum. True sufficient conditions, sometimes referred to as total conditions,[37] are needed for a genuine summit position. Such conditions require that for all movements, large or small, from the optimum in question, no other position can be reached at which "everyone" is better off.

Finally, we must remind ourselves that a Pareto optimum, or an ideal output, is but one of a large number of conceivable summit positions, each distinguishable from the others by a different pattern of welfare distribution.[38] It follows that, although there are

equilibrium under conditions of perfect competition satisfy the second-order conditions. Which stability conditions are intended are nowhere to be found, but presumably the Marshallian conditions are in mind—that the demand curve for each product cut the corresponding supply curve from above. Actually, the sufficient conditions for a (local) maximum are more complex, resulting as they do from the expansion of $d^2W < O$, W being the welfare function subject to the production constraints.

[37] See Hicks [96, p. 704]. The total conditions include the possibility of introducing a new good or ceasing to produce an existing good. Apparently no easily observable rules can be enunciated for the total conditions.

[38] This is clearly recognized by Hicks [96, p. 701] and, later, by Reder [207, p. 38] and by Samuelson [222, p. 231–232]. In fact, the general proposition that we cannot identify an ideal allocation of resources unless we commit ourselves to a specific welfare function was argued—though in more informal terms involving utility—as far back as 1936 by Harrod (R. F. Harrod, "Another Fundamental Objection to Laissez-Faire," *Economic Journal* [1936]).

On the other hand, Myint [189], who wrote of a "scientific welfare eco-

particular optimal positions corresponding to any given nonoptimal position which makes "everyone" in the latter position better off, a movement from this given nonoptimal position to *any* optimal position is not necessarily an improvement for "everyone."

We now turn to some of the outstanding applications of the optimum conditions. For the most part, the formal demonstrations involve little more than an inspection of the optimum conditions under alternative economic organizations. A practical difficulty in all the cases considered is that the optimum rules, corrected for differences between social and private valuations, must be met in *all* sectors for any welfare inference to be valid. If this stringent requirement cannot be met for any reason, there are no general rules to fall back upon; in particular, we cannot suppose that more conditions fulfilled are better than less. Again, we have so far ignored the consequence for the optimum conditions of the influence of the individual's welfare on the welfare of others. These two difficulties, along with others, will be treated in Section V. They are mentioned here in order to impress on the reader the rather provisional basis of the familiar welfare propositions which follow.

The case against monopoly in allocative economics[39] rested on its alleged restriction of output. This partial view of things was corrected by Kahn's ideal output[40] characterized by an equiproportional degree of monopoly in all lines of production. In so far as Lerner, Reder, and Little[41] reject this solution on grounds that the factor-product condition is not met, two points appear to have been overlooked. First, if Kahn's explicit assumption of a

---

nomics," seems to have put the matter too strongly in stating that the optimum conditions enable one to study "the purely mechanical efficiency of the economic system in satisfying individual requirements" without involving "any normative value judgments" [189, p. 118]. This language can easily convey the impression that allocative efficiency is something to the good which may be usefully pursued independently of any agreement on a desirable welfare distribution. But, as will be made explicit in Section III, an output combination that is "efficient" with respect to the existing welfare distribution may be "inefficient," and therefore nonoptimal, with respect to another, possibly more desirable, welfare distribution.

[39] I think it would generally be conceded today that questions of stability, technical efficiency, innovation, and the distribution of wealth and power capture the interest both of the economists and the public more than do questions concerning the optimum output.

[40] Kahn, *op. cit.*

[41] See bibliography, items 148, 207, and 161.

zero elasticity of the supply of all factors is accepted,[42] the factor-product condition is, in effect, fulfilled. Second, if the view is taken that Kahn's assumption is too far at variance with the facts to be acceptable, perfect competition fares no better than equi-proportional imperfect competition. For, as we have already pointed out, perfect competition is consistent with fixed hours of work in all occupations which, effectively, precludes opportunities for marginal adjustments by factor-owners.

In the belief that price equal to marginal cost was the correct rule for industry, the government intervening with taxes and bounties in order to correct for external effects, one slipped easily into the marginal cost-pricing controversy bedeviled by computational conundrums, problems of administration, monetary and fiscal policy, political power, and so forth. Allocative considerations alone, as it happens, have little to contribute.[43] An older element in the controversy goes back to Pigou's *Wealth and Welfare* of 1912, in which the author sought to demonstrate that output under competition was excessive inasmuch as rents which ought to enter into marginal costs were, instead, spread over average costs. The outcome of the discussion which followed this proposition was that—granted the prevalence of optimum conditions in all other sectors, and the coincidence of social and private benefits—the total increment of Ricardian rent and also, for that matter, all transfer rents on intra-marginal factors, should *not* in any case enter marginal costs. Such rents are not real costs but transfer payments, and there is no divergence, on these grounds, between competitive and ideal output.[44] However, we must remind ourselves again that price equal to marginal cost in all sectors is not by itself enough to meet the necessary conditions for an optimum. Further, even if these necessary conditions were met,

[42] This zero elasticity is to be taken to result from a combination of a zero substitution effect plus a zero wealth effect in the supply of factors.

[43] Few of the contestants in this field of controversy questioned the welfare basis of marginal cost pricing. For instance, the chief issues raised by Coase [48 and 49], Thirlby [236], Nordin [192], and Vickrey [243], among others, turned upon the practicability and other advantages of alternative methods of covering costs.

Despite its title, I can find nothing in Nancy Ruggles' article [217] that provides a welfare justification for marginal cost pricing.

[44] An excellent survey of this older controversy is to be found in Ellis and Fellner's 1943 paper [63].

and sufficient conditions also, there is no warrant for the assumption that such a summit position is, in any acceptable sense, superior to all nonsummit positions.

The marginal cost-pricing rule is yet less satisfactory when, as is generally the case, we envisage setting prices only for one or several industries, while having to acquiesce in a diversity of relationships between price and marginal costs in all other sectors of the economy. Finally, if it were decided, for lack of a better rule, to equate price to marginal cost in any case the particular methods used to cover costs in decreasing-cost industries have no direct allocative implications. They have welfare effects only inasmuch as they affect the real distribution of income in the economy.[45]

The taxation controversy is much of a piece with the monopoly one. Little,[46] in repudiating Henderson's allegation of an excess burden of indirect taxation,[47] argued that the alleged welfare superiority of direct taxation rested on its noninfringement of the existing ratios of prices to marginal costs. It was further required, however, that factor supplies were invariant, otherwise, whether taxes were direct or indirect, the factor-product condition was not met. In conclusion, since taxes on goods (including leisure) to which the individual is least responsive offend least against the optimum position, Little hazards the general statement, familiar from consumer's surplus analysis, that the least objectionable taxes are those on goods for which the individual's demands are least elastic. If there is a weakness in this analysis it is the restriction to a single individual which avoids the distributional complications.[48] For even a poll tax imposed on an already optimally or-

[45] In general, if an optimum were to be attained by universal application of the marginal cost-pricing rule, or on some other formula, one can go no further on a purely allocative basis. For there are no allocative requirements for the pricing of the *intra*-marginal units. Of the indefinite number of ways of covering costs (paying for fixed factors in the short period), including direct subsidies to the industry, two-part tariffs, discriminatory charges, all are consistent with the implementation of the allocative rule, though each affects in a different way the distribution of welfare. In this connection see Oort [194], especially the appendix.

[46] See bibliography, item 155.

[47] See bibliography, item 93.

[48] Essentially the same argument was put forward about the same time by Friedman [74]. He justifies his restriction of the analysis to a single individual by asserting his concern with "allocative" and not with "distributive" problems.

In justice to Friedman and Little, it must be allowed that they were explicit about many practical matters which forbade any sweeping policy conclusions.

ganized economy is not neutral if its proceeds are redistributed among the community. It shifts the economy to a different optimal position—one in which some people are better off and others are worse off.

With the popularity of the indifference-curve technique, the original Bickerdike case for "incipient" tariffs[49] was revised, first by Kaldor in 1940,[50] then by Scitovsky, by Kahn, Meade, Johnson, and Graaff,[51] to mention only the better-known contributors.

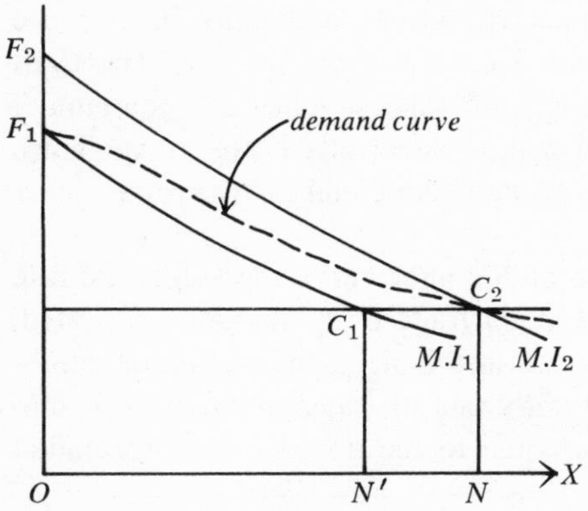

Figure 2

The basic idea is that although in a world of perfectly competitive economies free trade results in a world optimum, a country thinking only of its national welfare may increase its welfare, at the expense of other countries, by acting as a monopolist—selling less to foreign countries but on better terms. The simple demonstration that this is possible in the two-good, two-country model proceeds by use of Marshall's offer-curve technique plus the community indifference curves of the tariff country.

The intersection at *F* in Figure 2 of the offer curves[52] of countries

[49] C. F. Bickerdike, "The Theory of Incipient Taxes," *Economic Journal* (1906).
[50] See bibliography, item 122.
[51] See bibliography, items 81, 115, 119, 172, and 228.
[52] The offer curve for a country may be derived as follows: construct a terms-of-trade line tangent to the production frontier of a country already optimally organized. If these terms of trade differ from the initial domestic rate of substitution and transformation the new quantities of *X* and *Y* *produced* are indicated by the point of tangency of this line with the production-possibility curve; the new quantities of *X* and *Y* *consumed* by its point of tangency with the community

A and *B* reveals the free-trade equilibrium, country *A* importing *OX* of *X* in exchange for *OY* of *Y*, which is what country *B* imports in exchange for *OX*. By imposing a tariff on its imports, country *A* can reduce the domestic quantities demanded at any given international terms of trade, thereby reducing its effective-offer curve. The optimum tariff is one which generates an effective-offer curve, *A′*, intersecting *B*'s unchanged offer curve at *D*, at which point *A*'s community indifference curve, *I′*, is tangent to *B*'s offer curve.[53] The measure of gain effected by the optimum tariff is indicated by the movement from the community indifference curve, *I*, in the free-trade position, to *I′* with the tariff. The tariff is an optimum inasmuch as *I′* is the highest achievable community indifference curve consistent with *B*'s unchanged offer curve. Thus, it is not possible to move from *D* and make "everyone" in *A* better off.

For country *A*, the slope of *B*'s offer curve represents the rate of transformation through foreign trade of *Y*, the good exported, for *X*, the good imported. Seen in this light, the additional condition required is that country *A*'s rate of transformation of *Y* into *X* through foreign trade be equal to the domestic transformation

---

indifference curve. The length, along this terms-of-trade line, from the production tangency to the consumption tangency represents the exchange of goods; of imports (excess of domestic consumption over domestic production of one of the goods) for exports (excess of domestic production over domestic consumption of the other good).

Swivelling this terms-of-trade line about the production possibility curve continuously alters the lengths representing exchange. When they are measured from a common origin, and radiate into the northeast (and southwest) quadrant, the pencil of such lengths describe that country's offer curve. Unless the two countries have the same terms of trade in their initial no-trade positions, their offer curves must intersect in one or other of the two quadrants.

[53] Community indifference curves are discussed in the next section. I have assumed here a single set of community indifference curves reflecting a "satisfactory" distribution of welfare. The redistributive effects of a tariff are offset by direct transfers of income in order to ensure that no individual is worse off as, with the improved terms of trade occasioned by the tariff, we move to higher community indifference curves.

In Graaff's treatment [84, p. 49], what he calls a "Bergson frontier" takes the place of the community indifference map. Such a frontier is constructed as the inner limit of all those community indifference curves which for the community have equal welfare value. Any point on this frontier, therefore, indicates the minimum quantities of goods required to attain a given value of social welfare. A criticism of the usual treatment of optimum tariffs, which treatment accepts the optimum tariff position as superior, actually or potentially (i.e., using compensation tests), to the free-trade position, does not apply to Graaff's treatment. The Bergson frontier passing through *D* does not necessarily have a higher welfare value than that passing through the initial free-trade point, *F*.

of Y into X and also, since we assume perfect competition to prevail in A, to the domestic subjective rate of substitution of Y for X—the slope of the community indifference curve I' at D. If we regard the optimum tariff, t, as equal to the difference between (i) π, the domestic price ratio (equals $X'D/X'H$) and (ii) p, the actual terms of trade (equals $X'D/X'$), we can deduce that the formula $t = \pi/p - 1$ is equal to $X'O/X'H - 1$. But $X'O/X'H$ measures the elasticity of the foreign offer curve at D. Hence the optimum tariff, $t = E - 1$, where E is the elasticity of the foreign offer curve.

An alternative formulation put forward by Kahn,[54] in terms of the elasticities of the relevant demand and supply schedules, rather than in terms of the offer-curve elasticity, appears to lend itself better to estimation and may be derived directly from the optimum conditions in the above paragraph. Since the rate of transformation through foreign trade must equal the domestic rate of transformation, (a) the marginal cost of importing X divided by the marginal revenue from exporting Y must be equal to (b) the domestic marginal cost of X divided by the domestic marginal cost of Y. If we take the foreign supply curve of A's imports to be upward-sloping, the marginal cost to country A of importing X exceeds the foreign price of X by a proportion which varies with the elasticity of that supply curve. The foreign demand curve for A's export, Y, being downward-sloping, the receipts from an additional export of Y fall short of its price, again by a proportion which depends on the elasticity of that demand curve.

In the free-trade position, then, where the international price ratio is equal to the domestic price ratio, the (a) ratio, representing the true international rate of transformation, exceeds the (b) ratio; which is to say, that it costs more to transform Y into X through trade than through domestic production. One therefore proceeds to reduce exports and imports (both by the same value in order to maintain balanced trade) until—with the marginal cost of importing X falling, and the marginal revenue from exporting Y rising (the respective marginal costs in home production moving in the reverse directions)—the (a) ratio is brought into equality with the (b) ratio, and the optimum condition is met.

[54] See bibliography, item 119.

Since, however, the domestic consumers have regard only to (c), the ratio of the actual price of imports X to the price of exports Y, which ratio is always smaller than the (a) ratio in the absence of tariffs, the consumers' choice may be "corrected" by increasing the price of imports to the required extent by levying a tariff on imports of Y. The tariff which makes these ratios equal is the optimum tariff, and as its height depends upon the shape of the two curves mentioned, it can obviously be calculated with reference to their respective elasticities. Writing η_s for the elasticity of the foreign supply of imports, and η_d for the elasticity of the foreign demand for A's exports, the optimum tariff can be shown to have the form $\frac{1/\eta_s + 1/\eta_d}{1 - 1/\eta_d}$. Graaff has shown that this formula can be easily extended to cover any number of goods entering into a country's foreign trade.[55]

The assumptions of balanced trade maintained, say, through changes in the relative wage-rates of the two countries, of an unchanged level of employment in A, of universal competition and an absence of external effects, are exacting enough, to say nothing of the distribution problem. Even if we grant all this, the formulae, as Graaff points out,[55] do no more than reveal the relationships which are to obtain in the optimum situation. Guesses at tariff heights using the existing elasticities, if they can be obtained, may be wide of the mark, since the elasticities in question will themselves vary with the height of the tariff.

In conclusion, while there is little doubt that some countries may be in a position to improve their terms of trade with the outside world at some small sacrifice, if any,[56] in imports, the idea of an optimum tariff with its suggestion that there is some calculable set of tariffs which, in the absence of retaliation, is best for a country is all too facile. Quite apart from the stringent conditions and practical difficulties involved, the welfare significance

[55] See bibliography, item 84.

[56] If at the free-trade equilibrium B's offer curve were sufficiently inelastic (less than unity), then some tariff imposed by A can improve the country's terms of trade while also increasing the volume of its imports. To illustrate, if B's offer curve were B' in Figure 2, intersecting A at F', a tariff could reduce A's effective offer curve to intersect B' at, say, G. Country A now imports more and exports less.

of this optimum tariff is tenuous in the extreme. We already know that in the event that all the optimum conditions are fulfilled (including, here, the foreign-trade optimum condition) in all sectors, the best we can hope for is a Pareto optimum, a necessary condition for a maximum of social welfare. Since there are actually an indefinite number of such summit positions, each corresponding to a different initial pattern of welfare distribution, there are in principle an indefinite number of optimum tariffs. Until we have some rule, evolved from ethical considerations, by which we may choose among the alternative summit positions open to us, there is no warrant for moving to any one of them guided by a set of optimum tariffs calculated on the basis of the existing welfare situation—assuming such calculation practicable. For, as we shall affirm in Section III, there is no acceptable definition of welfare by which an existing nonsummit position may be judged inferior to *all* attainable summit positions.

III. The Choice of Welfare Criteria

With the advent of the "New Welfare Economics" in 1939 there began a period of cautious optimism. It was not to last long. Two years later, in an ingenious paper,[57] Scitovsky demonstrated that the apparently felicitous device of hypothetical compensation advanced by Kaldor and promoted by Hicks was quite capable of giving contradictory results. And, though the device was promptly amended to preclude the particular perversity uncovered by Scitovsky, the damage began to spread. Little's fastidious examination of 1949 left the idea of hypothetical compensation, as a criterion of welfare, in a dubious state.[58] It was left to Samuelson to push the logic of Scitovsky's initial discovery to its conclusion: that, in general—if we exclude comparisons between situations in one of which there is more of "every" good—it was not possible to rank alternative economic organizations on the basis of compensation tests.[59] Arrow's sweeping essay on social choice added to the skepticism which gathered force in the fifties,[60] so that when Graaff's

[57] See bibliography, item 227.
[58] See bibliography, item 154.
[59] See bibliography, item 221.
[60] See bibliography, item 14.

thesis appeared in 1957 [61] its elegant nihilism did little more than reflect the prevailing mood.

The controversy over welfare criteria was marked by greater critical insight, in respect both of ethical implications and the applicability of deducible propositions, than the more abstract dissertations on the optimum conditions. Interest in these criteria is, moreover, more easily sustained both because of the more explicitly ethical content and by virtue of a clear evolution of the compensation device which we follow in some detail, an evolution which, as it happens, links up eventually with the concept of a Pareto optimum regarded as a necessary condition for a position of maximum social welfare.

COMPENSATION TESTS

The formulation of the principle of hypothetical compensation[62] arose out of the controversies of 1938–1939 in the *Economic Journal*. Harrod,[63] illustrating the traditional acceptance of interpersonal comparisons of utility by reference to the repeal of the corn laws in 1846, had argued that the gain to the community as a whole might be regarded as exceeding the loss to the landlords only if the individuals affected were treated as equal in some sense. While he was prepared to go along with this, Robbins was not.[64] To him this assumption of equal capacities for satisfactions was unwarrantable.

Without challenging Robbins' view of the scientific status of interpersonal comparisons, Kaldor denied their relevance for prescriptive statements.[65] Indeed, according to Kaldor, the classical argument for free trade involved no such arbitrary element, the essence of the argument being that the government could so compensate the losers as to make "everyone" better off. The compensa-

[61] See bibliography, item 84.

[62] The terminology varies from time to time, and from one writer to another. The most common terms are compensation test, or compensation criterion; principle of compensation, or of potential or hypothetical compensation (with "overcompensation" frequently substituted for "compensation" in all these terms).

[63] R. F. Harrod, "Scope and Method of Economics," *Economic Journal* (September 1938).

[64] L. C. Robbins, "Interpersonal Comparisons of Utility," *Economic Journal* (December 1938).

[65] See bibliography, item 123.

tion test implied by this view was to be understood as an objective test of economic efficiency and, according to Kaldor, prescriptions based on it had a scientific status detached from any value judgment. Thus, whether one should compensate or not, he submitted, was a political question on which the economist could merely pronounce an opinion.[66]

Hicks,[67] who found much to admire in the structure of the traditional welfare economics while deprecating their foundations, eagerly grasped this notion of examining the efficiency of alternative economic organizations without reference to the question of distribution, and particularly without reference to the comparisons of satisfactions as between individuals.[68] Defining an optimum position along Paretian lines,[69] he pointed out that although there was not one but an infinite number of such optima, each differing

[66] Stigler [233] objects to the compensation principle inasmuch as its adoption would apparently sanction compensation of successful thieves for the amounts they would otherwise steal, thereby releasing resources engaged in maintaining law and order. In general, he argues, not only thieves and protected industries but anyone contemplating social mischief would, on this principle, be dissuaded from taking action by adequate compensation. As a principle, therefore, it is repugnant to our moral code.

But in fact the compensation principle asks only whether losers *could* be compensated: it does not require that they *should* be compensated. Consequently, from the successful application of the compensation principle to stealing, or tariff protection, nothing more may be inferred than that their removal would increase "efficiency." Whether, and in what manner, compensation should take place, if it should take place at all, is a question of distribution on which our moral sense has to be consulted. Indeed, the declared aim of the compensation test, as Kaldor stresses, is to separate the question of "efficiency" from that of distribution.

See also a comment on this paper by Samuelson [220].

[67] See bibliography, item 96.

[68] This, according to Hicks, was one of the three weak links in Pigou's valuation of the social income. The other two were: (1) the distinction between welfare and economic welfare (though this seems to be less a distinction of principle than of measurability), and (2) the measurement of the real value of the national dividend. However, as Hicks does point out, Pigou's welfare propositions refer to *changes* in the national dividend and, therefore, in no way depend upon his success in measuring the national dividend as a whole.

[69] Implicit in the definition of a Pareto optimum is a Paretian criterion that a position II is superior to I if, in moving to II, "everyone" is actually made better off. But its range of application is likely to be limited. It may be said that Kaldor's achievement consisted in transforming the Paretian criterion from an actual to a potential situation; II, that is, qualifies as the better position if, in the movement from I to II, "everyone" *could* be made better off. In effect, Kaldor followed Pigou's procedure in dividing welfare economics into propositions about the value of the product and those about distribution. Pigou's indicator for an increase in the national dividend, it should be recalled, was in fact just such a compensation test (*op. cit.*, pp. 50–55).

from the others by a particular distribution of welfare, one could lay down universally valid conditions for such an optimum.[70] If these conditions were not met the position was not one of optimum and, consequently, "everyone" could be made better off in moving to some optimum.

While Hicks followed Kaldor in using the notion of compensation as a wedge between efficiency and distribution, he was more cautious on the question of prescription and toyed with the idea of linking economic reform based on efficiency alone with some measure of actual compensation designed to make it more acceptable from the point of view of distribution, albeit not without reminding us that transfers of wealth might well reduce efficiency.

Scitovsky's paper, two years later,[71] is memorable chiefly for its apparently paradoxical demonstration, that having shown a position II to be more efficient than a position I on the Kaldor-Hicks criterion, the same criterion might well reveal, following the community's adoption of the II position, that I was now more efficient than II.[72] With this in mind, the new criterion suggested by Scitovsky was, as might be expected, that which required the result of the original Kaldor-Hicks test to be consistent with that of the "reversal" of this test—by which is meant the original test applied, now, to a movement from II to I. Only if *both* tests disclosed II to be better than I, or I to be better than II, was the Scitovsky criterion fulfilled. Any other outcome was ambiguous.[73]

[70] Hicks' marginal conditions required that the rate of substitution between any two goods (including factors) was the same for each individual and each producing unit. His stability conditions ensured that the position was one of maximum, and not of minimum. His total conditions (which in fact comprehended the stability conditions) would ensure the impossibility of improvement by introducing, or abandoning, any product or factor.

[71] See bibliography, item 227.

[72] It should be borne in mind, however, that positions I and II being compared were not, in the Scitovsky treatment, full optimum positions. In his main demonstrations they were two bundles of goods, each divided between a two-person community such that the exchange optimum prevailed in the division of each bundle.

[73] Scitovsky put it slightly differently. He considered two possibilities: (1) a II position in which redistribution of the II product made "everyone" better off than he was in I, and (2) a I position in which redistribution of the I product made "everyone" better off than he was in II. If (1) were possible and (2) impossible, then we could say that II was the more efficient position. Conversely, if (1) were impossible but (2) were possible, then I was the more efficient alternative. Whereas if both were possible we could say nothing. Other possibilities, such as II better than I by the original test and equal to I by the reversal test, were ignored.

To apprehend the nature of the Scitovsky paradox,[74] and some of the finer points emerging from the further development of welfare criteria by Samuelson and others, familiarity with two popular constructs in welfare economics, the community indifference map and the utility possibility curve, is of great expository value. The former is elaborated below and then employed to shed light on Scitovsky's initial and somewhat esoteric demonstration. The latter construct will be explained later, prior to a consideration of Samuelson's distinguished paper of 1950.

A direct analogy with the individual indifference curve suggests that the community indifference curve be a locus of combinations, or "bundles," of goods as between which the community is, in some sense to be defined, indifferent. It has been found useful to define this indifference in such manner that for any point on the curve (representing a bundle of goods which may be chosen by the community) it is not possible to make "everyone" in the community better off. The exchange optimum, therefore, obtains at every point along the community indifference curve. In consequence, at every such point the rate of substitution between goods is the same for each of the individuals in the community.

Let us illustrate the geometric construction of a community indifference map for a community of two individuals *A* and *B*, whose respective indifference maps are indicated in Figure 3.[75] Since we may form a community indifference curve from any pair of the individual curves, let us start by choosing a_1 and b_2. The community

[74] Scitovsky's attitude is less vulnerable than might appear from a reading of later criticisms. If he appeared to accept compensation tests as tests of efficiency he did so: (*a*) because the more acceptable Paretian criterion was likely to be satisfied very rarely, and (*b*) because in any case the "principle of compensated adjustment"—the fulfillment of the Kaldor-Hicks test plus actual compensation in order to make "everyone" actually better off, which gives the effect of implementing the Paretian criterion—obviously favored the status quo. Nevertheless, he was not willing to prescribe policy solely on the basis of these tests, and without reference to social justice.

Furthermore, he anticipated Samuelson in defining II to be more efficient than I if for every distribution of welfare each person in II could be made as well or better off than he was in I, a criterion which would be fulfilled if there was an increase in at least one good without there being a reduction in any good. Notwithstanding this generalization, he held that only two distributions really mattered—a position later taken up by Little in his more down-to-earth approach—that before the change and that after.

[75] This follows my treatment in 1952 [177]. Graaff has a similar geometric treatment. Scitovsky [228] and Baumol [24] also go into the construction of this curve in some detail.

indifference curve to be constructed therefrom is to have the property that, at all points along it: (i) the individuals *A* and *B* maintain their respective levels of welfare, a_1 and b_2, and (ii), as mentioned, the rate of substitution be the same for each individual for any division of the bundle of goods held in common.

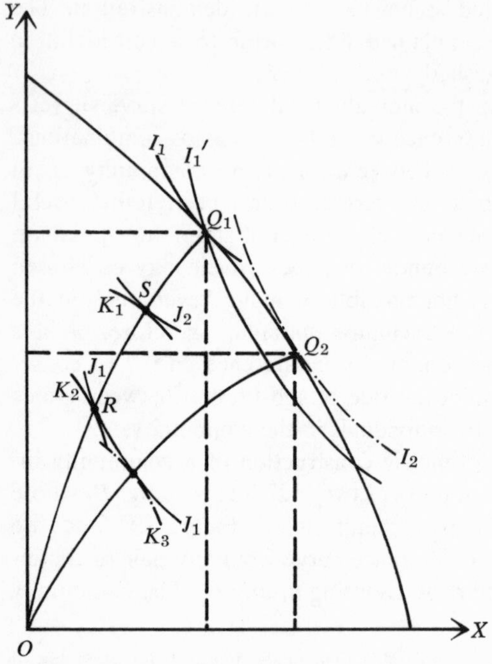

Figure 3

If, therefore, we place the origin of *B*'s map diagonally opposite to that of *A*'s origin and, keeping *B*'s axes parallel to those of *A*, move *B*'s map until b_2 just touches a_1 at, say *c′* in Figure 4, then the point O_b (the origin of *B*'s map) taken with reference to *A*'s origin, O_a, represents a point on the required community indifference map. Another such point would be O_b', *B*'s map having been moved downward to the right and adjusted so that, once again, b_2 just touches a_1, this time at *d′*. Clearly, by moving *B*'s map continuously downward to the right, and then upward to the left, b_2 at all times being placed tangential to a_1, *B*'s origin describes the community indifference curve I_1', having the desired properties (i) and (ii).

Two further observations are necessary before proceeding. First, given any point in the X-Y quadrant, say Q_1, as represented by O_b in Figure 4, the particular community indifference curve we

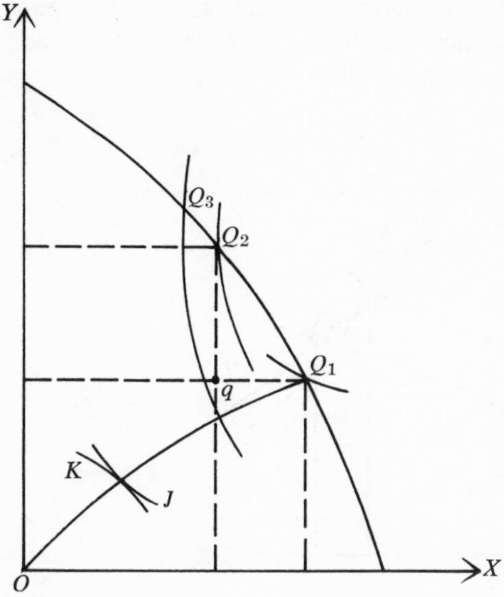

Figure 4

have constructed, I_1'—representing the sum of the individual welfares a_1 and a_2—is not the only community indifference curve which may pass through Q_1 having property (ii). For we could divide this bundle Q_1 between A and B in an indefinite number of ways, taking care always that, whatever the distribution chosen, the rate of substitution be the same for both individuals. Under this restriction, therefore, redistribution is confined to movements along the contract curve of Q_1. If, for instance, we move along the Q_1 contract curve from c' to c'', the latter point being the mutual tangency of a_2 and b_1, a new community indifference curve I_1'' can be generated from these individual curves in the way described. I_1'' and I_1' cannot, of course, be compared on the Paretian criterion —that "everyone" is better off on one of these community indifference curves compared with his being on the other—since in moving from I_1' to I_1'' individual B is worse off while A is better off. Indeed, we can derive a whole pencil of such noncomparable community indifference curves passing through Q_1, each corresponding to a different division, along the contract curve, of the Q_1 bundle. It is, clearly, a consequence of property (ii) that each of these community indifference curves passes through Q_1 at a slope parallel to the mutual tangency (on the contract curve) of the individual indifference curves from which it is generated.

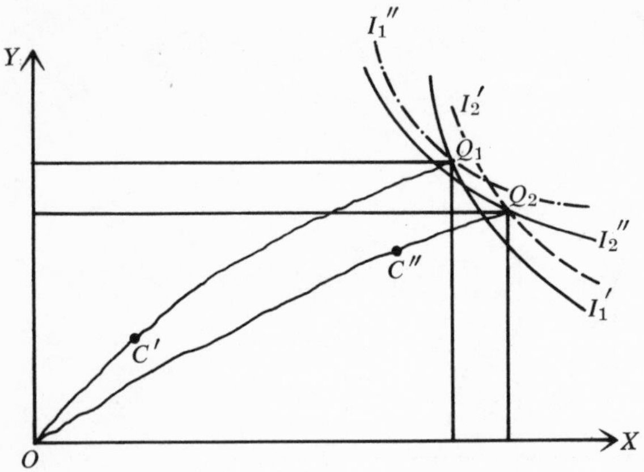

Figure 5

Second, if we use the Paretian criterion to rank the community indifference curves, its consistent application presents us with a map of nonintersecting community indifference curves.[76] For instance, having I_1' as representing individual welfares a_1 and b_2, we could proceed to construct I_2' from, say, a_2 and b_2, I_3' from a_3 and b_3, I_4' from a_3 and b_7, and so on—"everyone" being better off in each successively higher community indifference curve. Such curves we may call *comparable*. They form part of a consistent community indifference map. Obviously, quite a number of other

[76] It does not follow, however, that successively higher nonintersecting community indifference curves fulfill the Paretian criterion. Individual indifference maps which were identical and homogeneous would yield a unique set of nonintersecting community indifference curves. Irrespective of the manner in which the individual curves were combined, only one curve would pertain to a given bundle of goods.

consistent maps may be constructed on this principle, beginning with, say, I_1', though, in general, it will not be possible to move from a curve of one of these maps to that of another.

Figure 5 illustrates the Scitovsky case with two alternative bundles of goods, Q_1 and Q_2. The existing division of Q_1 between A and B is given by c' on the contract curve OQ_1, with I_1' representing the community indifference curve proper to that distribution. On the other hand, the existing distribution of Q_2 is indicated by c'' on the contract curve OQ_2, with the community indifference curve I_2'' corresponding to c''. If, now I_1' and I_2'' were directly comparable we could move directly from one to the other and fulfill the Paretian criterion of an improvement in the community's welfare. They are not comparable, however, and we therefore have recourse to the Kaldor-Hicks criterion, which devises comparability through hypothetical compensation. Through Q_2 we proceed to construct a community indifference curve I_2' that is comparable with I_1'. Apparently, then, there is some division of the Q_2 bundle—that from which I_2' has been generated—which does make "everyone" better off than he is with the Q_1 bundle. If we act on this criterion and arrive safely at Q_2, however, we discover that Q_1 beckons us with exactly the same happy prospect. For we may construct I_1'' through Q_1 comparable with and, as it happens, above I_2''.

The apparent paradox is easily explained. With the distribution c' of the Q_1 bundle, the common rate of substitution is, say, $2Y = X$. With X twice as valuable as Y for the community, the bundle Q_2, which differs from Q_1 in having, let us say, one more of X and one less of Y,[77] must be reckoned by the community as the more valuable of the two. Having moved to Q_2, however, the new distribution of that bundle is that indicated by c'', a distribution which happens to be associated with a common rate of subsituation $Y = 2X$. But on these relative valuations, Q_1 is, for the community, clearly the more valuable of the two bundles. This interrelationship between relative valuation and distribution is the source of elusiveness and paradox which runs through so much of the initial controversies on welfare criteria and index numbers.

[77] So small a difference between two bundles is adopted to suggest that we may effectively ignore those changes in the community's rate of substitution that result only from a movement along the community indifference curve.

LITTLE'S CRITERION

In respect of welfare criteria, Little's "Foundations" paper of 1949,[78] developing more systematically the ideas put forward in Scitovsky's 1942 "Note,"[79] represents the most critical opposition to the original Kaldor dichotomy between efficiency and distribution. He is no less critical of the purism of Robbins, since the impossibility of scientific interpersonal comparisons of welfare is not relevant to propositions about group welfare—though not for the reasons put forward by Kaldor, that they might be circumvented by the device of hypothetical compensation. It is not relevant simply because one no longer believes that propositions about group welfare require the adding together of the (cardinal) utilities of the various individuals.[80]

Value judgments, affirms Little, in particular those about distribution, cannot be avoided in welfare economics. We should, however, make them explicit and, if we wish to carry the reader with us, endeavor to make them widely acceptable. To say that a policy which meets the Kaldor-Hicks criterion increases the "efficiency" of society is, in effect, to recommend it. Whereas if the value judgments implicit in the criterion are bared, it is unlikely to find favor with many people. Compensation is, after all, only hypothetical: it is consistent with making the poor yet poorer. Hence, to announce, as did Kaldor, Hicks, and others at that time, that an objective method of detecting increases in "wealth" or "efficiency" had been discovered, is to mislead opinion by the use of persuasive words. Nothing had been discovered. Kaldor had merely coined a *definition* of efficiency, one whose ethical implications, as it happens, are hardly acceptable.

Turning to the more positive part of his analysis, Little explicitly favors the piecemeal approach to what he calls utopianism, or the all-or-nothing approach of Bergson, Samuelson, and others.

[78] See bibliography, item 154.
[79] See bibliography, item 227.
[80] Indeed, interpersonal comparisons of themselves are not value judgments but judgments of fact resting upon observation and introspection. A "desirable" distribution of real income is, on the other hand, obviously a value judgment. Thus, while we may agree on what constitutes an ideal distribution of real income, differences in our judgments of the facts may preclude agreement on the specific distribution of money, or goods, in the community.

The value premises on which his criterion will rest are: (i) that the individual is deemed to be better off in a chosen position than he is in any other position, and (ii) that a movement to a situation in which "everyone" is better off is a good thing. The criterion he lays down, reminiscent of Pigou's dual criterion, is that, in so far as welfare is affected only by the economic variables under consideration, the change to a new situation ought to be made: (*a*) if the new distribution is no worse than the old, and (*b*) if it is impossible to make "everyone" as well off in the original position as he would be after the change.

Three things are worth noticing: first, that Little does not commit himself to the extent that Pigou does in the matter of distribution, though one is left with the impression that, like Pigou, he would consider a general reduction of inequality, *cet. par.*, a good thing. Second, that part (*b*) of the criterion amounts to the fulfillment of the Kaldor-Hicks reversal test for a movement from I to II which Scitovsky had proposed to ensure consistency after the original Kaldor-Hicks test was met. Little refers to this reversal test as the "Scitovsky criterion." [81] Third, an implication in the first edition of the *Critique*[82] that comparisons of *relative* welfare distributions could be made. Such comparisons would require, as Arrow remarked in the review of that edition,[83] both the possibility of interpersonal comparisons and the measurement of cardinal utility.[84]

The particular method employed by Little in judging whether a movement from the initial situation I to an alternative situation II is an improvement for the community is to pose three questions: (i) Is the Kaldor-Hicks criterion satisfied? (ii) Is the "Scitovsky criterion" satisfied? (iii) Has II a better distribution than I? Since the answer to each of these three questions is either a yes or a no, eight different combinations of answers to (i), (ii), and (iii) are possible. In his second edition, in order to meet criticisms of his

[81] From now on, quotation marks will distinguish it from Scitovsky's declared criterion which required the fulfillment of the Kaldor-Hicks test, for a movement from I to II, *plus* the nonfulfillment of the reversal test.

[82] See bibliography, item 160.

[83] See bibliography, item 11.

[84] A comparison could be made, however, by use of the notion of comparability of distributions. If II′ represents a distribution of the II bundle which is comparable with the existing distribution of the I bundle, and if the initial distribution attaching to the II bundle is better than this II′ distribution, then the II distribution may be said to be better than the I distribution. It is along such lines that Little proceeds in his second edition.

earlier edition of the *Critique,* particularly those of *Arrow* and Baldwin,[85] Little considers the eight possible combinations first under assumption A: that purely distributional changes are not possible.[86]

We may usefully classify his results as follows: of four combinations (out of the eight possible) (i) and (ii) are both satisfied in two of these combinations, and are both *not* satisfied in the other two combinations, while the answer yes to question (iii) occurs only once, in one of the former pair of combinations. For that combination then, in which (i), (ii), and (iii) are satisfied, a movement from I to II is prescribed. Of the remaining four combinations, the answers to (i) and (ii) are opposites in all cases. In two of these cases, however, the answer to (iii) is yes, and therefore, as it transpires, a movement to II is prescribed in either case.

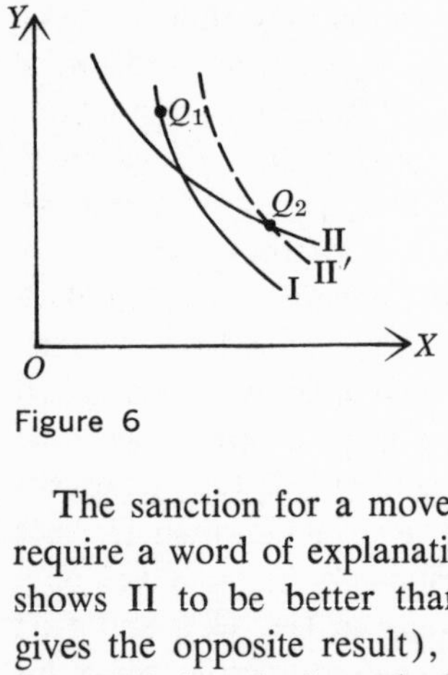

Figure 6

The sanction for a movement to II in the latter two cases may require a word of explanation. Suppose that the Kaldor-Hicks test shows II to be better than I (though the "Scitovsky criterion" gives the opposite result), it follows that a movement from I to II′—II′ being the hypothetical distribution of the II bundle which renders it comparable with that of the I bundle—would make "everyone" better off. We now make a further imaginary journey from II′ to II, II being the initial distribution of the II bundle. From (iii) being answered in the affirmative, we know that II is

[85] See bibliography, items 11 and 19.

[86] In his first edition Little made the arbitrary assumption that a redistribution of welfare was possible before the change to the new position, but not after, with results that were criticized by Arrow [11] and Baldwin [19].

better than, or at least no worse than, the II′ distribution of that bundle. The total welfare effect may then be regarded as a compound of two improvements: a movement from I to II′ which makes "everyone" better off, followed by a movement to II—which is to a better distribution of that bundle, or at least to one that is not worse.[87] We explain the other case in a similar fashion, though beginning the other way round. A distributional change from I to I″—I″ being that hypothetical distribution of the I bundle which is directly comparable with that attaching to the II bundle—is, by (iii), an improvement if anything. While, since the "Scitovsky criterion" is met, a movement from I″ to II makes "everyone" better off.[88] To conclude under assumption A, if the Kaldor-Hicks criterion, or the "Scitovsky criterion," or both, are met, and, in addition, the redistribution involved is, at least, not worse, then a movement from I to II is recommended.

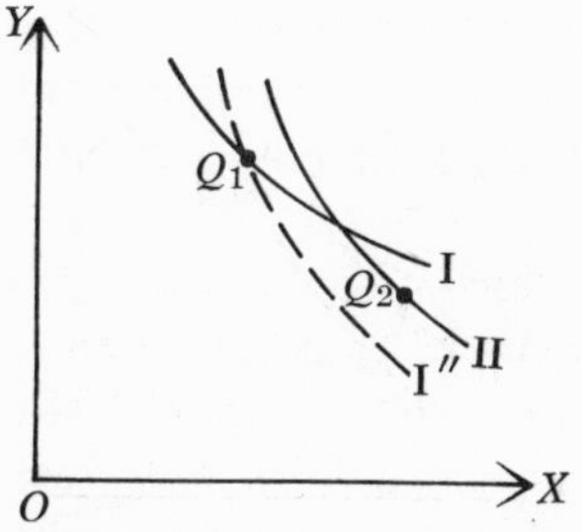

Figure 7

Following this exercise, Little considers these possible combinations under assumption B, that all distributional changes are possible. This means that "intermediate" positions such as II′ and I″ are not merely hypothetical but directly attainable as, of course, is any other distribution. The trouble about such an assumption, as

[87] In Figure 6 let Q_1 and Q_2 be the two bundles, and I and II their corresponding community indifference curves. II′ is a community indifference curve passing through Q_2 which is comparable with I. Hence the Kaldor-Hicks criterion is satisfied. If the community moves to Q_2 but maintains the II′ distribution "everyone" would be better off. A further improvement takes place in adopting the II distribution of Q_2.

[88] In Figure 7 the initial improvement arises from I″, which is a better distribution of the bundle Q_1, and one comparable with the II distribution of Q_2. A movement from I″ to II now makes "everyone" better off.

Arrow pointed out,[89] is that in the event of its adoption the logical procedure would be to move toward the attainment of an ideal distribution of welfare with any bundle of goods. Indeed, if all restrictions on direct redistributions were removed the only test open to us would be the straightforward Paretian criterion; we should ask: Is "everyone" better off with the ideal distribution of a new bundle, II, compared with the existing and comparable distribution of the bundle I?

SAMUELSON'S CRITERION

Further pursuit of welfare criteria is possible along a rather different route, one which begins with further consistency tests and leads inexorably to a concept of Bergsonian dimensions in which all the welfare potentialities inhering in the resources of an economy are displayed prior to eliciting some acceptable social-welfare function to select for us the ideal pattern of welfare. Our progress toward this concept will be facilitated by the employment of Samuelson's utility-possibility curve to which we now give brief attention.

In construction it resembles the production-possibility curve except that, along each of the axes, the welfare, or ordinal utility, of one of the individuals is measured on any arbitrary scale.[90] The boundary of all combinations of the individual utilities which are possible with a given bundle of goods forms the utility-possibility curve. If two individuals, A and B, share a bundle Q_1, such a curve may be mapped from data summarized along the contract curve of Q_1, since each point on the contract curve—and, for that matter, a corresponding point on the utility-possibility curve—may be viewed as providing the maximum utility to *B* consistent with a given utility to *A*.

The initial division of the Q_1 bundle, in Figure 8, is represented as the point c_1' on the utility-possibility curve Q_1Q_1. Since *B*'s utility cannot increase without that of *A* diminishing, the boundary Q_1Q_1 is downward-sloping to the right. Q_2Q_2 is the utility-possibility curve corresponding to the Q_2 contract curve, with c_2'' indi-

[89] See bibliography, item 11.

[90] With ordinal, and noncomparable utility, the scale used on each axis is arbitrary in everything except order.

cating the individual utilities corresponding to the existing division of that bundle. In order to compare the alternative bundles Q_1 and Q_2 using the Kaldor-Hicks criterion, we move along the Q_2Q_2 utility curve from c_2'', the existing distribution—increasing *B*'s welfare at the expense of *A*'s—to c_2', a point northeast of, and therefore comparable with, c_1' on the Q_1Q_1 curve. Having thus

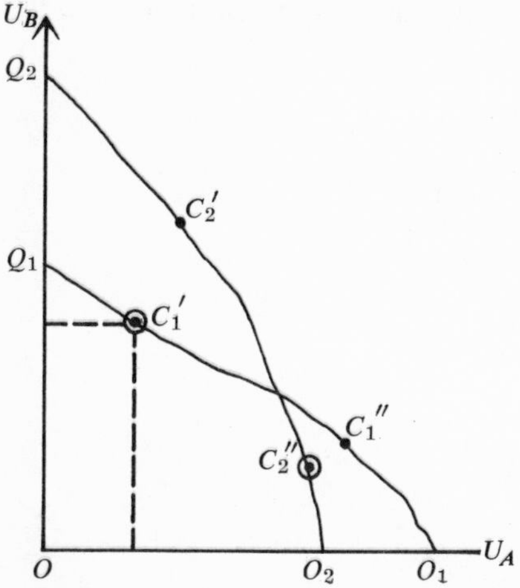

Figure 8

satisfied the Kaldor-Hicks test, we now try the reversal test, which will be based on the c_2'' distribution of the Q_2 bundle. From c_1' we move along Q_1Q_1 to c_1'', a point to the northeast of, and therefore comparable with, c_2'', in this way making both individuals better off with the Q_1 bundle.[91] Since Q_2 is superior to Q_1 by the original test and Q_1 superior to Q_2 by the reversal test, the criterion proposed by Scitovsky is not fulfilled. If the decision to move from one position to the other depended solely on these compensation tests we should have no warrant to change the initial position.

But suppose the Scitovsky criterion were met? Quite apart from the ethical objections voiced by Little and others to using compen-

[91] Though, admittedly, it summarizes the Scitovsky paradox with greater facility than the community indifference curve technique, the latter provides greater insight inasmuch as it points up the dependence of relative valuation on distribution.

sation tests as a sufficient criterion of an improvement in economic organization, we apparently run into logical difficulties if we persist in its application. For, as Gorman[92] has pointed out, the Scitovsky criterion may lead us round in circles if adopted as a welfare criterion. To use his illustration, c_1, c_2, c_3, and c_4 indicate the welfare distributions pertaining to four bundles of goods, Q_1, Q_2, Q_3, and Q_4 respectively, whose utility possibility curves are shown in Figure 9. Bundle Q_2 is easily shown superior to Q_1 by the

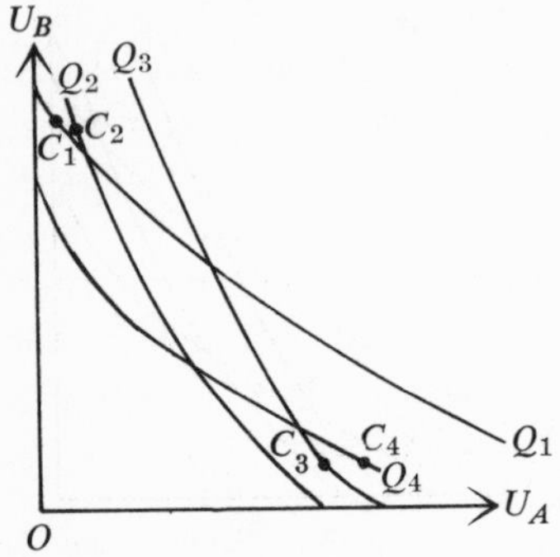

Figure 9

Kaldor-Hicks test, while Q_1 cannot be shown superior to Q_2 by the reversal test. Hence, by the Scitovsky criterion, Q_2 is better than Q_1. By the same criterion, Q_3 is shown superior to Q_2, and, again, Q_4 is shown to be superior to Q_3. Transitivity requires that Q_4 be superior to Q_1. But it is manifest from the figure that, by the Scitovsky criterion, Q_1 is superior to Q_4.[93] Clearly, the Scitovsky criterion—and, therefore, the Kaldor-Hicks criterion also—is not transitive, and could not be used alone[94] as a guide to policy without risk of contradiction.

[92] See bibliography, item 79.

[93] We could demonstrate this intransitivity just as well if, along the axes, we measured goods instead of utility, and treated the curves as community indifference curves, the points c_1, c_2, c_3, and c_4 being alternative bundles of goods.

[94] While Little's adoption of the "Scitovsky criterion" may appear vulnerable on these grounds, we must remember that his criterion also demands an acceptable distribution of welfare prior to any change being recommended. The Gorman demonstration of intransitivity does apparently depend on marked differences in the distribution of some of the bundles. Provided, then, that the acceptable range of welfare distributions was narrow, the fulfillment of Little's criterion would preclude, on distributive grounds, such contradiction.

Even for a straight choice between two alternatives we may be dissatisfied with the Scitovsky criterion. Though a movement from Q_1 (with the attached c_1' distribution) to Q_2 (with the attached c_2'' distribution) meets the Scitovsky criterion in Figure 10, we cannot allow that Q_2 is *potentially* superior to Q_1 when it is superior for only two alternative distributions of welfare; at least, not unless, in the nature of the problem, these two distributions are the only ones admissible. If, for example, we had to consider

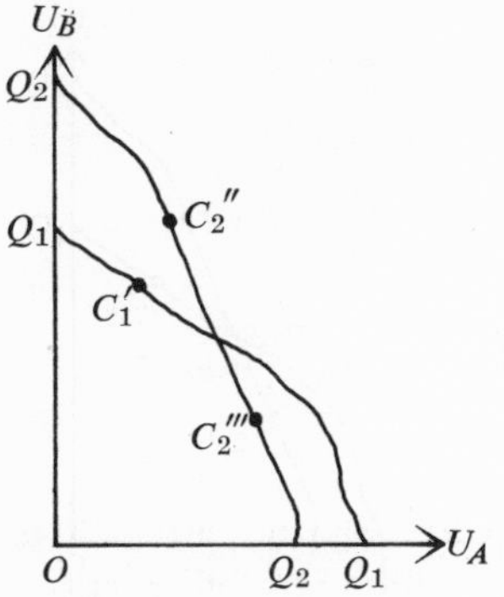

Figure 10

distributions comparable with c_2''', which would show Q_1 superior to Q_2, we could no longer assert that Q_2 was potentially superior to Q_1. Indeed, if, as Samuelson suggests,[95] we put aside for the present the question of distribution in the belief that, at a later stage, we may have the choice of any ("feasible") distribution, a much more stringent criterion is required to designate a potentially superior bundle; namely, Q_2 is potentially superior to Q_1 only if for every conceivable distribution Q_2 is superior to Q_1—if, that is, the Q_2Q_2 utility-possibility curve is at all points outside that of Q_1Q_1. A sufficient (though not a necessary) condition for Q_2 to be potentially superior to Q_1 and, to fulfill, therefore, Samuelson's criterion of an increase in "potential real income," is that Q_2 have more of "every" good than Q_1.[96]

[95] See bibliography, item 221.

[96] In view of Samuelson's welfare discussion in his 1950 paper being closely bound up with his examination of index numbers as indicators of a potential

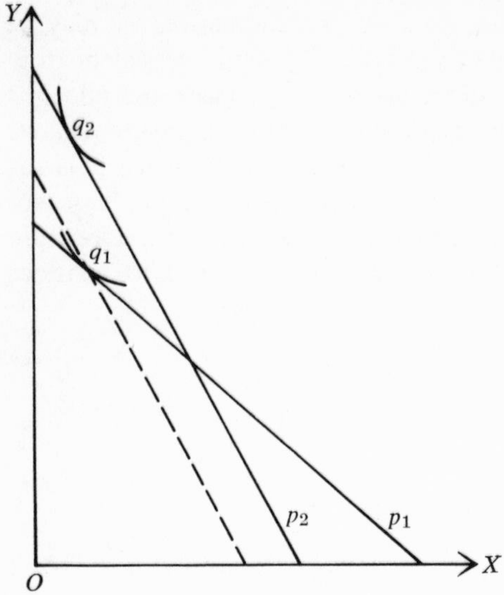

Figure 11

For some central range of the bundles on the production-possibility curve, all the corresponding utility-possibility curves will overlap. The outer envelope of these overlapping curves,

---

increase in the community's real income, a few words on the close relationship between index numbers and compensation tests may be of interest.

For the consistent individual,

$$\Sigma p_2 q_2 \geqq \Sigma p_2 q_1 \qquad (a)$$

implies

$$\Sigma p_1 q_1 < \Sigma p_1 q_2 \qquad (b)$$

From (a) we can infer that the q_2 bundle is preferred to the q_1 bundle, for in the II situation—that in which the p_2 prices are available—he spends on the q_2 bundle as much, or more, than the cost of the q_1 bundle. (This, indeed, is the interpretation of the (a) notation.) Thus, he could have had the q_1 bundle at the prices ruling in II, but chose instead to spend as much, or more, on the q_2 bundle—clear evidence of his preference for the q_2 bundle. Now, if instead of (a) we had the situation

$$\Sigma p_1 q_1 \geqq \Sigma p_1 q_2 \qquad (c)$$

similar reasoning would point to a preference for the q_1 bundle. Since he cannot prefer both q_2 and q_1, (c) is not consistent with (a). If (a) is established, we must cross out the greater-than-or-equal-to sign of (c) which, therefore, renders it (b). The sense of (a) and (b) in terms of indifference curves can be seen by the reader in Figure 11 without the need for comment.

In the case of the community, however, the simultaneous observation of (a) and (c) does not necessarily indicate inconsistency. In view of the intimate

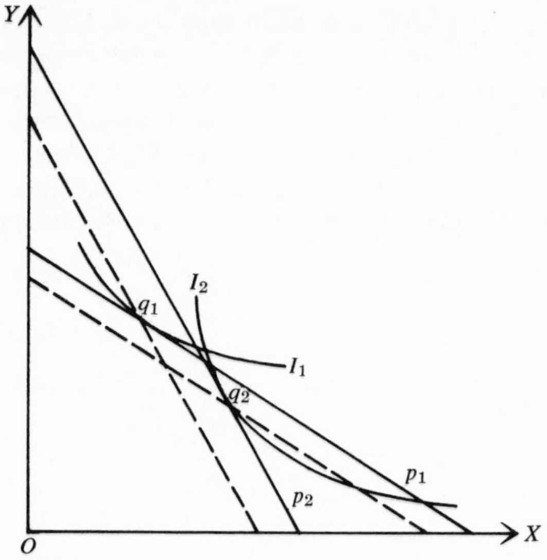

Figure 12

which we may refer to as the utility frontier,[97] is indicated by *FF* in Figure 13. Regarded as the boundary of all utility combinations possible with the given resources of the economy, *FF* summarizes the data which in principle can be made available without any ethical presuppositions other than: (*a*) that the individual is the sole judge of his own welfare, and (*b*) that the welfare of the community depends only upon the welfares of the individuals who

---

relationship between welfare distribution and relative prices, noncomparable indifference curves attaching to the bundles q_1 and q_2 may intersect as shown in Figure 12. With the p_2 prices q_2 has the higher value for the community, and (*a*) obtains. This situation corresponds to the fulfillment (for a movement from q_1 to q_2) of the Scitovsky reversal test—q_2 being preferred to q_1 when the comparison is based on the I_2 distribution of welfare. On the other hand, with the p_1 prices, q_1 has the higher valuation, and the index numbers give us (*c*). This situation corresponds to the nonfulfillment of the Kaldor-Hicks test, inasmuch as q_2 is not preferred to q_1, when the comparison between bundles is based on the I_1 welfare distribution.

Indeed, if we think now in terms of the Samuelson criterion, which requires that we compare q_2 and q_1 for all conceivable distributions of welfare, and, therefore, for an implied range of corresponding price ratios, q_2 is potentially superior to q_1 only if, for all such price ratios, q_2 costs as much or more than q_1. Again, a sufficient condition for this to occur is that the q_2 bundle contain more of "every" good than q_1.

[97] Samuelson [221] refers to it as the *situation* utility-possibility curve in order to distinguish it from the *point* utility curve of a bundle of goods.

comprise it. And only at a later stage, when choosing as between alternative combinations of individual welfares, are the ethics of distribution involved. The search for a satisfactory test of a potential welfare improvement using only compensation tests has—in its comprehension of all conceivable welfare distributions—joined with the concept of all existing production possibilities to issue in a construct, the utility frontier of society which, though

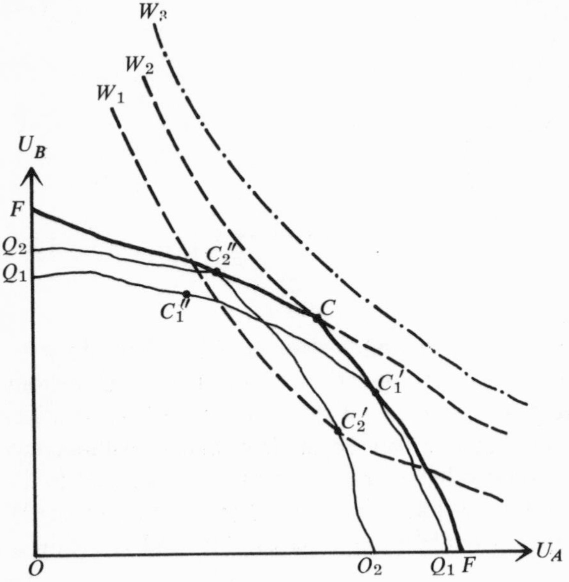

Figure 13

it contains no ethical presuppositions other than an acceptance of individual choice, provides the basic data of welfare possibilities necessary for a comprehensive social choice determined by any method.

It may be supposed that all welfare distributions on and within the boundary of Figure 13 can be reached by government policies or, if we wish to appear realists, we can follow Samuelson and include only "feasible" welfare combinations in the picture. The set of *W* curves in the figure emerges from some acceptable social-welfare function, each such curve being a locus of welfare combinations as between which society is indifferent.[98] If the social-welfare function is "of the Paretian type," to use Graaff's terminology, the *W*'s are ranked northeast from the origin; which is to say, if "everyone" is better off, then society is deemed to be better off—an ethical judgment that seems to have met with little opposition. *C* in Figure 13 is clearly the maximum social welfare for the particular Paretian type of social-welfare function chosen: of all the welfare combinations open to society that at *C* has, in the opinions formalized by the welfare function, the highest social value.

Disregarding, provisionally, the social-welfare function, let us briefly explore the properties of the utility frontier. The point c_1', as the tangency between Q_1Q_1 and the frontier *FF*, informs us that there is no distribution of any other bundle that can yield a situation in which "everyone" is better off than he is at c_1'. Since on this description c_1' is recognized as a Pareto optimum, all the necessary conditions—the exchange, production, and top-level optima—are fulfilled. Indeed, since the utility frontier is made up of tangency points such as c_1', this frontier constitutes a locus of Paretian optima.

A welfare combination c_1'' on the utility-possibility curve Q_1Q_1 is obviously not a Pareto optimum, being a point below the frontier *FF*. Exchange optimum obtains and we must assume—if *FF* is a genuine frontier—that production optimum also obtains. Top-level optimum, however, does not obtain, since a movement from c_1'' to, say, c_2'' involves a change of bundle which in effect makes "everyone" better off, thereby fulfilling the Paretian criterion. But such a movement does not fulfill the Samuelson criterion. For if we consider all comparable distributions of Q_1 and Q_2, for some of them, Q_2Q_2 will be above Q_1Q_1, while for others the reverse is true. Once it is appreciated that whether or not any efficiently produced bundle has top-level optimal properties—that rates of substitution in consumption and in production are equal—depends entirely on its distribution, any belief in the potential superiority of a Pareto optimum disappears. Any Pareto optimum will, of course, be actually superior to some particular range of compa-

[98] The reader is reminded that we have yet to determine whether a social-welfare function for society can emerge from the separate aspirations of the individuals comprising it.

rable nonoptimal positions. But since the optimal characteristic of a bundle depends solely on the distribution attaching to it, divested of that distribution it fares no better than the other efficiently produced bundles. No bundle, then, is superior to any one of the other efficiently produced bundles for *all* welfare distributions, and therefore no bundle can fulfill the Samuelson criterion.[99]

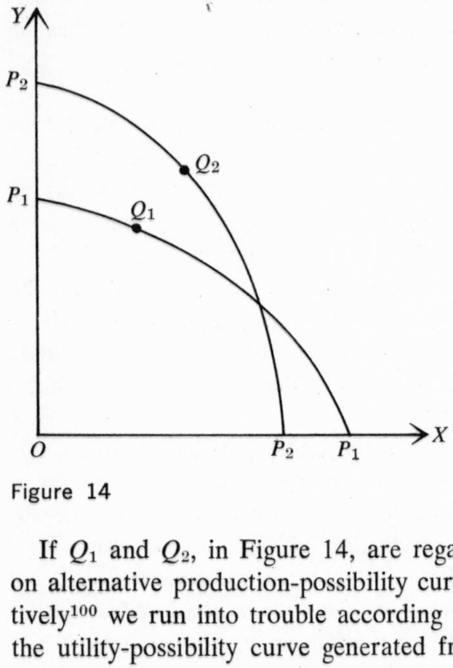

Figure 14

If Q_1 and Q_2, in Figure 14, are regarded as bundles of goods on alternative production-possibility curves P_1P_1 and P_2P_2 respectively[100] we run into trouble according to Samuelson. For though the utility-possibility curve generated from bundle Q_2 lies every-

[99] A similar treatment using community indifference curves can be found in [180], where it is shown that as optimal and nonoptimal positions are characterized, at top level, by the relationship between prices and their marginal costs, comparisons between such positions cannot even be made. Only when such a range of bundles (on the production-possibility curve) are divested of their optimal or nonoptimal characteristics can comparisons between them be made and, in the absence of a particular welfare distribution, no bundle can be demonstrated superior to any other.

[100] The meaning to be attached to a choice between alternative production frontiers is far from obvious. Other than international trade, which presents the community with alternative *consumption* possibilities, one expects, with the passage of time, that the entire production frontier moves outward. The choice of accumulating at a faster rate, then, translates into the choice of having the entire frontier move outward at a faster rate.

Even if, owing to the exhaustion of irreplaceable resources, some parts of the frontier shrink, the event is, surely, irreversible.

where above that generated from bundle Q_1, obviously the utility frontier of the production-possibility curve P_2P_2 will not lie everywhere above that of P_1P_1. If, now, the community experiences a shift from Q_1 on P_1P_1 to Q_2 on P_2P_2, producing more of all goods in the new position, the inference that a potential increase of real income has taken place would be false. This afterthought, however, is not very convincing.[101]

THE SOCIAL-WELFARE FUNCTION

We have already indicated that, in a manner analogous with the imposition of an individual's ordinal welfare function—in two dimensions, his indifference map—upon his budget constraint, to yield a maximum position, we can impose a Paretian-type social-welfare function upon the boundary of welfare possibilities to reveal the summit position for society. Actually, the original Bergson welfare function was designed to rank not the combinations of individual welfares but, more directly, the combinations of all those variables on which the individual welfares depended, in particular the goods consumed and the services rendered by each of the individuals in society. And, formally, this is how Arrow deals with it.[102] He was the first to make an attempt. Although the social-welfare function had received continual mention since Bergson's 1938 formulation, no instruction in the drafting of this grandiose design had been hazarded. Rather it had been invoked in the grand manner of Samuelson as a *deus ex machina* to crown the formal elegance of his "general equilibrium" welfare. Indeed, one could hardly hope to do more with so stupendous a concept —except, perhaps, to question whether such a thing could, in

[101] The sense of the word "potential" in this context is elusive. In the original Kaldor-Hicks criterion the statement that Q_2 is potentially superior to Q_1 would mean that a *redistribution* of the product Q_2 would make "everyone" better off. Pending the actual redistribution, that is, the superiority of Q_2 remains potential. But what of the assertion that a production-possibility curve P_2P_2 is potentially superior to P_1P_1, since, for any point on P_1P_1, there will be some point on P_2P_2 with more of "every" good? For not only is hypothetical distribution involved in this case but also hypothetical movements along the production-possibility curves. But if one can envisage movements from bundle to bundle along the curves, why not also between the curves? If such movements are admitted however, as it seems they should be, the comparison between the two production-possibility curves crumbles. Only the outer production frontier has meaning.

[102] See bibliography, item 14.

principle, be constructed so as to manifest the aspirations of a free society. This, in fact, was the task that Arrow set himself.

We are to imagine that each individual has his own precise notion of a suitable welfare function for society or, to use Arrow's terminology, that each individual has a particular "ordering," or ranking, of all the conceivable "social states"—each "social state" referring to a distinct combination of all the relevant variables in the economy that enter into the individual's welfare.[103] Suppose there are *m* distinct social states conceivable, and suppose that there are altogther *n* different ways of ordering these *m* social states,[104] the question to be answered is: regardless of which of these *n* different ways happens to be chosen by each of the individuals, will it be possible, always, by means of some rules that are ethically acceptable to a free society, to construct therefrom a corresponding social ordering of the *m* social states?

In order to be ethically acceptable, Arrow proposes that the social ordering to be derived from the individual orderings meet certain "reasonable" conditions: (i) it must be positively associated with the individual orderings;[105] (ii) if some social state were removed, as no longer relevant, society's ranking of the remaining social states must not be changed; (iii) the social ordering must not be imposed, either by custom or dictatorship.

After dismissing the rank-order method of voting,[106] and after a preliminary skirmish with the compensation principle,[107] Arrow

[103] Although it is allowed that the welfare of each individual may depend on those of others, inasmuch as the goods received and services rendered by every individual enter into the social states to be ranked, the formal treatment at no point draws on this complication.

[104] If we admit only "strong" ordering—no provision for indifference being made—*m* alternative social states can be ranked in *m* factorial different ways. The introduction of "weak" ordering—indifference being allowed—multiplies this number.

[105] This condition would exclude interpersonal comparisons of utility.

[106] See bibliography, item 14, p. 27.

[107] Since Arrow's rejection of the compensation principle on the grounds of inconsistency [14, pp. 34–45] stems from his adoption of a footnote suggestion by Scitovsky [228, pp. 94–95] that two bundles of goods whose community indifference curves intersect be regarded as "equally good," his demonstration is, perhaps, otiose. If anything, the principle of compensation cannot qualify for a social-welfare function meeting Arrow's conditions simply because of Arrow's axiom that for *all* alternative social states a social ordering must be derived, whereas it is generally acknowledged—notwithstanding Scitovsky's (unguarded?) proposal—that cases arise for which the compensation test gives an ambiguous answer, an answer which precludes judgment and prescription.

opens a full-scale attack with his "Possibility Theorem" designed to demonstrate the impossibility of meeting these conditions.

Though the problem has been posed on an astronomical scale, the proof is compact enough, involving, in the first instance, only two individuals and three alternative social states, *x, y, z*. Since among Arrow's axioms is the requirement that for every conceivable set of individual orderings there must correspond a distinct ordering for society, in the event that individual I prefers *x* to *y* and individual II *y* to *x*, we are obliged to infer that society is "indifferent" as between *y* and *x*. To state otherwise, for instance, that society prefers *x* to *y*, leads to logical implications which reveal individual I to be a dictator inasmuch as society's orderings will always coincide with his.

If, now, to take an awkward possibility, individual I has the ordering *x, y, z*, and II has the ordering *z, x, y*, we are required to infer, as just stated, that society is indifferent as between *y* and *z*. In addition, for both individuals, and therefore for society also, *x* is preferred to *y*. From which it follows—using Arrow's transitivity axiom—that, for society, *x* is preferred to *z*. But, since I prefers *x* to *z*, and II prefers *z* to *x*, we are bound to conclude, also, that society is indifferent as between *x* and *z*, which contradicts the conclusion of the previous sentence.[108]

Arrow concludes that, in general, a rule for passing from individual orderings to a social ordering consistent with his "reasonable" conditions cannot be found. Consistency would require an imposed or a dictated social-welfare function.

While the formal layout of Arrow's argument was impressive, it would not be unfair to suggest that the conclusion was hardly surprising. One does not have to venture beyond a vision of two stubborn men on an island with mutually opposite ideas about the proper division of labor, and the fruits thereof, to run into an impasse of this sort. Notwithstanding this opinion, Arrow's thesis caused some stir in academic circles. Several papers were published, productive more of symbols than of substance, urging modifications of Arrow's conditions in the attempt to keep the social-

[108] What this contradiction seems to reveal is that the "social indifference" arbitrarily—though in view of Arrow's axioms, necessarily—attributed to an opposition of values between individuals is not transitive, as we might well suspect.

welfare function from expiring.[109] But even if Arrow had proved that, in principle, a completely satisfactory transition from any set of individual orderings to an ordering for society was always possible, the route to the (continually changing) position of maximum social welfare would have been too arduous for the most accomplished econometrician to plot, to say nothing of prompting humanity to undertake the journey.

Summing up, there are three main ways of regarding compensation tests:

1. As sufficient conditions for prescribing a change to a new position by defining such tests as tests of "efficiency." It is doubtful if anyone holds this view today—or ever did without some qualification. If, however, it were adopted, and one aimed at a test which was to detach itself from any particular distribution, contradiction could be avoided only by espousing the Samuelson criterion. In view of the virtually infinite number of welfare distributions, such a criterion is not a practical proposition. But for the one situation in which the criterion is always satisfied—that in which one of the bundles has more of "every" good than the other—no such test is necessary.

2. Once proposed, the Samuelson criterion—requiring that the utility-possibility curve of one bundle be at all points outside that of the other—lent itself to the idea of an envelope of such curves, or a utility frontier encompassing all welfare possibilities latent in the resources at the disposal of the community. Each of the welfare combinations on the frontier corresponds to a position of Pareto optimum, but without some expressed partiality for one distribution of welfare over all others there is no acceptable case in welfare economics for prescribing a movement from a non-optimal position to any optimal position.[110] On the other hand, the formation of a "satisfactory" social-welfare function in order

[109] Hildreth [106] argues that if one individual barely prefers x to y while another desperately prefers y to x, the social choice should rank y above x. J. C. Wheldon [246] also considers bringing in interpersonal comparisons of welfare, as do Kemp and Asimakopulos [129], who further propose a "constitution" which entails measurable utility. Inada [113] proposes a less severe set of conditions which lead also to the Arrow result.

Other contributions, such as those of Little [162], Rothenberg [213], and Buchanan [44], are of a more philosophical nature.

[110] It may be stressed, however, that if society is not already at an optimum position there is scope for making "everyone" better off.

to determine a unique position of maximum social welfare is not only utopian, it is in principle impossible.

3. Returning to earth again, we may accept compensation tests but only as necessary conditions for policy prescription. For instance, in Little's piecemeal approach, if the Kaldor-Hicks and/or the "Scitovsky criterion" are fulfilled, then a movement to the new position is recommended provided, however, that redistribution is acceptable.

IV. Consumers' Surplus

One can readily sympathize with the high hopes originally entertained by Marshall for his doctrine of consumers' surplus as an instrument of social betterment. His definition of the individual consumer's surplus—the amount a man is willing to pay rather than go without the thing, over the amount he has to pay—had so immediate an appeal to subjective experience that, despite severe criticism of the doctrine and Marshall's own eventual loss of faith in it, the prospect of its extension as a practical tool of welfare analysis has tempted the ingenuity of several eminent economists, among whom the best known is Professor J. R. Hicks. In his *Value and Capital* consumer's surplus appeared as a by-product of his ordinal treatment of the theory of consumer's behavior. In this more acceptable ordinal form it was further refined and developed in a series of papers appearing in the *Review of Economic Studies* in the early forties.[111] The substance of these papers, along with some further reflections, may be found in his recent *Revision of Demand Theory*.

Myint, in his 1948 book,[112] champions the consumers' surplus technique as against the marginalism of Pigou. The marginal conditions, he contends, permit only of small adjustments within the neighborhood of the existing pattern of output. In contrast, consumers' surplus enables us to meet the Hicksian total conditions which encompass all ranges of output and, indeed, enables us to determine whether or not any particular good should be abandoned or a new one introduced. Again, it is frequently pointed out that the marginal conditions are inappropriate for goods that are

[111] See bibliography, items 100–103.
[112] See bibliography, item 189.

insufficiently divisible to enable the consumer to equate the value of the good to him with its market price. In such cases the value of the "marginal" unit—which may be the only unit purchased—might greatly exceed the price. So much at least may be said in favor of the technique of consumers' surplus. What of the criticisms? Before we consider them, however, and Hicks' attempts to meet them, let us glance briefly at the various definitions proposed.

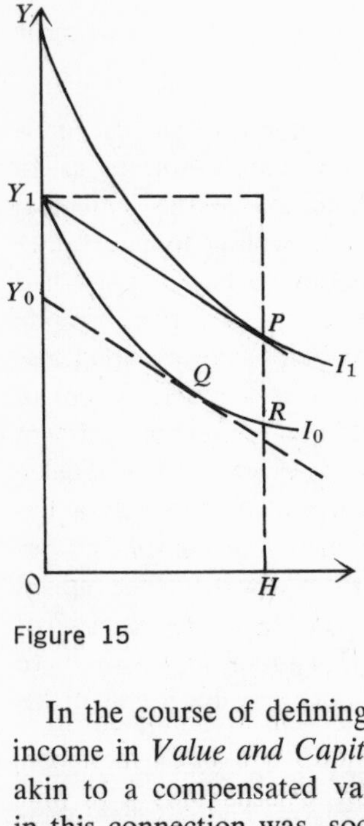

Figure 15

In the course of defining consumer's surplus in terms of money income in *Value and Capital,* Hicks suggested that the notion was akin to a compensated variation in income. The definition used in this connection was, soon after, shown by Henderson to differ from the original Marshallian definition,[113] the difference turning on the quantity of the good purchased. Marshall's definition corresponded to the sum of money that the consumer was prepared to pay for the privilege of being able to buy at the existing price *the amount that he was already buying at that price.* On the other hand, Hicks' definition concerned the sum he was prepared to pay for the privilege of being able to buy the good at the existing price

[113] See bibliography, item 92.

in whatsoever quantities he wished.[114] Inasmuch, then, as Marshall's definition involved a quantitative constraint, absent in the Hicks definition, the maximum sum of money that the consumer would be prepared to pay would be smaller under the former definition than under the latter.

In the same paper Henderson pointed to a further ambiguity: the compensating variation measure proposed by Hicks would differ according to whether the consumer had to *pay* for the opportunity to buy the new good X, or whether he was to *be paid* for abandoning the purchase of X. The same distinction clearly held if the choice was that between buying X at a lower price or at a higher price.

In reply, Hicks[115] carefully traced a relationship between four definitions of consumer's surplus and the Marshallian measure—the area under the individual's demand curve. The scheme required some new terminology in order to effect a double distinction: (*a*) that between the compensating variation (CV), for either a fall or rise in price, which compensation when paid or received is such as to leave the consumer in his *initial* welfare position, on the one hand, and, on the other, the equivalent variation (EV), again for a rise or fall in price, which involves compensation, paid or received, such as to leave him in the *subsequent* welfare position following the change of price,[116] and (*b*) that between the *price* compensating variation (CV_p), or *price* equivalent variation (EV_p), on the one hand, which covers those cases for which the individual is free to choose the quantity of the good in question, and, on the other hand, the *quantity* compensating variation

[114] Using Henderson's diagram on which Figure 15 is based, the Marshallian consumer's surplus is equal to PR. For if he were obliged to spend FR in buying OH of X he would be just as well off as if X were not available, whereas in fact he has to spend only FP. Hicks' compensating variation, however, is Y_1Y_0. For if the consumer is made to pay this much in order to retain the price P he will just reach Q on the indifference curve I_0, his initial welfare position in the absence of a price for X.

Note that since the issue in these earlier illustrations was whether to introduce X at a given price or not to introduce X at all, an all-or-nothing offer confronted the consumer.

[115] See bibliography, item 102.

[116] It follows, as Hicks points out, that (1) the CV of a *fall* in price from p_1 to p_2 (the maximum payment by the individual in order to have the new, lower price p_2, which payment leaves him at his *initial* welfare) is exactly equal to (2) the EV of a *rise* in price from p_2 to p_1 (the maximum payment by the individual in order to retain the old, lower price p_2, which payment leaves him at a new, lower level of welfare, which is equal to the initial welfare in (1).

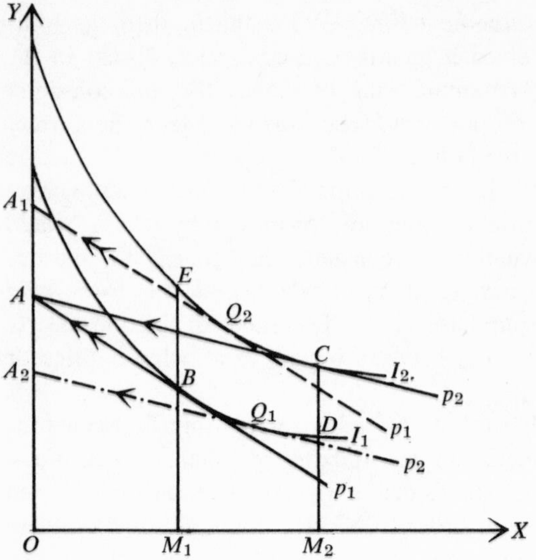

Figure 16

(CV_q), or the *quantity* equivalent variation (EV_q), to cover those cases in which—like the original Marshall definition—the consumer is restricted to the quantity purchased in the absence of compensation.[117]

[117] These four definitions are identified in Figure 16, in which, for brevity, we consider consumer's surpluses only for a fall in price from p_1 to p_2, the income of the individual—equal to all other goods at fixed prices—being measured as OA.

The CV_p is measured as AA_2, this being the maximum income the consumer will pay for the privilege of buying X at the lower price p_2. For with only OA_2 of his income left, he can move along A_2P_2 and just touch I_1, his initial level of welfare, at Q_1.

The EV_p is measured by AA_1, this being the minimum sum which the consumer will accept to relinquish the opportunity of buying at the lower price p_2. With this compensation and the old price he can move along A_1p_1 and at Q_2 just touch I_2, the welfare level he would reach if he did not relinquish p_2.

The CV_q is measured by CD. It is the maximum the consumer will pay for the privilege of buying at p_2 if, along with this privilege, he is constrained to buy OM_2 of X, the quantity which he would buy at p_2 in the absence of any compensating payments. Thus, if he buys OM_2 at p_2, he gets to C. He pays CD and gets to D, which is on I_1, his initial level of welfare.

The EV_q is measured by EB. It is the minimum the consumer will accept to return to the higher price p_1, if he is at the same time constrained to purchase OM_1, the quantity of X which in fact he would consume at p_1 in the absence of compensation receipts. Thus, consuming OM_1 at p_1 places him at B. The receipt of BE takes him to E, which is on I_2, the higher level of welfare he could have reached with p_2 in the absence of any quantity constraint.

It has been argued [179] that in all plausible circumstances we should consider using only CV_p and EV_p.

There is no analytical difficulty in extending these four definitions to simultaneous changes in the prices of many goods.[118] Indeed, they can be extended to cover not only all goods bought on the market but also all factors sold by the individual to the market, thereby involving rent in the same four-fold distinction.[119] In the absence of income effects, all these measures coincide, though in any case the differences between them are thought not to be important for practical measurement.

We are now faced with the rather more difficult task of making the transition from the individual to the community. Hicks attempts this by abandoning Marshall's assumptions about constant market shares and so forth, arising from his cardinal view of utility, as implausible and unnecessary. Without bothering our heads over interpersonal comparisons, if the area between the demand curve and the price is taken as a good approximation of the sum of the individual consumer's surpluses, however defined,[120] and if the area between the supply curve and the price[121] is taken to be a good approximation of the sum of the relevant producers' surpluses, however defined, we may add these areas algebraically as sums of money. If both areas are positive, or if the positive consumer's surplus exceeds the negative producers' surplus (in the case of decreasing average cost), the compensation principle provides a rationale for undertaking the investment in the good in question—or for retaining it if it is already in production. At least it does this if all the gains and losses to the community from the production of this good are summarized in this partial picture given by the market demand and supply curve. In general, this will not be the case. Problems arise when we trace out the effects in the rest of the economy, and it is to such problems that Hicks addresses himself in his "Rehabilitation" paper of 1943.[122]

If over the whole economy competition was perfect, and there was a complete absence of external economies and diseconomies, no apparent difficulty arises. The prices of the factors attracted to

118 Hicks, in his generalization of consumer's surplus [101], expresses them in terms of Paasche or Laspeyres variations plus income and/or substitution effects.

119 See bibliography, item 182.

120 For most purposes, the CV_p definition is appropriate.

121 Where the supply curve is above the price the producers' surplus is taken to be negative.

122 See bibliography, item 100.

the new project reflect their values at the margin in all other uses. If, however, prices exceed their corresponding marginal costs in other industries the values of the factors which move into the new project exceed their prices and, therefore, their cost to the new project. Since the opportunity cost of these factors to society exceeds their cost to the new project, some correction is called for and may be administered by raising the apparent marginal cost of the product under consideration by the appropriate percentage prior to measuring the net surplus. If this corrected net surplus, or social surplus, is positive the good should be introduced, and in the amount which makes the corrected marginal cost equal to price, notwithstanding that the commercial criterion, that of a positive producers' surplus, is not met.[123]

This treatment does not, however, face up to the chief difficul-

[123] The question of whether we are not double counting by adding together consumer's and producers' surpluses deserves some attention if only because of Marshall's warning in appendix K of the *Principles*. Obviously the issue turns on the meaning of producers' surplus. In the *Principles* it is used as a synonym for rents (not profits), which have been defined recently [182] in a manner symmetrical in all respects with consumer's surplus—as the *CV* or *EV* to the individual arising from changes in the prices of the factors that he sells to the market.

In an *n*-dimensional figure containing both goods' axes and factors' axes, we can regard the individual as both a consumer of goods, measuring the welfare effect of a change in the prices of goods along the goods' axes, and as a supplier of factors, measuring the welfare effect of a change in the prices of factors along the factors' axes. In principle, however, the welfare of all such price changes may be measured along any one, or any several, of the axes. After all, the net effect of any group of price changes is to place the individual on a higher, or lower, indifference surface, the difference between which and the initial indifference surface, being measurable along any one (or several) of the axes, as a *CV* or *EV*.

On a partial view, however, and thinking in terms of individual demand curves, we could add together the consumer's surplus arising from a decline in a group of product prices in the manner suggested by Hicks [99]—the *cet. par.* on successive goods, to include the lowered prices of goods whose consumer's surplus has already been measured. Alternatively, this same decline in a group of product prices could be regarded as giving rise to an increase in rent, or producers' surplus, for the individual, inasmuch as a fall in the price of any product he consumes is *pro tanto* a rise in his real income, or welfare. Now, the addition of an improvement in welfare of this sort, first as a consumer's surplus and then again in the guise of a producers' surplus, is obviously wrong. But this does not mean that there may not be some practical convenience in dividing a given gain of welfare into two parts: a part arising from changes in product prices and a part arising from changes in factor prices. An individual whose factors are attracted into the production of *X* and who, in addition, is enabled to purchase *X* at a lower price does in fact gain from both these circumstances. Therefore the total gain which places him on a higher indifference surface and which is, as suggested above, measurable in principle on any one of the axes, is, on this partial approach, split into a measure of the gain from the lower product prices plus a measure of the gain from the higher factor prices, which two measures add together to yield a measure of the total gain in welfare.

ties. Even within its own limited terms of reference, it does not answer the rather obvious question of what to do when some of the factors to be used in the new good *X* come from industries whose prices exceed their marginal costs in varying degrees, while others come from industries whose prices fall below their marginal costs, again in varying degrees. In principle, of course, there is little difficulty: we can value each factor to be used at the value it contributes elsewhere. But we have to abandon any simple practical rule, such as raising or lowering the cost curve of the industry in question.

Many of the chief difficulties in taking account of the repercussions in the rest of the economy are mentioned by Little,[124] whose main conclusions may be summarized as follows: the case for which Hicks' treatment is valid is that for which the introduction of a new good, *X*, affects only to a negligible extent each of the outputs of all other goods in the economy. However, cases in which other goods, say *Y* and *Z*, are closely related to *X* in consumption are more common. Suppose, for example, that *Y* and *Z* are close substitutes for *X*, and that everywhere price is equal to marginal cost. Now if both *Y* and *Z* are produced under constant costs there is little trouble. The area under the demand curve for *X* is then a measure of the consumer's surplus which meets the *cet. par.* requirement that all other prices be constant, and, in so far as the introduction of *X* causes consumers to switch from *Y* and *Z* to buying *X*, they are—for all intra-marginal units—made better off, the area between the demand curve for *X* and its price being a measure of their gain.[125] Since the assumption of constant costs ensures that no losses of producers' surplus take place in *Y* and *Z*, there is no need to correct the producers' surplus in *X*. Obviously, however, if price exceeded marginal cost in *Y* and *Z* the supply curve of *X* would have to be raised for reasons given above.

In the event, however, that *Y* and *Z* are not constant-cost in-

[124] See bibliography, item 161, Chapter 10.

[125] True, in so far as demand has shifted from *Y* and *Z* to *X*, the areas under the demand curves for *Y* and *Z* have shrunk. But this can be legitimately ignored, for no consumer can be worse off when *Y* and *Z* are available at the same price as before, and *X* is now cheaper (or newly available). In other words, the *cet. par.* being met in the measurement of the consumer's surplus in *X*, no further correction need be allowed for.

dustries difficulties begin to mount. Suppose they are increasing-cost industries, the consequent consumer's surplus in *X* measured in the usual way will be an underestimate. For in so far as the shift of output from industries *Y* and *Z* reduces their prices, when *X* is introduced, consumers are better off than if, as in the previous case, their prices remain constant. Yet the consequence of a decline in the prices of *Y* and *Z* is to reduce this shift of demand from *Y* and *Z* to good *X*, thereby, of course, reducing the area of consumer's surplus in *X*, notwithstanding the additional benefits accruing to consumers in this case as compared with the previous case. On the other hand, against any gain of producers' surplus in *X* must be set losses of producers' surplus in *Y* and *Z*. However, producers' surpluses are difficult things to measure, involving as they do the rents of all factors whose prices or occupations are changed as a result of introducing *X*. Profits, which are more closely identified with the area between the price and the supply curve, afford little clue to the magnitudes involved. Even in the special case above, we must be prepared for a rise in the prices of some factors, a fall in the prices of others, both groups of factors being found in many industries besides those of *X*, *Y*, and *Z*.

Though we have said nothing yet of divergences between private and social valuation, they require the same sort of correction as discrepancies in the ratios of prices to marginal costs. There is, however, still the familiar and inescapable difficulty arising out of the interdependence of valuation and distribution: in making the transition from the individual to the community, that is, we cannot escape the complication uncovered in Section III. Here, as there, only the Samuelson criterion can serve us without fear of contradiction for all criteria in which distributive considerations are to be set aside.

In order to separate this source of complication from that arising from closely related goods with increasing costs, let us suppose again that all goods other than *X* are produced under constant costs. The area enclosed between the demand curve for *X* and the price is a rough approximation to the sum of the individual consumers' CV_p given the existing distribution of welfare, prior to the introduction of *X*. The area between the supply curve and the price is yet a cruder approximation to the sum of the factor-owners' CV_p at the given welfare distribution. The algebraic sum of all individuals' CV_p regarded as consumers and as suppliers of factors, is therefore approximately represented by the area enclosed between the demand curve and the corrected supply curve.[126] Crude as this area is as an index of net gain in welfare arising from the introduction of X when all other goods are produced at constant costs, we are required by the Samuelson criterion to measure this social surplus for all conceivable welfare distributions. If for any welfare distribution this area of surplus is negative, there is no warrant, on grounds of "efficiency"—on the Samuelson criterion alone—for introducing X. On Little's approach, however, provided that we approve of the distribution which accompanies the production of X, we should introduce X if the social surplus is large enough to assure us that the sum of the CV_p must be positive. If it is positive, the Kaldor-Hicks criterion is met: with the old distribution (prior to the introduction of X) "everyone" can be made better off by producing X.

In sum, then, as a method of capturing data on which to exercise the compensation tests, consumers' and producers' surpluses suffer not only from the distributional complications common to comparisons based on such tests but also from difficulties in their measurement, largely owing to their essentially partial character. In view of this, one can sympathize with Little's comment that consumers' surplus is but a theoretical toy,[127] though it is putting the case a little too strongly. After all, what other practical procedures are open to us in a comparison of two situations?

V. Some Recent Obstacles

In order not to clutter up the main features in the developments over the last twenty years, we have set aside for separate treatment in this section a number of considerations, all of which appear,

[126] It is sometimes proposed that the sum of the CV's should exceed the sum of the EV's. But on Hicks' definition, if a price moves in favor of an individual the maximum he is prepared to pay for that price is the CV, while if the price moves against him the CV becomes the minimum he must receive in order not to be worse off than before. The gainers can therefore compensate the losers if the sum of all their CV's is positive.

The sense of this definition is further illustrated in the special case of an individual whose gain as a consumer exactly offsets his loss as a supplier of factors, his net CV being nil.

[127] See bibliography, item 161, p. 180.

on the surface of things, to reduce the applicability of welfare economics.

SECOND-BEST OPTIMA

The recent paper by Lipsey and Lancaster[128] was the culmination of a diversity of contributions[129] which sought ways of approaching a next-best solution whenever some particular institutional or policy constraint prevented the realization of all the conditions necessary for a true summit position. A common conclusion, albeit a negative one, was implicit in all these writings; namely, that if one or more of the optimum conditions could not, in the circumstances, be met in one or more of the sectors of the economy, one did not make the best of a bad job by proceeding blithely to fulfill the remaining conditions. We can illustrate this with a familiar problem: the determination of the output of a particular industry when it is known that in all other industries price exceeds marginal cost. Rather than equate marginal cost to price in this particular industry, we should choose an output for which price here, as elsewhere, exceeds marginal cost.[130] The new rule in this case is, of course, simple and obvious. If, however, some of the other industries were perfectly competitive, some monopolistic and others subsidized, there may not be a satisfactory second-best solution at all, and, if there is, the rules to be adopted may be far from simple.

A theorem embodying this negative conclusion is proved elegantly by the simple mathematics of maximizing a function of n variables subject to the usual constraints—such as the production function—*plus* an "artificial" constraint in the form of an *inequality* of one of the conventional marginal conditions. The first-order conditions resulting from this operation are not identifiable as the usual marginal conditions for an optimum but are relatively complex expressions. Indeed, without knowledge of the specific forms

[128] See bibliography, item 141.

[129] Some examples of the application of second-best theory may be found in Jacob Viner's *The Customs Union Issue* (1950); S. A. Ozga, "An Essay in the Theory of Tariffs," *Journal of Political Economy* (1955); J. E. Meade, *The Theory of Customs Unions* (Amsterdam: North Holland, 1955), also [172], [51], and [155].

[130] See Kahn, *op. cit.*, and the discussion in Section II. It is assumed, in this example, that the supply curves of all factors are of zero elasticity.

of the welfare and production functions we should, in general, be unable to translate such expressions even in qualitative terms—we should be quite unable to say, for instance, that in regard to, say, a good *Y* the price should be greater, equal, or less than its marginal cost.[131]

Though no logical difficulties arise in placing this theorem within the body of welfare analysis, it does seem, at first blush, to reduce drastically the applicability of such analysis. For it is too much to hope that welfare economists will be operating in an environment subject to no policy or institutional restraints. And it requires only that in one sector the conventional optimum conditions be abandoned as impracticable for the conventional optimum conditions to be irrelevant in the remaining sectors.

INTERDEPENDENT UTILITIES

Though recognition of the effect on the individual's welfare of the possessions of others is not new in the literature, Duesenberry was first to invest the idea with some formal analysis and to deduce therefrom some implications for welfare economics.[132] He attacks the problem by supposing a community of three people, each of whose welfare depends not only on his own income but also on those of the other two.[133] This interdependence, in effect, imposes additional constraints, so that the first-order condition of a maximum position for each individual is more complex than the usual one. Whereas with independent utilities the individual equates his (subjective) rate of substitution between product and factor to the marginal physical product, there are now, with interdependence, additional terms in the condition so as to take account of the welfare effect upon others of the addition to his welfare. Thus translating into value terms, if the value of the marginal product were

[131] Though the theory was not generalized to cover a community, the conclusion is applicable to the community. Thus, following the recognition of one or more policy constraints, pursuit of the remaining optimum conditions will not direct us to a point on the second-best utility frontier—a position, that is, in which, accepting the constraints, it is impossible to make "everyone" better off. To reach this second-best frontier, the familiar marginal equalities must give way to other more complex ones.

[132] See bibliography, item 60.

[133] Duesenberry simplifies further by assuming only one good and only one factor. But the results he reaches are sufficiently general for the purpose in hand.

equal to one pound the supply of the additional factors provided is not justified if it merely compensated the individual for the sacrifice involved. The one pound must, in addition, compensate others who are—let us assume—adversely affected by his one pound of additional income. Indeed, it must be enough to cover the effects of all subsequent adjustments to his own and to their incomes. If, of course, instead, the effects on others are beneficial, inasmuch as they rejoice in each other's good fortune, symmetrical reasoning shows that—since each individual in his own adjustment ignores the benefits he confers on others—the application of the conventional factor-product rule results in an output below the true optimum. In such situations no specific rules can be laid down without specific knowledge of the nature of the interdependence.

An interesting idea emerges from this analysis. Imagine, says Duesenberry, that, on balance, each income group is adversely affected by the income groups above but not by those below it, then a progressive income tax[134] would be a corrective in the right direction. Ideally, of course, the tax should suffice to cover all the initial and subsequent claims necessary to placate everybody in the lower-income groups, and the stronger is this envy of others,[135] the heavier must be the tax. In this connection the term "excessive" [136] is used to indicate a circumstance in which any net increase of output—for instance, more of "every" good without additional effort—will not advance the welfare of the community no matter how it is distributed. Indeed, any increase of output makes the community worse off, since, no matter how the additional goods are distributed, the additional envy generated cannot be adequately compensated out of these extra goods.[137]

[134] No reason is given why the tax should be progressive as distinct, say, from a proportional income tax.

[135] Envy of the possessions of others is frequently referred to, or classified under, "external diseconomies of consumption." But such terminology seems more appropriate to the tangible and, in principle, measurable effects on other people's enjoyment and convenience of the use by others of consumer goods. Such byproducts as air pollution, noise, mutual hindrance, and litter are obvious examples.

[136] See bibliography, item 84, p. 51.

[137] One might imagine that the existence of "altruistic" interdependence (enjoying others' good fortune) adds to the community's welfare while "egoistical" interdependence (resenting others' good fortune) reduces it, but this is not so. If I am made happy by the thought of those with higher incomes, or advancing incomes, I must be saddened reflecting on those with lower incomes, or declining incomes. If, on the other hand, I suffer mortification contemplating higher incomes, or advancing incomes, I shall feel triumphant in my own progress rela-

However, if the community were in so unfortunate a position, symmetrical reasoning would surely point to the possibility of improvement through a reduction of output. Empirical confirmation of the existence of excess envy does not therefore constitute a valid objection to the application of welfare analysis,[138] though the more complex conditions of substitution between factor and product are likely to involve guesswork rather than measurement, to say nothing of the political difficulty of a decision to reduce total output in order to restore a position of optimum.

What of the other marginal conditions of optimum? The general belief seems to be that a true optimum would require their modification also. But if excessive envy has been ruled out on the previous argument as evidence only of a failure of the true factor-product conditions, a failure which results in an output larger than optimum, the belief seems mistaken. Consider a movement from a position where initially there was a discrepancy of the factor rates of substitution as between one good and another to a position in which the factor rates of substitution were the same for the two goods. Since additional goods are made available without additional effort, there is some distribution of the additional goods which will—despite the existence of some (not "excessive") envy—make "everyone" better off. Top-level optimum remains unmodi-

---

tive to that of others. How much and in what way a person's welfare is affected by either sort of interdependence obviously depends on his age, his nature, his environment, his movement and position along the income scale, etc., there being no *a priori* reason to suppose that on balance his welfare is increased or reduced by either sort of interdependence. I owe appreciation of this point to Sir Roy Harrod.

Nevertheless, the argument that the application of the conventional factor-product condition results in too small an output in the case of altruistic interdependence and too large an output in the case of egoistical interdependence still holds. For the individual properly takes all his own feelings into account when adjusting the supply of his factors to their prices, but does not take into account the pleasures or pains experienced by others in the community whose welfares are affected by the size of his income.

[138] Though no formal development is undertaken here, it may be noted in passing that differences in the degree of envy experienced do not disturb this conclusion. We can easily see this by contemplating a situation prior to which the community's mutual envy is not such as to warrant any check on output. Thus we may imagine output to increase along with improvements in technology, this being permitted provided the additional product suffices to reward any additional factors involved and to placate additional envy generated. The additional envy may issue chiefly from one or a group of persons. Increased output is warranted, however, only so long as this additional envy, no matter how distributed, can be more than compensated out of the increase. Symmetrical reasoning applies to differences in degree of altruistic interdependence.

fied for the same sort of reason: if the relevant community indifference curve cuts the transformation curve there must exist a range of output possibilities for which "everyone" can be made better off. Finally, the exchange optimum, requiring the rate of substitution between all pairs of goods be the same for each individual, survives for similar reasons.[139]

DYNAMICS

No body of formal dynamic welfare analysis comparable with that of static welfare analysis exists. Reder made a modest attempt to erect some stylized structure in the shape of an extension of the optimum conditions to risk-bearing and the like,[140] but the concepts, even in principle, were scarcely measurable, and the ideas have not caught on. The fashion remains to court disillusion at the static level in a formal manner, and pessimism informally at the dynamic level.

On the question of capital accumulation, extension of the opti-

[139] By considering the effect on an individual's welfare of the consumption by another of particular goods, Henderson and Quandt [95] have concluded otherwise. They use two arguments: (1) In a model containing two individuals, each of whose utility function depends upon his own consumption and that of the other, the utility of one of them is maximized subject to a given utility of the other. The resulting expression differs from the familiar one (deriving from independent utilities) by having the ratio of the marginal utilities (to be equated to the price ratio) modified to take account of the losses or gains in the utility accruing as a consequence of the other's possession of the two goods. The interpretation placed on this mathematical expression by the authors is that the equality of rates of substitution is no longer the optimal condition. All that emerges, however, is that in the presence of interdependence the old formula no longer holds. It does not mean that the *ratio* of the modified marginal utilities are not, in equilibrium, equal.

(2) A graphical illustration in which, with an individual's indifference map drawn on the assumption of independence, the introduction of considerations resting on interdependence moves the individual from his initial (independent) optimum. This obviously will not do. In the two-good, two-person case, in which every combination chosen by one determines the combination of goods left to the other, each individual ranks every point in the box diagram according to the balance of advantage experienced—taking into account his response to the other's possessions—thereby generating a consistent ranking of his indifference curves. An optimum position under these conditions has the usual optimal property. In general, then, regardless of what goes into the individual utility functions, if rates of substitution between any two individuals differ, mutually advantageous exchange—provided the utility functions remain unchanged—is possible.

In any event, the community need not be very large before the individual will discount his influence on the consumption of others completely, accept the given prices, and seek a maximum position within his means, thereby equating his rates of substitution to those of the market.

[140] See bibliography, item 207.

mum conditions to intertemporal substitution had led to a proposed rule[141] that the quantity of money be adjusted so as to determine a rate of interest at which full-employment-saving and investment are equal. This rule is rejected by Graaff, among others, chiefly for two reasons.

First, the larger the existing holdings of bonds, the larger must be the supply of money in order to secure the full-employment rate of interest, a rate which therefore varies according to the volume of bonds in the economy. Indeed, if this is an objection, one might go further on the assumption of a wealth-saving relationship, popularly known as the "Pigou effect." For as Metzler has shown,[142] with such a relationship the rate of interest appears largely as a monetary phenomenon determinable by the government's control of the quantity of money. In response to changes in the quantity of money, changes in the price level shift the full-employment-saving schedule into equilibrium at the policy-chosen interest rate and investment level.

Second, the rate of saving depends not only on the current bond prices but also on expected future bond prices and, in addition, on variations in the general level of prices expected over time. But these prices, in turn, are influenced by the present and future saving of people, about which the individual saver and investor can have no clear information. Nor can the entrepreneur correctly estimate the productivity of his investment unless the investment plans of others, present and future, are known to him.

Now this second set of objections, though they may have particular relevance to capital accumulation, are surely general to all optimum rules. Unless direct information is available about everybody's present and future activities, or unless we can predict their effects on future prices, individuals are liable to make decisions they will regret and, in so far as they do make mistakes, incur "wastage" on the allocative criteria discussed. Sooner or later, there will appear "too much" investment in *X*, "too little" in *Y*, and so on. Obviously these are the inescapable consequences of uncertainty. But having determined the other optimum conditions explicitly in the absence of uncertainty and, for that matter, in

[141] See bibliography, item 16.

[142] Lloyd Metzler, "Wealth, Saving and the Rate of Interest," *Journal of Political Economy* (1951).

the absence of innovation, changes in taste, etc., we should be able to do no less for the conditions determining the rate of accumulation. Having done this satisfactorily, we may then consider the effects of uncertainty not only on the optimum conditions for capital accumulation but also, in general, on all the optimum conditions.

Keeping the analysis within a static framework, then, equality of the rate of return over cost with the marginal rate of time preference appears to be a required condition for the optimum rate of investment—always ignoring indivisibilities and divergences between social and private benefit, which may, of course, be of special importance in dealing with investment goods. For if this equality does not obtain, say the rate of return exceeds marginal time preference, there is scope for making some people, as borrowers and lenders, better off without making others worse off—provided, always, we abide, as we do in static welfare analysis, by people's immediate judgment of their own good. And though, as in the first objection, variations in the volume of bonds and money will influence the rate of interest and, therefore, the rate of accumulation, thus giving rise to the problem of additional conditions (connected, perhaps, with the distribution of welfare), this rule will still be necessary inasmuch as its nonfulfillment leaves room for some net improvement in the community's welfare.

If, on the other hand, we do decide to place the whole subject in a dynamic context, to consider, that is, the distribution of welfare over time in conditions of uncertainty and, indeed, in conditions of changing productive organization and social institutions, the inadequacy of the necessary conditions for an optimum position is apparent. It is with some such context in mind that Graaff abandons the conventional optimum conditions of capital accumulation and takes up the idea of a collective approach to this question. The things to be decided upon, all of which involve value judgments, are the choice of a time horizon beyond which we have no interest, the time distribution of welfare on our side of the horizon, and the amount, if any, of "terminal" capital equipment we bequeath to posterity beyond the horizon. These are not very firm materials to work with and, ere long, skepticism sets in and the whole lot is, in effect, emptied into the social-welfare function, there to meet a fate already prepared by Arrow.

The treatment of uncertainty *per se* is hardly more satisfactory. While there is a general case for spending on research and information services in order to improve expectations and guide business decisions up to the magic point at which the value of additional output attributable to such expenditure is just equal to such expenditure, the application of such an "optimum" rule is mainly guesswork. Again, some writers, such as Graaff, see proper to point out to us that, after all, uncertainty adds zest to life. One is already in danger of trailing off into banalities.

Treatment of the desirability of full employment, on the one hand, and stability, on the other; of government spending versus private spending; of standardization versus variety; of speed of adjustment as against comfort and security,[143] are subject in greater measure to the same pitfall, since on such broad issues the relatively simple goal of pushing outward the welfare frontier or of comparing situations on the basis of compensation tests, give way to vaguer ideas of what is proper, and yet vaguer criteria, if any, for their implementation.

VI. A Summing Up

Many of the modern writers on welfare economics take a poor view of its prospects. Little warns us, more than once, against the impressions of rigor and refinement in an analysis which ought to be employed only as a rough guide to policy, though "good common sense" would do as well. Graaff is less compromising. On a close examination, he asserts, every proposition in welfare economics is found wanting. It is more profitable and more honest to bend our energies to the development of positive economics in order to serve the public by providing policymakers with all the knowledge necessary to choose between alternative programs. On the other hand, Reder ends his book on a rather indulgent note, one from a theme made familiar to us by Galbraith's *Affluent Society*. We are a wealthy country, he urges, speaking of the United States, we can afford waste. Is it really worth while scrimping at the margin in order to squeeze the most out of our resources? If the implica-

[143] A rapidly adjusting economy imposes psychological strains on men and women which cannot easily be fitted into the welfare calculus. In this connection consult an informal and lively essay ("Progress Without Tears") by Honor Croome in *Lloyds Bank Review* (1959).

tion that welfare economics—which to Reder, but not to others, treats of scrimping at the margin—already enables us to squeeze the most out of our resources is granted, Reder's attitude might be justified, at least for the United States. But the strength of the recent attacks on welfare economics stems, rather obviously, from the belief in its being totally inadequate. If this be the case, there is no point to the judgment that the propositions of welfare economics are superfluous in view of the existing economic milieu. Therefore before passing judgment on the value for our economy of the study of welfare economics, let us briefly review some of the main objections to this study and consider how they might be met.

Though one can understand the general impatience with a subject which promises so much and, apparently, yields so little, Graaff's conclusions are too cavalier by far. Sweeping generalization is to be regarded askance, no less when it is purely negative. True, few welfare propositions can be predicated which are not, almost in the same breath, qualified out of existence. But this fact is, to a large extent, a consequence flowing from our ignorance of the world we live in. In recognition of it, we busy ourselves ferreting out of welfare analysis all those tacit assumptions that appear to say something about the economic universe.[144] But this purging of tacit empiricism has gone too far. Any generalization but the most trivial is sure to collapse when all bounds to technical and behavior possibilities are removed—when allowance is made for any and every imaginable situation. Under so exacting a procedure, it is not at all surprising that unambiguous prescription is hard to come by. What the subject badly needs is a strong infusion of empiricism to end its unchecked wanderings in the empyrean and to bring it down to earth feet first. Even the establishment of probabilities, or likelihoods, may enable us to escape the otherwise inevitable "perverse" cases thrown up, for example, by the interrelationship of welfare distribution and relative valuation.

The import of these remarks may be illustrated by reference to some of the difficulties already encountered, assuming, provisionally, that private and social valuations coincide.

[144] A parallel procedure in positive economics, as objectionable as it is common, is the "repudiation" of economic theorems simply because one can think up a less restrictive set of axioms.

The general second-best theorem certainly takes the edge off the marginal-cost rule in all existing types of economies, but, maybe, not more than that. If we grouped commodities into broad categories, on the basis of close substitution, a small departure from an ideal output (in terms of these broad categories) could not, perhaps, be sustained long without a movement in prices so marked as to attract factors to some industries and repel them from others. If there were evidence for this belief then: (1) the existing degree of commercial rivalry might suffice to keep us close to the community's utility frontier, and (2) the precise rule for a nationalized industry may not be important with this scheme in mind. If, for instance, there are no substitutes for the product of a nationalized industry, then regardless of whether the price is set equal to average cost, to marginal cost, or to something in between, the output demanded may be much the same. If, on the other hand, the nationalized industry produces a good, say electricity, for which other fuels are close substitutes, although the choice of the marginal cost or average cost may make an appreciable difference in the sale of electricity, the amounts demanded of all fuels taken together, measured in effective units, in some sense, may alter by very little. We should still be close to the utility frontier. Indeed, if we could rely upon existing enterprise, public and private, to keep us fairly close to an ideal output, we might abandon our concern with "utopia" welfare economics and pay more heed to the piecemeal approach. The compensation tests would then be serviceable in decisions to undertake entirely new projects. And though Little has spoken of consumer's surplus as a toy, it is hard to see how gains and losses on any scale can be computed without something of this sort. However, we are allowing that output in the rest of the economy is only roughly ideal. For this and other reasons given in Section IV, the area between the curves is only an approximation to the sum of the *CV*'s in the community. Only a slight gain in the practicable measure of the social surplus would not then be convincing evidence of the desirability of the investment in question.[145] Setting some mini-

[145] Sir Roy Harrod, in correspondence with me, points out that to reject all projects unless a sizeable gain can be expected from their introduction would be a very damping maxim, and if adopted would deprive us of the fruits of progress. If, from our experience of things, a small change can be recognized as connected

mal size of gain would have the added advantage of eliminating the possibility of contradictory answers which may arise when compensation tests are based on different distributions of welfare —though, on looking into the matter, we may have grounds for believing that, for all feasible distributions of welfare, the community indifference map, and hence, the corresponding outputs, vary but little.[146]

Turning to interdependent utilities, it must be admitted that if factor payments do not suffice both to compensate the factor-supplier for his additional sacrifice and to allay the heightened envy of others, existing output is too large. There is a temptation, in contemplating this circumstance, to lose patience with human cussedness[147] and to insist that if both the Smith family and the Jones family receive a 10 percent increase in their "real" income they *are* better off, even if they both sulk at the other's good luck. But while this may be salutary morals, if welfare is what people experience there is no escape for us in honest indignation. We may be wise to invest more resources in social psychology in the hope of making people more "rational," but in the meantime we have to concede that an all-around increase of worldly goods may not make people any better off and, indeed, may make them feel worse off.

Nonetheless, we must remind ourselves that the kinds and degrees of welfare interdependence are yet in the realm of conjecture. Common observation, and intuition, suggest that it is a stronger factor at higher living standards than at lower ones. In the poorer countries, where the bulk of the populations still struggle for bare subsistence, it may be negligible.

---

with a whole series of small changes whose sum results in a large change, then we should base our decisions, not on the data of each small change in isolation, but on the expected result of this large change.

[146] In the extreme case that the community indifference map remained unchanged for all distributions of welfare, allocative efficiency could be effectively separated from distributional considerations. In that event, "efficiency" tests, based on the compensation principle, could never contradict. Such a case, however, does not strengthen any prescription based on "efficiency" tests by themselves. (A sufficient condition for this extreme case to obtain exists when the consumption functions of all individuals are homogeneous and identical.)

Constant costs in the production of all goods do, of course, ensure unchanged relative prices, but do not ensure an unchanged combination of outputs, in response to redistributions of welfare.

[147] See bibliography, item 209.

In recognizing that no promising foundations for a dynamic economics have been laid, we must not overlook the difficulties intrinsic to that level of analysis. Though relative prices, outputs, and patterns of income distribution may be used, in certain circumstances, as indicators of changes in social welfare, for many of the dynamic factors that enter into welfare—time-paths of response, uncertainty, stability—no equally objective and measurable data exist, a deficiency which, in addition, makes agreement on norms more difficult. While this is a pity, it is not a fatal frustration. If we were more confident of our welfare economics at the static level of analysis it is not likely that we should be much inhibited by the recognition of unsolved dynamic problems. For whatever provision we make for uncertainty, patterns of response, capital accumulation, etc., practical criteria for improving the allocation of existing resources, and for choosing between alternative investment possibilities, could still be profitably applied.

Finally, though confidence may grow or decline as a result of empirical research, one thing should not be overlooked: the apparent trend toward economic egalitarianism apparently facilitates the application of welfare economics. For one thing, the stronger is this trend, the less we need worry about changes in the distribution of welfare causing contradictions in compensation tests. Indeed, in so far as equality is promoted by a highly progressive tax structure, the latter may be regarded as a sort of built-in compensatory device.[148] In the limiting case of completely equalizing taxes, gainers automatically compensate losers, thereby fulfilling the uncontradictable Paretian criterion while continuously maintaining an ethically unobjectionable distribution of income.

Again, as Duesenberry has pointed out, in a world in which the gains of higher-income groups are resented by the lower-income groups,[149] an income tax goes some way toward correcting the

[148] Even though the resultant pattern of consumption varies widely as between one welfare distribution and another, in so far as a progressive income tax narrows the range of possible welfare distributions, it reduces the likelihood of contradiction using the various compensation tests. In the limiting case of complete equalization no contradiction can arise—whenever "everyone" could be made better off, everyone in effect is made better off.

[149] There is no reason to believe, however, that a rise in the incomes of others of our group, or of the income groups beneath us, should be any less discomforting than an increase in the incomes of the groups above us. All increases of income, other than our own, amount to a loss of income status relative to some others.

conventional factor-product optimum condition by reducing the disposable marginal earnings of the factor below their value on the market. Indeed, not only does an income tax correct for social envy, this envy itself is reduced in so far as it is provoked by disposable rather than gross incomes. The more sensitive is the community in this respect, the steeper the progression of the tax necessary to correct the conventional conditions. In extreme cases only complete equality of disposable incomes solves the problem of interdependent welfares. In the nature of things, so extreme an institution is more likely to be encountered in an opulent society than in an indigent one.

CONCLUSIONS

It has already been suggested that explorations into the characteristics of the economic universe may show us a way round conceivable obstacles which have all too readily been adopted as logical impasses; that, provided we group commodities broadly, the allocative efficiency of Western economies—in the sense of being close to the utility frontier of society—may merit a high rating; and that a continuation of the trend toward income equalization reduces the need for correcting the conventional optimum for interdependent welfares while, at the same time, facilitating the application of criteria involving compensation tests. Yet, if all this is accepted it does not follow that the prospects of a rehabilitation of welfare economics are good. For one thing, there are several important issues—such as the choice between variety and dearness, on the one hand, and standardization and cheapness, on the other, or the proper division between private and public sectors of the economy—which the welfare economist can do little more than discuss in very general terms. For another, the notion of discrepancies between private and social benefit which, at first glance, appears a promising field for the application of welfare economics—and a salutary reminder of the limited capacity of the invisible hand—when pursued in earnest reveals grave difficulties. Certainly, the more serious objections to using index numbers, or consumer's surpluses, in the measurement of changes in social welfare do not reside in the tangle of interdependencies which has chiefly engaged the interest of recent writers. (If we do not believe that, over time measured in decades, the great majority of families in the Western world have higher real incomes in the index sense, we can always suppose a tax structure that effectively maintains income equality, in which case a rise in the appropriate index indicates a rise in the real value of goods and services of each family.) So long as we restrict ourselves to measuring in terms of private valuations, such a rise in the index may tell us little of welfare, or happiness, as experienced by individuals. Advances in the techniques of production, and the utilization of material possessions, have repercussions on people's welfare far beyond the initial anticipations of satisfactions.[150] Of course, such repercussions may be regarded as manifestations of a divergence between social and private valuations, but they are not thereby rendered amenable to measurement.[151] Taken together, however, they can be of decisive importance.

While accepting, therefore, "an expansion of the area of choice" as synonymous with an increase of welfare for the individual, and as an unexceptionable norm of policy, it requires an alarming degree of complacency to believe that a rising standard of living as commonly understood is the certain instrument of an expanding horizon of opportunities. Obviously the growth of material prosperity, and its dispersion among the populace, entails—by definition, we might say—more goods, and new kinds of goods, among

[150] The growth of private motoring provides a topical example. Each individual's enjoyment of his car varies inversely with the number of cars on the road. So long as cars increase faster than roads can be built the advantages—both for travel and ostentation—diminish. If we remind ourselves of the continual exasperation with which each motorist regards his fellow motorists, not to mention pedestrians, the inconvenience to the latter, the pollution of the air, the incessant noise, the problems of town planning, the growth of ribbon building and consequent spoiling of the countryside, the tying down of large numbers of police, the pressures on magistrates, to say nothing of the toll in killed and injured or the long-run effects on the national character, one may legitimately conclude that the yearly output of motorcars is too large by far, whatever the distribution of welfare.

[151] The cost of certain external effects, such as the smoke nuisance of factories, can be measured, roughly, by sample surveys. For an example, see Pigou, *op. cit.*, p. 185*n*. But where the discomfort endured leaves no material evidence it may be as difficult for the person afflicted to estimate the appropriate money compensation as it is for others to accept his estimate. In those cases, which are by far the most important, where the introduction of new types of goods (and their conditions of production) change for better or worse a whole way of life for the community, there is no hope of estimating the cost of the "external effects."

the mass of the people. But it is scarcely less obvious today that the concomitant subtopiazation of society involves a continual erosion of opportunities, at least for a sensitive minority.[152]

To sum up, if welfare economics is to be repudiated as a serious branch of study it is not for the logical difficulties which inevitably appear when generality of treatment is taken to encompass all imaginable relationships. These difficulties, and others, we have suggested, may be far from insuperable. It is rather that a study of welfare which confines itself to the measurement of quantities of goods and their distribution is not only seriously limited, it is—at least in those countries where the mass of people have advanced far beyond subsistence standards—positively misleading. For the things on which happiness ultimately depends, friendship, faith, the perception of beauty, and so on, are outside its range: only the most obstinate pursuit of formalism would endeavor to bring them into relation with the measuring rod of money, and then to no practical effect. Thus, the triumphant achievements of modern technology, ever-swifter travel, round-the-clock synthetic entertainment, the annual cornucopia of slick and glossy gadgets, which rest perforce on the cult of efficiency, the single-minded pursuit of advancement, the craving for material success, may be exacting a fearful toll in terms of human happiness. But the formal elegance of welfare economics will never reveal it.

[152] For instance, foreign travel, once suggestive of the lure and enchantment of far-away places, has become a highly organized mass exercise with small opportunity of avoiding motorized traffic, crowds of camera-happy tourists, and cynical tourist-hardened populations. For a particularly painful example of these things, read a report on "The Last Days of Andorra?" in *The Economist* (August 22, 1959).

Again, for those who enjoy a beach humming with portable radios, or the lakes teeming with motor boats, the world may be improving. But not for those whose tastes run to quieter things.

PART 2

CONCEPTS OF ECONOMIC SURPLUS

CHAPTER 2

Realism and Relevance in Consumer's Surplus*

Since the rehabilitation of consumers' surplus by Professor Hicks[1] several attempts have appeared to establish the most appropriate money measure of this concept, attempts accompanied by apologies for introducing into the concept refinements which are apparently of little practical importance. Consequently it is with some misgivings that I find myself fiddling about with this somewhat fragile notion of consumer's surplus, albeit not without hope that the result of the fiddling about will be to cause it to shed a little of its ostensible complexity.

After a consideration of the definition of the "Compensating Variation" given by Professor Hicks in his *Value and Capital,* and of the definition given in Marshall's *Principles,* Mr. Henderson in his article "Consumer's Surplus and the Compensating Variation"[2] finds himself with four alternative expressions for

* From *Review of Economic Studies,* 15 (1948), 27–33.

[1] J. R. Hicks, *Value and Capital* (Oxford: Clarendon, 1939), also "Rehabilitation of Consumers' Surplus," *Review of Economic Studies,* Vol. 8 (1941).

[2] "Consumer's Surplus and the Compensating Variation," *Review of Economic Studies,* Vol. 8 (1941).

consumer's surplus. Two of these he believes to be in accord with the definition of the compensating variation: one for a rise in price, and one for a fall in price. The two others he designates as "Marshallian" consumer's surpluses, again one for a rise in price and one for a fall in price.

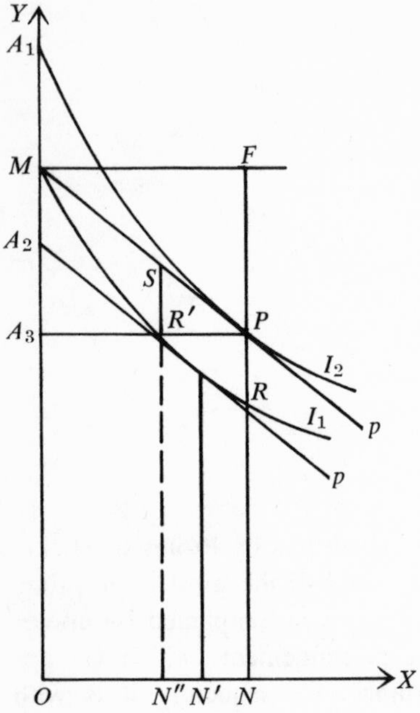

Figure 1

In his article "The Four Consumer's Surpluses," [3] Professor Hicks elaborates these distinctions (though now making each measure applicable to either a rise or a fall in price); generalizes them for both ordinary and "inferior" goods, and shows the relation between them with the use of "marginal diagrams."

Following these refinements comes Professor Knight's stimulating article "Realism and Relevance in the Theory of Demand." [4] On the methodological argument I dare not presume to pass

[3] "The Four Consumer's Surpluses," *Review of Economic Studies,* Vol. 11 (1943).

[4] "Realism and Relevance in the Theory of Demand," *Journal of Political Economy,* Vol. 52 (1944).

judgment, but in the last part of the article there is a criticism which we must examine of the original "Hicks-Henderson" measure of consumer's surplus (*PR* in Figure 1) and a proposal for adopting an apparently different method of reaching the required measure.

In all then there are five measures to be investigated. I hope to be able to show that, for either a rise or a fall in price, of these five only two are tenable in all familiar circumstances.

We can usefully start with some reflections on Professor Knight's approach, as there seems to be a marked divergence between his result and those put forward by Professor Hicks and Mr. Henderson (Figure 1).

Professor Knight argues: "The vertical distance *PR* is indeed the excess amount of money the individual would pay for *ON* of *X* offered as an indivisible block, over the amount *FP* which he does pay in the free market. But it is not the consumer's surplus. Henderson is correct in saying 'if the individual had spent *FR* in buying *ON* of *X* he would have been just as well off as if the commodity had not been available, whereas in fact he only has to spend *FP* on it.' But he overlooks the fact that the individual would also have been just as well off at any other point (than *R*) on the indifference curve I_1 (and as well off at any other point than *P* on I_2). Yet he recognizes that all the money measure of the difference in situation represented by the two curves is not the same at any two points on either—unless the curves are arbitrarily drawn in an admittedly indefensible way. The correct comparison with free purchase is clearly the point at which he spends the same amount of money for less *X* and not where he spends more money for the same amount of *X* . . . for if *X* had not been available he would have spent the amount on other things."

The last clause I take to mean that if the consumer could not buy *X* at a fixed price but only in a way which would leave him no better off he would not in fact spend any money on *X*. But if we accept this then it would be as unlikely that he would spend money on an amount of *X* less than *ON* (as the suggested comparison implies) as that he would spend on the amount *ON* itself.

However, Professor Knight continues: "To find the money measure of the consumer's surplus . . . we draw the horizontal line PA_3, cutting the indifference curve I_1 at *R′*. Spending the same amount of money *FP* under the indifference conditions the individual would buy A_3R' (or ON'') of *X* instead of *ON*; i.e. he would buy $N''N$ less than if he bought under market conditions."

By this method the consumer's surplus in terms of *X* appears to be $N''N$, and, leaving it in that form for the moment, it can be shown that the difference between this measure and the one criticized (*PR*, in terms of money), is not so great as may at first appear. They can be juxtaposed in a fairly simple manner if *Y* is temporarily looked upon as another commodity, to some degree a substitute for commodity *X*.

If the consumer starts with *OM* of commodity *Y* and a rate of exchange *p* is introduced he will move from his initial position on the indifference curve I_1 to a point *P* on the indifference curve I_2. The improvement in his situation is unequivocally the difference in "utility" between the situation represented by the curve I_1 and that represented by the curve I_2.

Measures of this difference between I_1 and I_2 must, of course, be completely vertical to be in terms of *Y*, or completely horizontal to be in terms of *X*. In the former case we are in effect comparing two combinations of *X* and *Y*, one combination from each indifference curve but with the amount of *X* held constant in each combination.

Now as the indifference curves are not parallel (except in rare circumstances where the income elasticity of demand is zero) there might be any number of measures of consumer's surplus in terms either of *Y* or of *X*, although properly interpreted each should indicate the same "real" gain. Nevertheless, attempts to interpret them must lead to a selection of the few which seem to fit in with any estimation of possible behavior. And of these, as we shall see, not all are equally intelligible.

The consumer having actually acquired, via *p*, an amount *ON* of commodity *X*, it would seem convenient to take a combination from each indifference curve, I_1 and I_2, each combination to include *ON* of *X*; i.e., combinations represented by positions *P* and *R* on curves I_2 and I_1 respectively. The difference between these two combinations is an amount of *Y* equal to *PR*. *PR* is the amount of *Y* by which a situation represented by the combination of goods at *P* is superior to a situation represented by the combination of goods at *R*. Now had the consumer started with an amount of X, instead of an amount OM of Y, it would have seemed equally as convenient to measure the difference between I_1 and I_2 in terms of X.

In fact PR', as a measure of consumer's surplus in terms of X, results in a similar way from taking a combination on I_1 and I_2 only, this time with an amount of Y, OA_3, held constant in each case.

This links up with Professor Knight's argument, for OA_3 is the amount of Y which the consumer is left holding after an expenditure of MA_3. And an expenditure of MA_3 with the price p gets him ON of X, and without p only ON'' of X, the difference being $N''N$ (equals $R'P$).

There seems to be little reason then for preferring $N''N$ to PR; one measure is as appropriate or as inappropriate as the other. However, in trying to bring out the supposed discrepancy between these two measures by translating $N''N$ into terms of Y there is a slip in the technique which has apparently been overlooked. For Professor Knight goes on to say: "The money value of this difference at the given price p is $R'S$. This is less than PR even if the curves are drawn according to Henderson's interpretation of Marshall's assumption, i.e. so as to have the same slope for the same X value, hence a uniform distance between them." [5]

But this sort of conversion into money takes the form of moving back along the price-line p away from the optimum position P to a less favorable position S. It is as though the individual, after reaching his equilibrium P, is forced to reexchange $N''N$ units of X (his surplus measured in terms of X) at the price p. But, in fact, to remain on the curve I_2 he can give up $N''N$ units of X only by receiving successively larger amounts of money[6] as determined by the shape of the curve I_2.[7]

[5] Henderson, *op. cit.*, p. 289.

[6] "Money" in these constructions is, as is often pointed out, taken to mean all other goods at set prices. We could only move back along a route identical with the price-line if we were concerned with an indifference map where "money" included the possibility of buying X at the price p, as well as all other goods at set prices. We could then use the sum of money received, representing the consumer's surplus, to buy back $N''N$ of X at the still possible price p. So nothing has been lost in the conversion to money at price p.

But obviously this sort of device is useless for discovering the consumer's surplus. Where "money" includes X at price p, the consumer's surplus is already *implicit* in "money" along with all other goods at set prices.

[7] With Professor Knight's marginal diagram (*op. cit.*, p. 314) the consumer's

This should at once be apparent if we reflect that if we made the conversion of a surplus in terms of X into a surplus in terms of money by multiplying by the price, then, as the price fell gradually toward zero, the consumer's surplus would gradually diminsh and finally disappear when the good became free.

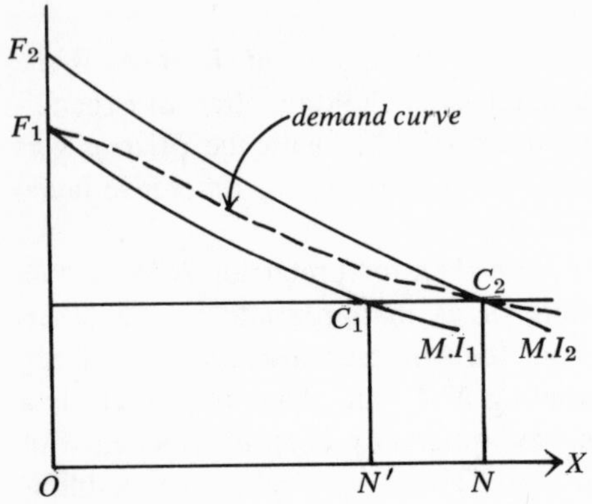

Figure 2

A further point considered by Professor Knight is the grouping of the definitions of consumer's surplus when a new commodity X is introduced at a price p. The two main definitions that result fall into the pattern of "compensating variation" and the "equivalent variation" as introduced by Professor Hicks with respect to a change in price in either direction.

If the price falls (or a price is introduced) the compensating variation asks what is the most that the consumer will pay in order to have the privilege of buying at the new price. The equivalent variation asks: If the new price is withdrawn, what is the amount of money that the consumer must be paid in order that he shall be as well off without the new price?

This latter sum is the same as would have to be paid if the lower price had previously been in existence and was now removed, i.e., if the price was to rise to what, in the paragraph above, was the old price. In such a case this sum will fully compensate

---

surplus can be measured by $x_t x$ in terms of X, but this amount of X cannot be converted into money by multiplying it by the price p in order to give the area $x_t nmx$.

him for the rise in price. The compensating variation for a rise in price is thus equal to the equivalent variation for a fall in price. The converse, of course also holds: the compensating variation for a fall in price is equal to the equivalent variation for a rise in price of the same magnitude.

Returning to the problem of an appropriate measure of the consumer's surplus when a price *p* is introduced we shall now see that *PR* is not above criticism.

As has been indicated, the vertical distance between any two indifference curves will narrow as we move to the right (the corresponding horizontal measure widening) for the marginal substitution of *Y*, or money, for *X* becomes greater as the consumer gives up *Y*, or money, to acquire more *X*. Money, that is, has a greater "value" as the individual is left with less of it—or, as some may prefer it, a greater marginal utility. The question arising from this is, what are the circumstances under which the individual could pay, or could be made to pay, an amount of money equal to the surplus? For this will determine his subjective valuation of money, and hence the appropriate amount of the surplus. More specifically, what are the likely circumstances surrounding the consumer's behavior which makes *PR* less appropriate as a measure of consumer's surplus than the compensating or equivalent variation?

If we suppose that the commodity *X* is one which can be bought at regular intervals, say every "week," then the consumers' surplus is properly concerned with a sum of money which can be added to, or paid out of, consumer's "weekly" income.

Now right at the start it seems unwarrantable to compare expenditures on *ON* of *X* with and without the price *p*, for the simple reason that before any price were fixed for *X* the individual would have no inducement to acquire any *X* at all, much less an amount *ON*, even if it were possible.

For instance, if the individual were on I_2 buying *ON* of *X* per "week" at price *p* and it was decided to squeeze the consumer as much as possible by charging him *PR* for a license to buy *X* at *p*, this might be successful the first "week." If he had already bought *ON* and was then obliged to pay *PR* for that "week's" license in order to keep what *X* he had already bought, then he would be brought back onto I_1. He would be no better off than if he had bought none of *X*. However, this ought not to apply to succeeding "weeks." For if the individual had any intelligence at all he would not begin future "weeks" by buying *ON* at price *p*. Anticipating this charge of *PR* he would lay it aside from his "weekly" income. But *PR* being smaller than MA_2, his net income after this deduction would be larger than *OM*. With the price *p* he could now get himself onto a somewhat higher indifference curve than I_1, buying an amount of *X* less than *ON* though slightly greater than *ON′*.

The compensating variation MA_2, however, passes the test, for with an income of *OM* he could pay MA_2 of it each "week" in getting the license to buy at *p*. This would continue to get him onto his I_1 curve: he would be no better or worse off than if *X* were not available.

Mutatis mutandis MA_1 is the equivalent variation. It makes the same "real" difference added to an income *OM* as does MA_2 subtracted from that income. If, from a situation in which the individual could buy *X* freely at *p*, *X* were no longer available (or though available there were no inducement to buy any), the individual would be back where he was before, not merely *somewhere* on I_1, but at *M* on I_1. In this position MA_1 would have to be added to his "weekly" income in order to place him on I_2.

These measures of consumer's surplus, MA_2 and MA_1, can be transposed onto the more popular marginal diagram (Figure 2). $M.I_1$ is the marginal indifference curve for *X* beginning with an income *OM*. The area under $M.I_1$ is built up from the increments of *Y*, or money, which the consumer would give up, as a maximum, for successive units of *X*. In a similar way, beginning with an income of OA_1, $M.I_2$ is marginal to I_2. The price *p* cuts $M.I_1$ at *ON′*, and $M.I_2$ at *ON*. Once the price *p* is fixed and the consumer begins to buy he begins to accumulate a surplus. The surpluses on each unit of *X* bought are in effect "paid in" to his income. As his valuation of every unit of *X* rises with every increment of surplus to his income (the "income effect") the whole marginal indifference curve shifts gradually to the right as successive units of *X* are bought. Because of the income effect the consumer ends by purchasing *ON* of *X* and not merely *ON′*. The demand curve is, of course, a locus of all these quantity-price relations and therefore passes through F_1 and C_2.

The compensating variation is the area F_1C_1p. The equivalent variation is the area F_2C_2p. As for PR (in Figure 1), this is equal to the area of the compensating variation F_1C_1p, less the smaller area C_1C_2D.

It will be found that the more appropriate measures of consumer's surplus for *changes* in price are also to be found along the Y-axis, and not along some vertical line passing through an amount of X purchased.

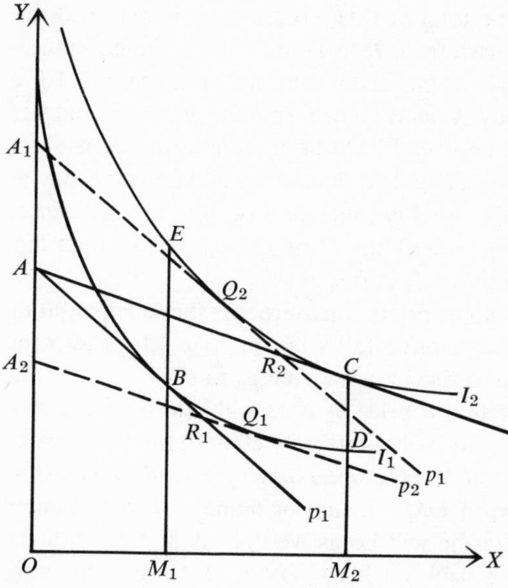

Figure 3

Suppose that the individual begins with an income of OA (Figure 3) and a price p_1, if the price then falls to p_2,CD would seem to conform with the Marshallian definition. It is the difference between the maximum amount of money he is prepared to pay if the price p_2 were now withdrawn (though not, of course, p_1) for OM_2 of X, and what he actually does pay for OM_2 of X given the price p_2.

BE might also qualify as a measure of consumer's surplus. It is the amount of money which, if p_2 were withdrawn (though not, of course, p_1), would have to be added to the combination B on I_1 (which is as far as he can gainfully move with p_1 alone) in order to bring him back onto I_2.

However, neither of these measures is acceptable for reasons mentioned in connection with the preceding illustration.

CD is derived from supposing the consumer to take OM_2 whether the price is p_2 or p_1. Now to acquire OM_2 when the price is p_1 he must proceed in two stages: he first buys OM_1 at p_1. He then moves along his I_1 curve, paying the maximum for successive units of X until he has a total of OM_2. But even if it were possible to move down his I_1 curve from B to D, there could be no inducement to act in this way; in fact if he were made to pay CD for a "weekly" license to buy X at the cheaper price p_2, he would not be just as badly off as he would have been without the license. He would be better off. For CD is less than AA_2, and he could pay as much as AA_2 from his "weekly" income OA for such a license: his residual income per "week" then being OA_2, p_2 could get him to a point Q_1, back onto the I_1 curve.

Thus AA_2 is the appropriate measure of the compensating variation in the case of a price fall from p_1 to p_2. It is also the equivalent variation for a rise in price from p_2 to p_1.

As for BE, it is true that if price p_2 were withheld from the consumer, left with only p_1, he would buy only OM_1 in future "weeks," and that if in some later "week" *after having already bought* his "weekly" consumption of OM_1, a sum of money BE is presented to him as compensation he will be as well off as he was with the price p_2, and therefore back on his I_2 curve. But again this does not follow for successive "weeks." If the consumer has any intelligence at all he will not continue to buy OM_1 at the price p_1, and then collect his compensation BE each "week." He will reckon BE as an addition to his former income OA before expenditure. But BE is clearly larger than AA_1, *and* AA_1 added to his "weekly" income OA is just enough to get him back onto the I_2 curve with the higher price p_1, which is still open to him. It follows that with a "weekly" compensation of BE added to his income he could get onto an indifference curve higher than I_2.

Thus, AA_1 is the appropriate measure of the equivalent variation for a fall in price from p_1 to p_2: it is the compensating variation for a rise in price from p_2 to p_1.

If it were possible to imagine a practical application, then, AA_2 and AA_1 would be the correct sums of money to work with. If the consumer were made to pay CD instead of AA_2 per "week" he would be paying too little; if he were compensated with BE instead of AA_1 per "week" he would be receiving too much.[8]

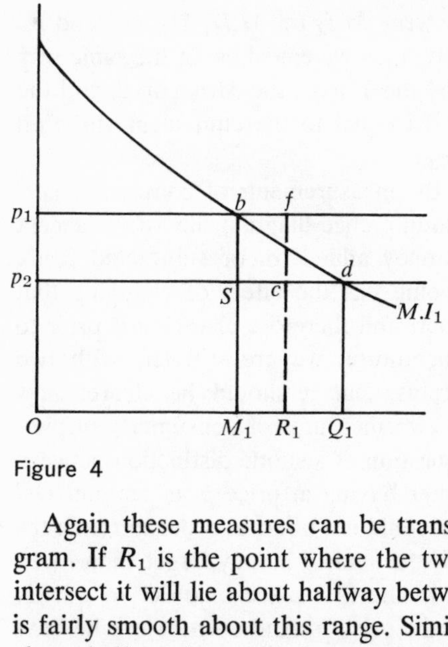

Figure 4

Again these measures can be transposed onto a marginal diagram. If R_1 is the point where the two price-lines tangential to I_1 intersect it will lie about halfway between B and Q_1 if the curve I_1 is fairly smooth about this range. Similarly R_2 may be taken to be about halfway between Q_2 and C. In that case the compensating variation (Figure 4), when the price falls from p_1 to p_2, is the area

[8] It might seem that if a sum of money equal to CD per "week" were charged as a direct tax at the end of a period, or a sum equal to BE per "week" granted as a bounty at the end of a period, the period being of such duration that the consumer does not connect it with his current purchases of OM_2 or OM_1, of X respectively, these measures of consumer's surplus might be vindicated.

Now unless great ingenuity was shown such a period would necessarily have to be long in relation to the "week" in order that the consumer should not allow the addition or subtraction of money to influence his expenditure. The total sum due, or owing, might, for instance, be added, or deducted, from the individual's income tax. But this poses additional difficulties. A sum of CD every week during the year is not the same to the individual as 52 times CD at the end of the year. There is now the element of time-preference. Moreover, his tastes and fortunes are likely to have changed.

The indifference curve technique in these instances is only usefully employed for periods so short that the accepted *ceteris paribus* propositions (referring to the constancy of income, of preferences, of all other goods purchased at set prices, and so on) are reasonably sure to obtain.

of the rectangle p_1p_2cf. Now if the marginal indifference curve $M.I_1$ is fairly straight between b and d, c (like R_1) being midway between g and d, the square $bfcg$ is about equal in area to the triangle bgd. The area of the rectangle p_1p_2cf is then about equal to the trapezium p_1p_2db, which then becomes our measure of the compensating variation.

If in this same diagram we write $M.I_2$ for $M.I_1$; M_2, Q_2, and R_2 for Q_1, M_1, and R_1 respectively, then we can show in the same way that the trapezium bounded by the Y axis, the $M.I_2$ curve, and the two price-lines contains an area equal to the equivalent variation for a fall in price from p_1 to p_2.[9]

To conclude, if we accept the measurements of consumer's surplus along the Y-axis of the indifference diagram, i.e., if we accept the view that any sum of money added to, or subtracted from, the consumer's "weekly" income has the effect of changing that money income to the consumer, and therefore changing it prior to laying out his "weekly" expenditure, we are still left with two measures of consumer's surplus. But it should be clearer now why we cannot avoid having two measures of consumer's surplus.

There is not, in fact, any question of a subtle distinction between ex ante and ex post. Even *after* buying at price p an amount ON of X (Figure 1) the consumer could not offer, in order to retain the privilege of buying at this price, a sum of money larger than MA_2, a sum which he could offer in the first place in order to qualify for the privilege of buying at the price p. And even *before* he buys any X at the market price p it would require a bribe as large as MA_1 to keep the consumer away from the market. Though MA_1 is the same sum as must be paid to compensate him if after he has bought ON of X at p the price p is removed.

The two different measures arise simply from the fact of the diminishing marginal utility of money. It is a distinction between what the consumer would *pay* (in order to get the lower price, or in order to avoid a higher price), and what the consumer must *be paid* (to induce him to forgo the lower price, or to accept a higher price). For what he would pay or pays is to be considered

[9] It should be noticed that these two measures respectively correspond to the "price-compensating variation" *HEph*, and the "price-equivalent variation" *HPCh*, for a fall in price from *H* to *h*, in the article by Professor Hicks, "The Four Consumer's Surpluses," *Review of Economic Studies*, 11 (1943), 34–35.

a *subtraction* from his money income; what he must be paid or is actually paid an *addition* to his money income. As has been mentioned, the difference between the two situations (the difference in utility) is unequivocal, but the sum of money required to express this difference is larger for an addition to an individual's money income than for a subtraction from it.

Finally, in the interests of brevity, the analysis has been confined to "normal" (or "superior") goods, but there should be no trouble in tracing out the same or symmetrical conclusions for "inferior" goods.

CHAPTER 3

Rent as a Measure of Welfare Change*

The definitions of economic rent in current use fall easily into two categories: (1) a payment in excess of that necessary to maintain a resource in its current occupation. Thus, Frederick Benham[1] tells us that rents are ". . . the sums paid to the factors which need not be paid in order to retain the factors *in the industry*." While to Kenneth Boulding[2] it is the payment to a factor ". . . in excess of the minimum amount necessary to keep that factor in its present occupation." The second category (2) is the difference between the current earnings of a resource and its transfer earnings[3]—the latter term signifying its earnings in the next best alternative use.[4] For instance, Paul Samuelson[5] says, ". . . we should term

* From *American Economic Review,* 49 (1959), 386–394.

[1] F. Benham, *Economics* (London: Pitman, 1945), p. 227.

[2] K. Boulding, *Economic Analysis* (New York: Harper & Row, 1948), p. 230.

[3] To impart precision to this measure of economic rent the period of adjustment should be specified, as should, also, the area of comparison—within the industry, region, country, or within the world as a whole. But since the inadequacy of this definition of rent prevails irrespective of these distinctions, I shall make no further mention of them in this chapter.

[4] Benham, *op. cit.*, p. 328.

[5] P. A. Samuelson, *Economics* (New York: McGraw-Hill, 1951), p. 593.

the excess of his income above the alternative wage he could earn elsewhere as *a pure rent*." Similarly, for George Stigler[6] the rent of a factor is ". . . the excess of its return in the best use over its possible return in other uses. . . ."[7]

While the first type of definition is, as we shall see, unavoidably ambiguous, the second type is yet more inadequate. Among other things it would require that, in the choice of occupation, men were motivated solely by pecuniary considerations.

I. A Measure of Rent as an Economic Surplus

For the purpose of revealing ambiguities in the existing definitions of economic rent and of demonstrating the logic of the proposed definition, we shall find it no less convenient and a good deal more suggestive to take our bearings from a more generalized version of the traditional theory of consumer's choice.

Rather than maximizing the utility function $W\{u(x_1, \ldots, x_n)\}$, over the range in which $\partial W/\partial x_r > 0$ for all x_r, subject to the usual constraint $\Sigma p_r x_r = Y$, where Y is the individual's income,[8] we require our individual, in possession of given resources, or assets, to maximize such a function subject to $\Sigma p_r x_r = 0$. At least one of the x's is negative in order to indicate a quantity supplied per period by the individual of a good or service and, of course, at least one of the x's is positive to indicate a quantity demanded per period of a good or service. The suggested constraint expresses nothing more than the proposition that, in all circumstances, the individual's current earnings are equal to the current value of his expenditure.[9] It is a significant amendment, however, because it brings to the fore the notion of simultaneous determination of the individual's allocation of his productive services and of his earnings in response to a given pattern of prices: an obvious point perhaps,

[6] G. J. Stigler, *The Theory of Price* (New York: Macmillan, 1952), p. 99.

[7] In all these cases the writers appear to be using "factor" in the sense in which I shall use the term "resource." And though, generally, I prefer to reserve the term "factor" for the productive service of the resource, it will avoid possible confusion if instead I adhere to the term "productive service."

[8] J. R. Hicks, *Value and Capital* (Oxford: Clarendon, 1948), p. 305.

[9] Strictly speaking his spending is equal to current earnings less current saving plus current dissaving. This could easily be allowed for without any modification of our conclusions. Over time, if his assets grow, his demand for goods and his disposal of productive services will, of course, alter. This problem is, however, common to all such static analysis.

but one frequently ignored in the analysis of the individual's demand and supply curves.

Maximizing the utility function subject to our new constraint, we derive the well-known equilibrium condition $\partial W/\partial x_r = \lambda p_r$ (λ being identified as the marginal utility of income) for all goods and services whether their magnitudes are positive or negative—whether, that is, they are demanded or supplied by the individual.[10] Or, dispensing with utility, we can write $\partial x_i/\partial x_j = p_j/p_i$ for any i and j.

It should be apparent that, although the substitution effect may be defined in the customary way, there can be no income effect, $\partial x_r/\partial Y$, since there is no necessary correspondence, using our new constraint, between changes in the individual's welfare and changes in his income, real or money. For with the new constraint, money income, Y, is no longer held constant; it is determined along with all the other variables. It may increase, remain unchanged, or diminish, with an improvement in the individual's welfare. In its place, therefore, we derive a *welfare* effect, $\partial x_r/\partial W$. In consequence, the effect on the quantity bought or sold of any chosen good or service of a given change in the set of prices is divided into a substitution effect and a welfare effect.

The implications of this less-restricted formulation, though straightforward enough, are worth recording. A change in the price of any good or service—whether it is supplied or demanded by the individual—changes, in general, the quantities of all goods and services which the individual buys and sells. Consequently it changes the value of his earnings and expenditure. A search for a useful definition of an "incentive good" might begin with the implication that a fall in the price of any consumed good will, *inter alia,* increase or reduce the amount of work done by the individual as a result of the operation of the welfare effect. But this will not be pursued here.

Having extended the customary confines of the theory of consumer's choice we may now develop the argument largely in terms

[10] Since we restrict ourselves to the range in which the marginal utilities of all goods and services are positive, the acquisition of goods and services from the individual's assets or resources subtracts from his total utility. Corresponding to the equilibrium conditions for goods purchased, the marginal utilities of the productive services supplied to the market are proportional to their corresponding supply prices.

of two or three goods or services, but deriving from our hypothesis a more symmetrical construction of the individual indifference map. Since $\Sigma p_r x_r = 0$, the price hyperplane passes through the origin of an n-dimensional indifference map and is negative in slope with respect to all the axes. This means that in order to acquire (or surrender) more of one good or service, other goods or services must be surrendered (or acquired).

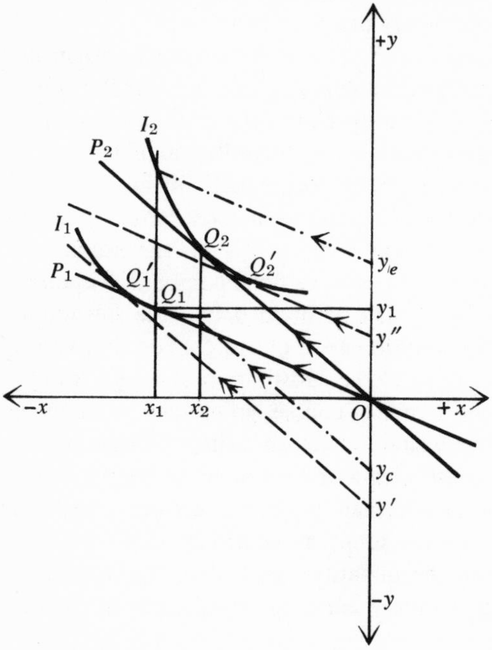

Figure 1

A two-dimensional cross section of this indifference map is represented in Figure 1. Any distance Ox to the right of the origin measures amount per unit period of x acquired by the individual. Any distance Ox to the left of the origin measures the amount of x per period given up by the individual. Similarly, Oy above the origin measures the quantity of y taken, and Oy below the origin, the quantity of y given up. Inasmuch as rent partakes of the nature of a surplus, and is to be measured in exactly the same way as consumers' surplus is measured, it is advantageous to consider in some detail the simple problem of the individual supplying x, say a single type of productive service, "labor," to the market in return for which y is demanded. Thus, we operate in the northwest quadrant of the figure. And though we may not do so in an n-dimensional treatment of the problem, confined as we are to two dimensions, we may find it convenient to regard y as all other goods at fixed prices, the only price which alters being the price of x, labor.[11] We now seek a precise measure of the difference in welfare resulting from alternative supply prices of labor.

If we construct a price-line P_1 passing through the origin and tangent to Q_1 on the indifference curve I_1, the individual is represented as in equilibrium, giving up Ox_1 of labor and acquiring in exchange Oy_1 of income y. We now perform the familiar Hicksian experiment in order to have the supply effects on all fours with those of demand. The price of x is now increased from p_1 to p_2, the individual's new equilibrium being at Q_2 on the indifference curve I_2. The change in equilibrium positions consequent upon the change in the price of labor may be divided into the substitution effect, Q_1 to Q_1', and the welfare effect, Q_1' to Q_2 (or alternatively the welfare effect Q_1 to Q_2' and the substitution effect Q_2' to Q_2). Although the welfare effect can, of course, go either way, it should be noticed that a positive welfare effect on x, implying an increase in the *demand* for x, constitutes a reduction in its supply, which is to say that a positive or "normal" welfare effect of a rise in the supply price of labor, or in the supply price of any good or service, is that of a reduction in the quantity supplied by the individual. The "backward-bending" supply curve of labor is, then, the out-

[11] This construction, and its later elaboration, are, I believe, to be preferred to the more common leisure-income diagram apart from the fact that the present diagram is derived directly from the more general condition in which the individual chooses to supply a combination of various goods and productive services to the market in amounts which depend upon the current set of prices: (1) Giving up leisure, a homogeneous good, does not have the same connotation as providing various kinds of services each of which requires a different skill and entails a different degree of hardship for the individual. (2) We need not evoke the artifice of a fixed amount of the good, leisure, say 24 hours a day, with the rather awkward result that an improvement in welfare may be represented along one axis as equivalent to more than 24 hours of leisure a day. In the construction used here, the shape of the indifference curves acts to limit the supply of any productive service furnished to the market, and our measure of welfare changes is in terms only of the good, y. Finally (3) the indifference map used here is the correct prior construction to that useful textbook diagram in which a downward-sloping line crosses the price-axis, to the right of which is represented the demand schedule and to the left, the supply schedule.

come of a strong positive, or normal, welfare effect, and not a negative, or perverse, welfare effect.

Suppose we are now to measure the increase in welfare following a rise in the price of x to p_2, we may follow Hicks' practice[12] and distinguish between two preliminary measures: the compensating variation (CV), and the equivalent variation (EV). The CV is the amount of y which, following a change in the price of x, has to be given to or taken from the individual in order that his initial welfare—indicated by the indifference curve I_1 in Figure 1—remain unchanged. In this instance, the individual's welfare being improved as a result of the price change, Oy' measures the CV. For if Oy' were taken from his income he could still maintain his initial welfare position on I_1, given that the higher supply price P_2 is available to him. The EV, on the other hand, is the amount of y which has to be given to, or taken from, the individual to ensure that he reaches the new level of welfare when the change in price does not apply to him. Since in this instance the increment in welfare is positive he is to receive a money equivalent. If he receives Oy'' he can just reach I_2, the new level of welfare, with the old price P_1.

The concept of rent as an economic surplus, it is suggested here, should be measured as a CV or an EV in a manner symmetrical in all respects with the concept of consumer's surplus. In the example above, it arises as the difference in welfare experienced by the individual from the rise in the supply price to P_2, P_1 being regarded as the most preferred alternative open to him.[13] The rent obviously becomes larger the lower the initial supply price P_1. In

[12] J. R. Hicks, *A Revision of Demand Theory* (Oxford: Clarendon, 1946), pp. 69–82.

[13] Though we are working with a single productive service, labor, the notion and the definition of economic rent may, just as in the analysis of consumer's surplus, be extended to several services with obvious modifications. If, for example, the individual is providing two services, x_1 and x_2, then a rise in the supply price of both services yields a CV rent which is the maximum he is willing to pay —prices of all goods and services other than those of x_1 and x_2 remaining unchanged—rather than forgo these higher prices. This measure remains the same, as we might expect, if we measure each in turn and add them: the rent when the price of x_1 rises, all other prices, including that of x_2, being constant, plus the additional rent when now the price of x_2 rises, all other prices remaining constant with x_1 unchanged at its new price.

This argument is symmetrical with that of Hicks on consumer's surplus (*A Revision of Demand Theory, op. cit.*, pp. 178–179), but the generalization on the conclusion of this paper goes further than Hicks'.

the limiting case, P_1 will be a no-transactions price tangent to an indifference curve at the point where it crosses the vertical axis.

Since the current definitions treat rent as a surplus which may be appropriated without any effects on the supply of the individual's productive services in his current occupation, it is important to ob-

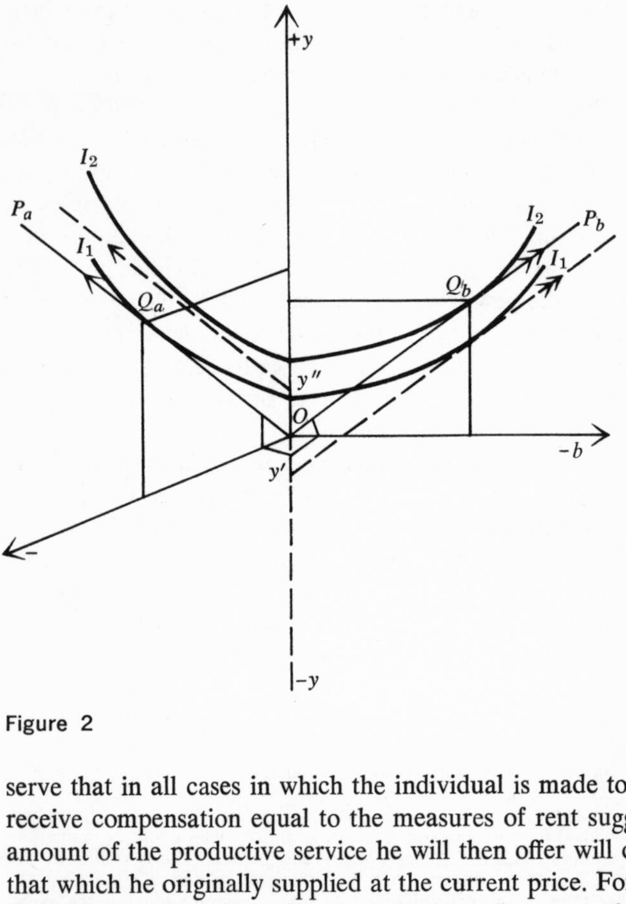

Figure 2

serve that in all cases in which the individual is made to pay or to receive compensation equal to the measures of rent suggested, the amount of the productive service he will then offer will differ from that which he originally supplied at the current price. For example, if, having reached Q_2 in Figure 1, he is made to pay the full *CV*, equal to Oy', he will no longer continue to supply Ox_2 of labor. Instead he will supply the amount indicated by the equilibrium point Q_1'—a larger amount than before if x is normal.

Finally it may be instructive to remove the restriction of a single occupation in our analysis and to consider briefly the case of the supply of productive services to two alternative occupations, *A* and *B*, in which, although the individual might choose to work part-time in each if that were feasible, he is obliged, owing to institutional arrangements, to work entirely in the one occupation or the other.

In Figure 2, a three-dimensional indifference map with a vertical *y*-axis and two horizontal axes, *a* and *b*, crossing at right angles, we cut a vertical slice along the negative *ay* plane and along the negative *by* plane as far as the *y*-axis and remove the segment. Hence, if we imagine our figure divided vertically into four quarters, we shall be looking into the space left after the removal of the vertical quarter in which *a* and *b* are both negative. The upper part of what meets the eye is represented in Figure 2. By removing the vertical quarter referred to, we have removed the possibility of combining employment *A* and *B*.

Despite the fact that both the rate of pay and the resultant earnings are higher in *A* than in *B*, the individual chooses to supply his services to *B*, his equilibrium there being at Q_b on the indifference surface I_2 compared with the alternative equilibrium position Q_a on I_1. Nonetheless, he enjoys a positive economic rent in the lower-paid occupation *B* which can be measured by the *CV*, Oy'—the maximum he is prepared to pay to remain in *B* when *A*, at the existing wage-rate, is the only alternative open to him. It can also be measured by the *EV*, Oy''—the minimum the individual must be paid in order to induce him to transfer his services from *B* to *A*.[14]

II. Comparison with the Marshallian Concept

Let us now compare our results with Marshall's concept of rent. Though the *Principles* do not contain a formal definition of rent, the sense of most of Marshall's dicta on the subject points to a definition of rent as a surplus above that necessary to elicit the pro-

[14] In all cases in which institutional arrangements preclude a combination of occupations—the individual having the choice only of putting the services of his resources entirely in *A* or in *B*—the coincidence of the four definitions and the Marshallian measure of rent no longer follow from a zero welfare elasticity, for the *EV* and the *CV* now arise from different cross sections of the individual indifference map.

ductive services of a resource.[15] This Marshallian definition, essentially that of category (1), suffers from the same imprecision as his definition of consumer's surplus.[16] For one thing, the surplus was treated as if it could be taxed away without affecting the supply of the productive service, which is manifestly false on our analysis. Once this is granted the difficulties are easily perceived. In order to persist with the Marshallian definition we have to interpret it to have reference to some unchanged amount of the productive service; either (a) the amount supplied in the equilibrium position resulting from the price change (Ox_2 in Figure 1), or (b) that supplied in the original equilibrium position (Ox_1 in Figure 1). In either case we are saddled with an improbable and cumbersome measure inasmuch as we have to compel the individual to supply an amount of the productive service other than that which he would freely choose. For instance, if we adopt (a) we derive what may be called, for convenience, the Marshallian *CV*, equal to Oy_c. It represents the maximum amount of money the individual would surrender in order to retain P_2 if at the same time he were constrained to provide no more than Ox_2 of productive service—Ox_2 being the amount supplied at P_2 when he is free to choose. As we should expect, the restriction on his choice of quantity reduces the maximum he is prepared to pay for the privilege of the P_2 price. In a like manner, if we adopt (b), the Marshallian *EV*, we are left with a measure Oy_e. It is larger than the *EV* proper, Oy'', since the minimum payment to him must be greater if he is now compelled to provide the original quantity of productive services Ox_1 at the original price P_1 *when his welfare is increased from* I_1 to I_2. There

[15] In particular see Marshall, *Principles* (London: Macmillan), pp. 155–162, 427–430. Elsewhere in the *Principles* Marshall talks of the additional earnings resulting from superior abilities as a surplus or rent (pp. 577–579, 623–627). What part of the additional earnings might be regarded as rent on the definition attributed to Marshall cannot be known without determining first what part of the additional earnings is necessary to attract the resource into that occupation. From the point of view of the firm, however, the additional payments for superior abilities must appear as efficiency payments.

[16] *Ibid.*, p. 124. Marshall was, of course, aware of the slippery nature of his consumer's surplus (though not, apparently, of his economic rent) and tried to cover himself by specifying a change in the demand price for a particular good whose real-income effect was so small in relation to the individual's budget that the marginal utility of money income could be taken, for all practical purposes, as constant. The trouble with this is that it is double-edged: ambiguity is reduced by reducing the significance of what is being measured. Ambiguity disappears entirely only when the price change under consideration becomes zero and there is nothing left to measure.

is obviously nothing strictly illogical about such definitions, but on the grounds of plausibility and convenience they are to be rejected in favor of the *CV* and *EV* proper.

If, on the other hand, a Marshallian *measure* of economic rent is taken to be the area above the supply curve of the services of the individual's resource[17]—a measure which seems to correspond with the category (2) definition if the individual's supply curve represents maximum earnings of successive increments of productive services in alternative uses—for this measure to be of any use requires (i) an upward-sloping supply curve, and (ii) exclusion of nonpecuniary considerations. Clearly this Marshallian measure, which is popular in textbooks, is inadequate since it represents no more than a first derivative of the locus of price-quantity equilibria of an indifference map. Nor is this derivative necessarily upward-sloping; it may be backward-bending in contrast to the *marginal* indifference curves which will always be upward-sloping. It appears yet more unsatisfactory if the restriction to pecuniary considerations is removed. We may then discover that differences between the earnings of the resource in its current occupation and those of the relevant alternative occupation are negative, a tribute to the individual's preference for his present occupation.

Hicks has done some admirable work in tracing the relationships between Marshall's definition of consumer's surplus, Marshall's way of measuring consumer's surplus (the area under the individual's demand curve), and the two precise measures *CV* and *EV* which were initially suggested by his indifference curve analysis. Important as these contributions were in clarifying our ideas on this tangled subject, it can be held that the tracing of these precise relationships assumes a far greater importance on the neglected supply side. For it is surely just there that we cannot reasonably suppose that change in price has negligible effects on the welfare of the individual inasmuch as the supply of any one of his produc-

[17] *Ibid.*, p. 811. Here Marshall graphically illustrates consumer's surplus and producer's surplus for an *industry*. But even if we interpret the industry's supply curve as a marginal curve, the producer's surplus could be identified with the rent of resources in that industry only under restricted conditions. On the other hand, it would hardly be inconsistent with Marshall's view of things to interpret the measurement of the individual's rent in a manner symmetrical with his suggested measurement of the individual's consumer's surplus (*ibid.*, pp. 125–127) as the area under the individual's demand curve.

tive services enters significantly into his budget. To the extent it does so, the area above the individual's supply curve, especially in the case of only one productive service, is a much less reliable index of the surplus welfare than the area under his demand curve for any one good.

In the special case in which the welfare elasticity of the supply of x is zero there is a coincidence of the *CV*, *EV*, Marshallian *CV*, Marshallian *EV*, and the Marshallian measure, the area above the supply curve. (This same coincidence obtains when the rent is reckoned as between the current and alternative occupations in the case in which the choice between occupations rests on a purely pecuniary basis.) While in general, a zero elasticity of supply with respect to price does not entail a zero welfare elasticity, in the particular case in which the former derives from a zero substitutability *plus a zero welfare elasticity*, these four definitions and the Marshallian measure all come to the same thing. The zero substitutability implies no alternative uses and therefore a set of vertical *marginal* indifference curves. The zero welfare elasticity implies that all the marginal indifference curves will coincide. Ricardian land is a favorite example of a zero elasticity of supply of this sort. Its characteristic is that it has only one use, say wheat production. As a consequence of this characteristic (i) it cannot move elsewhere in response to changes in relative prices (zero substitution effect), and therefore (ii) *all* of a given acreage of land of uniform quality is brought into wheat production in response to any positive price per acre (zero welfare effect).[18]

III. Conclusion

Little further reflection is required to recognize that consumer's surplus and economic rent are both measures of the change in the individual's welfare when the set of prices facing him are changed or the constraints imposed upon him are altered. Any distinction between them is one of convenience only: consumer's surpluses

[18] The indifference curves in this special case would all be horizontal (signifying zero elasticity of substitution) up to a distance representing the maximum supply of productive service from the given resource. At this distance they would all become vertical and, hence, coincide. Rent however measured would, on this vertical limit, be equal to the vertical distance between the two price-lines in question.

have reference to demand prices, economic rent to supply prices. Furthermore, no consideration of logic precludes our measuring the individual's gain—in terms either of the *CV* or the *EV*—from, say, a simultaneous fall in the price of a good bought and a rise in the price of a service provided.

Indeed, in general, if any one, several, or even all prices change for the individual, some demand prices and some supply prices rising, others falling, the resulting change in the individual's welfare can, in principle, be measured by either of our definitions. The *CV* is an exact measure of the transfer, to or from the individual, following a change in the set of all prices, in order to maintain his initial level of welfare. In this case the amount transferred is measured in terms of any one good, in combinations of various goods, or in a combination of all goods dealt in, always using the *new* set of prices. This is quite possible since, given a set of prices, the amount of any one good is equivalent in value to various combinations of some particular goods or of all goods. More usefully, an amount of money calculated at the given set of prices will suffice to measure the *CV*.

On the other hand, the *EV* is an exact measure of the transfer necessary to bring the individual's level of welfare into equality with what it would have been if he were not, as he is, debarred from the new set of prices. The amount of the transfer is now calculated at the *old* prices, and may be expressed in money or in any combination of goods at these prices.

PART 3

CRUCIAL ASPECTS OF WELFARE ECONOMICS

CHAPTER 4

A Reappraisal of the Principles of Resource Allocation*[1]

A rejection of the theories of welfare economics carries with it the judgment that there is at present no rule or method by which we may judge the relative efficiency of alternative forms of economic organization; indeed, that any conceivable set of production plans or any conceivable set of prices, no matter how arbitrary, are—in our present state of knowledge—to be considered as good as any others.

Few economists, even among those who are wont to treat welfare economics with extreme skepticism, will go as far as this to avoid courting the subject while economists of the liberal school who talk of a presumption in favor of the market mechanisms must, if they are to rationalize this presumption, invoke some theory of welfare. Put at its bluntest then it is in pursuit of an

* From *Economica* (November 1957), pp. 324–342.

[1] I am indebted to Mr. Ralph Turvey on whose advice I have removed a great deal of controversial and difficult material from a previous draft thereby increasing the readability and relevance of the present paper, to Professor James Meade for several important suggestions, and to Mr. Richard Lipsey for valuable and detailed criticism.

answer to the question, by what lights are we to distinguish between a good allocation and a chaotic one, that we are led willy-nilly into the domain of welfare economics.

Notwithstanding the logic of this conclusion a great deal continues to be written concerning economic efficiency which deliberately eschews the language of welfare economics, relying instead on apparently more acceptable criteria—for instance, the "common sense" rule that total receipts should be able to cover total costs supplemented, perhaps, by rules about marginal equalities. For the abiding impression seems to be that by confining oneself to the traditional rules governing the allocation of resources one somehow circumvents the tenuous concepts and fine paradoxes of welfare economics. After all, there are critiques and counter-critiques of welfare economics and in the process a great deal of smoke and subtlety is generated. But the principles of resource allocation are of more solid stuff. They are ever with us and in continual application.

This view, however, does not bear close examination. A by-product of this paper will be the demonstration that certain familiar welfare criteria and the so-called optimum conditions of resource allocation are raised on the same foundation: they stand or fall together. In fact the relationship is so close it is almost inevitable that allocative criteria be examined by the techniques which have proved so popular in welfare economics.[2]

I

It is hard to exaggerate how fundamental is the idea of resource allocation in the theory and application of economics. If competition or unimpeded international trade or mobility of capital and labor are good things, this is so, we are given to understand, because they are conducive to allocative efficiency. For opposite reasons monopoly, tariffs, price controls, and most kinds of taxes

[2] To those who have followed the development of the "New Welfare Economics" it can hardly be surprising that resource allocation should be linked with, and capable of being tested by, welfare criteria. If allocative criteria have managed to survive unscathed despite difficulties in formulating unambiguous welfare criteria the explanation is surely that the connection between the two, though apprehended, has not yet been made explicit.

are bad things. And if these judgments have been attacked the attack has not been leveled at the allocative principles on their own ground so to speak. Rather it is the relevance of these principles to the real world, the world of uncertainty, flux, and growth, that has been brought into question. Adjustments which may be demanded by allocative criteria alone, it is argued, may interfere with the more important factors making for growth.[3] Furthermore, to speak of resources being organized to meet the wants of the community is somewhat fanciful in view of the opinion that in advanced economies, at least, consumers may be persuaded to want almost anything if enough resources are devoted to the task of persuasion.

Weighty as these criticisms are I wish to make it plain from the start that my concern is with the narrower but less controversial aspect: with the validity of allocative criteria within their own limited framework. Let us be certain what this framework encompasses. First, it includes an unchanging population of "rational" and "responsible" beings. It is rational in two senses: (a) that the choices made by each individual in any situation are consistent with all his other choices and (b) that the well-being of the individual depends only on his own real income and not at all on those of others. Responsible in that each individual is taken to be the best judge of his own wants. Clearly both senses of rational are simplifications which may or may not be generally true, while individual responsibility is an ethical judgment without which nothing may be said about allocation. Furthermore—in order to ease the exposition but not necessary for its conclusions—the factor endowment of the economy is fixed[4] as also is the number of finished goods in the economy.[5] Arbitrary assumptions are usually made in order to deal with the government as a supplier of goods and

[3] For some very forcible arguments in this connection see Chapter 12 of Schumpeter's *Socialism, Capitalism and Democracy* (London: G. Allen, 1943). For a recent attack on allocation economics see P. Wiles, "Growth Versus Choice," *Economic Journal* (June 1956), also a comment on this article by K. Klappholz in the same journal for June 1957.

[4] Investment and saving can be, and often are, brought into the scheme of things since allocation has a time as well as a space dimension. We do not introduce it here simply because we are interested in testing the validity of the basic principles of resource allocation and not in their extended application.

[5] The introduction of a new good, however, may be treated in its effects on welfare as a reduction in the price of an existing good.

services.[6] But since our conclusions do not depend in any way upon such assumptions we will confine our attention to the market sector of the economy. Uncertainty, which gives rise to theoretical difficulties at many points, is conceded to be the preserve of dynamics, and is therefore excluded from an analysis which is basically static.

As to ethical presuppositions, other than individual responsibility already mentioned, we shall follow tradition in stating that the community as a whole is better off if at least one person is made better off and no person is made worse off.

We now proceed to inquire whether, within the confines of our assumptions and simplifications, a movement toward an optimum allocation of resources, defined with reference to the familiar marginal equalities,[7] is an actual improvement for the community in this sense.[8] If it is not an actual improvement is it, we ask, a *potential* improvement in accordance with the definition advanced in the "New Welfare Economics": that a situation II is to be preferred to a situation I if the community as a whole *could* be made better off by a movement to II. And in order to answer this ques-

[6] For some interesting controversy over the treatment of government activity see J. R. Hicks, "The Valuation of the Social Income," *Economica* (1940), in particular his section 6 on "Public Finance," and Simon Kuznets, "On the Valuation of Social Income—Reflections on Professor Hicks' Article," *Economica* (1948), Part I, section 3, also J. R. Hicks, "The Valuation of the Social Income—A Comment on Professor Kuznets' Reflections," *Economica* (1948).

[7] For a compact treatment of the relevant marginal equalities consult Melvin W. Reder, *Studies in the Theory of Welfare Economics* (New York: Columbia, 1947), in particular his Chapter 2.

[8] The answer, needless to say, is always affirmative if the community consists of only one individual. It is as soon as we have a community of two or more individuals that the problem arises.

In this connection the frequent assumption in the treatment of welfare or allocative problems, that the utility functions of the population are all homogeneous and identical, enables one to reach conclusions which are no more applicable to society than the conclusions arising from the analysis of a Crusoe economy.

This stricture is no less pertinent to "second-best" solutions which build on this restrictive simplification. In this connection one might consult a recent and very fertile approach by R. Lipsey and K. Lancaster, "The General Theory of Second Best," *Review of Economic Studies,* Vol. 24 (1957), where because of the explicit initial assumption of homogeneous and identical utility functions the welfare conclusions reached apply in effect only to an individual but not to society.

Unless, that is, we can find some way of justifying the criteria of an optimum allocation of resources for society all the interesting propositions about monopoly, controls, taxation, and trade barriers remain without any acceptable foundations. On the principle of first things first, then, we should seek to establish the apparently elusive rationale of the "first best" before pursuing the logic of the second best.

tion satisfactorily we shall, further, seek to be free from commitment in the matter of distribution—as indeed we ought to be if we are to accommodate the many economists who persistently invoke allocative criteria while shunning the question of better or worse distributions of welfare—by regarding II as superior to I only if it is a potential improvement over I for all conceivable distributions of welfare.

The conclusion of this paper briefly stated is this: that in principle an optimum allocation of resources is neither actually nor potentially superior on welfare grounds to a nonoptimum allocation of resources. Nevertheless, though an optimum allocation *per se* cannot be vindicated as a norm to be pursued some virtue may be detected in the "lower-level" optima of exchange and production. If, therefore, one disregards allocative criteria to the extent of trespassing upon these lower-level optimum conditions the welfare of the community is liable to be damaged.

In an endeavor to hold the interest of those readers who are not on familiar terms with some of the basic techniques of welfare economics the following two sections will be taken up in elaborating the properties of community indifference curves essential to the analysis and in examining briefly the various criteria put forward in the development of the New Welfare Economics. Readers already aware of the power, and limitations, of these constructs may pass on immediately to Section IV.

II

The need for a welfare criterion of the type now common enough in the literature arises from a consideration of the following sort of dilemma. The definition of an improvement in the collective welfare which commands general assent requires that at least one individual be made better off without any individual being made worse off. However, it is usually recognized that any change in the economic situation all too frequently affects the distribution of welfare in some degree. Consequently an actual improvement in welfare which conforms with the above definition is apt to be a rare event. To accept, therefore, only an actual improvement in this sense would be an extremely frustrating axiom for the welfare economist to adopt.

The formulation of a new welfare criterion by Kaldor and Hicks[9] was the outcome of an endeavor to circumvent this source of frustration by defining an improvement in the collective welfare in such a way as to be independent of the actual distribution of welfare among the individuals. The criterion alighted upon was one which involved a *potential* improvement in welfare: if everyone in the community *could* be better off by moving from an existing situation I to a new situation II—in other words, if the gainers from the movement to II could more than compensate the losers—then the criterion was fulfilled. Accordingly, the movement from I to II was to be treated as an improvement in welfare regardless of whether or not compensation was paid.

Soon after the formulation of this criterion Scitovsky proved that it was capable of self-contradiction.[10] Though the gainers might indeed be able to compensate the losers from a movement to II and yet remain better off than they were at I, this fact did not rule out the possibility that the losers in question might, after the movement to II, be in a position to bribe the gainers to agree to return to the I situation.

Subtle though this certainly was, it could be cast into a more obvious form and one through which the elusive nature of the apparent contradiction might be uncovered. The Kaldor-Hicks criterion made use of a comparison between two product aggregates I and II which was based on the distribution of welfare attaching to the I aggregate. To apply the Scitovsky reversal test, however, we must compare the two aggregates on the basis of the welfare distribution attaching to the II aggregate. The Scitovsky criterion was fulfilled if the result of this reversal test did not contradict that reached by the original Kaldor-Hicks criterion.

If the comparison based on the II distribution of welfare did in fact give a result contrary to that reached when the comparison was based on the I distribution of welfare then indeed nothing could be said of the potential welfare superiority of either I or II.[11]

[9] The criterion was suggested by N. Kaldor in "Welfare Propositions and Interpersonal Comparisons of Utility," *Economic Journal* (September 1938), and adopted by J. R. Hicks in his "Foundations of Welfare Economics," *Economic Journal* (December 1939).

[10] T. Scitovsky, "A Note on Welfare Propositions in Economics," *Review of Economic Studies,* Vol. 9 (1941).

[11] In a later paper, "A Reconsideration of the Theory of Tariffs," *Review of Economic Studies* (1942), Scitovsky says (pp. 94–95), "If [the community in-

Nor should we stop here. For if we are to remain truly independent of all welfare distributions there is no case for confining a comparison of I and II to criteria based on the particular welfare distribution attaching to each. A truly comprehensive criterion, and the one we shall adopt from now on, involves a comparison of I and II with reference to *all conceivable distributions of welfare*. This comprehensive criterion is fulfilled if II is shown to be superior to I for every conceivable distribution of welfare. Unless this criterion is fulfilled the possibility of contradiction is not fully eliminated.[12]

III

The reason why this apparent contradiction can arise in a comparison between two situations may be made clear with the aid of Figure 1. The point *P* in the coordinate system with origin *O* fixes the quantities of *X* and *Y* available to the community. *P* may also be regarded as the other corner of the conventional box diagram for these quantities of *X* and *Y* which are to be shared between two individuals, *J* and *K*. The mutual tangency, and the individual ordering, of the two sets of indifference curves, representing respectively the welfare functions of the individuals *J* and *K*, are indicated at several points along the contract curve *ORSP*.

Irrespective of the manner of division of the total product *P* between the two individuals the community indifference curve must, of course, pass through point *P*. But the *angle* at which it

---

difference curves through two given situations] intersect . . . according to our convention we must regard the two situations as equally good." This conclusion is hardly acceptable. Unfortunately Arrow, in his *Social Choice and Individual Values,* elected to treat this unwarrantable conclusion as a proposition of the New Welfare Economics (pp. 44 ff.) and—manipulating a self-contradictory relationship as if it were instead a transitive one—discovered, not surprisingly, that it led to a self-contradictory conclusion.

[12] That the fulfillment of the Scitovsky criterion—that is, the Kaldor-Hicks criterion and the Scitovsky reversal test both yield the same result—is by itself insufficient to guard against contradiction has been amply demonstrated by W. M. Gorman, "The Intransitivity of Certain Criteria Used in Welfare Economics," *Oxford Economic Papers* (February 1955). Given that the relevant community indifference curves intersect, Gorman shows that, with more than two situations to compare, the Scitovsky criterion may be intransitive and, if consistently applied and acted upon, the community may be led into a clear reduction of its welfare. Only the comprehensive criterion is necessarily transitive and free from all possible contradiction.

passes through P depends directly on the division between them of this aggregate product. Since at each point on a properly constructed community indifference curve[13]—and therefore also at the particular point P—the rate of substitution of Y for X must be the same for each individual, the locus of efficient divisions of the total product between the individuals is given by the contract curve $ORSP$.[14]

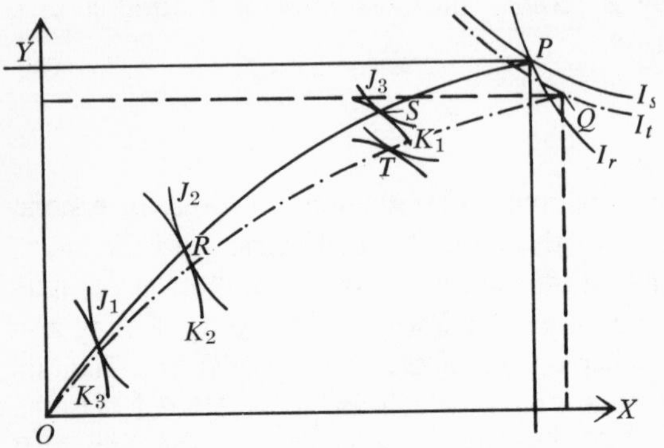

Figure 1

However, for any two points along the contract curve, representing two different divisions of the product P, the rate of substitution of Y for X is, in general, different for both individuals. For example, if we divide the product P between the two individuals in the manner indicated by R on the contract curve, the community indifference curve I_r passing through P (and representing along its length the sum of the individual welfares determined by this division) is parallel to the slope of mutual tangency at R. If, on the other hand, we begin with a division between the two individuals which is indicated by S on the contract curve, the

[13] For a simple geometric construction of a community indifference map derived directly from individual indifference maps, see my paper, "The Principle of Compensation Reconsidered," *Journal of Political Economy* (August 1952).

[14] A division of the product given by a point off the contract curve is inefficient since by exchange both individuals can improve themselves. For the present we shall consider only those divisions of the product traced out by the contract curve. The exchange optimum is therefore fulfilled as indeed it will be in any economy in which each product has only one price and people are free to buy all they want.

community indifference curve I_s passes through P at an angle parallel to that of the mutual tangency at S.

In general we may say that the rate of substitution at P, and therefore the slope of the community indifference curve at P, is uniquely determined by the division of the product between the individuals as represented by a point on the contract curve.[15]

If we now introduce another combination of goods, Q, with similar possibilities of division between these two individuals, we can again construct a whole pencil of community indifference curves passing through Q. In order to make a welfare comparison between P and Q we must select two community indifference curves, one passing through P and one passing through Q, that are *comparable* with each other; which is to say that the two curves selected may be regarded as parts of a properly constructed community indifference map—a map in which a higher indifference curve denotes that no individual is worse off and that at least one individual is better off.

This condition of comparability is less restrictive than it may first appear. For any one community indifference curve derived from some particular division of P, such as I_r, there will be many community indifference curves passing through Q each deriving from a slightly different distribution along Q's contract curve, which are directly comparable with I_r.[16] Consequently all these

[15] Paul Samuelson, in his paper "Social Indifference Curves," *Quarterly Journal of Economics* (February 1956), rejects community indifference curves simply because, as distinct from individual indifference curves, they do not enable welfare to be determined uniquely from the given amount of the products. They are then, according to Samuelson, not capable of generating group demand or of being of much service in the technique of revealed preference.

Now one can always "fix" a community indifference map, making the welfare of the community depend only on the quantities of the goods involved, by using some method such as lump sum transfers in order to maintain constant the initial distribution of welfare. This is in essence what Samuelson's "social indifference curves" amount to. Such a construction, however, is rather a vehicle for bypassing the crucial problem posed by the interdependence of prices and distribution than a device for its investigation.

That is to say, if the community indifference curves have to be constructed with due regard to this interdependence constraint it is not a defect in them but a virtue. Properly understood it makes explicit a relationship which we overlook to our cost, a relationship which plays a key role in this paper.

[16] These curves are not, of course, comparable with one another (since as we pass from one to the other one individual has a little more, the other a little less) but any *one* of them is comparable with I_r. Whichever one we choose to work with, to the exclusion of the others, it will, in a comparison of the two positions, give us the same answer.

comparable curves will at all points be above I_r. All of them will reveal the same thing, that Q is above P for the community as a whole.[17]

As we cannot legitimately talk of the same or similar welfare distributions existing at different levels of collective welfare[18] we shall, for terminological convenience, speak of any two distributions of welfare from which two comparable community indifference curves are generated as being *comparable welfare distributions*. For the same reason a comparison of, say, P and Q using I_r on the one hand and, on the other, any one of the comparable community indifference curves passing through Q, may be spoken of as a welfare comparison *based on* the I_r indifference curve or, alternatively, a comparison of P and Q *based on* the R distribution of welfare.

Suppose now that the aggregate of goods represented by Q differed from that represented by P in its having one less of Y and one more of X and that we chose to make a welfare comparison of P and Q based on I_r, I_r being the community indifference curve generated from the existing division at R of the product P. If the community's rate of substitution at R, and therefore also at I_r as it passes through P, were $2Y{:}1X$ then I_r is practically sure to pass below Q. On a comparison based on the R distribution then, Q is a better welfare position for the community than P.

If instead we chose to compare P and Q on the basis of the T division of the product Q, I_t is the community indifference curve generated for Q, a comparable one for P being I_s. If with the

[17] Since we shall continue from now on to deal with comparable community indifference curves it may be worth while emphasizing that in moving from a particular community indifference curve to one above that is comparable with it, the only condition to be fulfilled is that at least one member of the community be better off, none being worse off. Thus, a higher comparable curve may entail an improvement for all the individuals in the community, for some of the individuals, or only for one individual, no one being worse off. Having somewhat different distributions of welfare such curves will be slightly different from one another but, as stated, any *one* of them will be comparable with the curve below.

Having chosen one comparable community indifference curve with reference to the one already given, they both form part of a consistent indifference map—indeed, they could, on this principle of construction, form part of many such maps each differing in some degree in the arrangement of the curves above and below this pair. The curves of such a map cannot, of course, intersect.

[18] We cannot, for example, say that in a situation II everyone in the community is 20 percent better off than he was in a situation I, and that therefore the distribution of welfare remains unchanged, without admitting cardinal utility into welfare.

division T the community's rate of substitution were $2X:1Y$ the community indifference curve I_t will almost certainly pass below P. A comparison based on the T distribution of welfare would then reveal P to be a better welfare position for the community than Q.

If P is taken to be the initial situation, and Q the new alternative situation, the Kaldor-Hicks criterion is fulfilled by a movement to Q. For, beginning with the existing distribution, R, everyone *could* be made better off by a movement to Q. Having moved to Q, but compensation not having been paid, the welfare distribution is now that indicated by T. The relative valuations of the two goods are, as a concomitant of the new distribution at T, so changed that once again it is apparent that everyone can be made better off by a movement back to P—I_s being a higher community indifference curve comparable with I_t.

This is the essence of the Scitovsky paradox. And it has been shown that it stems from the interdependence of relative prices and welfare distributions.[19]

IV

The apparent contradiction which can arise with the use of these welfare criteria has, however, been demonstrated only for a comparison of given product aggregates without reference to the conditions under which they are brought into being. If we wish to bring these criteria into relation with the traditional principles governing the proper allocation of resources—which ensure that each class of factor is distributed over the economy so that in all

[19] It may be noted in passing that if, as in the above example, the I situation appears superior to II when a comparison is made with the II distribution (or, in Figure 1, if P appears superior to Q when the comparison is made using the distribution pertaining to the latter) it may *not* be interpreted as if "potential losers could bribe potential gainers to oppose the change to II" as in fact it very frequently is. For this expression turns the apparent contradiction into a real one. It says (i) that individual J can bribe individual K to make the change to II while, *at the same time,* (ii) individual K can successfully bribe J to oppose the change. Or, in other words, everybody could be made better off (i) by moving to II and (ii) by staying at I. These are logically contradictory propositions. Both cannot simultaneously be correct.

Stated correctly, the apparent contradiction should read: (i) individual J could bribe individual K to make the change from I to II, but (ii) *having made the change* to II, and no compensation having been paid, individual K could bribe individual J to return to I.

lines of production the value of its marginal product is the same—we must bring the production conditions into the picture.

In taking account of these conditions, however, we may for the present allow that production is efficiently organized; that the rate of substitution between any two factors is the same in the production of all goods in the economy.[20] On the other hand, we have already seen that the use of community indifference curves implies that the rate of substitution between any two goods is the same for all individuals. Therefore, in an economy where all firms maximize profits without recourse to discrimination between individuals and without regard to the supply curves of the factors, the two "lower-level" optima—the production optimum and the exchange optimum—will be simultaneously realized. Granted this much, we can focus our attention on the significance of divergences in the ratios of prices to marginal costs.

What is now to be examined is what we may call an economic *plan*. The plan is identified by a particular aggregate of goods from the many producible with the resources at the disposal of the economy *plus* the differential in the ratio of the product prices to the ratio of their respective marginal costs. For brevity this differential may be referred to as the *price-cost ratio*. In diagrammatic terms, whereas the community's aggregate of goods is represented by a point on the coordinate system, a plan is represented by the intersection, or tangency, of a community indifference curve with the production possibility curve—the angle between them, if any, measuring the price-cost ratio.

Now in the absence of all forms of external economies, the "ideal" allocation is said to be found in a situation in which marginal cost everywhere is equal to price or, on our simplification of fixed factor supplies, in which the ratio of price to marginal cost is the same for all products. Any situation, or plan, having this "ideal" allocation is commonly spoken of as a complete optimum

[20] It is not necessary, of course, to hold factor supplies fixed to describe a production possibility curve. We need only assume consistent preferences of factor owners as between the alternative types of activity open to them, including leisure. A production possibility curve could therefore be constructed in such a way that at every point along it the additional condition is met that the rate of substitution for any class of factor as between one activity and another is the same for each factor owner at the margin.

and is represented diagrammatically by the tangency of the community indifference curve with the production possibility curve.

Can we now compare two optimum plans, such as Q_1, with the community indifference curve I_1 in Figure 2, and Q_2 with com-

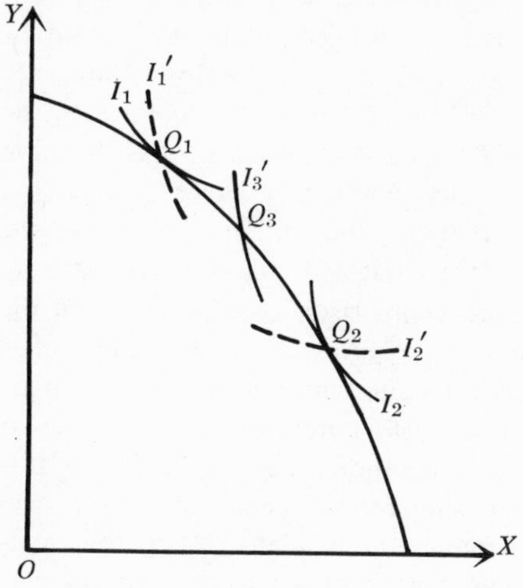

Figure 2

munity indifference curve I_2? The answer is no, and the reason easy to illustrate. For if we hypothetically redivide the aggregate product Q_2 in order to derive therefrom a community indifference curve, say I'_2, which is comparable with I_1 in the sense defined, then in effect what is now being compared with the optimum situation at Q_1 is no longer an optimum at Q_2 which has a welfare distribution comparable with that attaching to Q_1, but instead a nonoptimum plan at Q_2, since I'_2 *cuts* the production possibility curve at Q_2. The same thing happens of course if we try to base the comparison on the I_2 community indifference curve by redividing the product Q_1 between the individuals so as to generate I'_1, a community indifference curve comparable with I_2.

We conclude that welfare comparisons between optimum plans is logically impossible: the attempt to make use of such comparisons entails a destruction of the essential characteristic of at least one of the optimum plans—the equality of the ratio of prices and marginal costs.

Moreover, and this is more to the purpose, we can demonstrate by analogous reasoning that, in principle, an optimum plan cannot be made comparable with a nonoptimum plan and therefore cannot be said to be superior to it. Consider, for example (Figure 2), the optimum plan Q_1 with the community indifference curve I_1, and the nonoptimum plan Q_3 with the community indifference curve I'_3. To attempt a comparison of the two plans through the medium of a community indifference map based on the I'_3 curve requires a comparable community indifference curve through Q_1, say I'_1. But this manifestly destroys the optimum characteristic of the plan at Q_1, and therefore vitiates the desired comparison. In a like manner an attempted comparison based instead on the community indifference curve I_1 requires the construction of a community indifference curve passing through Q_3 at an angle differing from the original, in this way contravening the particular price-cost characteristic of the nonoptimum plan at Q_3. Hence it is not possible, in principle, to compare by means of hypothetical compensation optimum with nonoptimum plans or, for that matter, optimum plans with one another.

The words *in principle* should be stressed, for there may be cases where the community indifference curves initially attaching to the plans to be compared already form part of a consistent community indifference map. Here a direct comparison is possible without invoking the technique of hypothetical compensation (which, as we have just seen, destroys the price-cost ratio characteristic of at least one of the plans). Since the two plans are directly comparable—for instance, plan Q_1 with I_1 and plan Q_2 with I'_2—one is actually and unambiguously superior to the other. When, however, two plans are not directly comparable in this way, a comparison of potential welfare is, in the nature of things, impossible.

It is surely at this juncture that we sense acutely the need to answer the question: what virtue resides in an optimum plan that is absent in a nonoptimum plan? And the answer will, I think, emerge most clearly if we compare an optimum and a nonoptimum plan with a particular aggregate of goods common to both—let us say the optimum plan Q_1 with I_1 and the nonoptimum plan Q_1 with I'_1 in Figure 3.

Of the optimum plan at Q_1 it may be asserted that, with the particular division of the aggregate Q_1 as summarized in the community indifference curve I_1 at that point, no improvement is pos-

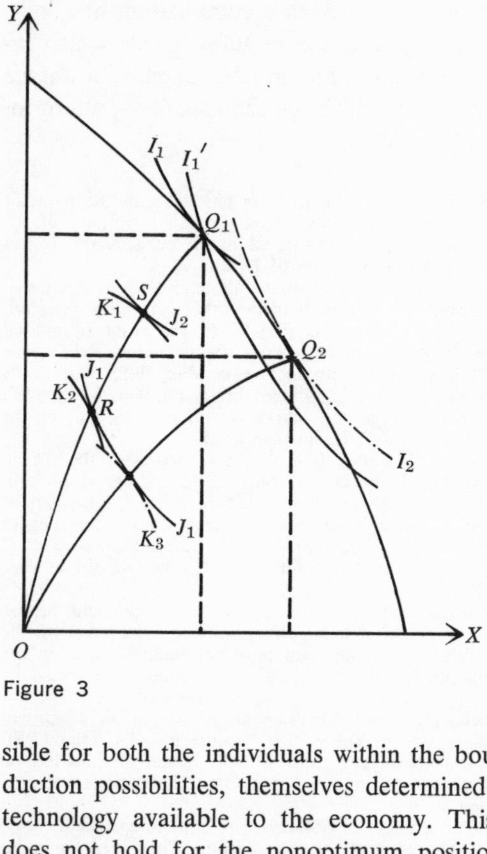

Figure 3

sible for both the individuals within the bounds of the given production possibilities, themselves determined by the resources and technology available to the economy. This statement, however, does not hold for the nonoptimum position at Q_1—that is, for the division of the aggregate product Q_1 which is summarized in the community indifference curve I'_1 at that point, for we can clearly construct a community indifference curve comparable with I'_1 which is an improvement for both individuals and yet is below the production possibility curve along some of its length. One such comparable community indifference curve, I_2, will just touch the production possibility curve at a point Q_2 thereby forming an optimum plan at that point. With this resulting division of the aggregate product Q_2 no further improvement for both individuals is possible.[21]

It is manifest therefore that for each point on the production possibility curve, representing as it does a combination of goods, there corresponds a *unique* distribution of those goods which invests it with the properties of an optimum and therefore a *unique* community indifference curve which determines the pattern of individual welfares.[22]

[21] In more detail, I_1 at the point Q_1 in Figure 3 is parallel with the point of mutual tangency S on the contract curve $ORSQ_1$, the respective welfares of the individuals J and K being denoted by the individual indifference curves J_2 and K_1. I_1 therefore represents the proper summation of K_1 and J_2.

Since I_1 is above the production frontier at all points save Q_1 it is not possible for either individual to become better off without the other becoming worse off.

On the other hand, I'_1 at the point Q_1 is parallel to the point of mutual tangency at R and represents the proper summation of the individual indifference curves J_1 and K_2. But as I'_1 is below the production frontier along part of its length it is obvious that both individuals can be made better off. This is achieved, for example, with the community indifference curve I_2 which is tangent to the production frontier thereby forming an optimum plan at Q_2.

For simplicity of construction, however, I_2 is drawn to represent the special case in which all the improvement in welfare accrues to the individual K, individual J remaining as well off but no better off than before. Thus I_2 becomes the proper summation of J_1 (whose extension across the contract curve pertaining to the product Q_2 is possible inasmuch as the origin of J's indifference map at O remains unchanged) and K_3 (measured from individual K's new origin at Q_2), where K_3 is of course above K_2.

[22] It may well be emphasized that an optimum has a sensible and precise meaning but one *inseparable from the distribution of welfare.* Any point on the production frontier may qualify for an optimum position, each of such optima being tied to a particular distribution of the quantities of goods represented by that point.

This inseparability has been recognized by Professor Meade in his *Theory of International Economic Policy,* Vol. 2. On p. 76, for instance, he writes, "Efficiency demands that the production programme should match the distribution of income which is judged proper on grounds of equity. The two sets of considerations cannot be separated."

Certainly there is no inconsistency in Meade's concern with allocative efficiency for he explicitly admits interpersonal comparisons. Thus there is in his system of welfare an "optimum" distribution of welfare.

In strict logic, of course, we cannot select an "optimum" distribution of welfare as an *a priori* concept without invoking cardinal utility, for the choice of distribution is constrained by the possibilities provided by the range of optimum allocations. In other words, we can only compare the actual quantities distributed among the individuals for each point on the production frontier when each point is treated as an optimum. Having chosen among the various distributions of goods among the individuals that which we judge to be most desirable, we have

We conclude therefore that so long as we have no rule for the ranking of welfare distributions (a) comparisons between optimum plans are not possible and (b) comparisons between optimum and nonoptimum plans are, in general, not possible. They are not possible because whenever the distribution of one of the plans has to be altered for the purposes of comparison—welfare distribution being inseparable from relative prices—the identity of one of the plans is destroyed. (c) If the optimum and nonoptimum plans to be compared already form part of the existing community indifference map then the method of hypothetical compensation is superfluous, the optimum being actually and unambiguously superior to the nonoptimum.

Conclusion (c) is, however, not so much of an exception as it may first appear, not merely because as the number of individuals in the commuity increases the likelihood of this eventuality rapidly diminishes but because of our aim to be neutral as between different welfare distributions. If, from an existing nonoptimum plan we move directly to a comparable optimum plan, everyone being better off, this improvement in welfare is unambiguous for the existing distributions of welfare. For other distributions of welfare the previously optimal plan is a nonoptimum plan and, as such, it will be actually inferior to some other plans, optimum and nonoptimum; which is to say, once more, that only by abandoning the endeavor to be neutral in the matter of welfare distributions—or, more positively, by selecting one reachable distribution of product quantities above all others available from the given resources—can we define an unambiguous optimum position.

The full force of these conclusions must now be apparent. Far from an optimum allocation of resources representing some kind of an ideal output separable from and independent of interpersonal comparisons of welfare, a particular output retains its optimum characteristics only insofar as we commit ourselves to the particular welfare distribution uniquely associated with it. *If, therefore, we insist on eschewing interpersonal comparisons of welfare the*

---

effectively isolated the optimum position for society compared with which all other possibilities are unambiguously inferior.

Nevertheless, any change in tastes or in resources nullifies this ideal position and once again we have to choose among the new range of optimum positions for the most desired distribution of the product quantities.

logic of choice impels us to be indifferent as between "good" and "bad" allocations of resources.

To those who, like myself, do not at first take kindly to these conclusions some additional persuasion may be necessary. Let us then turn aside from the price-cost constraints imposed by allocative criteria and briefly reconsider the matter in the light of the more familiar welfare comparisons. Toward the end of Section II we stated that in order for our results to be truly independent of welfare distributions we were required to employ the comprehensive criterion which would define II as an unambiguous potential improvement over I if, for all conceivable distributions of welfare, II proved to be superior to I.

Now in a comparison of the two particular product aggregates in Section III we illustrated the possibility of alternative welfare distributions giving contrary results. If we now introduce the constraint that the product aggregates to be compared are points on a production possibility curve contrary results are certain. Therefore the comprehensive criterion can never be fulfilled. For there will be always, at least, two sets of comparable community indifference curves which give contrary results. One set will be based on a welfare distribution yielded by the community indifference curve which passes through one of the two points at a tangent to the production possibility curve—say I_2 in Figure 3. The other set will be based on the welfare distribution which is derived from the community indifference curve tangent to the production possibility curve which passes through the other point—say I_1 in Figure 3. These two sets of community indifference curves will always intersect, one set based on I_2 revealing Q_2 to be superior to Q_1, the other set based on I_1 revealing Q_1 to be superior to Q_2.

It follows—provided we do not opt for any particular pattern of welfare—that no one of these possible combinations of goods represented by the production possibility curve is unambiguously potentially superior to any other. But each one is superior to all others for some distribution.

Only by preferring above all others, on account of the welfare distribution it entails, the community indifference curve passing tangentially through a particular point on the production possibility curve can we avoid contradiction, since we thereby commit ourselves to *the* optimum; that is to say, only an indifference map built around our chosen community indifference curve has a right to be considered, all other indifference maps built around other tangential community indifference curves being irrelevant. Hence, to repeat our conclusion, there can be no proper allocation of resources independent of a judgment as to the best distribution of welfare.

V

The conclusions reached in the previous section may indeed give us pause, for the principles governing the proper allocation of resources, and therefore the notion of an optimum, have long enjoyed an unshakable eminence in the theory and application of economic policy. As was suggested at the begining of this chapter, if they were challenged at all the challenge was directed toward their restrictive assumptions. Granted these assumptions, however, and due allowances being made for divergences between private and social costs, equalizing the marginal conditions was the accepted and apparently inescapable formula.

What is left of this formula? If there is now nothing to choose between an optimum and a nonoptimum situation are we to go on to say that any arbitrary system of quantities and prices is as good as any other? Fortunately this is not the case. Though the top of the edifice, the complete optimum, has been shown to be illusory the lower levels of optima are fairly substantial. In particular, the exchange optimum which we required for the construction of the community indifference curves and the production optimum which was necessary for the construction of the production possibility curve may be vindicated, the former completely, the latter partially.

In regard to the exchange optimum, if individuals place different relative valuations on the same range of goods, some at least can profit by exchange until the rate of substitution between pairs of goods is the same for each individual in the community. Irrespective of the distribution of welfare, a movement to or toward an exchange optimum is an unambiguous *actual* improvement in the welfare of the community. In other words, some people will always be better off—and none will be worse off—if exchange between individuals of their initial product endowments is permitted,

As for the production optimum, this in general is less certain. Within limits it fulfills the comprehensive criterion. For if it is not fulfilled—if the ratio of the marginal physical products is not the same in all lines of production—then we are at a point inside the production possibility curve, say at *q* in Figure 4. Any combina-

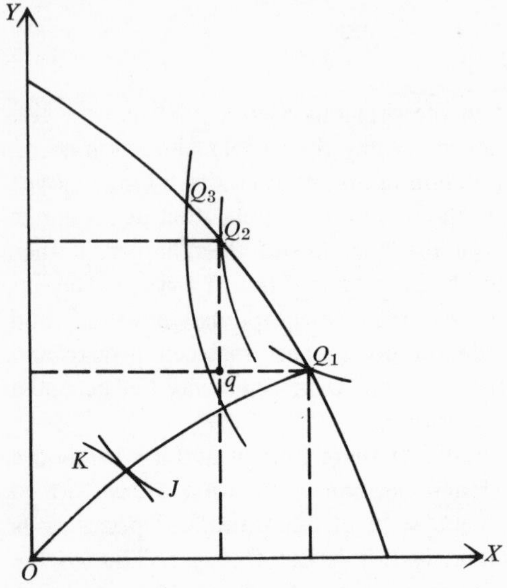

Figure 4

tion of *X* and *Y* on the segment of the production frontier between Q_1 and Q_2—the segment contained in the quadrant northeast of *q*—represents a net addition to output without additional sacrifice by the community. Hence for *any* conceivable welfare distribution existing at *q* and a comparable distribution of any product combination along the segment Q_1Q_2 the latter combination yields a higher welfare for the community. This is clear common sense since, starting from *any* distribution, some additional products can be distributed to make all or some of the individuals better off without making anyone worse off.[23]

[23] To put the matter diagrammatically, consider the production-optimum output Q_1 (Figure 4) as divisible between individuals *J* and *K*, and examine the extreme case in which the whole of the output Q_1 accrues to the first individual. His preference for *X* over *Y* being stronger than that of individual *K*, the com-

Provided, then, that a movement to, or toward, a production optimum is one which entails the production of more of one good without reducing the production of another the new output will be unambiguously *potentially* superior to the old output. It need hardly be added that the further removed is the economy from the production optimum the greater is the scope for unambiguous potential welfare improvements.

To sum up, we began our inquiry by affirming that all questions concerned with allocation economics lay within the domain of welfare economics and therefore could be treated with and tested by the techniques evolved in welfare economics. Starting, therefore, from a widely acceptable definition of an improvement in the collective welfare—that the community is better off if no one is worse off and at least one person is better off—we proceeded to inquire whether a movement toward an optimum allocation of resources results in an unambiguous improvement either in the *actual* or in the *potential* welfare of the community. We concluded (1) that an exchange optimum is perfectly reliable. From any nonoptimum position at this level individuals who avail themselves of exchange opportunities will better themselves without harming anyone else. A movement to, or toward, an exchange optimum is therefore an unambiguous actual improvement in the welfare of the community. (2) A production optimum is less reliable. A movement to or toward an optimum production point is an unambiguous potential

---

munity indifference curve passing through Q_1—in effect the indifference curve of individual J—is as flat as it can be at Q_1, any subsequent distribution in favor of K entailing an anticlockwise movement about Q_1 of the community indifference curve. Even if it were perfectly horizontal about Q_1 it must pass above q and, therefore, above the comparable community indifference curve passing through q. An analogous argument holds for the community indifference curve passing through Q_2 at the northern tip of the segment. Even if all the product accrues to K, the community indifference curve—in effect the indifference curve of K—passes above q and, therefore, above the comparable community indifference curve passing through q. Consequently, any other community indifference curve which may be generated through points Q_1 or Q_2, or through any points on the segment Q_1Q_2, will *a fortiori* pass above the comparable community indifference curve passing through q.

If, however, we move outside the Q_1Q_2 segment we can no longer ensure this result. If, for example, in equalizing the ratio of the marginal physical products of the relevant factors we move from q to Q_3, a point on the production frontier at which a lot more of Y but a little less of X is available than at q, it is possible to conceive of an extreme distribution—say all, or almost all, of the product accruing to individual K—such that the community indifference curve generated will pass below q, as in Figure 4, and therefore below any comparable community indifference curve passing through q.

improvement with certainty only if the movement toward the optimum entails an increased production of at least one good without reducing the production of another good. (3) Granted that the exchange and production optima are achieved, the "top-layer" optimum, reached by equalizing the ratio of prices to marginal costs, is in general no improvement actual or potential as compared with a nonoptimum position. Failing interpersonal comparisons, no optimum at this level is superior to a nonoptimum. Put otherwise, in a noninterpersonal welfare economics there is no case for equalizing the ratios of prices and marginal costs.

VI

Many propositions in economics require modification in the light of these conclusions. For instance, monopoly may continue to be condemned for various reasons but no longer for the reason that in an otherwise competitive economy it causes a malallocation of resources. More generally, it can no longer be maintained that an aggregate output in which the ratio of prices to marginal costs is the same for all products is in any way ideal, or to be preferred on welfare grounds to an aggregate output in which this ratio differs from one product to another.

As another instance, the long controversy between the welfare effects of direct and indirect taxation now takes a new turn, and it may be of general interest to describe this briefly before ending.

Since we are to be concerned with the *excess* burden of taxation we may follow custom and suppose that any tax the individual pays is directly refunded to him. If then, after the tax the community as a whole, on any chosen criterion, is worse off, the method of taxation imposes an excess burden.

On the basis of partial analysis it was for some time widely believed that indirect taxation imposed burdens on the economy from which direct taxation was free. About a decade ago the question was reopened by several economists, among them Henderson,[24] who demonstrated that direct taxes imposed a welfare burden on the individual inasmuch as he would be better off if, instead, the same amount were collected by a poll tax. Nevertheless, argued

[24] A. M. Henderson, "The Case for Indirect Taxation," *Economic Journal* (1948).

Henderson, indirect taxation was worse still, for it was equivalent to an income tax with its concomitant loss of welfare *plus* an additional loss of welfare arising from the tax-distortion of product prices.

Three years later, Little[25] attempted to prove that, in general, there was nothing to choose as between direct and indirect taxation. Illustrating his thesis with three goods, two products and leisure, he pointed out that an income tax, inasmuch as it raised the price of income relative to that of leisure, in effect raised the prices of the two products relative to that of leisure. There was no essential welfare difference between this effect and that of an indirect tax on either or both of the two products.

However, an investigation of the welfare effects of taxation on the individual may yield results different from those which arise when we reexamine the matter at the community level, for it is at this level that relative prices and welfare distributions are interdependent.

If we remove the assumption of fixed factor supplies and assume that no institutional rigidities prevent the individual from equating his rate of substitution between leisure and X and Y to the resultant market rates of exchange between these three goods, the production possibility curve for products X and Y which emerges may be viewed as the cross section, at a certain level of leisure for the community, of a three-dimensional production possibility surface, any point on which indicates a combination of total X, Y, and leisure available for distribution among the community. This total amount, or level, of leisure is, of course, determined along with the total amounts of X and Y by the point at which the community indifference surface touches the production possibility surface.

An indirect tax on X alone, or on X and on Y, alters for each individual the preferred pattern between leisure and the quantity of X and of Y consumed. A direct tax on income, being an equiproportional tax on X and Y, does the same thing. Either tax moves the economy to a new aggregate combination of X, Y, and leisure. In this new position, however, the community indifference surface *cuts* the production possibility surface in a manner which reflects

[25] I. M. D. Little, "Direct Versus Indirect Taxes," *Economic Journal* (1951).

the divergences between marginal costs and the new market prices. Either tax position has the characteristics of a nonoptimum position.

Formally, then, the argument moves on lines parallel to those of Little. The conclusion we reach does not contradict that of Little, though it is more radical. The interpretation of this formal similarity is, however, quite different. Since Little was dealing with a single individual he constructed a unique indifference map and derived a unique optimum. Both direct and indirect taxation took the individual to essentially similar sub-optimal points and were therefore equally indictable on welfare grounds. A poll tax, or a tax on earnable capacity, did not move the individual from his optimum and was therefore clearly preferable.

If we turn to consider the community as a whole, any direct or indirect tax not only causes a divergence between marginal costs and prices of some or all of the products, but concomitantly alters the distribution of welfare among the individuals. In general the new community indifference surface which cuts the production possibility surface is not comparable with the initial community indifference surface. Once again, therefore, we are constrained to employ the method of hypothetical compensation in order to compare the two positions. We have already demonstrated, however, the impossibility of comparing, in general, nonoptimum and optimum positions at the highest level or, put more strictly, the impossibility of having any optimum unambiguously potentially superior to any nonoptimum position.

In the absence of interpersonal comparisons and provided, as we have assumed, that all taxes leave us somewhere on the production possibility surface, we cannot on welfare grounds justify any choice as between a poll tax, a direct tax, an indirect tax, or no tax at all.

CHAPTER 5

Second Thoughts on Second Best*

While formal demonstration of the general theorem of second best[1] is, in substance, unassailable since, like other impossibility theorems,[2] its negative corollaries rest securely on the posited absence of empirical limitations, it must be admitted that its forceful presentation several years ago disturbed us somewhat and carried just so much farther the process of disillusion with conventional welfare economics. Not that we had any right to be disturbed, for it is clear enough now that in talking of optimum conditions we were, in any case, saying precious little; no more, in fact, than (assuming the appropriate degree of differentiability in our functions) that a constrained maximum entails necessary conditions. This much being conceded, the second-best theorem does no more than point

* From *Oxford Economic Papers*, N.S., 14 (October 1962), 205–217. Reprinted, with minor revisions, with the permission of The Clarendon Press, Oxford.

[1] See R. G. Lipsey and Kelvin Lancaster, "The General Theory of Second Best," *Review of Economic Studies*, Vol. 24 (1957).

[2] For instance that of K. J. Arrow, "A Difficulty in the Concept of Social Welfare," *Journal of Political Economy*, Vol. 58 (1950).

out that, if additional constraints are imposed, the necessary conditions for a maximum are in general more complex.[3] The obvious corollary follows that, in order to identify a maximum position in these conditions, it is necessary to forsake the optimum conditions that are strictly relevant only to the simple case of a single and familiar constraint.

It might seem proper then to say no more on the matter until a great deal more of information has been unearthed about the economic world we live in. But with welfare economics in the dumps now in consequence of several attacks in the last decade, those who have not yet abandoned hope will be prompted to scrutinize these theorems more closely if only with a view to setting limits to the gradual erosion of confidence in the subject. In regard to the second-best theory, for instance, we may admit that *in general* one can say nothing in the absence of universal optimization; further, that the vast and intricate knowledge required in order to derive quantitatively exact second-best solutions will be denied us in the foreseeable future. Yet we may still be able to indicate certain easily conceived conditions that permit us to say something useful; in particular we may be able to discover circumstances which enable us to derive guidance from the familiar optimum rules even though these rules are not universally met.

I

In order to face second-best theory on its chosen ground, we must ignore throughout complications arising from the possible dependence of a person's utility on the utility enjoyed by others, and from divergences between private and social benefit.[4] In short, we shall adopt all the assumptions necessary to warrant the proposition that a situation of perfectly competitive equilibrium entails an ideal allocation of resources. In addition to such assumptions, the employment by Lipsey and Lancaster of a unique utility function to illustrate and demonstrate their theorem is, of course, a permissible procedure. It can hardly be supposed that the introduc-

[3] *Ibid.*, p. 26.

[4] The argument would remain unaltered if we corrected outputs in order that the value of the *social* marginal product of each class of factor were the same in all uses.

tion, instead, of a community of persons, each having a distinct utility function, would in any way detract from the formal conclusions they reach. Nevertheless, in the search for mathematical convenience some finer points have been overlooked which, if recognized, would have led to greater caution in their interpretations.

Thus, to take up a minor point first, the general case in which the utility function differs as between individuals presents no easy adding-up problem. Such a utility function depends upon the distribution of incomes, which incomes themselves depend upon factor and product prices. In the very process of approaching some optimum the distribution is being altered, with the result that the initial optimum aimed at may cease to be relevant. But if one has to be careful in moving from nonoptimal positions, one cannot feel very easy about optimal positions either. A Pareto optimum, as everyone knows, has the property that movement away from it in any direction cannot make some people better off without making others worse off, a property whose implications have been made explicit in the controversies over compensation tests. It has since been recognized that inasmuch as the set of product prices is itself a function of the distribution of the social product, the value of that product when it displays optimal characteristics is a maximum only for the distribution associated with that price set: it is a best position for society only in the sense that there is no movement from such a position that could make everyone better off.[5] Translated into the language of compensation tests, a movement from any nonoptimal position to an optimal position meets only what Little has called "the Scitovsky criterion."[6] It does not necessarily meet the Kaldor-Hicks criterion: in other words, a movement to an optimum does not ensure that everyone in the optimum position could be made better off than he was in the nonoptimal position. Thus movements as between optimal and nonoptimal positions are prone to the same paradoxes as are movements as between nonoptimal positions themselves. In both cases, it is

[5] Where we could assume the existence of second-order derivatives at all points on the community's indifference map, we could go farther and say that any movement from a Pareto optimum would take us to a position in which everyone could be made worse off then he was at the Pareto optimum.

[6] See T. Scitovsky, "A Note on Welfare Propositions in Economics," *Review of Economic Studies,* Vol. 9 (1941), where a "reversal" of the Kaldor-Hicks test is proposed. By "Scitovsky criterion fulfilled," Little meant that from the new position gainers could not be bribed by losers to return to the old position.

possible that each of the alternative positions appears superior in the light of its corresponding distribution, and a choice between the associated distributions becomes necessary if only for the purpose of reaching a determinate solution.

The implication of these preliminary remarks for second-best theory is that its occasional positive contributions carry no more weight than "first-best" contributions. For instance, the Corlett and Hague[7] theorem that, in the absence of a poll tax, some system of excise taxes weighted in favor of goods complementary with leisure is superior to an income tax[8] was derived with the aid of a unique utility function. Once we bring into account that a change in the tax structure in general alters the distribution of income, and therefore the community utility function, it can no longer be asserted that the community as a whole is better off with the proposed tax system. For we can no longer be sure of meeting the Kaldor-Hicks test—of reaching a position in which everyone could be made better off with the new system than he was in the old income-tax system. Indeed, the Kaldor-Hicks test can contradict the result of the "Scitovsky test," and we can but conclude that movements to a second-best position, no less than movements to an optimal position, must be subjected to more searching criteria, such as those proposed by Little, before they can be comfortably accepted.

Having said all this, however, and recalling that "the Scitovsky criterion" plus a "better" distribution of income in the new position was one of the criteria suggested by Little, we may carry on with the argument on the supposition that a movement to an optimal position is a good thing.

II

A further, and also a relatively minor, point arises from the method of proof of the general theorem used by Lipsey and Lancaster. Translated in terms of sectors of the economy, the constraint takes the form of a ratio of two prices being unequal to the ratio of

[7] "Complementarity and the Excess Burden of Taxation," *Review of Economic Studies,* Vol. 9.

[8] On the rather far-fetched assumption that such goods, when identified, turn out to be complementary with leisure in much the same degree for all taxed individuals.

their marginal costs. Maximizing with respect to this constraint in addition to that of the transformation surface is enough to yield a quite complicated set of necessary conditions.[9] But in economics this constraint is really equivalent to two constraints—for example, price 10 percent above marginal cost in X and 50 percent above marginal cost in Y. Indeed, if there were only one constraint, say price in Y being 50 percent above marginal cost, the second-best solution is well known and quite straightforward: set the prices in the remaining $n-1$ sectors 50 percent above their corresponding marginal costs.[10] This solution, as it will transpire, is no less of an optimal solution than one wherein every price is set exactly equal to its marginal cost,[11] though, of course, it carries with it a different distribution of income. Consequently, if there is a price-marginal cost ratio common to all the constrained sectors in the economy, the rule is simple: adjust output in all the remaining "free" sectors until the same ratio prevails there also.

Another issue, less obvious than the above, is obscure both by the form of the general proof and the two illustrations preceding it. In the former, the additional constraint consists of negating one of the necessary conditions for an initially restrained extremum where, as we have seen, these conditions are cast into ratio form. In the latter—the illustrations—it takes the particular form of setting price equal to marginal cost in one of the constrained sectors, greater than marginal cost in another constrained sector, and finding a second-best solution for the free sector. As a result

[9] Their general proof proceeds as follows: in order to maximize some function $F(x_1, \ldots, x_n)$ subject to a constraint $\phi(x_1, \ldots, x_n)$, use the Lagrange method and maximize $W \equiv F - \lambda\phi$. Necessary conditions are $F_i = \lambda\phi_i$ $(i = 1, \ldots, n)$.

Now impose an additional constraint $F_1/F_n = k\phi_1/\phi_n$ $(k \neq 1)$, and maximize

$$W - \mu(F_1/F_n - k\phi/\phi_n).$$

The necessary conditions become

$$F_i - \lambda'\phi_i - \mu\left\{\frac{F_nF_{1i} - F_1F_{ni}}{F_n^2} - \frac{k\,\phi_n\phi_{1i} - \phi_1\phi_{ni}}{\phi_n^2}\right\} = 0 \quad (i = 1, \ldots, n).$$

[10] See R. F. Kahn, "Some Notes on Ideal Output," *Economic Journal* (1935).

[11] It is occasionally asserted that price-equals-marginal cost meets a further optimum condition that is not met in equi-proportional monopoly, namely the leisure-income condition. This mistaken view is corrected in Section III, where it is pointed out that perfect competition, no less than imperfect competition, is consistent with the worker's being *unable* to equate income and leisure at the margin. He cannot adjust the hours of his work given the rate for the job but must also accept as a constraint the hours per week that go with the job.

of this method of attack, attention is focused on top-level optima, also on a particular kind of additional constraint, and, therefore, on a particular kind of second-best solution.

In order to remove these limitations, consider a popular three-tier optimum scheme: (1) an exchange optimum, in which rates of substitution between all pairs of goods (including, where necessary, *negative* goods—meaning factors supplied by individuals) are the same; (2) a production optimum, in which rates of substitution between pairs of factors are the same for each good produced in the economy; and (3) top-level optimum, in which the subjective rate of substitution between each pair of goods is equal to their technological rate of substitution.

However, before investigating the implications of this division for second-best theory, the reader should be reminded that in so far as the *individual* is concerned, utility maximization is an *assumption,* an assumption from which we may deduce necessary conditions. Again, for the firm, cost minimization is an assumption (a corollary of profit maximization) from which, again, we may deduce necessary conditions. It follows that the introduction of additional constraints of the form $f_i/f_j \neq p_i/p_j$ (the p's being prices) is not admissible for the individual or for the firm. If the f's are the marginal utilities of pairs of goods, this inequality is precluded by implication of maximizing behavior of the individual. If the f's are the marginal physical products of pairs of factors in the output of any good, then the inequality is again precluded by implication of the cost-minimizing axiom applied to firms.

On the community level, however, where it is no longer legitimate to suppose a unique utility function and to ignore distribution of the product, there can be no *assumption* of maximization; indeed, there would hardly be a problem if there were. One seeks instead the fulfillment of necessary conditions. If they are all fulfilled, we are enabled to *deduce* a maximum in some sense—in fact, in the sense indicated by a Pareto optimum. One or more of these conditions may well be unfulfilled in one sector or in several sectors. If there is no possibility of intervening in such sectors we are faced with the problem of prescribing a second-best solution.

These reminders, as it happens, do enable us at once to say something useful when considering constraints operating on levels

(1) and (2), though we shall also have quite a bit to say, in Section IV, about top-level constraints.

Thus, in so far as the individual is correctly apprised of all constraints, budget and otherwise, he must be deemed to attain a correct maximum solution—whether first or second-best—in virtue of the maximizing assumption. Even though it exceeds our mathematical ability to derive the specific conditions necessary for this maximum, they are implicitly realized: for whatever the individual's choice is, it has to be accepted as the best solution in the circumstances facing him. Once satisfied with his choice, we can but infer the condition that the marginal utility per penny expenditure is the same in all lines that are freely available at given prices and, therefore, that the ratio of marginal utilities must be equal to the ratio of these prices.

One can therefore immediately modify one serious impression left by the general second-best theorem to the effect that, if there are one or more constraints, the familiar optimal rules can no longer serve us. For we have just seen that whenever the individual's initially free choice is openly interfered with in the market there is no need for the economist to intervene. The individual finds his own way to maximize his utility. To illustrate, we can use the labor market where, in the nature of modern industrial organization, it is not feasible to permit the individual to choose the number of hours to work at each job. The optimum condition that requires the worker's subjective rate of substitution between each factor and product be made equal to the relevant real wage rate[12] cannot be met. Nor, therefore, can this subjective rate of substitution between factor and product, through its equation with the real wage rate, be equated to the technological rate of substitution between factor and product.[13] Each worker, constrained to accept, say, a forty-hour week in a particular firm, must then infringe the factor-product condition and make a decision on an all-or-nothing basis from the range of occupations and firms. He will accept some

[12] This is the rule for adjusting the position as between income and leisure and for determining the number of hours to be worked in each occupation.

[13] One could assume, as is common, a zero elasticity of supply of the factor (compounded of a zero substitution and a zero welfare effect), but it would be too much to assume that the fixed supply of the factors, independently decided upon by each worker, coincided exactly with the amounts required by the industries in question.

employment if his rent is positive—defining rent as the maximum sum he would pay to enter the employment in question when compared with other alternatives—and, by assumption, seeks that employment that maximizes his rent.

But the rent maximizing choice on the all-or-nothing basis, and the consequent infringement of the factor-product condition, does not thereby nullify the applicability of the remaining optimal conditions. In meeting some of them we can ignore the interpretation of the calculus that would have us deal in small units, say hours of labor, and instead apply the optimal rule in terms of the amounts in which factors are customarily hired. Thus, in the production of each good the value of the "marginal" product of each type of labor must be the same when the "marginal" product is now measured as the minimum amount of labor that can be hired. Translated from factor to product terms, the price of each product must again be equated to its corresponding social marginal cost, the units of product being measured as the amounts produced by the successive weeks of hired labor. The top-level optimum condition continues then to be held in the same form, amended only by the unit of measurement. The production optimum, requiring the same factor rate of substitution in all goods, which when met, describes the boundary of the production transformation surface, is amended in exactly the same way. The exchange optimum condition, however, remains unamended. Finally, if in addition to a general factor-product constraint another constraint is introduced in the form of a monopolized good, the familiar second-best solution—that all other goods' prices be raised above social marginal cost in the same proportion—continues to apply.

III

We now turn to additional constraints which face individuals *qua* consumers. Two types will be considered—a constraint on the quantities purchasable and discriminatory pricing. In order to avoid constant qualification, we shall start in both cases from a position of over-all optimum.

Introduce first a rationing system for a particular good, X. Clearly, if the ration is to make any difference to the consumer, it must be smaller than the maximum amount of X he would choose to buy at the current price. We shall assume this to be the case and, further, so as not to evade problems, we shall allow that, in general, the marginal valuation of the rationed quantity of *X* differs from one person to another.

Before examining how matters stand on level (1), the exchange level, let us turn for a moment to see how things fit in on the other two levels. If the shortage of *X* were the result, say, of a harvest failure, levels (2) and (3) would have no relevance. We could then, with a clear conscience, pursue the familiar optimum conditions notwithstanding the rationing constraint.

Alternatively, the rationing of *X* may arise from the social policy imposed by the government, it having been decided that, all liberal arguments notwithstanding, people should buy less of *X* than they would buy if it were produced by unrestricted private enterprise. There must then necessarily be an output constraint on the production of *X*. But whatever the output that is deemed socially proper, it should still be produced efficiently. The economy, that is, must still produce on its production frontier and, therefore, the rule for factor combination must still hold—the production optimum (2) must be fulfilled. As for top-level optimum, inasmuch as the ratio is assumed effective, the marginal valuation-marginal cost ratio in *X* exceeds that in all other goods—though, of course, it will vary as between individuals. If, for the moment, however, we assume that for all individuals this ratio is the same, it might be thought that a second-best solution would involve merely raising all other prices above their corresponding marginal costs in the same proportion. But since this solution would entail an expansion of purchases of *X*, its adoption would necessarily defeat the government's social policy. If, therefore, we accept the social policy of the government, we are not at the same time at liberty to seek a second-best solution of this sort.

We return therefore to the exchange level, recognizing once more that individuals have different marginal valuations of *X*. Obviously, if consumers are permitted to sell their ration, *X* will acquire a market price at which anyone can buy or sell *X*. Apparently no one will be made worse off and some will increase their welfare. The method of securing a correct second-best solution on this exchange level would appear to be that of simply allowing a free market for *X*. Yet, once more, if in pursuit of this social policy the exchange of X as between persons were prohibited by the government, a second-best solution of this kind must be ruled out of order. In that case each individual has to accept the rationing constraint, and maximizes therefore with that constraint in mind. The substance of these remarks is, of course, unaltered if more than one good is rationed by the government.

What of the case in which relative product prices differ as between consumers,[14] so violating the exchange optimum? Once again it should be manifest that the damage cannot be repaired by any new directives on the production level, since any departure from the rule for efficient production necessarily entails that, whatever the resulting output combination, it is smaller than is potentially producible. As for top-level rules, nothing useful can be accomplished by juggling with price-marginal cost ratios as between the various products, since the fault arises not from differences in such ratios but rather from different prices of the same product—some firms, or some industries, having two or more prices for exactly the same product. Indeed, if for any reasons this constraint is accepted, there is nothing one can do to improve matters by altering the other conditions. If, however, there is no warrant for this discriminatory pricing, it ought not to be accepted as a constraint. The government can act to remove it either by making such discrimination a legal offense or by disseminating relevant information among the buying public.

Both these forms of constraint may also operate at the production level. If the quantity of some input (raw material or factor) were arbitrarily rationed among a number of firms, each being forbidden to buy additional supplies from the other, cost of production would differ among them.[15] Firms that were least rationed (in terms of their output of the good in question) would produce at a lower cost than the others. By assumption each firm minimizes

[14] If relative prices were the same to each person but money prices differed as between them, exchange optimum would remain unaffected.

[15] A rationing system applied at the production level is quite consistent with market equilibrium. Although there will be only one price for each commodity on the market, the firms that are least rationed (relatively to their outputs), and therefore make larger profits, will be unable to expand and replace other firms so long as the rationing system is in force. In the case of price discrimination, however, if there are no limits on the amounts that can be bought, firms that are enabled to buy inputs at a lower price will eventually displace less favored firms and competitive long-run equilibrium would be restored.

its cost by attributing a virtual price to this rationed input, but since these virtual prices differ as among the affected firms, the production optimum is not met, and the resultant output combination is to be found on an inferior range of production possibilities. If we now suppose that, for reasons of social policy, one cannot escape the constraint, the inferior locus of production possibilities has to be accepted, and one makes the best of this inferior locus by invoking the rule for a top-level tangency solution—in effect, an equi-proportional, price-marginal cost ratio for all goods. In sum, notwithstanding the constraint which infringes the production optimum, we achieve a correct second-best solution by realizing top-level (and exchange) optimal conditions.

These remarks are equally relevant for a production constraint in which the costs of some given input are made different to different firms.[16]

IV

The impression from the preceding section is that, in virtue of the assumptions about the behavior of the individual and the firm, constraints imposed at the two lower-level optima do not cause much difficulty. Rather it is at the top level that the significance of second-best theory finds scope. There it does correct the view that if one or more sectors of the economy are "out of line," and for any reason cannot be brought into line, the best thing to do is to go ahead and maximize within the remaining sectors—in the belief that if, after all, the constraints are genuine, there is nothing

[16] If, however, rationing were instead on an *industry* basis, the less-favored industries would suffer a steeper rise in prices relative to marginal costs (where the marginal cost of the good in question included the marginal cost of the rationed inputs, *not* their market value to industry). Moreover, since the marginal value of the rationed inputs, regarded as internal prices, differed as between industries, the conditions for the production optimum would be infringed. The combination of outputs produced will, therefore, be somewhere inside the locus of production possibilities.

If one rejects these constraints as undesirable, then obviously one takes steps to abolish them. If, on the other hand, they are accepted as part of a desirable social policy, the fact that their implementation takes us away from an optimal position—or, rather, an optimal position built on market valuations—must also be accepted.

Similar remarks apply to price discrimination on an industry basis. If it is regarded as undesirable, it can be overcome by legislation and by other means. If, however, it is part of the government's social policy, there is no getting closer to an optimum without in some degree undoing the objectives of that policy.

one can do about them, and one may as well concentrate therefore on reshuffling factors in the remaining sectors in order to maximize the value of their social product. However, equalizing the value of the marginal products in the controllable, or free, sectors does have repercussions on the value of the outputs in the constrained sectors. This follows from the simple proposition that, given an interdependent system, in response to a movement along any market demand curve, prices and quantities purchased in all other sectors cannot both be held constant. Thus if there were a *quantity* constraint in the production of X, any reallocation in the free sectors would in principle alter the price of X and, therefore, the value of the marginal product of factors used in X. If, alternatively, there were a *price-marginal cost* constraint in X, a reallocation of factors in the free sectors would in principle entail a change in the output of X. In either case then the value of output in X is altered. There is no warrant, therefore, for concluding that the set of all relative product prices thrown up from the process of optimizing in the free sectors only will be that at which the value of the social product of the entire economy (including, that is, the value of the product in the constrained sector X) is greater than it could be for any conceivable nonoptimal arrangement in the free sector.[17] This is the common sense of the second-best theorem when applied to top-level situations.[18]

[17] Put otherwise, the implication of the tangency solution of the top-level optimum is that, at the ratio of product prices associated with it, the output combination has a value higher than any other output combination producible with the community's resources (measured in terms of any of the n goods regarded as numeraire). But maximizing in this way the value of $n-x$ goods with only part of the total resources of the economy is to ignore the prices and the outputs of the remaining x goods. When account is taken of them, plus the constraints attaching to them, the pattern of outputs in the whole economy at the resulting $n-1$ relative prices might not be that which yields a greater value than any other output combination of the $n-x$ goods that is consistent with the constraints on the remaining x goods.

[18] One has, of course, to admit the same sort of deficiency in the "piecemeal" approach in sub-optimal situations. Thus, to assert that a movement of some factors out of X, where the value of the marginal product of factors is low, into Y, where it is high, will increase the value of the social product, and will therefore constitute a movement toward an optimum, is to ignore these secondary repercussions on all other market valuations. Each such transfer of factors from one product to another in principle alters all demand prices and, indeed, all factor prices also. Only in circumstances in which we can safely neglect these repercussions on all other prices can we proceed along this route with hope of approaching closer to an optimum—to a position in which there is no further scope for such factor transfers.

But although nothing in general may be said at this level, and we cannot hope for quantitative estimates of a multitude of relevant interconnections in order to make decisions in specific cases, we need not shrug our shoulders and say nothing at all. For one thing, it would seem very reasonable to believe that (i) the smaller are the constrained sectors relative to the remaining ones, and (ii) the larger are the initial discrepancies in the price-marginal cost ratios of the free sectors as compared with the constrained sectors, the surer we are to improve matters by optimizing in the free sectors alone than by standing by and sadly sucking our thumbs under the sign of second best.[19] We shall not improve matters quite as much as we might have done if we could have alighted on the complex of exact second-best rules and could have applied them at no greater cost. But by adopting the simple and familiar rules for the free sectors we may not be very far from this hypothetically ideal position. It is reasonable to believe this because the larger the initial discrepancies as between the free sectors of the economy, and the greater the part of the total economy accounted for by these sectors, the farther away is the economy from an optimum. If, then, we applied a single price-marginal cost rule to all the free sectors, at the end of the process the economy could not be far from a complete optimum. For if the constrained sectors that remain out of line were small, then a relatively small reshuffling of factors as between the free and the constrained sectors could—if the constraints were removable—take us to a complete optimum.

In fact we may go a little farther. The larger are the differences in price-marginal cost ratios as between industries in the free sectors relative to these differences in the constrained sectors, the more certain we are to improve matters—to come closer to an ideal allocation—by adopting as a rule for all the free sectors any one of the price-marginal cost ratios in the constrained sectors.

[19] To be more cautious, we should require as a sufficient condition that all the goods (whose outputs will be affected by the process under discussion) be roughly equal substitutes. If the market substitutability of the goods were exactly equal, for each 1 percent that price is in excess of its marginal cost the output of any such good would be x percent smaller than the price-equals-marginal cost output. Under these conditions, the smaller are the contrained sectors relative to the free sectors, the smaller is the amount of unavoidable misallocation. Again, for any given size of the free sectors, the larger the initial price-marginal cost discrepancies, the larger the amount of "potential improvement."

These remarks bring us to another proposition; namely, that if we had to choose a price-marginal cost ratio common to all the free sectors such a ratio should lie somewhere within the range set by the highest and the lowest ratios of the constrained sectors. To illustrate, if *X* and *Y* were the two constrained sectors at the extremes of the range of constrained sectors, *X* having a 50 percent markup over marginal cost and *Y* having a 10 percent markup, then the markup to be set for the free sectors should be between 10 percent and 50 percent. This is intuitively plausible, for if, instead, the markup set for the free sector is above 50 percent or below 10 percent, we widen price-marginal differentials and, inasmuch as we thereby increase the movement of factors that would be necessary for a complete optimum to be achieved, we move farther away from an optimum.

Nor need we stop here. We could surmise that the price-marginal cost ratio to be adopted by the free sectors would not be far removed from a correct second-best solution if it were calculated as an average of the ratios of the constrained sectors, each such ratio being weighted by the value added of that sector. Thus, if the value produced in the constrained sector *X* were large relative to that in the constrained sector *Y*, the rule to be adopted would be nearer to a 50 percent markup than to a 10 percent markup. Again, this has intuitive appeal. If we suppose *Y*'s output dwindling toward zero, the markup to be adopted gradually approaches 50 percent: it reaches 50 percent in the case already mentioned, that in which all the constrained sectors have the same 50 percent price-marginal cost ratio. This rough result does, however, assume that the goods produced in the constrained sectors are about equal substitutes with the goods produced in the free sectors of the economy. But the closer the substitutes the greater the change in outputs for a given differential in price-marginal cost ratios. As between complements, however, even large differentials in price-marginal cost ratios entail small changes in the patterns of outputs. In consequence, the more substitutable is a good produced by the constrained sectors with those in the free sectors of the economy, the more weight it should carry in striking an average; the more complementary it is with goods in the free sectors, the less weight it should carry. To illustrate briefly, suppose there are three highly substitutable goods in the free sectors of the economy, wine, beer, and cider, the constrained good being glass bottles. Since glass bottles accompany the purchases of each type of refreshment, a rise in the price of bottles reduces somewhat the demand for wine, beer, and cider. In the extreme case in which they are bought in fixed proportions, the rise in the bottled drink could be attributed as much to the contents of the bottle as to the bottle itself. If the fixed proportions are the same, in value terms, for each of the three drinks, it is a matter of indifference to the consumer if the price of the bottle alone rises, or the price of the drink alone rises, or whether the rise in price is spread partly on the bottle and partly on the drink. Thus in the case of extreme complementarity as between the good in the constrained sector and those of the free sectors, we could ignore completely the price-marginal cost ratio of any good in the constrained sector and proceed to an optimum simply by imposing a common ratio on all goods in the free sectors. If, now, wine entered the constrained sectors, since it is a strong substitute for cider and beer, the larger the discrepancy between its price-marginal cost ratio and that adopted for cider and beer, the larger the change in outputs demanded as compared with a situation in which all three had the same price-marginal cost ratio. In this case we should ignore the price-marginal cost ratio of bottles completely but we should bring those of beer and cider into equality with that of wine in order to reach a correct second-best solution —one which, in this particular case, happens to be no different from that of a Pareto optimum.

Finally, there may be circumstances in which one may justify optimizing in some broad sector of the economy while explicitly neglecting what takes place in the remainder of the economy, circumstances which are frequently invoked in partial analysis. If the changes in outputs and relative prices in this broad sector happen to have negligible repercussions in the rest of the economy, we can proceed along these lines. For maximizing the product of this broad sector by equalizing the value of the marginal products of each factor class does not, by assumption, affect the value of the output in the rest of the economy. Thus, without doing any worse in the rest of the economy we can do better by reshuffling factors so as to maximize the social product in this broad sector. The same argument would, of course, apply to some geographical area which had tenuous economic links with the rest of the economy.

V

This is about as far as we should be prepared to go in offering practical suggestions which, although admittedly rough and ready —a sort of "third best"—are much superior to the rather paralyzing conclusion that unless all optimal rules are everywhere met nothing at all may be said, a conclusion that is too often eagerly embraced as an anodyne against further thought. If second-best theory has a positive contribution to make it is that of serving notice that, in the presence of constraints, slap-dash optimizing, wherever one can, may not improve matters: one has, in that case, to proceed cautiously—which is rather different from not proceeding at all.

Indeed, to descend for a moment to the exigencies of the real world, since time is taken to adjust the sizes of industries in response to continual changes in the over-all pattern of demand, it is unlikely that at any instant of time we shall, even in the absence of all such constraints, attain a Pareto optimum, much less that we should for long maintain it. We can only hope to be moving in that direction most of the time and not to be too far away from an optimum for any prolonged period. It should not bother us too much then if we cannot pick out exact second-best solutions provided that we are able to adjust frequently towards positions which are fairly close to optimal.

Treated in this way and regarded in the light of the last paragraph, second-best theory has had a good deal of its sting drawn. And this seems to point to a moral. Much of the recent disillusion with welfare economics has arisen from the rather depressing spectacle of familiar universal propositions being tripped up by facile possibility theorems of this sort. But though it is fashionable to wallow in skepticism about welfare propositions we can and must do better. We can turn our ingenuity to more constructive purpose by attempting to determine the range of conditions under which welfare propositions hold, or hold approximately, and to discover methods that enable us to come within satisfactory distance of an ideal position whose attainment is not practicable.

CHAPTER 6

The Recent Debate on Welfare Criteria*

Three areas of development may be distinguished in theoretical welfare economics, (1) that which, aiming at complete generality, seeks to develop the formal apparatus necessary for attaining a unique social optimum. The set of conditions determining the boundary of production possibilities, or of the utility possibilities, is the more acceptable product of this approach, no rules for the selection therefrom of a unique social optimum, other than purely tautological ones, being provided. However, although recent contributions within this area have elaborated optimal conditions to cope with indivisibilities, nonconvexity, and other such awkward possibilities, more prominence has been given to discussions about the theoretical possibility of constructing, under certain circumstances, an apparatus of social choice to enable the unique social optimum to be reached. Though it lends itself to some fascinating philosophical speculation one must be inordinately optimistic to

* From *Oxford Economic Papers,* N.S., 17 (July 1965), 219–236. Reprinted with the permission of The Clarendon Press, Oxford.

expect welfare propositions to emerge in the foreseeable future from these investigations.

(2) The more traditional interest in resource allocation closely associated with the development of the theory of value had elements of both a general and a partial approach to welfare problems. On the one hand, there was a stress on the allocative rules—in particular, the equality of marginal products in all lines of production—often coupled with the belief that every additional sector in which the rule was met placed the economy closer to optimum. On the other, there was the development of such partial concepts as consumer's surplus and rents and, to some extent, social cost often in connection with a comparison of the merits of various types of taxes and bounties. In this field can also be placed the propositions of second-best theories and many recent contributions intent on refining the concepts of consumer's surplus, social cost, and external effects.

(3) Beginning with the so-called New Welfare Economics, an interest over the last 25 years has sprung up in the possibility of formulating simple welfare criteria. The attempt to order all possible social states is consciously repudiated in the search only for sufficient criteria, based on widely acceptable value judgments that enable the community to choose between specified alternative forms of economic organization.

What hope there is for evolving a practical welfare economics seems to me to lie in this last field of endeavor. Justification for commending it to the attention of readers can count on more than this belief, however. The familiar rules of resource allocation, and their growing application through the spread of mathematical programming techniques, can be vindicated by recourse to those judgments of fact and value made explicit only in the search for satisfactory welfare criteria. Until such criteria are established, all recommendations deriving from allocative rules must be acknowledged as tentative and provisional.

The welfare criteria to be considered here are those initially proposed by Little[1] and since then subjected to much criticism. Though, as mentioned above, they can produce only an incomplete ordering, certain attributes are desirable, even essential: (*a*)

[1] See I. M. D. Little [**9** and **10**] esp. chapter vi.

the ethical judgments made should command a consensus,[2] and (*b*) the criteria should be logically tenable; in particular, they should be conceptually clear and unambiguous and, also, consistent in themselves if mutually contradictory recommendations are to be avoided.

Misgivings about whether Little's criteria did in fact possess these attributes have been the source of all the recent controversies. The questions raised in this connection may be grouped under three broad headings which we shall consider in the order that follows:

1. The meaning of the alternatives under comparison, Q_1 and Q_2, and intermediate points such as H and J in Little's analysis.
2. Distributional problems in the application of Little's criteria.
3. Transitivity of the two parts of the criteria, and the question of consistency of the criteria as a whole.

I

Prior to the analysis of the chief issues in the recent debate the reader should remind himself that it took place within the confines of Little's assumption A: that direct income transfers were not possible. Thus, only those distributions directly associated with the situation under comparison could be reached. Under that assumption the criteria proposed had two parts, a Pareto part involving a test of hypothetical compensation, and a distributional part. A position Q_2 was to be regarded as socially preferred to Q_1 either (1) if the change from Q_1 to Q_2 met the Kaldor-Hicks test —everyone[3] could be better off in the Q_2 position than he was in Q_1—and the distribution in Q_2 was better[4] than in Q_1, or (2) if

[2] One could sidestep methodological discussion by making these criteria conditional upon a consensus, or by pointing out to the individual that by accepting certain factual and value judgments he is logically impelled to accept the outcomes of applying the criteria—always under the assumption, of course, that they produce noncontradictory results.

[3] We can assume perfect divisibility of goods and factors, also that each person's welfare is increased if he has more of any goods or supplies less of any factor. Though these assumptions are not necessary for the argument they would warrant the abbrevation "everyone better off" for the more usual definition of a Pareto improvement: "At least one person better off and nobody else worse off."

[4] Actually, Little only requires that the distribution in Q_2 be *no worse* than in Q_1. However, the logical status of his criteria can hardly be weakened by substituting the stronger requirement, that Q_2 have a *better* distribution than Q_1.

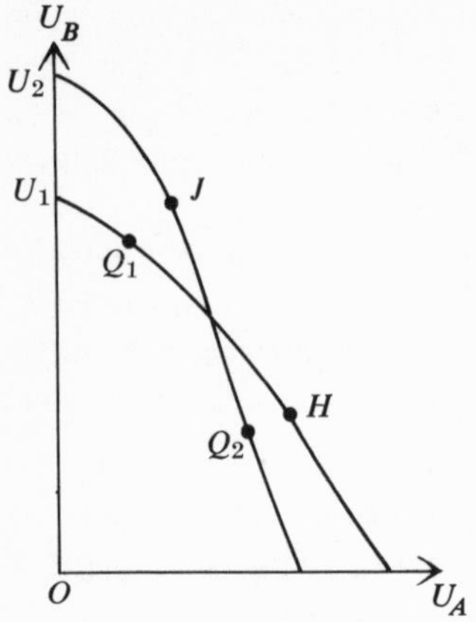

Figure 1

the same change met the "Scitovsky" test[5]—that in changing from Q_2 to Q_1 everyone could not be made better off than he was at Q_2[6] —and, again, that the Q_2 distribution was better. Obviously if both criteria were met, Q_2 would be socially preferred to Q_1.

Since Scitovsky had shown in 1941 [**20**] that the fulfillment of the Kaldor-Hicks test ranking Q_2 above Q_1 could be simultaneously contradicted by a reversal test that ranked Q_1 above Q_2, and it was later recognized that the "Scitovsky" test (the negation, in fact, of the latter reversal test) establishing the superiority of Q_2 could also be contradicted by a reversal test,[7] it is fitting that any demonstration of the force of Little's argument should be tested by assuming the appropriate reversal test to give a contradictory result in each case. At any rate this has been the practice, the standard method of representing the two criteria being shown in

[5] I follow my custom of writing "Scitovsky" in quotes since Little inadvertently misrepresents Scitovsky's criterion [**10**, p. 101]. Scitovsky proposed that Q_2 be regarded as superior to Q_1 only if both the Kaldor-Hicks test was met and the reversal of the Kaldor-Hicks test negated. This latter test, the negation of the reversal test, is what Little refers to in Table I [**10**, p. 101] when he speaks of the Scitovsky criterion.

[6] "Strong" ordering has always been assumed in the discussion of these criteria: if, for example, in moving from Q_2 to Q_1 everyone could *not* be made better off, it is accepted that everyone in Q_1 could be made worse off than he was in Q_2.

[7] Initially, in connection with the problem of index numbers as indicators of changes in welfare, see Kuznets [**8**], also Hicks' reply [**4**]. The reader who feels a bit rusty on these concepts will find a simplified treatment of their rationale in my *Survey* paper [**16**, pp. 218–228].

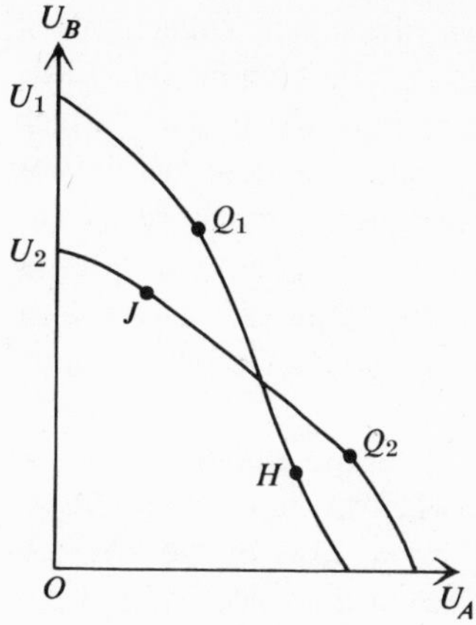

Figure 2

Figures 1 and 2. In a two-person community *B*'s utility is measured on the vertical axis, *A*'s utility on the horizontal axis.[8] In both diagrams the initial position is taken to be Q_1 on the U_1 utility possibility curve, the alternative position being Q_2 on the U_2 curve. In Figure 1, the Kaldor-Hicks test is met in a movement from Q_1 to Q_2, since by moving from Q_2 along U_2 a position *J* can be reached at which both individuals are better off than they were with Q_1. In Figure 2 the "Scitovsky" test is met since by moving along the U_1 curve from Q_1 to *H*, both individuals are worse off than they were with Q_2. We need only add that, in some sense, Q_2 has a better distribution than Q_1, to meet, in each case, the requirements of one of Little's criteria establishing the superiority of Q_2 over Q_1.

No more than this conventional apparatus is needed in analyzing the issues raised in the controversy.

II. The Meaning of Points Q_1, Q_2, and H, J

Although little has been heard in the recent discussion about the meaning of alternative organizations represented by Q_1 and Q_2 to which the criteria are to be applied, the tacit understanding

[8] There is no need to assume cardinal utility nor interpersonal comparisons. Apart from moving downward from left to right the shapes of the curves are arbitrary.

being that they are to be regarded as alternative collections of goods distributed in a certain way among the community, Little had actually suggested other interpretations [**10**, p. 102] which I take up first as a ground-clearing operation. Indeed, Little was under the impression that he had illustrated the nature of the paradox of hypothetical compensation tests by initially interpreting Q_1 and Q_2 as positions chosen by a quantity-adjuster *B* in response to prices P_1 and P_2 set by a monopolist *A* in an economy composed of a given collection of goods.[9]

Presumably each individual already has some amounts of *x* and *y* and there remains to be shared between them the amounts of *x* and *y* indicated by the lengths of the two axes of the box diagram in Figure 3. The indifference curves of the price-setter *A* rise

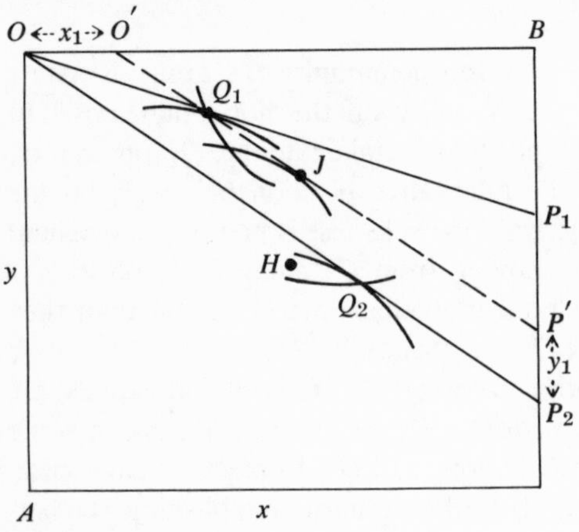

Figure 3

as we move in the northeast direction, those of *B* rising as we move in the southwest direction. The initial position is Q_1 chosen by *B* when faced with price P_1. If *A* now sets price at P_2 so that Q_2 is chosen, both individuals can be made better off than they were in position Q_1.

Construct $P'O'$ parallel to OP_2 to pass through Q_1, and transfer

[9] No other interpretation of Q_1 and Q_2 was explicitly introduced in the first edition of the *Critique*. In the second edition, the same box diagram was retained to illustrate the Kaldor-Hicks and "Scitovsky" criteria before alternative interpretations of Q_1 and Q_2 were discussed.

an amount of y_1 or x_1 (or any appropriate combination of both at the P_2 price) from B to A. B is now faced, in effect, with a price line $O'P'$ and, therefore, chooses J. But at J both individuals are on higher indifference curves than they were at Q_1, Q.E.D. The reverse is then proved by constructing, instead, a line parallel to OP_1 and passing through Q_2, the amount of y represented by the vertical distance between OP_1 and this line being transferred from A to B after A's raising the price from OP_2 to OP_1. The position H chosen by B represents a higher indifference curve for both parties as compared with Q_2.

However, this demonstration is unconvincing and when pressed against Little's analytic framework it tends to disintegrate. If, as Little allows, the monopolist is free to set prices, then, even if he began by setting price P_1 so inviting position Q_1, by continuing to set prices further exchange could move them to J (or any other mutually beneficial division) without recourse to this unnecessary and devious route which Little associates with the Kaldor-Hicks test. Indeed, since direct transfers of goods between them are also allowed, nothing is to prevent an exchange which takes them in one bound from Q_1 to J, or some point of mutual tangency. The paradox generated therefore arises only from the inability of A (the monopolist, price-setter, and transfer-arranger) to think straight, not from some inescapable economic relationships. If A had any sense and arranged matters so as to move to a position J on the contract curve to start with, such a "paradox" could no longer be demonstrated.[10]

The other interpretation of Q_1 and Q_2 suggested by Little, that they could be factor endowments described by a frontier of production possibilities, must also be rejected, since one could establish the hypothetical superiority of the outer frontier, arising from the Q_2 endowment, only if it were possible to move freely along

[10] How Little is able to represent such a case by a pair of utility possibility curves on his diagrams in Figure VII [**10**, p. 104] is something of a mystery. According to Little [**10**, p. 102], each utility possibility curve gives the maximum utility attainable by one person given the utility of the other, this maximum depending upon what is fixed. If the set of goods *and* prices are fixed, he goes on to say, the curve traces out the utility levels of each person as direct transfers are made from one to the other. Allowing complete freedom of such direct transfers, however, would surely discover the contract curve itself as being the utility possibility curve. But there is only one contract curve and, therefore, only one utility possibility curve.

these frontiers choosing any collections of goods and, therefore, any of the distributions directly associated with them. But if the full range of distributions are realizable the second part of Little's dual criteria, which asks whether *the* distribution associated with Q_2 is more desirable than that associated with Q_1, is no longer applicable.

The upshot is that we must perforce continue to view Q_1 and Q_2 as alternative collections of goods in the customary way.[11]

Let us now return to the intermediate points H and J which have elicited much more controversy. Kennedy in 1953 [**5**] had argued that there was no need for such intermediate points; that a person should be able to compare Q_1 and Q_2 directly. Replying to this charge in his second edition of the *Critique* [**10,** p. 106] Little emphasized two things: the difficulty of specifying the new position Q_2, and the absence of well-ordered preferences by someone doing the ranking. It failed, however, to impress others. Robertson called it "lame" [**19,** p. 228]. Robertson's understanding of the matter was that in moving (in thought) from Q_1 to H the total supply of such factors (work, saving, risk-taking)[12] should remain unchanged, a view, however, rejected by Little [**11,** p. 230] who laid it down that a point such as H, northeast or southwest of Q_2, is that collection of goods reached by a lump sum transfer from Q_1.[13] Such an intermediate point, he argued, is a "potential reality," and though incentives should not be affected inasmuch as lump sum transfers are involved, there can be wealth effects which, in general, alter the total supplies of the factors. On reflection it would seem that Robertson was correct though he might well have gone further and included as unchanged the collection of goods at H as well as the supplies of factors. In the

[11] A fourth alternative, that a movement along the utility possibility curve represents "what would actually happen as money was shifted between the individuals, the points being determined by the actual price and output policies . . ." [**10,** p. 102], is not taken up at this point. Such an interpretation involves intermediate points H and J that have quantities of goods different from Q_1 and Q_2, an interpretation which I discuss in the latter part of this section and reveal to be untenable.

[12] How risk-taking should be conceptually measured in this context is not at all clear.

[13] In the same note [**11,** p. 230] Little, in reply to a criticism of Professor Meade, made it clear that Q_2 being distributionally preferred to Q_1 is to be taken to mean that some point H to the S.W. or N.E. of Q_2 which could actually be reached by lump sum transfers from Q_1 is better than Q_1. We consider this further in Section III below.

first place, the "potential reality" that Little wishes to make of H is a rather fuzzy concept.[14] One may be uncertain of economic consequences and one may have to do some guesswork in applying criteria to alternatives in the real world, but the criteria themselves rest on pure concepts, and if they are to be vindicated at all they must be crystal clear on the conceptual level in the first place. If it cannot be known whether the factors increase or decrease, or whether the goods increase or decrease in the imaginary journey from Q_1 to H, it has yet to be made plain by reference to Little's value judgments why it is a matter of indifference. Secondly, if H is a different collection of goods than Q_1, as well as being distributed differently—so as to be comparable, in some sense, with the Q_2 distribution—then, *in general,* it cannot be any easier to compare Q_1 with H than Q_1 with Q_2. In fact H simply ceases to have any essential characteristics of an intermediate point.[15] Thirdly, and most important of all, it is just not true, as Little asserts, that wealth effects involved in redistributing the collection must alter the factor supplies. For by continuously varying the price set as redistribution takes place one may ensure optimal exchange conditions so that, moving along the contract curve in effect, the total collection of goods and factors does not alter.[16]

[14] Dobb's criticism of this interpretation of H is more explicit. If it were accepted, he says, it would be better to banish "the terminology and apparatus of the older compensation debate and to say simply: 'there is no pretence that H is the equivalent of Q_1 in all respects save distribution: it is simply a point which it would be feasible to reach in given circumstances from Q_1; and when I say Q_2 is better than Q_1 I merely mean that such a point exists to the south-west of Q_2 which is preferable to Q_2.' " [**2,** pp. 769–770].

[15] A. K. Sen [**20,** pp. 774–776] interprets Little's position more intelligibly (1) by appointing H to a position outside Q_1's utility possibility curve and (2) by some other collection H which is worse than Q_2 though better than Q_1 then one can rank Q_2 above Q_1. But to accept this interpretation of the procedure would be a virtual abandonment of the attempt to formulate objective (or, rather intersubjective) welfare criteria. For what Sen is describing is a purely personal ranking with H no longer uniquely defined but merely a position any particular economist might chance to think on. Economists could, under this procedure, consistently take up opposite positions.

[16] Individual indifference curves encompassing factor supplies can be constructed [**15**] and the maps of various individuals compounded into community indifference maps in the usual way [**16,** pp. 221–224]. For any given collection of goods and factors there will be a "contract curve" giving a range of factor and product prices associated with the efficient distribution of these factors and products.

This concept incidentally lays to rest the shade of an old and favorite dilemma, brought to light by Meade in this connection [**13**], the conflict between equality and incentives. For the community is now seen to be ordering alternative collections in one of which there may be fewer factors and goods but which may not,

If this contract curve is defined, like the utility possibility curve, as the maximum satisfaction available to one person for given levels of satisfaction enjoyed by the other persons, the property that at any point along it the goods rate of substitution for each person be the same[17] is exhibited only in the absence of external economies or diseconomies of consumption. Nonetheless, even in the presence of such external effects there exists a clearly defined contract curve and so, also, a clearly defined utility possibility curve. Since none of the arguments put forward in the recent controversy invoked these external effects, and since in any case no essential part of the analysis is altered by their consideration, no further reference to them appears in the rest of this paper.

III. The Question of Distribution

By substituting some single criterion such as maximizing social utility[18] or by invoking the concept of a social-welfare function we can, of course, continue to evade this issue. Apparently one measures total social utility by adding the individual utilities, presumed to be cardinal and comparable. In the absence of an agreed interpersonal cardinal measure we might accept as judgments of fact that tastes and capacities for enjoyment are pretty much the same, at least given time for human adaptation. We might further agree that the marginal utility of money income persistently diminishes after subsistence income. Ignoring the effects on the total product of a more equal distribution, we should then infer that an equal distribution of income issues in the maximum of total utility. It does not seem likely, however, that if the evidence revealed prodigious differences in the capacity to enjoy money and/or significant ranges of increasing marginal utility of income, that many of the Cambridge economists would have accepted the distributional implications. Rather, I imagine, they would jettison the maximizing objective and come down in favor of a more equal distribution of income for its own sake. In the last resort, if distribution does matter then it should be separately acknowledged as

---

however, preclude its meeting the tests of hypothetical compensation. [See also **17**, p. 236.]

[17] See my *Survey* [**16**, pp. 228–229] and also Little's statement at the top of p. 102 [**11**].

[18] See Kennedy [**5** and **6**].

a judgment to be taken into account explicitly in any welfare criterion; certainly not left as a by-product of some single-minded pursuit in the hope that certain features in the real world would act to ensure that the resulting distribution would not be at variance with our ideas of fairness.

As for leaving it to the social-welfare function to specify the distribution, although many symbols have been expended in the endeavor to prove that under "reasonable" conditions it is not possible to generate a social ordering from individual ones, it would not matter much if the contrary were established. Not only is any hope of obtaining such orderings from individuals chimerical; if such information were to be had it would certainly reveal orderings with wide and irreconcilable differences. The social-welfare function solution to this problem has no affinity with the ideal distribution which informs the distributional requirement of welfare criteria, like those of Little, that begin *ab initio* from value judgments designed for general acceptance and which, in any case, serve only an incomplete ordering. For such welfare criteria, a better or best distribution, is envisaged as a *structure,* one that holds irrespective of any of the conceivable permutations of individuals in the community.[19] On the fairness of a structure of distribution wide agreement may well be possible, while it is not in the least likely that much agreement would emerge if each individual were asked, instead, to write down *inter alia* the share of goods, or income, or wealth, to be received by himself, by Jones, by Smith, and by Robinson, and so on. We should think a person unworldly if he did not give his family and friends high priority, and unusually detached if he did not occasionally regard himself as rather worse off when, though his command over goods remained unimpaired, those around him managed to improve their lot. Such personal rankings, the stuff out of which social-welfare functions are supposed to be formed, along with the existence of "interdependent utilities" would, therefore, seem to have no part to play in

[19] It is for this reason that one of Arrow's strictures [**1**] of Little's *Critique* [**9**] is, perhaps, not so relevant as it appeared. The view that distributional comparisons of different collections imply both interpersonal and cardinal utility (which belief, if valid, would in any case apply no less to distributional comparisons of a single collection) is not true if one is concerned with comparing distributional *structures,* something which is feasible enough if we are content to work with the structure of money, income, or wealth.

the distributional judgment which enters into such welfare criteria.

Several minor points can be dealt with quickly. I had suggested [**17,** p. 238] that "more equal" distribution could be substituted for the noncommittal term "better" distribution, since more specific statements, or statements about the pattern of some contemplated improvements in distribution, always made it clear that, for the West at least, more equal was synonymous with better. Some additional constraints might well be desirable[20] but otherwise the judgment that a more equal distribution of a given product was not likely to meet with opposition. It is of no analytic consequence, however, and were I shown to have misinterpreted the consensus in this respect I should gladly withdraw. In addition, I proposed that we cut the Gordian knot rather than forever be entangled in bitty arguments about real and money income or wealth [**18,** pp. 345–346]; indeed, that in a predominantly market economy our distributional value judgments could be expressed directly in terms of money—a value judgment that a more equal distribution of money incomes in allocating a given collection of goods was a social improvement might command widespread assent. Again, however, this proposal is no more than an attempt to fit some clothing on the bare part of Little's criteria and does not constitute any criticism or even any formal amendment of them. It should be noticed, however, that in a world in which there happened to be great variations in the capacity for enjoyment, the achievement of equality implies that aggregate utility could be raised by transferring income from those with smaller to those with larger worldly appetites. The forfeiture of this potential access of utility, even if we knew exactly how to realize it, is an implication I find easy enough to accept though I am aware of its power to upset others.[21]

[20] A reduction in some measure of dispersion about the mean income is obviously consistent with a group of the very poor suffering a reduction in their average income. If compensation for such a group were not feasible, the relevant constraint would operate to prevent fulfillment of the criteria, notwithstanding that distribution was more equal in the Q_2 position.

[21] Sen's criticism of the equality thesis [**20,** p. 777] amounts to concern with the possibility of this implication, though he chooses to illustrate his point with a two-person world in which *A* is a cheese lover having all the cheese and *B* a beer lover having all the beer, in an economy rich in cheese though poor in beer. In the process of reaching welfare equality *A* has to sacrifice large quantities of cheese which, however, add very little to *B*'s satisfaction. Without invoking so restrictive an example it should be clear that what is at issue is the large loss of utility by *A* with no commensurable gain by *B* in the pursuit of equality of total

IV. Consistency and Transitivity

In his review [**13**] Meade pointed out that it was possible both for H to be distributionally preferred to Q_1 and for J to be distributionally preferred to Q_2 which, if accepted, would carry the interpretation that Q_2 was distributionally preferred to Q_1, and at the same time Q_1 was distributionally preferred to Q_2, so that in Figure 2, for example, we should be able to show, on Little's criterion, that Q_2 is socially preferred to Q_1 and vice versa. One could, of course, guard against this possibility by requiring in the "Scitovsky" application of Little's criterion (illustrated in Figure 2) that, whenever any point H was distributionally preferred or indifferent to Q_1, all possible points J be distributionally worse than Q_2. Similarly in the Kaldor-Hicks version of the criterion (illustrated in Figure 1) we should require that for any Q_2 distributionally preferred or indifferent to J, Q_1 is distributionally worse than all possible points H.

This constraint is a bit clumsy, however, and would add to the difficulties of applying the criteria. We might discover a simpler way to avoid this possible contradiction if we could first ascertain how it arises. It soon transpires that the possibility of contradiction in the criteria is latent in the value judgments on which they are based: (i) that a change which makes everyone better off is a social improvement, and (ii) that a better distribution of the given product is a social improvement.[22] For if we effect a social improvement by realizing an ideal distribution of the product, and then effect a further social improvement by a Pareto improvement that gives the whole of the increase to one individual, the resulting distribution will be less than ideal; thus, a movement that ranks as a social improvement by reason of the (i) judgment may simul-

---

utility, an issue which is quite adequately illustrated, as above, by the more traditional concern with differences in capacity for enjoyment.

[22] See Little's *Critique* [**9**, p. 111 and p. 116]. Since Little's intermediate point H is open to the interpretation of being a collection of goods different from Q_1, he does not talk of a better distribution *of the given product* but merely of a better distribution of welfare. Though reasons have been given to reject this interpretation, the argument in the text is, nonetheless, still applicable even if H did represent a different collection from Q_1.

taneously appear as a socially inferior position in virtue of the (ii) judgment. The seed of the contradiction is sown.[23]

The way it insinuates itself into the criteria can be demonstrated quite simply if we suppose interpersonal cardinal utility, by reference to Figure 4, with the ray R_0 representing an ideal

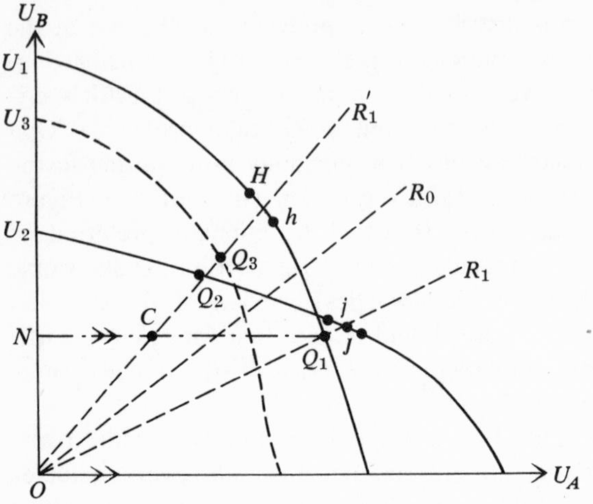

Figure 4

distribution of income, rays on either side being a worse distribution the further they are from R_0. Rays R_1 and R'_1 are distributions that are ranked as equally desirable.[24] It will, further, be an advantage to adopt the following notation:

d to indicate distributionally preferred. (Since strong distributional ordering is generally adopted, Q_2dJ implies $J\,\tilde{d}Q_2$.)

p to indicate Pareto preferred (in Figure 4 JpQ_1, and therefore $Q_1\tilde{p}J$).

> to indicate socially preferred on either of Little's criterion ($Q_2 > Q_1$ implies $Q_1 \ngtr Q_2$).

[23] Kennedy [**6** and **7**] pointed out correctly that the two parts of the criteria are different in kind and therefore not transitive. See also Dobb [**2**, pp. 767–768]. I agree with this point, although I conclude that nontransitivity, in this instance at least, does not *necessarily* lead to contradiction. For we can take precautions to guard against this eventuality [**18**, p. 343].

[24] The argument in the text is facilitated by this construction which helps us to keep our distributional bearings, but it holds as well for the usual construction of utility possibility curves.

Confining our attention to the U_1 and U_2 utility possibility curves, the Kaldor-Hicks-Little criterion takes the following form:

$$Q_2 dJQ_1, \quad \text{therefore} \quad Q_2 > Q_1 \qquad (a)$$

However, it is no less true that

$$Q_1 dHpQ_2, \quad \text{and therefore} \quad Q_1 > Q_2 \qquad (b)$$

The explanation of this paradox is not difficult. The ordering JpQ_1 admits a latent contradiction inasmuch as it is simultaneously true Q_1dJ. If the same relationship exists between H and Q_2 as exists between J and Q_1, and Q_1 and Q_2 are distributionally indifferent, we have the result that Q_2dJ and Q_1dH at the same time as JpQ_1 and HpQ_2, the rankings from which (a) and (b) are derived. Indeed, we can go further. Since there is a whole range of possible intermediate points like J and H, in the northeast quadrant of Q_1 and Q_2 respectively, by altering the position of such points—though without in any way altering the properties of Q_1 and Q_2, the collections under comparison—we could reach a consistent result that $Q_2 > Q_1$, or a consistent result that $Q_1 > Q_2$, or else (taking H and J to be the intermediate points) the result that both $Q_2 \not> Q_1$ and $Q_1 \not> Q_2$.

The need for some further restraint in the choice of such intermediate points is fairly obvious not only to eliminate contradictability and also the arbitrariness of an apparently consistent result, but also because value judgments that can be made to pull in opposite directions do not provide a steady enough foundation on which to raise welfare criteria. What was suggested therefore [**17,** p. 242] was that judgment (i) be amended to (i′) that society is better off if everyone is better off *without the distribution being made worse*. And to ensure that this judgment is met in applying such criteria, intermediate points such as H and J are required not merely to be Pareto comparable with Q_2 and Q_1 respectively, but "equi-comparable" also—which term serves to indicate the requirement that everyone at H or J be better off (or worse off) in the same proportion as compared with Q_2 and Q_1 respectively. The difficulty of discovering what would constitute a proportional increase in the welfare of all the individuals concerned is to be resolved simply by couching the distributional value judgment in terms of money.

Following these proposals, two further implications of such welfare criteria were pointed out by Kennedy [**6**]. First, that the unambiguous fulfillment of Little's Kaldor-Hicks Welfare Criterion is consistent with a movement to a smaller collection of goods. Thus, if we suppose for the moment that the ray R'_1 in Figure 4 represented a better distribution than the ray R_1, we should legitimately infer from the (Kaldor-Hicks) Little criterion that Q_2 is socially preferred to Q_1. However, Q_3 being northeast of Q_2 and along the same ray R'_1 is—by either judgment (i) or (i′)—socially preferred to Q_2. Consistent application of the criterion would take us from Q_1 to Q_3 on the utility possibility curve U_3 which is generated from a collection having less of every good than the collection U_1 on which Q_1 is to be found.[25] Second, that judgments such as (i′) and (ii) can be boiled down to judgment (iii) that there is a social improvement if the distribution of welfare is better, provided that not everyone is made worse off.[26] The limiting case which such a judgment could be made to cover is that in which, although the distribution has improved, everyone in the community is worse off except one person whose welfare remains unchanged. In a two-person community such a case is illustrated in Figure 4 by a movement from Q_1 to a point C on the ray R'_1 which is in some degree a better distributional arrangement than the ray R_1. Such a limiting case could also involve a limiting shape for the U_2 utility possibility curve. J would coincide with Q_1 and the portion of the curve from J to N would run parallel with the horizontal axis. If, however, we are reluctant to accept a movement along the contract curve, from an initial position in which B has all the goods, which makes B no worse off while making A continuously better off, at least for some range, then the limiting point C must be in some degree higher than Q_1. (iii) would have to be revised to read (iii′) that there is a social im-

[25] Granted the proposed amendments, however, intransitivity is not involved. Since Q_3 has a *better* distribution than Q_1 it cannot be shown inferior to Q_1—which is one good reason for substituting a *better* distribution for Little's *no worse* distribution.

[26] To which one ought to add for completeness the judgment (i′) itself, that there is a social improvement even if the distribution remains unchanged provided everyone is made better off [**18**, p. 349]. Since it adds little to (iii), and its inclusion does not affect the rest of the analysis, we shall omit further reference to it.

provement if the distribution of welfare is better, provided at least one person is better off.[27]

It is important to notice in passing that these two implications depend in no way upon the proposed value judgment (i′) and the consequent constraints imposed on the intermediate points *H* and *J*. They are implications of Little's criteria applied to alternative collections of goods however the intermediate points are interpreted.[28]

V. Further Reflections on Intransitivity

Since the two parts that make up each of Little's criteria rest on judgments that are different in kind they cannot, according to Kennedy, be treated as transitive, as they are by Little. Moreover, as we have indicated above, a movement that fulfills the unamended Pareto value judgment (i), may tacitly negate the distributional value judgment (ii), and, if this happens, mutually contradictory rankings may be derived. One way of overcoming this deficiency has been discussed at some lengths in the preceding section. Before going on, however, it is pertinent to inquire whether there exists any other consideration which might prevent the emergence of contradictory rankings. It could be alleged, for instance, that the original Little criteria are consistent with the ordering of what Graaff [**3**] has called a Pareto-type welfare function—one in which society is better off if no person is worse off and at least one is better off—or, possibly, that a Pareto improvement is never to be regarded as a worse distribution of welfare. Now, apart from the ethics of the matter, neither proposition can in fact save the original criteria. If they are supposed to be consistent with a Pareto-type ordering the constraints necessary

[27] It might be argued that external economies of consumption could result in a left-to-right upward sloping portion of the utility possibility curve, leading to the conclusion that a Q_2 may be found in which *both* individuals are worse off along R_1' and yet, by these criteria, Q_2 is socially preferred to Q_1. However, if the contract curve is defined, as it ought to be, as a locus of positions in which both individuals cannot be made better off, such upward sloping ranges, if they could be observed in the real world, would not form part of the effective utility possibility curve.

[28] This should be emphasized because of the impression conveyed that they arise only in consequence of the proposed revision of Little's criteria [**18**, p. 347].

to ensure this attribute should be clearly indicated, whereas no hint of their nature is to be found. As for the proposition that a Pareto improvement can never be judged a worse distribution, even if it were acceptable the effect would be merely to ignore the possibility of latent contradiction in the criteria. If, for example, in Figure 4, we assert that a latent movement from Q_1 to J is not only a Pareto improvement but a distributional improvement also, similarly for a movement from Q_2 to H, it would not prevent the outcome that Q_2 is socially preferred to Q_1 and Q_1 socially preferred to Q_2. We conclude that contradictory results can be insured against only by adopting value judgment (i′) instead of (i) and, therefore, in applying the criteria making use of equi-comparable intermediate points or—since the latter can be effectively employed by recourse to money distributions—by comparing the money distributions of Q_1 and Q_2 directly. Alternatively the judgments (i′) and (ii), as also these amended criteria, can be boiled down to a single judgment (iii), or (iii′) in which, again, money distributions are compared. True, when the criteria are transformed into judgments such as (iii′), that society is better off if distribution is improved and at least one person is better off, their luster is somewhat diminished. Nevertheless, experience of their application may give more satisfaction if in most cases the Q_2 adopted yielded something of a premium above this acceptable minimum. We might hope to find that in many cases quite a lot of people were made better off in addition to the distributional improvement.

Finally, even though the adoption of (i′) effectively bars the way to contradiction, we may not feel altogether comfortable. Considerations of symmetry at least would suggest that we also amend judgment (ii) to some sort of (ii′). And there is something to this. For we may rank Q_2 above Q_1, for instance, on the ground that Q_2 is distributionally preferred to J which is distributionally as good as, and also Pareto preferred to, Q_1 (see Figure 4). We can now choose a Q_3 that is distributionally as good as Q_2 and Pareto preferred to Q_2, in which case we rank Q_3 above Q_2 and, *a fortiori,* above Q_1. Yet we have already shown that Q_3 can have smaller amounts of every good than the collection Q_1. If we wanted to avoid such an outcome we should have to require, in comparing Q_2 and Q_1, that Q_2 is not only distributionally preferred to J but also Pareto preferred to it—or, at least, not Pareto inferior. This desideratum would be ensured if the distributional proviso (ii) were amended to (ii′), that there is a social improvement if the distribution of welfare is better provided no one is made worse off.[29]

This amended judgment (ii′) may seem pretty stringent, and it is obvious that, like (i′), it cannot be met by confining the change to a given collection of goods. Yet (i′) and (ii′) are not very different: (i′) is "strong" on the Pareto requirement and "weak" on distribution, the reverse being true for (ii′). An improvement that meets (i′) *alone* can be expected to meet (ii′) alone, and vice versa, since an improvement in which distribution is no worse and everyone better off may be expected to be one in which distribution is also better. The stringency really arises from requiring Pareto *and* distributional improvements in *both* movements, from Q_1 to the intermediate point, say J, and then from J to Q_2 also. Having to meet them successively in this way amounts to a judgment (iv) that there is a social improvement when everyone is better off and the distribution also is better off. Such a judgment is likely to command a wider consensus than, say, (iii′) though it is unlikely to be met as often as (iii′) and, in a large community, one would be surprised if it were ever completely met.

[29] The implications of the intransitivity of a dual criterion and the need to impose further constraints to avoid contradiction can be illustrated by a homely example in which a person ranks various shades and qualities of some blue woollen material, preferring brightness of color and softness of texture. For BbA, read cloth B is preferred to A on grounds of brightness. For CsB read cloth C is preferred to B on grounds of softness. Applying, now, the logic of a dual criterion we would reason: (1) $CsBbA \rightarrow C > A$. However, it is not impossible that brightness and hardness are inversely related, so that comparing the same pairs in the reverse order for opposite qualities, we should reason: (2) $AsBbC \rightarrow A > C$.

To avoid contradictions of this sort, one could now lay down that $BbA \rightarrow B > A$ only if $A\tilde{s}B$. Assuming that statement (i) is allowed only after ensuring $A\tilde{s}B$, this effectively prevents us from asserting (ii). This requirement is analogous to that part of the proposed amended judgment (i′) that reads "provided the distribution is not made worse." But the requirement $A\tilde{s}B$, though sufficient to prevent contradiction, is not wholly satisfactory. We should further want to lay down that $CsB \rightarrow C > B$ only if $B\tilde{b}C$, otherwise $CsBb$, $sA \rightarrow C > A$ has C superior to B superior to A, notwithstanding the possibility that C is preferred to B on grounds of softness only and therefore when B, and indeed A also, may be brighter than C. It is for analogous reasons I suggest above an additional amendment to (ii). In an incomplete ordering guided by a sufficient criterion based on two nontransitive qualities, it seems to be the only satisfactory way of proceeding, though obviously it must reduce its successful application to such criteria.

VI. Summary and Conclusions Relevant for Resource Allocation

It is well known that a movement from a nonoptimal position Q_1 to a fully optimal position Q_2 meets the "Scitovsky" compensation test, though it may fail the Kaldor-Hicks test: in other words, a redistribution of the Q_1 collection that made it comparable with the existing distribution of the optimal collection Q_2 would always reveal Q_2 as Pareto superior to Q_1, although it is simultaneously possible that a redistribution of the optimal collection Q_2 that rendered it comparable with the existing distribution of the Q_1 collection would reveal Q_2 to be Pareto inferior to Q_1.[30] Since the outcome of a hypothetical compensation test between optimal and nonoptimal positions depends, as it does also in such tests as between two nonoptimal positions, upon the distribution on which the test is based, it would appear that one could be sure of an unambiguous answer only after deciding which was the relevant distribution. If one agrees that the relevant distribution is the better distribution one is in fact led into contemplating dual welfare criteria—that is, criteria with distributional as well as Pareto requirements—as much to avoid ambiguity as for the ethical concern with distribution itself.

What has emerged from the recent controversy, however, is that unless these dual criteria are more carefully formulated than they were by Little the ambiguity remains after the distributional judgments are included in them. We have indicated that a point *H* distributionally preferred to Q_1 is not inconsistent with a point *J* distributionally preferred to Q_2—or, in long hand, that a distribution of Q_1 comparable with the distribution of the optimal collection Q_2, which is judged better than the actual distribution of the Q_1 collection (on which grounds we assert Q_2 to be better distributed than Q_1), does not rule out the possibility that a distribution of the optimal Q_2 collection made comparable with the Q_1 distribution is better than the actual distribution of the Q_2 collection (which we interpret to mean that Q_1 has a better distribution than

[30] See [14] esp. pp. 332–337. This is one of the reasons why the supposed demonstrations that for any country free trade (or restricted trade) is better than no trade at all are unsatisfactory.

Q_2). Thus even an optimal position with a better distribution (in the Little sense) does not necessarily establish itself as being unambiguously superior to a particular nonoptimal position.

In the endeavor to eradicate this further source of ambiguity it was found necessary to amend Little's judgment (i) to (i′) and, in consequence, it was found expedient to define uniquely the intermediate points *H* and *J*. In order to implement the more precise criteria, however, two further steps could scarcely be avoided. Though *H* and *J* were made conceptually precise, there was still the problem of how, in the real world, we should determine such points. If the transition to the real world is ever to be made I cannot see how we can avoid accepting the distribution of money incomes, or wealth, as an index of the distribution of welfare. Nor does this step seem to me at all questionable. If there was broad acceptance of the distributional judgment (ii) when framed in terms of money we could legitimately circumvent much of the fastidiousness on this question. Granted this much, however, the points *H* and *J* become otiose since their structures of distribution in terms of money are now no different from the distributional structures of Q_2 and Q_1 respectively. In applying these dual criteria, then, we should be able to compare the distributions of two alternative collections Q_1 and Q_2 directly without recourse to intermediate positions.[31]

Having gone so far, however, it would seem that we need not go to the trouble of employing these criteria based on hypothetical compensation. For once we seek to justify the two parts of the criteria by reference to judgments (i′) and (ii) we become aware that, taken in succession, they yield (iii′), with distribution measured in money terms, which can be applied directly to Q_1 and Q_2. The dual welfare criteria become unnecessary. And since by definition of a Pareto optimum it is not possible to have an optimum position in which all individuals are worse off (or even in which all individuals are no better off) than any nonoptimal position, any optimal position Q_2 that has a better (money) structure

[31] If, for any reason, we continue to use dual welfare criteria based on distributional judgments in terms of money and hypothetical compensation tests between Q_1 and Q_2, though we many not in practice have any need for intermediate points such as *H* and *J*, we might still want to retain them merely in order to illustrate how meeting those dual criteria issue in the fulfillment of judgments (i′) and (ii).

of distribution than the nonoptimal position in question enables (iii′) to be met.[32]

REFERENCES

1. Arrow, K. "Little's Critique of Welfare Economics," *American Economic Review* (1951).
2. Dobb, M. "A Further Comment on the Discussion of Welfare Criteria," *Economic Journal* (December 1963).
3. de V. Graaff, J. *Theoretical Welfare Economics.* Cambridge: Cambridge, 1957.
4. Hicks, J. R. "The Valuation of the Social Income. A Comment on Professor Kuznets' Reflections," *Economica* (August 1948).
5. Kennedy, C. M. "The Economic Welfare Function and Dr. Little's Criterion," *Review of Economic Studies,* Vol. 20 (1952–1953).
6. Kennedy, C. M. "Welfare Criteria—a Further Note," *Economic Journal* (June 1963).
7. Kennedy, C. M. "Two Comments (II)," *Economic Journal* (December 1963).
8. Kuznets, Simon. "On the Valuation of Social Income—Reflections on Professor Hicks' Article, Part I," *Economica* (February 1948).
9. Little, I. M. D. *A Critique of Welfare Economics.* 1st ed. Oxford: Oxford, 1950.
10. Little, I. M. D. *A Critique of Welfare Economics.* 2nd ed. Oxford: Oxford, 1957.
11. Little, I. M. D. "Welfare Criteria, an Exchange of Notes. II. A Comment," *Economic Journal* (March 1962).
12. Little, I. M. D. "Welfare Criteria, an Exchange of Notes. IV. A Rejoinder," *Economic Journal* (March 1962).
13. Meade, J. E. Review of *A Critique of Welfare Economics.* 2nd ed. *Economic Journal* (March 1959).
14. Mishan, E. J. "A Re-appraisal of the Principles of Resource Allocation," *Economica* (November 1957).
15. Mishan, E. J. "Rent as a Measure of Welfare Change," *American Economic Review* (June 1959).
16. Mishan, E. J. "A Survey of Welfare Economics, 1939–1959," *Economic Journal* (June 1960).
17. Mishan, E. J. "Welfare Criteria: An Exchange of Notes. V. A Comment," *Economic Journal* (March 1962).

[32] Meeting judgments (i) and (ii) in succession, which amounts to meeting (iv), is a good deal more ambitious. A movement from a nonoptimal to an optimal position that has both a better distribution and more of all goods than the nonoptimal one may still leave some individuals worse off and, therefore, fail to meet (iv).

18. Mishan, E. J. "Welfare Criteria: Are Compensation Tests Necessary?," *Economic Journal* (June 1963).

19. Robertson, D. H. "Welfare Criteria: An Exchange of Notes. I. A Note," *Economic Journal* (March 1962).

20. Sen, A. K. "Distribution, Transitivity and Little's Welfare Criteria," *Economic Journal* (December 1963).

21. Scitovsky, T. "A Note on Welfare Propositions in Economics," *Review of Economic Studies,* Vol. 9 (1941).

CHAPTER 7

Reflections on Recent Developments in the Concept of External Effects*[1]

I

An all-pervading interdependence is what makes economics so intractable a subject. Walras' algebra, which represented the relationships between prices and quantities as a system of equations, was one of the first explicit demonstrations of how everything could depend on everything without entailing circular reasoning. So far as positive economics is concerned the only relationships to be considered are those which are believed to be operative: that a man feels worse off in consequence of the change of fortune or behavior of other men is by itself nothing to the purpose of positive economics. In order for such facts to qualify as agenda for an economics that seeks to formulate predictive hypotheses these feelings must have some impact on observable economic magnitudes—on the prices and the quantities of goods and factors. But for a norma-

* From *Canadian Journal of Economics and Political Science.*

[1] My understanding of the papers by Professor Meade and by Professors Davis and Whinston has very much benefited from correspondence with them.

tive study, at any rate for a study that is manifestly concerned with human welfare, such reactions of men to the behavior of others is no less relevant simply because it does not register on the existing economic mechanisms. Indeed, it is just because these reactions fail to influence the working of the market that they are of particular interest to economists concerned with resource allocation.

External effects (external economies and diseconomies), broadly defined, encompass this desideratum. The larger they are in range and magnitude the smaller is the faith that can be reposed in the allocative virtues of the market mechanism even when working under ideal circumstances. Assuming sufficient divisibility, any economic organization is deemed satisfactory (in the Pareto sense, that no factor movements can make everyone better off) only (i) if the market tends to a solution in which the value of the marginal product, as measured by market prices, of each factor class is the same in all uses in the economy, and (ii) if all relevant effects, as defined by the welfare economist, make their impact on the pricing system. Universal perfect competition is believed to meet the requirement of the first condition, but it does not in general meet the requirements of a Pareto optimum if the latter condition is not met; in short, if there are external effects. One of the roles of the economist, as envisaged by Pigou, was to lift the lid off these external effects in order to reveal "divergencies between marginal social net products and marginal private net products," and to suggest appropriate adjustments of market prices in order that the set of outputs to which a purely competitive market tended would be displaced by one that was truly optimal; one in which the value of the *social* marginal products (*SVMP*'s) of the factor classes were the same in all uses.

It is now well recognized, however, that if the degree of competition (or of monopoly) differs as between industries so that the market (or "private") value of marginal products (*VMP*) are not equalized in the first instance, a seemingly proper correction for external effects may just as well move us further from, rather than nearer to, an optimal position. Doubtless the authors of recent contributions to the literature of external effects were aware of this though they did not always trouble themselves to be explicit enough in their partial analysis to convey the point that after "correcting" the outputs in question, the economy would be at an optimal position only if initially the *VMP*'s of factor classes were the same in all uses. Since the most casual observations suggest that the economy does not in fact achieve, or tend toward, "market efficiency"—defined as a situation in which everywhere *VMP*'s are equalized (or in which prices are equal to market marginal cost)—it might be inferred that such "corrections" of output in the presence of external effects are unwarrantable; indeed, that unless one could first be sure of a tendency toward market efficiency before adjusting outputs for *all* external effects, one could not know whether the new allocation was better or worse than the old. For all that, welfare economics can no more reach conclusions applicable to the real world without some knowledge of the real world than can positive economics. If it transpired that although market efficiency were not realized we were never too far removed from it, and if it were discovered that some external effects were very large indeed, we should certainly have a case at least for investigating the consequences of making adjustments for these external effects as if everywhere else in the economy the *SVMP*'s were already equalized. The larger the external effect in question, the more we may feel that making the requisite adjustment is likely to improve matters, notwithstanding the existing deviations from an optimal position. Certainly if adjustments for certain external effects were known to involve negligible changes of factor and product prices in the rest of the economy, we could legitimately talk of a Pareto improvement.[2]

The attention given to external effects in recent literature is, I think, fully justified by the unfortunate albeit inescapable fact that as societies grow in material wealth the incidence of these effects grows rapidly. Indeed, some particular abuses have become so phenomenal that it would not be hard to make out a case for *ad hoc* intervention.

It remains to justify this further excursion into the field. The literature over the past thirty years or so has done much to iron out inconsistencies, to suggest new classifications and to propose effective policy measures. But this development has not been en-

[2] For discussion about the significance and limitations of second-best theory, see my paper "Second Thoughts on Second Best," *Oxford Economic Papers* (October 1962).

tirely beneficial. As things stand today, the term is evocative of interdependencies of various kinds all carrying the implication that the perfectly competitive solution does not suffice. Otherwise it is far from being unambiguous[3] in consequence of misapplications or, in another interpretation, of arbitrary extensions of the original meaning. If the cutting edge of this powerful analytic tool is to be restored, some attempt must be made to chip away much of the accumulating accretions of meaning that have attached themselves to this term over time. Its range of usefulness and its limitations may then be displayed by appropriate classification.

The papers that are discussed in connection with this attempt to free the term from much extraneous matter are, all of them, well worth reading in their own right. If I appear to make use of them only to illustrate certain deficiencies in our current stock of ideas on the subject, it is not from any lack of appreciation of their high qualities. But their merits must speak for themselves since in this paper I shall address myself chiefly to a critical examination of the contributions of others in order to give shape to a consistent and comprehensive analysis of the concept of external effects.

II

In view of the many aspects of the problem to be discussed it will be an advantage to set out, first, a list of twelve propositions argued in this paper. Some of them are arguments in themselves and require no further elucidation. Each of the others, however, contains to some extent conclusions reached in the rest of the paper where the treatment is built around the contributions of a number of authors, Scitovsky, Duesenberry, Ellis and Fellner, Meade, Davis and Whinston, Coase, and Buchanan and Stubblebine, in that order. The sections of the later discussion most relevant to the proposition in question are indicated in brackets.

1. [Section A] Despite occasional recourse to the word "dynamic" to indicate a writer's concern with the problems of this

[3] Even mathematical formulations are subject to ambiguity. Expressing a firm or industry's cost, revenue, or profit as a function not only of its own outputs and inputs but also of those of other firms or industries (see Sections A and F) hardly reveals the essential character of external effects. For there is nothing to prevent one from reading into such a function a statement of general interdependence as in the Walrasian system.

world, the concept of external effects is rooted in comparative statics. But this should not be taken to mean that the concept of external effects is inapplicable to the actual world of flux and change. If comparative statics were not relevant to the real world we should indeed have to jettison most of our economic theory. The mere fact that the adjustment of supply to demand in all goods is being continually interrupted by changes in taste and technology is obviously not inconsistent with the key concept of the market as a mechanism of adjustment, a mechanism which, at any moment of time, produces prices that make for an equilibrium of the initial forces of demand and supply. The introduction of the concept of external effects is meant to suggest only that certain economic arrangements be superimposed on those generated by the market, so that, at any moment of time, the economic system tends to realize, not so much an equilibrium of the market forces, but an equilibrium which accords with our notions of an optimum allocation.

2. External effects may be said to arise when relevant effects on production or welfare go wholly or partially unpriced. Being outside the price system such external effects are sometimes looked upon as the by-products, wanted or unwanted, of other people's activities that immediately or indirectly affect the welfare of individuals.[4] Although these effects clearly come within the domain of welfare economics their study has generally been restricted to their allocational aspects. The distributional aspects, necessarily associated with allocative adjustments are, of course, of crucial importance in welfare economics. But by convention they are excluded from the analysis of external effects.[5]

The external effects in production may be exhibited by a production function of the form $x = x(a_1, \ldots, a_m; \bar{a}_n, \ldots, \bar{a}_w)$ where x is output, $a_1, \ldots, a_m$, the priced inputs, and $\bar{a}_n, \ldots, \bar{a}_w$, the unpriced inputs. We must interpret carefully, however. First,

[4] Which means that an industry's output can be affected by means other than through the movements of existing priced factors. It also means that though an individual's "real income" remains unchanged (the prices of the existing goods he buys and the factors he sells remaining unaltered) his welfare may be changed by the activities of neighboring industries and individuals.

[5] How useful this procedure is as a basis on which to make recommendations depends upon an empirical question. If, for example, it transpired that for all acceptable income distributions the corresponding optimal outputs were much the same, then a movement toward an optimal set of outputs may properly be thought of as a provisional movement in the right direction. Redistribution could then be undertaken as a separate rearrangement.

$\bar{a}_n$ may be an unpriced factor but, not being scarce, it should in any case bear a zero price—though it may also be regarded as a factor having potential allocative significance should it ever become scarce (see Section E). Secondly some of the $\bar{a}$'s may be positively priced albeit inadequately, in which case their social values in alternative occupations are not equalized. There remains, therefore, some residual service (or disservice) of the $\bar{a}$ in question where marginal social value remains unpriced. These unpriced "bits and pieces" then are to be included in the $\bar{a}$'s. Analogous remarks apply if x, instead, were an individual's welfare function, and the a's and $\bar{a}$'s the goods and services (and disservices) available to him.

These remarks add up to a comprehensive definition of external effects. It is, however, highly convenient to make a distinction at the start between what I shall call (1) external effects *internal* to the industry, and (2) external effects *external* to the industry.

In regard to (1), if some factor used in industry A is, say, undervalued in consequence of the industry's internal organization, there does not occur any alteration in its production function. Nonetheless, as a result of the relative under-pricing of that factor, the factor combination in A is not optimal. In the economy as a whole, therefore, factor rates of substitution are not everywhere equalized, which implies that the combination of goods produced by the economy is not to be found along the maximal production possibility boundary. Once the factor is properly priced, however, both the production optimum condition and top-level optimum are simultaneously met: a general Pareto optimum position is reached on the outermost production possibility boundary. Thus once industry A adjusts itself for optimal output, the external economy internal to A vanishes completely. The familiar examples of external economies internal to an industry (though external to the firm) arise in competitively organized industries in which a scarce factor such as land, fishing grounds, highways, goes unpriced or inadequately priced. They are discussed in more detail in Section C.

In regard to (2), however, inasmuch as industry A generates external economies *external* to itself, it alters the production function of some other industry, say B, and this *does* affect the technological possibilities of production. If B were a perfectly discriminating monopolist and, therefore, already producing an optimal output, the resulting effect on B's cost curve indicates the new optimal output which B will now produce. A's output alone will require correction insofar as the external economy, or diseconomy, generated varies with its own production. Once effected and a Pareto optimum realized, however, the presence of this external effect is not—in contrast to (1) above—completely eradicated. For the new optimal position is to be found on a production possibility boundary that is along some of its range either above or below (according as the effect is an economy or a diseconomy) the hypothetical production boundary that would exist in the absence of the external effect which is external to the A industry.

If, on the other hand, B were a competitive industry its mode of responding to this external effect on its production would involve generating external effects internal to itself, so that its output would also require correction. If, for example, the initial effect of an external economy external to A were to lower industry B's supply curve but caused it also to rise more steeply as B expanded, each firm in B would attend only to the additional cost to itself of expanding its production. Since each firm ignores the additional cost of its expansion borne by all other firms, the resulting supply curve for B is not the marginal curve required for optimal output determination.

3. [Section A] The above definition excludes a large group of possible cost-saving effects on industry arising from such factors as better information about investment plans (especially about investment in complementary products), the pooling of risks, better training facilities, and the like. It also excludes the need for such terminological innovations as "pecuniary" external effects (as distinct from technological external effects). Either such effects are in fact technological, and are therefore external effects proper,[6] or else the need for correcting competitive outputs is attributable to causes other than external effects as defined (and argued in Section A), or, finally, they are features necessarily associated with inelastic factor supplies.[7]

[6] Viner [**16**, p. 217] suggests the term external pecuniary economies to cover reductions in the cost to industry A as it expands its purchases of materials and services from a falling cost industry B. (In our terminology, they are external economies internal to the competitive industry A.)

[7] Viner [**16**, p. 220] also suggests the use of external pecuniary diseconomies to cover the case of rising supply price as a result of rising factor price when output expands. But rising supply price is inevitable in any economy where factor supplies are less than perfectly elastic and production functions are homogeneous

4. [Section B] Although the interdependent-utility case may be expressed in the same functional form as external effects on consumption, it may be expedient to exclude its classification under external effects. It is possible, of course, to approach welfare economics in a positive frame of mind, and to concern oneself with all those factors that may affect the welfare of the individual. Welfare propositions may, in principle, be tested if we agree to accept people's opinions about their welfare as evidence. Traditionally, however, this branch of the subject has always been concerned with the social and ethical implications of various welfare criteria. In proposing such criteria economists have drawn on basic values that are apparently widely acceptable in the Western communities for which such criteria are fashioned. One can well imagine that the costs of the more tangible external diseconomies, such as obstruction, noise, smoke are readily accepted as such by a consensus. Indeed, anyone who is able to rationalize the working of the market cannot consistently ignore external effects. If, on the other hand, a man were bold enough to complain that the mere fact of others becoming better off saddened him considerably, we may have some sneaking sympathy with him. But it is hardly likely that practical measures would be contemplated which were calculated to impoverish others in the hope of restoring his spirits. A widely acceptable social-welfare function, that is, could quite conceivably take cognizance of all the Pigovian external effects while excluding the pangs of envy or ill-feeling induced by the knowledge of other people's good fortune.

Even if, on inspecting a fair sample of the population, such reactions were shown to be widespread, and people were persuaded to take them seriously, they would be far more difficult to measure than the Pigovian external effects. In fact no government has ever proposed taking account of them. It may be argued, however, that progressive taxation is, among other things, an indirect way of appeasing these unworthy feelings, though the greater is the equalizing effect of such taxation, the less scope remains for resentment at income differentials. In an egalitarian society, it would not be income differentials, but presumably differences in public

---

of degree one. And if the industry is competitively organized, the equilibrium output—the point where each firm equates its average cost *including rent* to price —is the optimal output.

recognition and in manifest ability that would be the source of resentment. It might be universally agreed that such inescapable differences did give rise to feelings of resentment, and no less universally agreed that this was a vice and not a virtue and should not therefore be included in a social-welfare function.

5. The form in which external effects have been presented in the literature is that of partial equilibrium analysis; a situation in which a single industry produces an equilibrium output, usually under conditions of perfect competition, some form of intervention being required in order to induce the industry to produce an "ideal" or "optimal" output. If the point is not made explicitly, it is tacitly understood that unless the rest of the economy remains organized in conformity with optimum conditions, one runs smack into second-best problems. The output adjustments of the particular sectors under consideration can be strictly regarded as the completion of an optimal position only where such adjustments culminate in universal fulfillment of the optimal condition that *SVMP*'s for each factor class be the same in all employments. Nevertheless, the customary analysis is restricted to that artificial setting corresponding to partial analysis in positive economics, so that one proceeds as if the sector(s) under survey is (are) alone in need of adjustment. At all events this is the setting in which one has a license for speaking of an optimal output, such output being attained when the product price is set to equal social marginal cost or, going back a step, when the *SVMP*'s in that sector are equal to their factor prices. There can be no methodological objection to continuing this practice provided always we have at the back of our minds the necessary limitations of such partial allocation analysis.

6. [Section A] The area of the economy under survey must be stated, however. If people outside the chosen area are, on balance, made worse off when those inside the area are, on balance, made better off this fact is of no concern to the insiders. This value judgment is implied in any recommendation that optimal tariffs be imposed. A free-trading economy with perfect competition in each sector is therefore a sub-optimal situation. To attain a Pareto optimum requires that the marginal value of exports to this economy (less than the price of exports) and the marginal value of imports (greater than the price of imports) be taken into account and trade adjusted so that the rate of transformation through trade be equal

to that through domestic production (and also equal to the domestic rate of substitution). One could, by an uninhibited stretching of the concept, talk of domestic factors producing uncompensated services abroad, and therefore enter a bid to include this phenomenon under the heading of external effects (see Scitovsky [**15**]). But it is more apposite to recognize that a single area can exploit potential gains in virtue of its monopoly power.

7. [Section C] Turning to the Pigovian categories, it can be shown that, in the external diseconomies internal to the industry case, it makes no difference whatsoever to the determination of optimal output whether we talk of external effects, as does Pigou, or whether, like Knight, we talk about the need for private ownership to impute a rent to the scarce resource. In other words, if we observe that long period equilibrium is such that diminishing *average* product is set equal to factor price (in terms of product, by all firms then without reference to, or recognition of, the scarce fixed factor), we may legitimately argue that optimal output requires that we attend instead to the diminishing marginal product of the variable factor (or to increasing marginal cost of the product). But if we go further and explain the diminishing returns to the variable factor by reference to a scarce fixed factor the imputation of a rent to this fixed factor, equal to the value of its marginal product ensures, in perfectly competitive equilibrium, that the variable factor also receives the value of its marginal product. (In terms of product supply curves, the average cost to the industry, *including* rent, is equal always to the marginal cost in terms of the variable factor alone.)[8]

[8] It would seem that the production-on-consumption, and consumption-on-consumption categories fit conceptually at least into this dual approach, and that private ownership of the unpriced good or factor would provide an automatic corrective. For instance, if people separately owned the fresh air they breathed, they could be induced to sell some of it to the smoky factory for pollution. If each person owned his own quiet, so that nobody could legally invade any part of it without paying him his minimum price for a portion of it, optimal output would be assured. But though this extension of the Knightian approach is suggestive there might be difficulties even though it were possible to organize a market for fresh air or quiet. For any person who was not honest would not reveal his response to the market price, but hold out for as much as he could get, which tactic would pay since the buyer could not proceed while any single individual held out; substitution between the units of quiet is not possible, the quiet of each person in the area being strictly complementary from the standpoint of the buyer. To the buyer, it is a case of all-or-nothing; in fact an example of indivisibilities.

Nevertheless, if such a market could be made to work, say by giving each per-

8. [Sections D and F] If an external effect external to the industry is variable, say a by-product jointly produced with some other marketed product, and either consumed directly or made use of as an input by other industries, there exists a virtual demand schedule for it which, could it be realized in a competitive market, would ensure optimal outputs, all relevant factors receiving their *SVMP*'s. In circumstances where such unpriced products cannot be appropriated and marketed, the tax-subsidy solution is always available. Alternatively, a merger of the two industries would provide the proper corrective, assuming always that the concern produces, or is made to produce, the competitive output. The case for a merger is, as Davis and Whinston [**3**] point out, stronger on grounds of practical administration for those variable external effects that are reciprocal as between two firms or industries.

9. [Sections D and H] A useful classification of external effects external to the industry can be based on two distinctions: (1) between the industry generating the external effect and the industry absorbing it, and (2) between overhead and output-variable external effects. In the simple instance of an industry A having external effects on B's production, either industry, both industries, or neither industry may have to adjust outputs. Whether their competitive outputs have to be adjusted in order to realize optimal outputs—whether, that is, the external economies have allocative significance—does not, however, depend upon the output-variability or otherwise of the external effect. Variability is neither a necessary nor a sufficient condition for allocative significance.

10. [Section G] Most of the journal literature follows the custom of ignoring the cost incurred in making necessary arrangements to ensure that optimal outputs are in the process of being realized. Coase [**2**] is an exception, though his emphasis on these unavoidable costs appears more as an attack on the Pigovian doctrine than as a quite obvious consideration that ought to be brought into the picture on a second approximation. There may be cases where no additional cost, or very little, is involved, as when the government collects the additional revenues without additional

---

son a legal property right to his quiet, or fresh air, etc. it would ensure optimal output: for whenever the aggregate value placed on the collective good exceeded its worth to the party (or parties) who would otherwise reduce or destroy it, he (or they) would be unable to proceed.

personnel and firms make provision to pay it at no extra cost of administration,[9] but generally we have to allow for additional costs. If these costs vary with output they have to be added to social marginal cost and they therefore further reduce the optimal output. If, however, these costs are a lump sum, then in order that it be worthwhile to correct existing output the lump sum must be smaller than the gain in social valuation (or, in the case of external diseconomies, the reduction of social loss) from moving to the optimal output.

11. [Sections G and H] In the particular case in which variation in the output of industry A inflicts damages on B's production the marginal value of such disservices should be reckoned, as Coase correctly pointed out [**2**], not as the marginal value of the product destroyed, but as that value *minus* the prices of the factors thereby released and regarded as perfectly mobile within the period in question. It should also be apparent that if the factors are not indifferent as between the various occupations open to them, we should have to add to the losses suffered by the immobile factors in B all losses of rents borne by the variable factors that are obliged to move from B to employment they consider inferior. This analysis is obviously symmetric for the case of benefits conferred by A on B.

In this connection it is also useful to stress the point made by Buchanan and Stubblebine [**1**] that—provided we ignore the welfare, or "income" effects[10]—the reduction in A's output necessary to render it optimal can be achieved whether A pays sums equal to the marginal damage inflicted on B, or whether instead A receives such sums on condition that it reduces its outputs.[11] Inasmuch as the latter corrective is adopted, expansion of A's output by one unit of product x involves foregoing a sum equal to the marginal loss sustained by B. Thus producers of x are effectively

[9] Though even in such cases, people who are more occupied in collecting taxes without any increase in pay may be regarded as worse off. In real terms, then, costs of the new economic arrangements may be unavoidable.

[10] A more general treatment of the sort of situation envisaged by Buchanan and Stubblebine, one in which welfare effects are not ignored, is given in [**10**].

[11] The damaged parties will generally have some incentive to approach the producers of x (if they can organize themselves without too much cost) since there is scope for bargaining when the maximum they would pay to be rid of a certain number of units of x exceeds the profits made on these units by the x-producers.

subjected to an opportunity cost for every additional *x* product produced. The effect on their output is then no different from that of an excise tax equal at every point to the estimate of the marginal damage.

12. [Section G] Finally, there is a proposition so obvious that it is in continual danger of being overlooked. The existence of external diseconomies external to an industry, though consistent with optimal outputs after the necessary adjustments are made, unavoidably involves some loss of social value compared with a situation in which such diseconomies are absent. In other words, an optimal output in the absence of these external diseconomies is superior to an optimal output that is adjusted for their presence. Indeed, the loss from the introduction of a particular external diseconomy is not to be estimated by the required adjustments in outputs which may conceivably be slight. This may be appreciated without much effort if we consider the *removal* of some external diseconomy inflicted on others by industry A whose product has a low demand elasticity, this being clearly equivalent to a technological improvement that reduces the social costs of production. In a partial equilibrium analysis, in which changes in all other factor prices and in other product prices can be neglected, this gain may be estimated by the increase in consumer's surplus in the case of constant costs. The social loss arising from the introduction of this external diseconomy is, of course, the negative of this gain.

Put somewhat differently, if the producers of the good *x* were compelled to compensate the losers exactly for the damages borne by them after output of *x* had been reduced to the optimal size and the price raised to meet the social marginal cost, the sum paid over would—in the absence of welfare, or "income," effects—exactly represent the social loss. True, this sum is a transfer payment from manufacturers of *x* to the group of individuals in question. But since the manufacturers become worse off and the group becomes no better off as a result of being exactly compensated for damages sustained, society as a whole is worse off in the presence of external diseconomies by an amount exactly equal to this sum levied on the manufacturer.

One advantage of looking at things this way is that it becomes immediately apparent that if the manufacturers could discover some less costly method of coping with the diseconomies they would, on the profit-maximizing hypothesis, at once adopt it. If, for example, the compensation they must pay exceeds the cost of installing and maintaining smoke-preventing devices, they change to the latter, and from this to any further cost-saving device. And there is clear social justification for this action, since it implies that the cost to society of eliminating this source of diseconomy altogether is yet smaller than that of sustaining it with outputs adjusted optimally.[12]

III

We now turn to a summary and critical examination of the crucial aspects of the contributions mentioned, beginning with that of T. Scitovsky.

A. The chief impression given by Scitovsky's paper [**15**] is the classification as "pecuniary external economies" of economic phenomena that seem to fall readily into already familiar categories.[13] From the many examples given in the literature on the industrialization of underdeveloped countries he infers a definition of external economies which he alleges is much broader than, though it includes, that appropriate to equilibrium theory. This definition marks them out as having the characteristic that they include interdependencies among producers *through* the market as well as interdependencies that do not pass through the market. If $P_1 = G(x_1, c_1, l_1; x_2, c_2, l_2, \ldots)$, where P_1 is the profit of the firm one, x_1 its output, and c_1, l_1 its inputs, the remaining

[12] One might, therefore, be tempted to argue that one of the economic advantages of putting the burden of compensation on firms rather than allowing it to fall on other people (even though these people can effectively organize in order to compensate the damaging firms, so inducing them to curtail their outputs to optimum) is that it would provide a strong incentive for these firms to undertake research into ways of eliminating the sources of the social diseconomy, thus providing an incentive to reducing social loss in the economy.

[13] In private correspondence Professor Scitovsky indicated to me that he was not at all anxious to introduce into the subject a new concept of external economies; that in fact he was engaged merely in drawing attention to the many different meanings given to external economies especially in the literature on underdeveloped countries. The qualifying adjective "pecuniary" was proposed by him only in order to separate the various new meanings from the traditional concept used in equilibrium analysis, which concept is preserved by the term "technological" external economies. He agrees with my conclusion that there is no need in economic analysis for this concept of "pecuniary" external economies, and that his illustrations of them all fall into already familiar economic categories.

symbols after the semicolon refer to those outputs and inputs of other firms which give rise to these pecuniary external economies or diseconomies.

In explicating the nature of such pecuniary external economies, Scitovsky talks of investment in an industry resulting in increased output which leads to lower product and higher factor prices. When these benefits accrue to firms as profits they are "pecuniary external economies," though (according to Scitovsky) Marshall would call them (together with benefits accruing to persons) consumer's and producers' surpluses. These benefits should be taken account of whenever investment decisions are made. What is to be maximized, then, is not only profits but the sum of both profits and pecuniary external economies. This situation is to be compared with that of equilibrium theory in which, under the usual assumptions, the maximizing of profits by each firm[14] and the maximizing of satisfaction by each person bring about an optimal situation, one in which consumer's and producers' surpluses are maximized.

These conflicting views, he goes on to say, are resolvable if we discover those limitations of general equilibrium theory that render it inapplicable to the problems of investment. And he finds these limitations in the following considerations:

(a) Perfect divisibility, and therefore the marginal equalities, cannot always be met. Output may therefore exceed or fall short of the hypothetical optimum. The alternative investment that yields the highest profits need not be best for society as a whole. This proposition was recognized in 1844 by Dupuit who discovered the proper criterion, not in the actual profitability but in the hypothetical maximum profitability attainable by perfect price-discrimination,[15] though neither Dupuit, nor Hicks later, indicated the role of indivisibilities which renders the above test necessary.

[14] Since the orthodox position has it that in a perfectly competitive equilibrium all firms make zero profit, it may be that Scitovsky had in mind the area above the upward sloping industry supply curve, something which, possibly, he identifies with producers' surplus.

[15] Given divisibility, the hypothetical maximum profitability is also reached at the output where price equals marginal cost, if this hypothetical magnitude comprises both consumer's and producers' surpluses. The marginal-cost-pricing rule should not be under attack, but the profitability criterion when the term is confined to the profits of the firm or industry.

(b) General equilibrium theory, being static, is inapplicable to the theory of investment. According to equilibrium theory the closer to equilibrium is the system the closer it is to an optimum. But investment need not bring the system closer to equilibrium, and when it does not do so the results of equilibrium theory do not apply. Profits, under competition, are an index of disequilibrium and act to bring the system closer to equilibrium. Yet, profits may understate the desirability of, say, cost reducing investment in A if no account is taken of the initial increase in profits of B which uses products of industry A. Only when equilibrium is reestablished in both industries do the conclusions of equilibrium theory become applicable, and investment in A becomes the socially desirable amount. But this amount of investment is greater than that at the first stage before industry B began to adust itself. Scitovsky concludes that whenever investment results in pecuniary external economies its private profitability understates its social desirability.

Elaborating further, Scitovsky argues that an expansion of the A industry may lead to increased profitability in the B industry if (i) B produces inputs for A, (ii) B produces substitutes for inputs used in A, (iii) B produces products complementary with A, (iv) B is consumed by persons who benefit by A's expansion. In such circumstances vertical integration is not enough. Complete integration is necessary to eliminate divergencies between private profit and public benefit. So far as investment is concerned, therefore, profits in a market economy are a bad guide to economic optima, and are a worse guide the more decentralized is the economy.

Before moving on, Scitovsky re-states his argument in the following terms: In a decentralized economy a supplementary system of communications is necessary so that each producer can learn about the decisions of others and coordinate his decisions with theirs. But market prices reflect the economic situation as it is, and not as it will be, and are therefore ineffective in coordinating investment decisions that come to fruition only over a long period.

(c) Investment in the export industries is less desirable, and investment in import-competing industries more desirable, from a national standpoint than from an international standpoint. Here the divergence between private and public benefit arises from failure to exclude pecuniary external economies and diseconomies that accrue to foreigners and are reflected in the profits of export- and import-competing industries. The degree of divergence between national welfare and private profit depends on the elasticities of the foreign import-demand and export-supply schedules as shown by Graaff in his "Optimal Tariff Structures" (*Review of Economic Studies,* 1949–1950).

While much of Scitovsky's argument appears reasonable, it should be evident that there is no need for a new category of pecuniary external economies. The analysis and the illustrations all seem to fit into already familiar pigeon holes. There is, for instance, nothing in the four cases mentioned in (b) above that calls for any revision of existing concepts. Take case (iii), in which the products of A and B are complements, by way of illustration: if, as a result of technological advance, industry A finds it profitable to invest in expanding its capacity the expansion of its sales will increase the demand for the complementary product of B. Industry B also will be confronted with a rise in the rate of return on its capital and will undertake investment to meet the increased demand for its product. If both continue to respond in this way, the equilibrium solution is the optimal one. On the other hand, A might find it profitable to expand only if it could collect the rise in the price of B's complementary good (consequent upon the reduction in A's price). Unless there was cooperation between A and B, this potential gain may be left unexploited. However, the underestimate of A's contribution is not the result of an external diseconomy imposed by B's activity. It is the result of a market relationship between the demand for the two products. In conditions under which relevant information is inadequate there can be underinvestment in complementary goods just as there can be overinvestment in substitute goods.

Scitovsky's (a) category is recognizable as the problem of indivisibilities that results in decreasing average inclusive cost over the relevant range, and is properly appreciated in a static setting. As for the considerations grouped under (c) they are evidently no more than a restatement of the—again static—optimum tariff doctrine. The country is analogous to an imperfectly competing firm selling more only at a reduced price and buying from an increasing cost industry. Such a firm can maximize its profits by producing an output at the intersection of a curve that is marginal to its sales curve and a curve that is marginal to that of its input purchases.

Thus the considerations dealt with under (a), (b), and (c) appear to be clearly distinguishable phenomena, with little to be gained in analytic acuity by investing them with a blanket term, pecuniary external economies. Scitovsky's restatement towards the end of (b) provides a clue that he is concerned with the problem of inadequate information available to industries and firms of the investment decisions of other industries and firms. This is a feature making for economic waste and though it may not justify centralized planning it would warrant some research into practical methods of improving the communication of relevant information among firms. One could hardly take exception to such recommendations, but one can make them forcibly enough without recourse to the terminology of pecuniary external economies.[16]

B. Towards the end of his well-known book on the consumption function, Duesenberry [**4**] devoted a chapter to those relationships that, broadly speaking, are formally embraced by the term external effects, but are sometimes spoken of as interdependent utilities. It is customary to ignore this interdependence in any initial treatment of a Pareto optimum. Indeed, in any systematic treatment it is one of the last complications to be faced up to.

Expressed in purely mathematical terms, this interdependence

[16] Of course, there can be many other ways of extending the traditional meaning of external effects to comprehend other features of industrial development that seem to call for the intervention of some agency other than those commonly associated with the market. For example Rosenstein-Rodan, in considering some particular circumstances of economic development, tells us that: "The planned creation of such a complementary system [of industries producing goods that are, broadly speaking, complementary in consumption] reduces the risk of not being able to sell and, since risk can be considered as a cost, it reduces cost. It is in this sense a special case of 'external economies.' " [**14**] If "this sense" has reference to cost reduction, it would seem that technical innovation, migration, risk pooling, three-shift systems, managerial training, increased competition, cheap foreign credits (more centralized planning for some, more market and decentralized planning for others), and any number of economic phenomena must all be gathered under the umbrella term, external economies. Such indiscriminate coinage must have the inevitable result of reducing to zero the analytic power of the original concept.

is not distinguishable from Pigovian external effects relating to uncompensated services and disservices. For the welfare of any person *A* depends not only on all the prices facing him but *inter alia* directly on the goods consumed and factors provided by other persons making up the group or community. Alternative and less general formulations have the welfare of this individual *A* depend on the expenditure, the income, the wealth, or the utility of each member of the community. Whatever the precise formulation, however, conditions necessary for a Pareto optimum have to be reconsidered in the light of this interdependence.

If we start with zero elasticity in the supply of all factors in order to postpone the question of income-leisure adjustments we can look first at the "lower-level" optimal conditions. *If* any increase in goods that were made possible by reshuffling the factors could always be so distributed among the community as (assuming sufficient divisibility) to make everyone better off, then the condition for a production optimum—that the ratio of marginal products of all pairs of factors be the same in all uses—would continue to be applicable to the community. For if it were not met, then regardless of the existing distribution, everyone would not be as well off as he might be if it were met. If, on the other hand, the community happened to be in such a position that no increase in material output could be so distributed as to make everyone better off,[17] a Pareto optimum would call for a reduction in material output in favor of more leisure—a reduction therefore in the demand for factors in general. Nevertheless, having decided on the magnitude of the reduction in goods necessary to restore optimality, the resulting quantities of goods are all to be produced by factor combinations that meet the above-mentioned optimal production condition.

However, we now remind ourselves that Duesenberry was concerned not with the case of fixed factor supplies but with variable factor supplies in which he assumes that the individual has a continuous choice between income and leisure. Since no individual makes voluntary correction for the impact of his choice on others' welfare, constraints on his factor supply are required if his contribution is to meet the optimum condition that the technological

[17] The case referred to by Graaff [6] as "Excessive external effects in Consumption."

rate of substitution between factor and product be equal to the *net* subjective rate of substitution between them—the word *net* indicating that the product, or income, demanded by the individual in return for his increment of effort has now to be reduced by the amount of compensation payments to others whose welfares are adversely affected.[18]

In the absence of this correction, the individual's supply of factors, and therefore the outputs produced, are excessive, and a

[18] To illustrate, consider an initial nonoptimal position in which person *A* is offered \$5 to surrender one more unit of leisure in order to perform the work in question whereas \$2 would just have sufficed. If nobody is made any worse off when it becomes known that he accepted the offer, the Pareto criterion to a better position is met; for *A* is better off and nobody is worse off. If one or more members of the community do feel aggrieved at his acceptance of the offer but would just recover their equanimity if less than \$3 were distributed among them, then again the new position is a movement in the right direction. If, however, the minimum sum required to placate each of these good souls who begrudge *A* his good fortune exceeds \$3, his acceptance of the offer leads to a socially inferior position. For if he returns to the status quo ante, thus foregoing his \$3 rent, he could be fully compensated by those others while they would remain better off than if he had accepted the offer.

We are, therefore, justified in subtracting from *A*'s *VMP* (equal, in competition, to factor price) the full compensation necessary to prevent any of the others feeling worse off. Only if this adjusted *VMP* still exceeds his supply price is the Pareto criterion met.

A simple example taken from Duesenberry [**4**, pp. 97–101] of a three-man community producing one good with one factor, labor, indicates the sort of formal factor-product conditions to be met within the interdependent case.

Given that u_1, u_2, u_3; x_1, x_2, x_3; and y_1, y_2, y_3, are respectively the utility indices, the amounts of labor supplied by, and the products (or incomes) of the three individuals, we determine the value of the x's and the y's that maximize community welfare $W = W(u_1, u_2, u_3)$ subject to $y = u(x)$ and to u_1 and u_2 being held constant at u^o_1 and u^o_2,

$$\text{where } u_1 = \phi_1(x_1;\, y_1) \tag{1}$$
$$u_2 = \phi_2(x_2;\, y_2, y_1) \tag{2}$$
$$u_3 = \phi_3(x_3;\, y_3, y_2, y_1) \tag{3}$$
$$\text{and} \quad y \equiv y_1 + y_2 + y_3$$
$$\psi(x) \equiv \psi(x_1, x_2, x_3)$$

Thus for given values of u^o_1 and u^o_2 we are able to determine a single maximum point on the three-dimensional utility-possibility boundary corresponding to the third individual's maximum utility. By varying u^o_1 and u^o_2 through all possible values we describe the complete utility-possibility boundary for this community subject to the production function $\psi(x)$ and the individual's utility functions (1), (2), and (3).

The necessary conditions for such a maximum turn out to be

$$\frac{\partial \psi_1}{\partial x_1} = -\frac{\partial y_1}{\partial x_1}\left(1 - \frac{\partial y_2}{\partial y_1} - \frac{\partial y_3}{\partial y_1} + \frac{\partial y_2}{\partial y_1}\frac{\partial y_3}{\partial y_2}\right) \tag{i}$$

$$\frac{\partial \psi_2}{\partial x_2} = -\frac{\partial y_2}{\partial x_2}\left(1 - \frac{\partial y_3}{\partial y_2}\right) \tag{ii}$$

$$\frac{\partial \psi_3}{\partial x_3} = -\frac{\partial y_3}{\partial x_3} \tag{iii}$$

welfare optimum can be attained only by contracting the supply of factors and output.[19]

C. The Ellis and Fellner paper [**5**] rightly emphasizes the proposition that, contrary to an initial allegation by Pigou (later corrected), no divergence between the ideal of perfectly competitive output results when product supply curves slope upward in consequence of rising factor prices: for though a rising supply curve reflects a rising minimum average cost equilibrium for each firm, such average cost does include the rents paid to the intra-marginal factors. An important asymmetry between rising and falling supply curves was therefore recognized by the authors: in rising supply price the increase in average cost to the industry *includes* intra-marginal rents, which rents are *not* reckoned as true social costs but as transfer payments. When such rents are excluded, however, the same supply curve can be regarded as a true *social marginal* cost curve for the industry. In contrast, a downward-sloping supply curve was indicative of falling average *social* costs, and the relevant output was to be determined by taking a cost curve marginal to this.[20]

The third equation re-states the familiar "independent" case, the L.H.S. being the positive rate of transformation between product and labor and the R.H.S. being the (negative) rate of substitution of the third individual between product (net of all direct taxes) and labor. Since the third individual's income does not affect the welfare of the other two individuals, his marginal effort must produce enough to satisfy only his own preferences.

The product arising from the increment of effort by the second individual, however, must suffice to compensate not only the efforts of the second individual but to make up for any loss of welfare experienced by the third individual in response to the increased income of the second. Hence the bracketed term on the R.H.S. of (ii) in which $\frac{\partial y_3}{\partial y_2}$ being negative indicates the exact compensation to be paid to individual 3 in order to maintain unchanged his level of welfare for every additional dollar increase in individual 2's income.

The terms on the R.H.S. of equation (i) reveal that the product arising from the increment of labor by the individual on the L.H.S. must be enough to compensate individuals 2 and 3 for losses consequent upon the increase in individual 1's income, and further to compensate individual 3 for the compensating addition to individual 2's income.

[19] It is evident that if, instead, the others were cheered at *A*'s enrichment we should *add* to *A*'s *VMP* the maximum sums they would pay for the pleasure of knowing that he had availed himself of the offer. If this sort of interdependence predominated (which is much to be doubted) then, unless the standard rule were corrected for these responses, the supply of factors and aggregate output would be below those required for a Pareto optimum.

[20] It would be more accurate to say that the downward-sloping supply curve *may* reflect only increasing returns. For it is clearly possible also that as output is expanded factors important to this product rise in price. The rents accruing to

However, in the course of their excellent exposition the authors made two interrelated distinctions that do not appear to stand up well to close scrutiny: (a) a distinction between rising costs, or diminishing returns, due to a fixed factor on the one hand, and, on the other hand, rising transfer costs due to that increase in the price of factors necessary to induce them to move from other industries, and (b) a further distinction between both the phenomena mentioned in (a) and a rising supply curve due to "the wasteful exploitation of natural resources."

As for (a), I think it would now be generally conceded that there are no differences in kind. The effect on the supply price of any good of those factors whose supply elasticity to the industry is zero is essentially the same as the effect of those factors whose elasticity to the industry is somewhat greater than zero though less than infinity. In general, one may affirm that any inelasticity in the supply of the factors adds rent elements to the supply curve of the product. And since this average curve for the industry includes infra-marginal rents (rising transfer payments), the true average cost (excluding rent) is below it.

Turning to (b), Ellis and Fellner write [**5**, p. 253] that their preceding analysis is not concerned with "genuine diseconomies" arising from such phenomena as the smoke nuisance, the wasteful exploitation of natural resources, etc. And though they have a reference to Knight's paper on social costs, they fail to point out that Knight, in contradistinction to Pigou, regarded such things as road congestion not as instances of divergence between private and social net product but as instances of wasteful exploitation of a natural resource; something that would not occur if the resource in question were treated as private property and its rent maximized.

Knight's interest in the debate arose from Pigou's conclusion that free enterprise could lead to excessive investment in industries having upward-sloping supply curves; in particular he was interested in the example given by Pigou of traffic congestion. We need not follow the actual example of the distribution of trucks

---

intra-marginal factors are included in the average cost which, however, continues to fall because of the predominance of scale effects. Nonetheless, if we excluded these intra-marginal transfer payments the true average social cost would fall yet more rapidly, and so also, therefore, would the true *marginal* social cost.

between a good and bad road, the essential point being, as Pigou saw it, that the owner of each additional (equally efficient) truck on the road would have regard to the cost only so far as it affected him and would ignore the increase in the average cost of driving simultaneously imposed on every other truck. In open competition, therefore, the number of trucks on the road increases until the average cost incurred by each equals the maximum price each can afford to pay for the right of way. In order to take account of the diseconomies each additional truck inflicts on the preexisting number, Pigou constructs a curve marginal to this average curve, optimal output being then determined at the point where this marginal cost is equal to the maximum price the trucks are able to pay. Since this optimal output would not be brought about by competition, a case could be made for government intervention in the shape of an excise tax on all trucks equal, at each point, to the difference between the average and the marginal curve.

Knight's response to this argument was crucial: if good land were free, output would also be excessive. If, however, such land were put under private ownership and properly "exploited," output would not be excessive since diminishing marginal returns to the variable factors would realize the maximum rent for each piece of land. Similarly, if a road were put under private ownership and its rent maximized the number of trucks also would be optimal, a point made clearer perhaps if, as suggested by Knight, we think of the owner of the road hiring the trucks (instead of truck owners hiring the use of the road). The rent levied by a private owner for the use of the scarce resource therefore serves the socially useful purpose of limiting output to the point at which marginal cost equals product price (or factor price equals *VMP*).

Nevertheless, Pigou's external diseconomies approach is not shown incorrect by Knight's analysis, which, of course, is itself entirely correct. For, at least in the production-on-production category, the external diseconomies referred to by Pigou arise precisely because a scarce factor is used as though it were free. Thus if limited land that would otherwise command a price were made freely available to competitive firms, each firm in reaching long-run equilibrium would ignore the effects of its expansion on the variable costs of all other firms and one could legitimately talk of a social cost being imposed by each additional firm on the outputs of all infra-marginal firms. An excise tax equal at each output to the difference between average and marginal cost would compel the competitive industry to regard its marginal-cost curve as a (average) supply curve (since the height of the average cost to industry *including* this excise tax is then equal to the true marginal cost without it) and so be led to produce an equilibrium output equal to the optimal output.

Exactly the same result follows if, instead, the limited land is put under private ownership, either to a single owner, or to a group of owners, or divided up among competitive firms. If, for example, the last course is adopted, each firm, taking the price of the product as fixed, maximizes revenue by exploiting its average cost curve which, because of the limited land he holds, is upward-sloping.[21] He achieves this by producing an output at which a curve marginal to his average cost curve cuts the price line. The horizontal summation of these marginal-cost curves yields an industry supply curve for a period during which land cannot be augmented, a supply curve that cuts the price line at the optimal output.

Some additional light is shed on both interpretations if the analysis is expressed in factor units, in particular if we follow custom and suppose only two factors, labor and land. Pigou could be said to have concentrated on the variable factor, labor, and to have discerned that, if no price were attributed to land, competition would result in an equilibrium employment at which *average* product was equal to the wage rate and at which, therefore, *marginal* product was lower than the wage rate and, therefore, lower here than in alternative uses. Knight, on the other hand, focused attention on the other factor, land; if it were treated as though it were free, the whole of the product would be distributed to labor alone. Thus, while labor would be "under-exploited," receiving a wage in this employment (equal to average product) above its marginal product, land would be "over-exploited," its marginal product in this employment being in excess of its rent

[21] We should here assume that uniformly efficient labor is readily available at a fixed wage, otherwise, as indicated earlier, we should have to make further allowance for net rents received by labor as output expands.

(which is zero). Both approaches are valid, each representing one side of the same model. If Knight was explicit about the "over-exploitation" of land, implicit in Pigou's vision of the over-employment of the variable factor was this notion of its "under-exploitation"—its *VMP* in this use being less than its wage, and less, therefore, than its *VMP* in alternative uses.[22] It follows also that the policy proposed by each writer, where it is practicable, results in the required optimal output. If with Pigou one interprets this reduction of average product of infra-marginal firms as a social cost, as one may well do if economic institutions do not compel competitive firms to take account of it, the imposition of an excise tax does ensure that it is taken into account. Alternatively, one could argue, as Knight does, that *if* a proper rent were imputed to land, perfectly competitive firms, whose average costs now include rent, would themselves tend to promote an optimal output.[23]

Knight's prescription is, then, only one of a number of possible prescriptions. And the cause, or explanation, of the overproduction should not be attributed to the absence of his particular prescription—that is, to the absence of private ownership of a scarce factor. Indeed, Knight's analysis carries an implication about distribution also, which is incidental to but not necessary for, optimal output.

D. Meade's paper [**9**] falls into the production-on-production category in a competitive situation, and although he resorts freely to calculus to obtain precise expressions of the adjustments required the essential arguments may be expressed in ordinary language. We are to concentrate attention on two industries, A and B, which, presumably, may be thought of as comprising a small segment of the economy in the remainder of which we assume that

[22] It may be observed in passing that if diminishing returns *to scale* prevailed, *all* cooperating factors would be paid their corresponding average products, and all marginal products would be lower than factor prices, which would indicate over-production of the product in question. But then competition is not consistent with production in the diminishing-returns-to-scale range.

[23] The revenue yielded by an optimal excise tax is, of course, exactly equal to the maximum rents that could be charged, both being equal to the difference between average variable cost and marginal cost times the equilibrium output (or, alternatively, equal to the difference between average product of labor and its marginal product times the equilibrium employment then determined).

everywhere factor prices are equal to their corresponding *VMP*'s.

Two types of external effects in this category are distinguished: (I) "unpaid factor," in which there are constant returns to scale for society as a whole, but less than constant returns for the individual industry, and (II) "creation of atmosphere," in which we have constant returns to scale for each industry, but more than constant returns for society as a whole. He gives two examples for each type: (a) one-way effects, and (b) reciprocal effects.

For I(a) we have the picture of an apple-growing industry, A, situated close to a bee-honey industry, B, in which the bees feed on apple blossom (which is, therefore, the "unpaid factor"). Any expansion of industry B alone soon runs into decreasing returns to scale. Only if apple blossom is increased in the same ratio as honey bees—and, therefore only if industry A increases in the same proportion as B—do the returns of B remain constant.

Labor in A provides not only apples but, in effect, cooperates in providing honey also, since apple blossom is a by-product of the planting and tending of apple trees. Indeed, for every set of apple and honey outputs there corresponds a *VMP* of apple-growing labor, composed of its marginal contribution to the value of apples plus its marginal contribution to the value of honey. According to Meade, correct social accounting should require that the marginal value of the honey component attributable to labor in A be actually paid to labor in A. Capital in A should have its return supplemented on the same principle. And since labor in B is supposed, by Meade, to receive its proper *VMP,* the excise subsidies to labor and capital in A have to be paid from the proceeds of a tax on the returns to capital in B (since the return to capital is treated by Meade as a residual from the total value of the honey output after labor in B has been paid its *VMP*).

Meade's *ad valorem* tax on capital in B is, then, calculated as the marginal honey value contributed by an apple *times* the apple output, *divided* by the total capital used in B. Alternative methods for correcting outputs are: (i) a subsidy paid on the *output* of apples itself rather than on the apple-producing factors plus a tax on honey, or (ii) the integration of the two industries which would then yield constant returns to the joint product of apples and honey.

The reciprocal relationship, I(b), can be illustrated by assuming that, besides feeding on the apple blossom, the bees fertilize the apple trees.[24] The *VMP* of apple labor therefore includes not only the direct marginal increment of apples and the increase in the value of honey arising therefrom, as in the previous example, but also the increase in the apples resulting from the increase in the bee population associated with the aforementioned increase of honey, and, as a result of this increase of apples, a further increase in the output of honey with the associated increase of bees fertilizing more apples, and so on, to a convergent series. An analogous argument holds for bee labor. These mutual repercussions are, of course, easily solved by simultaneous equations. According to Meade, in the absence of intervention in the competitive industries the wage of the apple laborer is equal only to his direct *VMP*, whereas it ought to exceed the value of his direct marginal product by the sum of the indirect effects on honey and apple production. An analogous prescription applies to the bee-keeping laborer. Capital, which takes the residual product in the two industries, is therefore required to subsidize these supplementary payments to labor in the two industries, since only in this way will factor payments exactly exhaust the product in the two industries.

Since these two examples provide all the essential elements of Meade's method, it may be as well to appraise the value of these prescriptions at this stage in his exposition. We shall then find it easier to dispose of the remaining examples.

Consider Meade's treatment of the first example, I(a), an example of an external economy external to A. In accordance with the Pigovian concept of the *SVMP*, if marginal labor in apple farming causes an increment in the output of honey, in addition to apple output, the value of this honey increment is to be added to the market marginal product of labor in order to obtain the true *SVMP*. This prescription should, however, apply to *all* factors and, it is further required, in order to realize a Pareto optimum,

[24] Whereas Meade's expression for I(a) is $\begin{cases} x_1 = H_1(L_1, C_1, x_2) \\ x_2 = H_2(L_2, C_2) \end{cases}$

that for I(b) is $\begin{cases} x_1 = H_1(L_1, C_1, x_2) \\ x_2 = H_2(L_2, C_2, x_1) \end{cases}$

where x_1 is honey output, x_2 is apple output, and L_1, L_2, and C_1, C_2, are the amounts of labor used in honey producing and in apple growing, and the amounts of capital used in honey producing and in apple growing, in that order.

that the *SVMP* of each factor be the same in all alternative uses. In a perfectly competitive situation there will, of course, be only one price for each class of factor so that the latter condition is realized if the *SVMP* of each factor is proportional to its factor price—though, for simplicity, and to avoid unnecessary controversy, we can say *equal* to its factor price.[25] If we began with this condition prevailing in every sector of the economy except in the A and B industries where *VMP*'s only were equal to corresponding factor prices, on recognizing that the *SVMP*'s in apple farming exceeded their *VMP*'s, these *SVMP*'s may be made equal to the ruling factor prices only by expanding apple output relative to the outputs of other goods including that of honey. *Per contra,* since for the honey industry, apple blossom though beneficial is a scarce resource whose invariance leads to diminishing average returns to capital and labor in that industry, honey output of the competitive honey industry would have to be reduced in order that the *SVMP*'s of those factors be equal to their ruling prices.

This analysis may be cast in a yet more familiar form. It is well known that from the above factor condition we can easily deduce a corresponding condition for optima in terms of product units: that, in the production of all goods, outputs must be such that price is equal to social marginal cost.[26] Inasmuch as a part of the market marginal cost in the A industry is offset by the value it contributes to the B industry, A's social marginal cost curve lies below its corresponding market curve, the socially optimum output therefore exceeds the equilibrium output. If the B industry is competitively organized, as we assume, apple blossom is treated as a free good and we require a curve marginal to the supply curve (which is rising, even though rents imputable to scarce apple blossom are excluded) in order to determine the optimal honey output.

Now these product, or factor, conditions by themselves suffice

[25] Reasons for the view that proportionality is sufficient, even in the absence of fixed factor supplies, are given in [**II**, see especially pp. 208–212].

[26] Although this is the more familiar condition when couched in terms of product units, it is no less valid, as in Pigou's treatment [**13**], to deduce the condition that the social marginal value of the product be equal to its (market) marginal cost, in which the word *social* requires that we add to, or subtract from, the market value of the product the marginal effects on all other products. What is incorrect, however, is to equate marginal social product with marginal social cost, since it would involve counting the same external effects twice.

to determine optimal outputs. And it does not advance matters to treat the service of capital in any of these cases as a residual factor (as the reward of the entrepreneur, or the hiring agent) which has to be taxed in order that the complementary factors may receive more than their *VMP*'s on the assumption that factor payments exhaust the product. If, in a full-employment economy, an industry is to receive an excise subsidy there are any number of ways of collecting the required revenue, each with effects on income distribution—which redistribution effects may be ignored in the pursuit of the purely allocative problem of meeting the Pareto conditions.[27] Thus the exhaustion of the product problem has relevance only for the distributional aspects of welfare, not for the purely allocative aspect that is being investigated by Meade. This being the case, the particular type of production function—in particular whether returns to scale are constant, diminish or increase—is irrelevant to the allocative analysis.[28]

[27] There are, to be sure, allocative problems associated with the raising of taxes; for instance, it can be argued that a poll tax is, on allocative grounds, superior to an income tax which is superior to an unequal system of excise taxes. If there are such problems then, clearly, a Pareto optimum is not realized until the conditions are met in the raising of revenues also, but this contingency is quite consistent with the distinction between distributional and allocative effects. Concern with the problem of product exhaustion is unambiguously distributional.

[28] To elaborate this last point in connection with Meade's examples, although the character of the production functions may well be of interest for various reasons, it is not *per se* central to this question of external effects. What is central is the existing organization of the market. To be specific: we do not discover the existence of an external economy in apple production from the information that the output of honey is homogeneous of degree one in capital, labor, and apple blossom, and homogeneous of less than degree one in capital and labor alone. For if all honey producers became aware of the need for apple blossom as a complementary input in honey production, any increase in the demand for honey without a corresponding increase in the demand for apples would be met at a lower cost by those firms which produced both honey and apples (assuming the price of apples to remain unchanged as output increased somewhat).

Industry A, in effect, is producing a joint product, apples and apple blossom. If the blossom could be sold separately, we should indeed have a demand schedule for each of the joint products and the sum of their prices in equilibrium would give the true social valuation of one apple plus the accompanying blossom. At this equilibrium, therefore, the optimal output is realized, since if we subtract the demand price for blossom from the marginal cost of apples-plus-blossom, we are left with the social marginal cost of an apple alone exactly equal to its demand price. External effects have been "internalized" into the price mechanism. Similar remarks apply no less to production functions homogeneous of degree greater than one. If such increasing return industries were competitively organized their equilibrium outputs would be below optimum. The government might then have to rectify matters by granting an *ad valorem* subsidy to such industries. If, on the other hand, any of these industries were controlled by perfectly dis-

Finally, since any excess *SVMP* over the factor price in A has been made to vanish by expanding the output in question, it would be appropriate either to pay a subsidy to apple farmers according to the number of factors hired or to offer them an excise subsidy on the apples, financing this transfer in any way we choose (provided, of course, that the tax-raising techniques do not conflict with the universal fulfillment of the optimum conditions). Similarly, and in so far as external diseconomies prevail internal to the production of honey by reason of the limited amount of apple blossom, the contraction of output (from the market equilibrium) required to equate the *SVMP*'s of the hired factors to their corresponding prices calls for a tax on the hire of factors in the honey industry, or an excise tax on the honey. Thus the specific method used to transform the market equilibrium output set into the optimal output set is a problem that is conceptually distinct from the allocative problem under discussion. Too much attention to it has frequently led, as in this case, to unnecessary complications or restrictions in the application of the optimal conditions.[29]

The introduction of reciprocal external effects, as in Meade's example I(b), detracts in no way from the above remarks, though obviously the estimating of such effects will, in practice, be more difficult. Each industry must be induced (a) to take account of the advantage external to itself that it confers on the other and, inasmuch as they are both perfectly competitive industries, (b) to take into account also the diseconomies internal to itself of expanding its output if the useful by-product it receives is scarce. If the *SVMP*'s of each factor in the two industries A and B exceed their *VMP*'s in the same proportion, then no change of outputs would be called for provided these industries comprised the whole economy. If, however, they are only a small part of the economy, as is assumed here, they will have to expand at the expense of the rest of the economy.

Let us now turn briefly to Meade's two examples of "atmosphere-creation." For example II(a), we regard industry A as wheat farming, and industry B as timber growing. Again we can

---

criminating monopolists, no external economies would be evident, and intervention could not be justified on purely allocative grounds.

[29] Some of the evidence for this statement may be found in [12, especially Chapter 3].

suppose land is free, the only paid factors being labor and capital. Constant returns to scale are observed in each industry, but if the level of timber output is increased the output of wheat is raised due to the rain-inducing effect of trees. If we include timber, therefore, in the wheat production function, it would appear that it has increasing returns to scale. As in the first example, Meade derives an expression to show that the *SVMP*'s of labor and capital in timber exceed their corresponding *VMP*'s by the value added to wheat production in virtue of their rain-inducing effect. As in the preceding example, timber output should be expanded until the *SVMP* of each factor there is equal to that factor's price, either through subsidizing the hire of factors in timber production or through payment of a subsidy per unit of timber equal, at each timber output, to the marginal value that timber ultimately contributes to the value of wheat. Other schemes for reaching an optimal position may be more feasible, including a merger between industries that would effectively internalize these otherwise external effects.

In II(b) we have the case where, in addition to timber encouraging wheat output, wheat output has beneficial effects on the growth of timber.[30] So again, "the infinite chain of action and reaction" can be solved by simultaneous equations, otherwise the substance of the argument remains unchanged. The *SVMP* of all factors are above their *VMP*'s, and if they are above by the same proportion then there is no need to change the level of outputs in A and B provided that A and B industries comprise the whole economy. If, on the other hand, they are but a segment of the whole economy, both timber and wheat expand at the expense of products in the remaining sectors.[31]

[30] Whereas in the II(a) example the equations take the form:

$$\begin{cases} x_1 = H_1(L_1, C_1)A(x_2) \\ x_2 = E_2(L_2, C_2) \end{cases}$$

(x_1 being wheat output and x_2 being timber)

in the II(b) example they are written: $\begin{cases} x_1 = H_1(L_1, C_1)A(x_2) \\ x_2 = H_2(L_2, C_2)A_2(x_1) \end{cases}$

There does not seem to be any good reason for not writing them in the form $x = H\ (L, C, x)$ as in the "unpaid factor" case.

[31] It should be noticed in passing that industries A and B are now to be recognized as increasing-returns-to-scale industries; thus the sum of the factor payments when optimal outputs are produced—when factor prices equal *SVMP* in each industry—will necessarily exceed the total value of the outputs in A and

A final case III considered by Meade is that in which the output of these two industries depends directly on the total employment between them of a given class of factor. For instance, an increase in the total labor force could improve the efficiency of production in each industry.[32] Constant returns to scale for each industry are apparent only if this positive relation between the labor force and efficiency is ignored. But when we allow for it, labor's *SVMP* exceeds its *VMP*. A per unit subsidy for the competitive industries is required in order to expand employment to the point where the *SVMP* of labor equals the ruling wage-rate.

In conclusion it seems doubtful whether it is worth pressing Meade's distinction between I, II, and III. The classification into "unpaid factor" and "atmosphere" is too particularized to offer a general analytic distinction. After all, the essence of an external effect in the production case is the existence of an unpaid factor or, to use the appropriate Pigovian nomenclature "uncompensated services or disservices." Irrespective of the other characteristics of the relevant production functions, whenever increases in the output of industry A raise the output of industry B, the *VMP*'s of all A's factors are to be revised upward proportionally. If some but not all of A's factors affect B's output either directly, or in connection with B's factors, the *VMP*'s of such A factors may have to be revised in different proportions.

E. We turn now to an interesting feature brought out in Meade's simple first example I(a) in which the bees of B industry feed on the by-product, apple blossom, of the A industry. Although the external effect runs in one direction only, from A to B, the output of both industries may require correction—that of industry A which generates the effect because its activities influence B's level of production, and industry B which absorbs this effect—at least if the production of B is competitively organized (so that long period equilibrium positions are along the industry's average rather than its marginal supply curve). This implication invites consideration

---

B, unless they are engaged in price discrimination which is, however, precluded by the assumption of competition. While they remain separate industries, they can be induced to produce optimal outputs only if they are subsidized.

[32] Meade's equations for this case are:

$$x_1 = H_1[L_1, A(L_1 + L_2), C_1]$$
$$x_2 = H_2[L_2, A(L_1 + L_2), C_2]$$

of circumstances in which either the output of A or B alone, or neither, requires correction.

It should be noticed that in the I(a) example, the external economy generated varies directly with A's output. Industry B absorbs the external economy—its cost curve shifts downward—but, because perfectly competitive, it produces so as to manifest an external diseconomy internal to the industry. Nonetheless, external effects that vary with output do not provide a *sufficient* condition for allocative significance—for correction of outputs notwithstanding perfectly competitive pricing. If, for example, the apple blossom resulting from A's activities was, relative to B's requirements, so abundant that diminishing returns to B's paid factors did not set in, adjustment in neither industry's output would be required. In such circumstances we may (following a suggestion by Buchanan and Stubblebine [**1**]) regard the external economy generated by A as "infra-marginal," inasmuch as a sufficient *reduction* in A's output would bring it within range of its influencing again B's total production. By the same logic we might call the external effect absorbed by B "ultra-marginal" on grounds that a sufficient *expansion* of B's output would make apple blossom once again a scarce input, and which, being used without payment in a competitive industry, would result in a divergence between *SVMP* and *VMP*. However, so long as apple blossom is, like "the casing air," free and general, it should be treated accordingly and priced at zero.

Nor is variation with respect to output a *necessary* condition for allocative significance. Imagine a competitive industry C which, in order to produce any output at all, generates a fixed volume of noise, which noise impedes the efficiency of labor employed in a neighboring and competitive industry D. Only if the net returns which a perfectly discriminating monopolist could extract from the C industry exceeded the cost of the damage should industry C be permitted to operate at the normal competitive output: otherwise it should cease to produce altogether.[33] As for industry D's

[33] Although the cost of the noise damage is an overhead it should not be charged to industry C as an overhead since it would have the long-run effect of reducing C's output to the point at which price was equal to average cost including this overhead. This adjustment would be incorrect since, from this reduced output, any reexpansion of C's output would not be accompanied by

output, if the same proportional reduction in the efficiency of each laborer is assumed there will be a parallel upward shift of the average variable cost curve with a consequent reduction in the volume of D's production.[34] No correction of D's new market equilibrium is necessary since at this output the resulting increase in price is equal to the increase in marginal factor cost.

If, on the other hand, C generated a fixed volume of smoke which, though it initially lowered the efficiency of D's labor force, became less damaging to labor's efficiency the greater the expansion of D's output, the higher average costs of producing D good would decline with increases in its output. And this is allocatively significant for a competitive industry D which would contract its output to the point where average cost equals price, a smaller output than the optimal output at which price equals marginal cost for the industry. One could concoct further examples, but enough has been said to suggest a useful four-fold classification resting on two separate distinctions: that between the industry generating and the industry absorbing the external effect on the one hand, and, on the other hand, that between output variable and overhead external effects.

1. Overhead external effects generated by industry A and also by the recipient industry B.
2. Overhead external effects generated by A but experienced as output-variable external effects internal to the competitive B industry.
3. Output-variable external effects generated by A but experienced as an overhead external effect by B.
4. Ouput-variable external effects generated by A and also by the recipient industry B.

---

additional noise damage and indeed would initially create market value in excess of marginal factor cost.

[34] No losses are suffered by D industry in its new equilibrium since in the long run all factors are mobile, and those no longer employed there continue to receive the ruling rate of return in other lines of production. Even if C were legally compelled to compensate the owners of D, the sum paid over would not induce any expansion in D's output. It would appear as a transfer payment from the owners of C to those of D. The only welfare justification of any such transfer in those circumstances would be on distributional grounds; for instance, a transfer to the consumers who suffer a loss of "surplus" in virtue of the higher price and output-reduction of the D good.

These external effects may be economies or diseconomies, and any of these four cases could be, though in the particular circumstances may or may not be, allocatively significant.[35]

F. Instead of discussing external effects as between industries, Davis and Whinston [**3**] choose to work with two competitive firms A and B,[36] with the interrelation expressed in terms of cost curves rather than in terms of the production function. The total cost of the product in each firm depends, in general, on the quantities produced by both firms.

Estimating welfare as the difference between social benefit (which they measure by the price of the product) and social cost[37] the exercise consists (i) in showing that the private maximum net revenue does not always maximize welfare as defined (which nobody will deny) and, more important, (ii) in showing that under

[35] An example of 1 would be a project for a single giant airliner the vibration from which made it impossible to operate a pottery industry. Only if the net profit that could be realized by a perfectly discriminating monopolist operating the airliner was large enough to cover the cost of compensation of all net pottery value foregone (equal also to the net revenue extractable by a perfectly discriminating monopolist) should it be built.

An example of 2 would be the pollution of a river in a degree that is invariant to the output of a large works, and has the effect of increasing the cost of fish proportionally to the catch. If the gains from maintaining the works (as measured above) exceed the fishing losses and if this were the only river providing fish to the economy, the new market equilibrium would reveal a reduction in the output and a rise in the price of fish which would not require correction.

An example of 3 would be Pigou's factory whose smoke damage varied with its output, but which falls as an overhead on the neighboring population.

An example of 4 could be Meade's apple blossom and bee-honey case, producing at levels that made external economies allocatively significant for both industries. Alternatively, we could turn to his example of rain-inducing timber production which increases wheat output. Although timber should be expanded to the point at which price is equal to social marginal cost, no correction to the consequent equilibrium output of wheat need be contemplated if the effect imparted to wheat is proportional to its total production; or, in other words, if the average cost curve is shifted proportionally downward.

[36] The reasons given for this decision may not convince everyone: (1) the firm is an entity that fits more easily into the analysis, (2) firms are the decision units, (3) external effects may involve aspects of duopoly which remain even when the number of firms expands, (4) using the firm as an entity gives greater generality than the traditional approach, (5) we do not run into the aggregation problem.

[37] But if the two firms are in competitive long-run equilibrium, average inclusive cost is equal to price, and therefore maximum profits are zero. On this interpretation welfare would be zero—which makes more sense if two competitive firms produce a negligible part of the total output than if a duopoly situation is envisaged. Nevertheless, since the necessary condition for a welfare maximum, whatever the market organization, is that price-equal-social-marginal cost, we need have no hesitation in going along with their analysis.

certain conditions the popular tax-subsidy proposal is impractical.

The aspect of the problem treated under the first proposition is that of mutual dependence. If in general one writes the two cost functions for A and B respectively as:

$$(1)\quad \begin{cases} c_1 = c_1(q_2, q_1) \\ c_2 = c_2(q_2, q_1) \end{cases}$$ (where the c's are total costs, the q's are output quantities, and the subscripts 1 and 2 refer to firms A and B respectively),

then the necessary condition for a welfare maximum is price = inclusive marginal cost for each firm. Thus, for

$$\left.\begin{aligned} \text{firm A, } p &= \frac{\partial c_1}{\partial q_1} + \frac{\partial c_2}{\partial q_1} \\ \text{and for firm B, } p &= \frac{\partial c_2}{\partial q_2} + \frac{\partial c_1}{\partial q_2} \end{aligned}\right\} \qquad (2)$$

Each firm, however, ignores the effect on the marginal cost of the other firm of any variations in its own output. Firm A, for instance, ignores the value of $\partial c_2/\partial q_1$ since this affects only the cost of B's output. And as a separate firm B cannot control the value of $\partial c_2/\partial q_1$, though necessarily the value of this term must affect its total profit. Acting as profit maximizers only, firm A sets $p = \partial c_1/\partial q_1$, and firm B sets $p = \partial c_2/\partial q_2$.

Clearly it is only when $\partial c_2/\partial q_1 = \partial c_1/\partial q_2 = 0$ that the profit-maximizing outputs of the two firms coincide with the welfare-maximizing outputs in equations (2). However, since we are dealing with external effects, the value of these terms cannot be zero. There will, therefore, be a divergence between the profit-maximizing outputs and the welfare-maximizing outputs of the two firms.

Furthermore, the cost functions in (1) may take either of two forms, "separable" or "nonseparable." If the former, they are written

$$\left.\begin{aligned} c_1 &= f_1(q_1) + g_1(q_2) \\ c_2 &= f_2(q_2) + g_2(q_1) \end{aligned}\right\} \qquad (1a)$$

A's profit-maximizing output is unique since its marginal cost, $\partial f_1/\partial q_1$, depends only on A's output q_1. Nevertheless, its profit depends upon B's output; in fact on the term $\partial g_1/\partial q_2$. It is inferred therefore that variations in B's output have the result of vertically displacing A's *total* cost curve—though clearly without altering the uniquely determined profit-maximizing output given by the familiar tangency condition. The impact of this external effect on A's output is, then, strictly intra-marginal. Analogous remarks apply to firm B.

This unique determination of profit-maximizing outputs irrespective of the action of the other firm is associated, by the authors, with the game theory of dominance.[38]

The nonseparable cost functions, on the other hand, cannot be split into the sum of two separate functions each containing the output of one firm only as in (1a) above. No general form of the nonseparable function is furnished by the authors, but it is clear that in any specific form it must contain a term involving the product of q_1 and q_2 in order that the *marginal* cost of, say, firm A, $\partial c_1/\partial q_1$, be a function not only of q_1, its own output, but also of the level of B's output, q_2, which obviously adds to the firm's difficulties in finding its profit-maximizing output.

The authors go on to associate this nonseparable case (entailing interdependence of maximizing outputs) with nondominance in game theory, since this interdependence, or absence of row-column dominance, is the "essence of nondominance." As in the analysis of duopoly, there is no widely accepted method of determining the firms' outputs (at least not without positing further information concerning expectations).

The chief conclusion reached by the authors is that although the "classical tax-subsidy solution" is difficult to achieve in the separable case, since the government would have to obtain sufficient information to determine optimal outputs for both firms through a solution of simultaneous equations,[39] such a solution is almost

[38] The pay-off matrix with which they illustrate the opportunities facing two such firms, though interesting in itself, seems to me to have only a superficial and formal connection with the substance of their preceding analysis. In game theory firms no longer maximize with known demand and cost functions; they are minimizing given discrete alternatives, under conditions of uncertainty regarding the stratagem to be adopted by the other firm.

[39] Indeed, each time there is a change in the demand conditions or in the existing technology, recomputation would be necessary. Provided the market structure remains competitive—so that each firm treats the price as a parameter—a profit-maximizing merger would be mutually beneficial and would also ensure optimal outputs.

impossible to achieve in the nonseparable case. True, the welfare outputs are determinate and are, in principle, solvable by simultaneous equations, but the outputs that the two firms seek to adopt are not determinate (as they are in the separable case). And this makes it practically impossible for the government to calculate optimal taxes or subsidies. In that case a merger which "internalized" the external effects might be the more practical solution.

The importance of this contribution appears to me to turn on two empirical questions: 1. An obvious question arising from the authors' distinction: viz. whether the external effect arising from, say, B's output is such that it alters A's overheads but not its variable costs or, put otherwise, that it alters A's total cost though not its marginal cost; or whether it alters A's marginal cost also. 2. Whether such external effects—generated by either separable or nonseparable cost functions—move generally in one direction only; for example, an external effect, imposed on A by B, though not on B by A. Or whether such external effects are, as in the authors' treatment, more commonly reciprocal.

I should think that a good part of the practical difficulties emphasized by Davis and Whinston may be attributed to the mutuality assumption in their analysis rather than to nonseparability proper. Indeed, one of the features of the familiar examples of external effects which one tends to associate with the "classical tax-subsidy solution"—for instance, some of Pigou's external diseconomies (smoky factories and sparking engines)—is the determinate change of competitive output necessary to realize ideal output once the external effect in question is introduced. The tax-subsidy adjustment was not implausible simply because the external effect was deemed to run one way only.[40]

It is the mutuality of the external effects, in short, that is the villain of the piece. In such cases one can agree that a merger may be the least expensive solution. Since it is in the direct interests of both firms it is also likely to come about in the absence of penalizing legislation.

[40] If such effects were uni-directional, say from B to A only, and also *separable*, then indeed no correction of A's profit-maximizing output would be necessary, though correction of the output of B, which is generating the external effect, would be required.

If, on the other hand, the damage is unilateral—which, I am suggesting, has been the more common supposition—then, in the case of a diseconomy, it is in the interest of the damaged party alone to approach the damaging party in the hope of bribing him to reduce the activities causing the damage. However, in the production-on-consumption diseconomies, such as the smoky factory instance, the group who are damaged may be too large and too widely dispersed to organize themselves effectively. In such instances the government can expedite matters by taking the initiative.

G. In a learned paper, replete with case law, Coase [**2**] criticizes what he believes to be the "traditional approach" to the problems of damages inflicted by one firm on another—external diseconomies of production-on-production.

He begins by pointing out that any restraint imposed on B, the firm that damages another firm A, is obviously also a hindrance on B's operation. The real question is whether B should be allowed to harm A, or A to harm B.[41] There follows some detailed discussion of an example in which steers bought by a cattle-raiser cause increasing marginal crop losses to an adjacent farm. Given the assumption of constancy for both the product price and the variable factor price, three things finally emerge: (1) that in general it does not matter who has to compensate whom in the determination of the optimum output.[42] It is the same optimal output whether the cattleman is by law compelled to pay the farmer for the damage caused by his steers, or whether the farmer takes the initiative in bribing the cattleman to buy fewer steers.[43] (2) If factors can move into alternative occupations without loss, the esti-

[41] Later on, Coase tells us that the courts are usually aware of the mutuality of inconvenience, and the general doctrine has been that, since economic activity tends to promote welfare, people in the vicinity must put up with some "not unreasonable" degree of discomfort. This is doubtless an interesting fact about the courts' response to the problem. But what is the answer of the economist to this question? Coase does not provide the solution, and, indeed, it cannot be provided in a purely allocative context. However, by invoking distributional effects, criteria for such problems may be provided, as shown in [**10**].

[42] In the production-on-production case in which firms are profit-maximizers, this is valid if one is concerned only with allocative issues (and is not interested in the distribution of welfare). But it should be apparent that where the individual or group is involved, different welfare effects as between conflicting groups can make a difference in the optimal output according as a question of who compensates whom is answered.

[43] In so far as market arrangements arise "spontaneously," those who suffer injury must, in effect, bribe those who inflict it.

mate of the damage in question has reference only to loss of the rents of the unmovable factor.[44] (3) Compensation equal to this estimate of damage is an upper limit: alternative ways of combating the damage, or reducing it, may be available, and these, if they cost less, should be adopted in the interests of maximizing the value of the social product with given resources. In the example above, the cattle-raiser would be ready to pay $1 for a fence rather than $2 to the cattleman to avoid crop damage. All these points are well taken.

Four law cases follow, which seem to illustrate the uncertainties of the law rather than ambiguity in the current economic doctrine, after which the respective costs of market arrangements and administrative arrangements are taken into account since, according to Coase, economists have tended to overestimate the advantages of government regulation. The unexceptionable conclusion is reached that the cheapest method of adjustment to optimal output should always be employed.

There is then a digression purporting to reveal the inadequacy of Pigou's position, as understood by Coase, that additional state action is required to remedy market imperfections, an inadequacy he believes is demonstrated by Pigou's example of divergence between private and social net product arising from damage done to a surrounding wood by the sparks from a railway engine. Pigou's argument that the railways should be obliged to compensate for the damages caused is not accepted by Coase who continually emphasizes the costs of reaching and maintaining business agreements. If there were no costs involved in reaching agreements with people having property adjoining the railway line, it would not matter whether the railway were made liable for

[44] If an additional steer caused crop damage of $12 a year estimated at existing market prices, and $10 of the costs of that crop is labor, the remaining $2 being a rent to the farmer-owner, it should be a matter of indifference to the farmer-owner whether (i) damages awarded him $12 *provided* he continued to cultivate the patch of land in question exactly as before, or whether (ii) damages awarded to him were only $2, but with no conditions attached—in which case he would abandon its cultivation. However, it is not a matter of indifference so far as allocation is concerned. If option (i) were adopted, the final contribution of $10 worth of labor to growing crops on this patch of land is nothing, since anything produced is doomed to destruction by the additional steer, whereas if that much labor were transferred elsewhere it would contribute $10 to the social product. If, on the other hand (ii) were adopted, only when the profit on the additional steer exceeded $2 would the land be taken over for cattle-raising rather than crop-raising.

damages or not.[45] But if it were too expensive to reach such agreements, would it then be socially desirable to make the railways legally liable for damage? If we may ignore the cost of implementing the law, the conclusion that Coase appears to reach[46] is that to make the railways liable could result in a greater cultivation of crops than if they were not liable, and a greater cultivation than is socially warranted. For in the latter case the landowners would be indifferent whether their crops were damaged or not. They would continue to cultivate all damageable areas, including, therefore, those areas in which the damage exceeded the cost of the movable factors. The correct procedure in such cases, concludes Coase, is to estimate the total social product yielded by alternative arrangements.

The argument seems unnecessarily ingenious. Assuming divisibilities, if "reasonable" compensation were to be paid by the railways, land would be withdrawn from cultivation whenever the damage exceeded the "profit" (or rent) of that land. And reasonable compensation should not, of course, exceed the total loss of "profits" (or rent) from the land. Indeed, this dictum is in accordance with the conclusions of Coase's own extended treatment of the example of crop-damaging steers.[47] Nor does it matter whether these compensating payments—reckoned as the value of the

[45] If the railway were not legally liable for damage, all agreements reached would involve some transfer from landowners to the railway companies in consideration of the companies' taking action to reduce potential damage to the land.

[46] I say "appears" to reach, because the lengthy, indefinite, and somewhat repetitious arguments on pp. 31–34 of his paper [**2**] are difficult to assimilate. On p. 31 Coase writes that "it also seems likely that he [Pigou] was mistaken in his economic analysis." On pp. 32–33, he asserts that "A change from a regime in which the railway is *not* liable for damage to one in which it *is* liable is likely therefore to lead to an increase in the amount of cultivation on lands adjoining the railway. It will also, of course, lead to an increase in the amount of crop destruction due to railway-caused fires." Finally, on p. 34 he asks, "How is it that the Pigovian analysis seems to give the wrong answer?" And he goes on to assert that Pigou did not notice that his analysis was dealing with "an entirely different question"; that the analysis as such is correct, but the conclusions illegitimate; that a "comparison of private and social products is neither here nor there"; and that "the proper procedure is to compare the total social product yielded by these different arrangements." The exact interpretation of these seemingly elusive arguments is, however, less important for our purpose than the establishing of the essential correctness of Pigou's analysis in those circumstances where the costs of implementing arrangements may be ignored.

[47] Of course, if the market-value compensation to be paid to the landowner were always *conditional* upon his actually cultivating the land that is expected to be damaged by engine sparks then Coase's conclusion would follow. But I find no evidence for interpreting Pigou's proposals in this fashion.

"profits," or rents forgone—are paid by the railway to the landowners or by the landowners to the railways. In either case the correct output will be reached.[48]

The reemphasis put by Coase on certain propositions should help to combat superficial misunderstandings about social cost;[49] their calculation is, in practice, very difficult, and implementation of any new arrangements, whether by the government or "through the market," carries costs which should not exceed the apparent reduction in the loss of social value in the hypothetical case of costless readjustments. Nevertheless, throughout the paper the impression was conveyed (though perhaps unintentionally) that the existence of alternative methods for reducing social diseconomies was a consideration that somehow vitiated the essential Pigo-

[48] In the absence of any legal liability by the railways, if one acre of wheat land (with no alternative use) is damaged by engine sparks to the extent of $8, and if $5 is the "profit" or rent of that acre, it would be taken out of cultivation in order to limit the loss to $5. If the railways could reduce this damage to zero by taking off one coach, and if the profit of that coach were estimated at less than $5, then it would pay the landowner to compensate the railways fully for the removal of that coach. If the profit on that coach exceeded $5, however, the landowners would find it cheaper to take that acre of land out of cultivation and suffer a loss of $5. Since this hypothetical behavior minimizes social loss, it is the correct allocative solution.

The same result, however, would occur if the railways were legally compelled to compensate the landowners for running the "marginal" coach. If the additional profit yielded by the extra coach exceeded $5, it would pay to compensate the landowner to the extent of $5 and run the coach. If, on the other hand, the profit on that coach were less than $5 it would pay them to remove the last coach.

To put it in a nutshell, the question to be asked is simply whether more value is created by allowing the marginal coach to run and inflict this damage or by removing the coach and growing the crops. And, at market prices, the answer is the same irrespective of which side has to compensate the other.

[49] In a minor key are some lengthy criticisms of Pigou's analysis. My impression is that such criticisims arise from focusing on one or two passages to the neglect of the relevant chapters as a whole. Although it would be out of proportion to deal with such textual criticisms in a short survey of recent developments, I should like to give one example:

Coase draws attention to Pigou's remark that factory owners installing antismoke devices render to the community uncompensated services—implying, according to Coase, that such factories should be subsidized. (Even if this were so, any concern over it must be on distributional grounds, since such subsidy would be quite consistent with an optimal output). However, if the reader consults p. 184 of *The Economics of Welfare* [**13**], I think he will go along with me in affirming that Pigou's sentence construction there was perhaps chiefly to blame for this misinterpretation. Nonetheless not only does Pigou point out at the bottom of the page that this smoke inflicts a heavy uncharged loss on the community, but the footnotes on the same and on the following page make it unmistakable that the factory owners who do *not* install antismoke devices are deemed responsible for inflicting damage on the local population. The analysis, therefore, calls for the installation of such devices from their net revenues, or for the curtailing of output to the point where price equals social marginal cost.

vian doctrine that optimal outputs entail equality in all uses of the social value of the marginal net products of the factors, and that when the market solution did not yield this equality, government intervention to promote optimal outputs by various devices, including taxes and subsidies, should be considered. This is far from being the case, however, and since a point of substance is at issue, it is worth devoting a paragraph to its exposition.

Whatever the optimal adjustment happens to be in the face of inescapable external diseconomies, their existence implies that society is worse off than it would be if the world were such that these diseconomies did not accompany the production of certain goods. Consider the academically favored case of a smoky factory in which damage done is positively related to the factory's output, and let us suppose further that in consequence proper action has been taken and output curtailed to the point where the excess of marginal valuation (given by the market price) over marginal cost is large enough to just cover the value of the marginal social damage. At this optimal output the sum of money that would just compensate for the social damage sustained is a correct index of the inescapable net loss of social value attributable to the manufacture of the product[50]—regardless of whether the loss is borne by the local population, by the manufacturer, or by the community as a whole through the incidence of direct taxation. If it now transpired that the group adversely affected were willing to move from the neighborhood for a sum smaller than this, the minimum sum they would accept as compensation would represent the net loss of social value resulting from the external diseconomy. Again, if a completely effective antismoke device were invented that was yet cheaper than compensating payments for migrants its installation (with output reexpanded to the point where price-equals-market-marginal cost) would entail a yet smaller net loss of social value—regardless, as always, of who actually foots the bill for these devices. It should also be apparent that adoption of the lowest cost method of dealing with inevitable external diseconomies is required by the Pareto condition for an optimum: namely, that aggregate

[50] This sum can be represented diagrammatically by the area between the market marginal cost curve and the social marginal cost curve above it over a range from the price-axis to the socially optimal output.

social value cannot be increased by any reshuffling of the productive factors at the disposal of the economy.

H. We can wind up this survey with some brief comments on the short paper by James M. Buchanan and Wm. Craig Stubblebine [**1**] which, though following the traditional treatment, aimed to clear up some popular misapprehensions about external effects, in particular those that fall into the consumption-on-consumption category. In connection with variable external effects, they draw a useful distinction between wholly *infra*-marginal external effects which—as we saw in section E—require no modification of the competitive output, and marginal external effects which are "Pareto relevant" or "allocatively significant" in our usage where output can be altered so that everyone concerned could be made better off. If there is an eventual loss of A's welfare associated with some further increase in B's activity (or consumption) it becomes necessary, in order to achieve an optimal position, to reduce B's output (thereby reducing A's loss) until B's excess valuation per dollar of cost is large enough to equal A's (now smaller) loss of marginal valuation per dollar of cost.[51]

What is emphasized in the paper is that Pareto optimality is consistent with the continued existence of the external effect (contrary to slipshod usage that gives the impression that an external effect has always to be "removed" before an optimum is reached), and that, ignoring "income effects," the decision as to which party compensates the other does not affect the optimal output. The law might compel B to compensate A for damages. Without the law, however, it would still be in A's interest to bribe B to move to this optimal point.

IV

A word in conclusion. The most that can be expected from a critical survey of this sort is some disclosure of further features

[51] This marginal case they illustrate with a nice example of B's choosing the height of a fence, H_B, to build between his garden and A's garden. This is much higher than the height H_A that would have been chosen by A. The optimal height is H_O, somewhere between H_A and H_B, and is that height at which the marginal valuation of A's loss is just equal to the marginal valuation of B's loss. No movement from this point can make both better off.

of interest in the over-all logical structure, some delineation of hitherto vaguely discerned connections and, perhaps, some classification that will sharpen the theoretical analysis of allocative problems. Allowing for the inevitable deficiencies, the picture that emerges is, I hope, coherent if not convincing. Certain patterns that at first seem unfamiliar or labored may, after reflection, appear acceptable enough or even obvious links in a routine elaboration of the traditional conceptual framework largely associated with the pioneer work of A. C. Pigou.

REFERENCES

1. Buchanan, J. M., and W. Craig Stubblebine. "Externality," *Economica* (November 1962).
2. Coase, R. H. "The Problem of Social Cost," *Journal of Law and Economics* (October 1960).
3. Davis, O. A., and A. Whinston. "Externalities, Welfare, and the Theory of Games," *Journal of Political Economy* (June 1962).
4. Duesenberry, J. *Income, Saving and the Theory of Consumer Behaviour.* Cambridge, Mass.: Harvard, 1949.
5. Ellis, H., and W. Fellner. "External Economies and Diseconomies," *American Economic Review,* Vol. 33 (1943). Reprinted in *Readings in Price Theory*. Chicago: Richard D. Irwin, 1952.
6. de V. Graaff, J. *Theoretical Welfare Economics.* Cambridge, Eng.: Cambridge, 1957.
7. Knight, F. H. "Some Fallacies in the Interpretation of Social Cost," *Quarterly Journal of Economics* (August 1924).
8. Marshall, Alfred. *Principles of Economics.* 8th ed. London: Macmillan, 1925.
9. Meade, J. "External Economies and Diseconomies in a Competitive Situation," *Economic Journal* (March 1962).
10. Mishan, E. J. "Criteria for External Effects," *American Economic Review* (September 1961).
11. Mishan, E. J. "Second Thoughts on Second Best," *Oxford University Papers* (October 1962). Reprinted in this volume. See pp. 141–156.
12. Oort, C. J. *Decreasing Cost as a Problem of Welfare Economics.* Amsterdam, 1958.
13. Pigou, A. C. *Economics of Welfare.* 4th ed. London: Macmillan, 1946.
14. Rosenstein-Rodan, P. N. "Problems of Industrialization of East and South-East Europe," *Economic Journal,* Vol. 53 (June 1943).
15. Scitovsky, T. "Two Concepts of External Economies," *Journal of Political Economy* (April 1954).
16. Viner, J. "Cost Curves and Supply Curves," *Zeitschrift für Nationalökonomie,* Vol. 3 (1931).

CHAPTER 8

Pareto Optimality and the Law*

Over the past few years it has been generally recognized that the nature of any optimal solution depends, for two quite different reasons, on the existing distribution of income [**10**]. Inasmuch as the distribution of income is itself influenced by legislation—through taxes and subsidies, through price regulation and controls, and through a vast and growing public expenditure on goods and services—the optimal solutions attainable must depend also upon the laws of a country. In a modern economy in which external effects are rapidly spreading, the influence of the law both on the determination and the attainment of optimal solutions makes itself felt in yet other ways. In cases of conflicting interest, according as the law, deliberately or by default, places the burden of reaching optimal arrangements on one party or group rather than the other, both the characteristics of the optimal outcome and the costs of its attainment are altered. And the more important, as a

* From *Oxford Economic Papers* (November 1967). Reprinted with the permission of the Clarendon Press, Oxford.

component of welfare, are the external effects in question, the greater, in these respects, is the impact of the law.

I

This paper, then, is concerned primarily with demonstrating (1) that the characteristics of an optimal solution are not uniquely specified but depend, in general, on the existing law, (2) that the costs incurred in realizing an optimal outcome, and the question therefore of its "feasibility," also depend upon the existing law, and finally (3) that an optimal solution emerging from conflicts of interest is optimal only with respect to an implicit constraint requiring the area in question to be used in common by the groups or persons having conflicting interests. Once separate areas, or separate facilities, are introduced solutions appear that are Pareto superior to the familiar constrained optimal outcomes. The first two propositions are particularly relevant in connection with external diseconomies which, when uncorrected, engender conflicts of interest. The expositional scheme used here, however, can just as well be extended to cover external economies.

Since the analysis has more heuristic than operational value, the problems of measurement are not touched upon. Nor do we introduce algorithms for determining solutions in the n-unit case. Again, though the treatment of external effects must be regarded as an exercise in partial statics, we circumvent familiar second-best obstacles by keeping to the path of *ceteris paribus* which, in this connection, requires that consequent changes in all prices, other than those directly under examination, be negligible: an "improvement" within the sector under survey is, therefore, on the Pareto principle, an improvement for the economy as a whole, irrespective of the condition of the economy prior to this improvement.

We introduce, in addition, a number of simplifications into the analysis which facilitate the exposition without restricting unduly the range of its applicability: (1) The activity, exemptions from which involve compensatory payments, is measured over a given period without reference to the pattern of its distribution within that period. (2) The income, or welfare, effects, with respect to the activity in question, are taken to be "normal." (3) The compensatory payments used throughout the paper are defined as compensating variations. (4) The money equivalent of the net benefits arising from any Pareto improvement within the area in question is in all cases passed on to the government for distribution outside that area. A few words about each of these:

1. Formally one can choose a period small enough as to make the question of the pattern of distribution within it appear trivial. But a limit is placed on the shortness of the period by the requirement, in any solution, that successive periods carry the same distributional pattern; for the characteristics of the solution must, within the framework of static analysis, be repeated in all periods. This neglect of the pattern of distribution within a period of minimum duration is convenient and frequently realistic, but not always. An example will be given in a later footnote to suggest how improvements may be brought about by changing the pattern of the distribution of the activity within the period.

2. A "normal" welfare effect, implying that an improvement in the individual's welfare raises his demand for the good, also implies that the maximum sum he will pay for a given amount of it (or, alternatively, the minimum sum he will accept to forgo a given amount of it) will rise with an increase in his welfare. It has the further implication that the maximum he will pay for a thing, provided the thing is a good,[1] is less than the minimum sum he will accept to forgo it.[2] Although the "normal" welfare effect is plausible for the sort of activities exemplified in this paper, the results do not in the least depend upon it.

3. In a general treatment of external effects—one that is not restricted to spillover effects that can be costed through the market—the distinction should be made between a compensating variation, *CV*, defined more generally as a measure of the money transfer necessary, following some economic change, to maintain the individual's welfare at his original level, and an equivalent variation, *EV*, defined more generally as a measure of the money transfer which, in the absence of the change in question, affords the individual an equivalent change in his welfare [**10**, p. 610]. Exactly

[1] If, instead, it were a "bad" there is a maximum sum he will pay to divest himself of it, and a minimum sum he will accept as compensation for bearing with it.

[2] A discussion of this implication will be found in my paper [**10**, p. 603].

the same distinction between *CV* and *EV* arises if we consider a reversal of some specific law from being, say, permissive with respect to an activity to being prohibitive.

To illustrate, if from a state of permissiveness with respect to smoking, a no-smoking order were introduced, the *CV* of a nonsmoker who gains from the change of law would be measured as a maximum sum per period, say $20, this being the amount he is willing to pay to have the permissive law reversed. The *EV* measure would be a transfer to him of some minimum amount, say $22, in lieu of the contemplated no-smoking order. If, later, the no-smoking order were revoked the *CV* would be a payment to him of this minimum sum, $22, while the *EV* would be a maximum sum of $20. The smoker's welfare is affected in the opposite way, but the pattern is equally symmetric.

Thus, if we are interested in the effects wrought by a reversal of the law, it would appear that for each person affected by the state of the law four measures of exact compensatory transfer are required; a *CV* and an *EV* corresponding to each of the two states of the law. However, it is evident from the above illustration that there is only a single difference notwithstanding the four measures, the individual's *CV* and *EV* for the introduction of the no-smoking order being equal, respectively, to the *EV* and *CV* for a reversal of that order. Hence, for two alternative states of the law, one the reverse of the other, we need consider only the *CV* or only the *EV*. And our choice, here, will be influenced by the definition of a Pareto improvement as one that makes everyone affected better off (or some better off and others no worse off), beginning from the status quo. By adopting the *CV* measure, rather than the *EV*, we enjoy the convenience of identifying a Pareto improvement with a positive sum arising from the algebraic total of the *CV*'s of all the individuals affected by the change in question. For those who are affected by a change can be divided into gainers and losers. The *CV* of each gainer is the maximum sum he would now pay (a sum which, if paid, would leave him no better off than he was before the change). The *CV* for each of the losers, on the other hand, is the minimum sum he can be made to accept as a quid pro quo (a sum which, if paid to him, would leave him no worse off then he was before the change). If, with respect to some change, the maximum sum the gainers would be willing to pay exceeds the minimum sum the losers would accept, that is, if the algebraic sum of the *CV*'s is positive, that change offers a Pareto improvement.[3]

Reversing the law, we shall still want to ask whether a Pareto improvement can be effected by a change from it. We must again ask, that is, whether the algebraic sum of the *CV*'s is positive.

4. In comparing the distribution of welfare in the initial situation under the existing law with that which would emerge if the laws were reversed, we begin in each case from a position in which the external effects are uncorrected. Those made better off in reversing the existing law will subsequently be made worse off if, later, the law reverts to its previous state. The important implication, to be demonstrated, is that the outcome of each decision rule which may realize a Pareto improvement starting from the initial situation (with external effects uncorrected) is not uniquely determined. In general such outcomes will depend upon the law under which potential Pareto improvements are envisaged. Granted this much, it becomes a matter of great convenience that when comparing, under the existing law, the magnitude of the gain from one arrangement B with that of a previous arrangement A, the individual *CV*'s continue to remain the same as those determined in the initial (uncorrected) situation notwithstanding any consequent redistribution of welfare resulting from the first, A, arrangement. Put otherwise, if the net benefit, *NB*, of an arrangement B, is the algebraic sum of the *CV*'s compared with the initial situation under the existing law, and the *NB* of an arrangement A is similarly defined, then it would be convenient to reckon the *excess* net benefit of B as compared with the net benefit of A as $\{NB(\text{B}) - NB(\text{A})\}$, where $NB(\text{B})$ and $NB(\text{A})$ are, respectively, the net benefits of B and of A, both measured with respect to the initial, uncorrected, situation. This desideratum may be accom-

[3] If, instead, we adopted the *EV* measure, the *EV* of each of the gainers from the change would involve a minimum sum to be paid to him (enough to compensate him to forgo the change). The *EV* of each loser, on the other hand, would involve a maximum payment from him (leaving him no better off than if he accepted the change). If the algebraic sum of the *EV*'s were negative, an over-all Pareto loss results from *not* introducing the change. This is awkward in respect both of sign and of interpretation—for this sum need not always be negative when the algebraic sum of the *CV*'s is positive.

plished by requiring that, after full compensation is paid within the group, the amount left over, the positive sum associated with an *NB* from any adopted arrangement, be paid in to the government which may distribute it among people in the rest of the economy, for instance among the poor there. No individual within the group affected, therefore, is left better off or worse off than he was in the initial situation under the existing law in virtue of a positive *NB* arising from an A, B, C, or D arrangement. Nonetheless any positive *NB* constitutes a Pareto improvement for the economy as a whole, on this scheme, inasmuch as no one in the group is worse off and some others in the rest of the economy are made better off.

II

Prior to a more general formulation we shall consider the fairly common case of a population of individuals, firms, or families, the members of which are located within a given area. Each member enjoys the product of his own activity while, in varying degrees, resenting the products of the same activity of others. An example which may help to fix our ideas is that of a beach daily occupied by individuals, or families, each of which enjoys the sound of his own radio while disliking the sounds generated by each of the others. No distortion of the central features of the analysis arises from supposing that, notwithstanding differences in location of neighboring radios, differences in volume or program, each individual dislikes equally the noise created by any r numbers of radios, which noise however is more objectionable to him, by a determinate amount, than the noise produced by any $(r - 1)$ radios.

The existing state of the law, which we assume is permissive, is denoted by L, the reverse state of that law, $\bar{L}$, being prohibitive. Whichever state of the law prevails, however, agreements reached by mutual consent to exempt one or more individuals from the existing law are always sanctioned. Under the permissive law L, then, each individual would have to be paid some minimum compensatory sum before agreeing to exempt himself from the existing freedom to play his own radio. On the other hand, in order to exempt some other individual from the existing law L, he is prepared to pay some maximum sum by way of compensation.[4]

We construct in Table 1 a simple numerical example, in which the relevant data under the L law for four individuals, W, X, Y, and Z, are shown.

W	−14	6	5	4	1
X	−33	9	7	3	−14
Y	−35	16	15	10	6
Z	−25	10	9	8	2

TABLE 1

The first positive figure, 6 in the W row, indicates the maximum sum individual W would pay to have the first other radio turned off, whether it be that of X, Y, or Z. The following figure, 5, is the maximum sum he is prepared to contribute as compensation for any second radio that is turned off. The last figure, 4, is the maximum sum he will pay for the last remaining radio (excluding his own) to be turned off. This diminishing magnitude of the positive row figures for each person implies the "normal" assumption of diminishing marginal utility (or, more precisely, marginal valuation) of a good—quiet, in this instance. The corresponding "normal" case implied under the $\bar{L}$ law is increasing marginal disutility of the "bad"—radio noise, in this instance. Thus, under the $\bar{L}$ law, the W row would read 14, −4, −5, −6. Since the broad conclusions to be reached in this section about the ranking of the outcomes A, B, C, and D, are not affected if, instead, we assumed increasing marginal utility of a good and diminishing marginal disutility of a bad, we confine ourselves throughout the paper to the "normal" case. Some particular features of the "perverse" case are, however, indicated in Appendix 1.

The −14 in the W row indicates that 14 is the minimum sum required by individual W as compensation for surrendering his right under the L law to play his radio; i.e., to exempt him from the L law. We may assume that this sum is invariant to the number of other radios that are playing.[5] All other rows are interpreted in the same way.

[4] If the exemption is agreed upon for a particular individual, it is agreed, that is, to preclude his radio from the beach. If the law instead were prohibitive, an exempted individual plays his radio freely.

[5] This "independence" assumption, stating that the value to the individual of

On the right hand side of the table is a column of figures, 1, −14, 6, 2, which are in fact the row totals. The figure 6 corresponding to the *Y* row, for example, being the total of compensatory sums proposed by *Y* to exempt every radio on the beach (including his own), is to be interpreted as the net value to *Y* of a reversal of the existing *L* law to $\bar{L}$. In other words, *Y* is prepared to pay a maximum sum of 6 to have the beach change from an area in which all radios are permitted to play into one in which all are prohibited from playing their radios. The total for the *X* row, −14, reveals the minimum sum, 14, which *X* would regard as adequate compensation for replacing the *L* law by the $\bar{L}$ law.

With this information, and provisionally ignoring all costs incurred in moving from the status quo to any other arrangement, let us appraise four alternative rules or methods for reaching a decision on whether, and how, to depart from the initial situation under the *L* law, in which everyone is playing his radio: A, single-outcome voting, B, single-outcome bargaining, C, Pareto mixed outcome, and D, a separate facilities outcome.

A. This rule requires each individual to vote whether or not to reverse the existing *L* law into the $\bar{L}$ law, a majority to carry the decision. Bargaining between them being prohibited, each individual only weighs the advantage of listening to his own radio against the disadvantage of being exposed to the sounds of all

---

playing his own radio is determined independently of the number of other radios that are playing, is not plausible. It is more reasonable to expect the value of his own radio playing to be enhanced as other radios are switched off.

Taking 33 to be the minimum sum acceptable to individual *X* for not playing his radio when all others are permitted to play, if the first alteration in the initial situation, that in which all four were playing, was agreement to have one individual, say *W*, turn off his radio, the minimum sum acceptable to *X* might now rise to 36. The additional 3 that *X*'s own radio playing is now worth could be added to the amount he is willing to pay for the first other radio to be turned off, making it 12 instead of 9. If another radio turned off added a further 3 to the worth of his own radio playing the next sum would be revised from 7 to 10, and so on. But this adjustment is possible only up to the point at which *X* itself is exempted, after which it becomes irrelevant. If, for example, *X*'s radio playing were excluded first, the positive figures would remain without revision. Without the independence assumption then, only when agreement has been reached on which individuals are to remain playing their radios, and which are not to play, are these negative numbers finally determined.

It is not, however, worth elaborating the problem to allow for this interdependence since, as we shall indicate in later footnotes, the qualitative results to be established do not depend on the independence assumption.

the others. If his row total is positive he votes for the $\bar{L}$ law, otherwise he votes for a continuation of the *L* law.

In our numerical example, individuals *W, Y,* and *Z* all vote for the $\bar{L}$ law, *Y* alone voting for a continuation of the *L* law. By the A decision rule, then, common agreement is secured to transform the permissive area into a prohibited area.

B. This decision rule differs from the one above in that each individual's vote no longer counts as one but, instead, is weighted according to the value of net advantage, or disadvantage, he attaches to a change from the *L* law. *W*, *Y*, and *Z* between them offer a maximum of 9 for the change to $\bar{L}$. Individual *X*, however, requires at least 14 as compensation.[6] In consequence the existing *L* law continues.

Under the provisional assumption of costless implementation of new arrangements, the B outcome can be regarded as Pareto superior to the A outcome, in that, wherever the B outcome differs from the A outcome, as it does in our example, it is possible to make everyone better off by substituting the B outcome for the A outcome. The A outcome in the above example, entails a negative *NB* of 5 for the group as a whole as compared with the initial situation, since a change to $\bar{L}$ makes *W, Y,* and *Z* better off by 9, a sum which, if paid to *X,* would fall short by 5 of adequately compensating him. Compared with the B arrangements, then, the A outcome leaves *X* worse off by 5 with *W, Y,* and *Z* no better off and is, consequently, Pareto inferior to B.

C. The Pareto mixed outcome differs from B in the device of exempting one or more individuals from the existing *L* law, the others remaining subject to that law.

If one individual alone were persuaded not to play his radio, his loss is given by the negative number in his row, and the gain of each of the others by the first positive number in their rows. If the algebraic sum of these numbers were positive, the exempted individual could be fully compensated with some payment left over as *NB* going to the government. For a second individual a positive

[6] The independence assumption involves no sacrifice of plausibility when decision rules A and B are applied to the initial situation, since for each individual the value of his own radio playing is to be estimated under the condition that all the other radios are being played.

NB is also possible if his negative number is more than offset by the sum of the second positive numbers in the rows of the other three, and so on. There are 4!, or 24 different ways of ranking the four individuals in successive order of exemption, an optimal ordering being one which produces the largest positive *NB* (if any) from the first *r* individuals—*r*, in our example, being any number from one to three.[7]

Let us suppose that this has been done, and the result set out in the Matrix *I*(*L*) below. The matrix arrangements differs from that in the table in the reordering of the rows necessary for an optimal outcome and in the placing of the negative numbers along the principal diagonal. The numbers carry the same interpretation as that in the table, and the row totals remain unaltered. The figures along the bottom of the matrix are the column totals, and these are significant for implementing the C decision rule.

Reading down the *W* column, the first element, −14, is *W*'s compensatory payment for exempting itself, *W*, from the *L* law—a minimum payment of 14, that is, is required by *W*. The 10 below is *Z*'s compensatory payment for exempting *W*, a maximum of 10. The 9 and the 16 are, respectively, the maximum payments from *X* and from *Y* to exempt *W* from permission to play his radio. The amount by which the sum of these payments to prohibit *W* exceed the compensation required by *W* is given by the algebraic total of the *W* column, 21 in this instance, and is the positive *NB* of exempting *W* alone from the *L* law as compared with the initial situation. The algebraic total of the next column being 3, we infer that the exemption of individual *Z,* in addition to individual *W*, adds another 3 to the *NB,* a total *NB* of 24 as compared with the initial situation. Further exemptions would not be admitted. For the exemption of *X* and/or *Y* would serve only to reduce the total positive *NB* of 24, since each of their algebraic totals are negative —the compensatory payments offered falling short of the minimum sums required.[8]

[7] If *r* were equal to four, *NB* would be the same as for the B outcome irrespective of the ordering.

[8] If we remove the independence assumption, the negative numbers may be higher (absolutely) in the resulting matrix for the remaining radio players *X* and *Y* than they are in the table. If so, the negative column totals for *X* and *Y* would be higher (absolutely) than they appear in the Matrix *I*(*L*). If, for example, the figures —33, and —35, were revised respectively to —36, and —40, and the *X* and *Y* column totals therefore to —12, and —25 respectively the

Compared with the initial situation (and, in this instance, also with the B outcome) the C outcome confers a positive *NB* of 24.

	W	*Z*	*X*	*Y*	
W	−14	6	5	4	1
Z	10	−25	9	8	2
X	9	7	−33	3	−14
Y	16	15	10	−35	6
	21	3	−9	−20	−5
	→				

MATRIX *I*(*L*)

D. This rule requires that we substitute for the given areas to which the C outcome was constrained two separate areas, one to be placed under the *L* law and one to be placed under the $\bar{L}$ law, the law in each area being binding on all members placed therein. One can seek an algorithm for selecting individuals for the two areas so as to maximize *NB*. Alternatively, one can reveal an increase in *NB* over that resulting from the C outcome[9] if, as in this example, some but not all of the column totals are positive, by placing in the separate $\bar{L}$ area those exempted under the C procedure (those having positive column totals), and placing the remainder in the separate *L* area. In this paper we restrict ourselves to demonstrating this latter proposition. Accordingly, we place *W* and *Z* in the separate $\bar{L}$ area and *Y* and *X* in the separate *L* area.

The increase in *NB* over the C outcome is easily shown by partitioning the *I*(*L*) Matrix with reference to the C outcome; i.e., by drawing a broken line separating the columns *W* and *Z* from the other columns, and a broken line separating the *W* and *Z* rows from the other rows, as indeed is shown in the matrix.

NB from exempting *W* and *Z* would be increased by 8, to 32 altogether. To *X* and *Y*, the worth of their permission to play when *W* and *Z* are excluded is enhanced by 8. This should be clear whether we add this 8 to the sum of their minimum payments, as here, or whether instead we had revised upward their maximum payments to *W* and *Z* by a total of 8.

[9] On the sufficient condition that, under a total-prohibition law, the individual is indifferent with respect to the size of the area.

Let us identify the N.W., N.E., S.W., and S.E. submatrices respectively as V^{11}, V^{12}, V^{21}, and V^{22}.

(a) Now, in the C outcome, in order that *W* and *Z* together be fully compensated for their exemption from the *L* law, their joint net minimum compensation requirement of 23—equal to the negative of the algebraic sum of the elements in V^{11}, −14, 10, 6, −25,—has to be met by joint payments to them from the group *X* and *Y*.[10] Once *W* and *Z* are placed in a separate $\overline{L}$ area, however, their required compensatory payment of 23 has no longer to be met. As a result *X* and *Y* between them dispose of an additional 23 as compared with the C outcome.

(b) However, *W* and *Z* have been moved from an *L* area into an $\overline{L}$ area.[11] From their row totals, 1 and 2, we know they are willing to pay a joint sum of 3 to change to an $\overline{L}$ area. Under the D arrangement they are placed in such an area without payment. They are therefore better off by this amount 3 as compared with the C outcome.[12]

The excess *NB* as compared with the C outcome is therefore 23 plus 3, or 26.[13] In summary, *NB*(D) − *NB*(C) has two com-

[10] These latter payments, however, equal to 47, or the sum of the elements in V^{21} (9, 16, 7, 15), exceed the required joint compensation of 23 by the amount 24, which, as already indicated, is the *NB* arising from the C outcome compared with the initial situation.

[11] If we removed our rule on the separate facilities arrangements, *W* and *Z* could be made yet better off by changing, by common consent, their separate $\overline{L}$ area into a separate *L* area. Indeed, in the limiting case, the maximum net benefit accrues if each individual were placed in a separate *L* area. In order to highlight the practical alternatives we ignore these possibilities.

[12] If the new totals for *W* and *Z* were negative, they would be added algebraically to the negative of the sum of the V^{11} elements, so reducing excess *NB* compared with C.

Again, if it so happened that the algebraic sum of the elements in V^{11} was positive, there would be no additional gain to *X* and *Y* from no longer having to make up a required compensation for exempting *Z* and *W*. For in such a case *Z* and *W* between them provide more than enough compensation for one another. However, in such a case the *Z* and *W* row totals are that much larger—by at least 23, that is. Separation of *Z* and *W* into an $\overline{L}$ area would then provide them with an excess benefit of more than the 3 in the text example (by at least 23).

[13] If, for this case also, we remove the independence assumption, the negative elements for *X* and *Y* may again be revised upward (absolutely) owing once more to the exclusion of *W* and *Z*—in this arrangement, because of their being placed in an area separate from the *L* area for the *X* and *Y* group. If we assume the figures were revised upward (absolutely) by a total of 8, this revision holds both for the C outcome and the D outcome. Consequently the excess *NB* from moving from the C outcome to the D outcome remains unchanged at 26.

ponents (a), $-V^{11}I$ for X and Y, and (b) $V^{11} + V^{12}$ (equal to row totals for W and Z). Hence, NB(D) $-$ NB(C) = (a) + (b) = $V^{12}I$. In this example $V^{12}I = 26$.[14] In the absence of all costs associated with the change from one arrangement to another, these decision rules A, B, C, D, are ranked in ascending order of positive NB.

III

We now compare these results with those which would obtain if, instead of the L law, we started with the $\overline{L}$ law. In our example, the initial situation is now one in which radio playing is totally prohibited and, as in the preceding section, we go on to consider the possible improvements of permitting exemptions by common consent according to each of the decision rules. Each individual would now pay some maximum sum for permission to play his own radio but would require some minimum compensation to suffer any of the others to play his. Perfectly symmetrical results are assured by assuming that each individual has a zero welfare effect with respect to radio sound, whether his own radio sound or someone else's. Under this assumption the matrix remains unchanged in every respect save that all the signs are reversed. The resulting Matrix $I(\overline{L})$ is shown on page 238.

A. Individuals W, Z, and Y vote for remaining with the $\overline{L}$ law, and therefore have a majority over X's solitary vote for the change to L. Under this rule the area is voted, as before, to be an $\overline{L}$ area, all radio playing prohibited.

[14] An alternative method of estimating this measure of excess NB is to sum the row-wise improvements for each individual in the D solution compared with the *initial* situation, and subtract this estimate of NB(D) from the known NB(C). (a′) For X & Y, the improvement in being left in a separate L area consists in their no longer having to offer payments equal to $V^{21}I$ to exempt Z & W, both of whom are now placed in the separate $\overline{L}$ area. As a result of this saving the joint minimum compensation necessary to move X and Y from a separate L area goes up by $V^{21}I$, or by 47 (compared with the original minimum joint compensation of 8 in the shared L area). (b′) For W & Z, as indicated in the text, the improvement in being placed in a separate $\overline{L}$ area, indifferent to the shared $\overline{L}$ area, is equal to their row totals, 3, which $= V^{11}I + V^{12}I$. Thus NB(D) = (a′) + (b′) $= V^{21}I + V^{11}I + V^{12}I = 50$. NB(C), the W and Z column totals $= V^{11}I + V^{21}I = 24$. Therefore, $NB(D) - NB(C) = V^{12} = 26$ as above.

	W	Z	X	Y	
W	14	−6	−5	−4	−1
Z	−10	25	−9	−8	−2
X	−9	−7	33	−3	14
Y	−16	−15	−10	35	−6
	−21	−3	9	20 ←	5 ↑

MATRIX $I(\bar{L})$

B. Individual *X*, however, can bribe the other 3 to change to the *L* law, and yet show an *NB* of 5. Again, therefore, the *L* law is the outcome.

C. The arrows serve to indicate the order of exemptions under the C rule (the reverse of the order under the *L* law), *Y* and *X* being successfully exempted from the $\bar{L}$ law. The *NB* is given by their column totals as 29, an excess of 24 over the *NB* yielded by the B outcome.[15] The result, again, is no different from that of the C outcome under the *L* law: in both cases, *X* and *Y* will continue to play their radios and *W* and *Z* will be prohibited from playing theirs.

D. Placing the *X* and *Y* individuals in a separate permissive (*L*) area and *W* and *Z* in a separate prohibited ($\bar{L}$) area again increases the *NB* compared with the C outcome. In claiming their exemption from the $\bar{L}$ law under the C rule, *X* and *Y* were required to meet the compensatory demands of *W* and *Z*; i.e., *X* and *Y* were required to pay 26—equal, with sign reversed, to the algebraic sum of the elements in submatrix V^{12}. With the *W* and *Z* removed to a separate area this payment is no longer necessary, and the excess *NB* from the reduced *X* and *Y* columns is 26. In fact this 26 equal to $-V^{12}I$, is, once again, equal to the excess *NB* of the D outcome over the C outcome,[16] since *W* and *Z* are

[15] In general we should expect the *NB* yield by the C outcome to be different under the $\bar{L}$ laws as, in general, the optimal outcome will be further from the initial state under one law than under the other.

[16] Again this result may be checked by comparing the row totals under the D outcome with those in the initial situation under the $\bar{L}$ laws. (b′), *W* and *Z* are neither better off nor worse off. From being in a joint area where all are prohibited they are now in a separate area where all are prohibited. (a′), *X* and *Y*, on the other hand, are better off. From being in a shared prohibited

no better off and no worse off in the D outcome, in which they are placed in a separate prohibited area, than they would be remaining in a joint prohibited area under the C outcome and being compensated for the radio noise created by the exempted group *Y* and *X*.[17]

Greater interest, however, attaches to a comparison of the results under L and $\bar{L}$ when we remove the restrictive assumption of zero welfare effects for each individual. If, now, an individual is, on balance, better off in the initial (uncorrected) situation under the $\bar{L}$ law as compared with the L law, all his compensatory payments, positive and negative, will be revised upward (absolutely): if he is worse off under the $\bar{L}$ law all such payments will be revised downward. Individuals *W, Z,* and *Y* are each better off under the $\bar{L}$ law, since each, when under the L law, would have paid, on balance, some positive sum to have the L law reversed. The reverse is true only for *X* who, when under the L law would have had to be bribed to agree to reverse the L law. Matrix $I'(\bar{L})$ is constructed with these revisions in mind.[18] The negative row totals for *W, Z,* and *Y* are each larger (absolutely) in this new matrix than they were in the Matrix $I(\bar{L})$. The positive row total for individual *X,* on the other hand, is now smaller than it was in that matrix. As a result of these alterations, only the new A

$\bar{L}$ area they are prepared to pay, for being placed in a separate L area, a sum, 55, equal to $V^{22}I$, the algebraic sum of their reduced rows. Since the D outcome would in fact place them in the separate L area, this sum is pure surplus. $NB(\text{D}) = (\text{a}') + (\text{b}') = V^{22}I = 55$. $NB(\text{C})$, equal to the *X* & *Y* column totals, $= V^{12}I + V^{22}I = 29$. Therefore, $NB(\text{D}) - NB(\text{C}) = V^{22}I - V^{12}I - V^{22}I = -V^{12}I = 26$, as above.

[17] The reader will have noticed that under the $\bar{L}$ law, we calculated the excess *NB* for the D outcome without a contribution from the *W* and *Z* group while under the L law we added their row totals to the surplus of *X* and *Y* to arrive at the excess *NB*. This apparent symmetry arises from the fact that under the L law, *W* and *Z* are *not* (necessarily) indifferent as between being placed in a separate quiet $\bar{L}$ area and being exactly compensated under the C outcome as to be no worse off than they were under the initial $\bar{L}$ law (where all had permission). In contrast, under the $\bar{L}$ law, *W* and *Z* *are* indifferent as between being placed in a separate $\bar{L}$ area and being exactly compensated under the C outcome as to be no worse off there than under the initial $\bar{L}$ law (where all four were prohibited in a joint area).

[18] The magnitude of the alterations made to the compensatory payments in the Matrix $I'(\bar{L})$ are obviously exaggerated. This does not matter in a purely illustrative example. The significance of this asymmetry in important instances will be argued later.

outcome is the same as that in the symmetric Matrix $I(\bar{L})$. The outcomes of applying the decision rules B, C, and D, however, are all different.

	W	*Z*	*X*	*Y*		
W	15	−6	−6	−5	−2	
Z	−12	29	−11	−9	−3	
X	−8	−6	30	−4	12	
Y	−18	−16	−11	37	−8	↑
	−23	1	2	19	−1	
				←		

In the B outcome with the *symmetric* Matrix $I'(\bar{L})$, individual *X* by 14 to 9 prevailed over the other three to change to the *L* law; in the new matrix *X* is prevailed upon by the other three, by 13 to 12, to remain with the $\bar{L}$ law. As for the C outcome, whereas only *X* and *Y* were exempted from the $\bar{L}$ law under the symmetric matrix with an *NB* of 29, in the new matrix *X, Y,* and *Z* are exempted with an *NB* of 22. Turning finally to the D outcome, if we continued to place *X* and *Y* in a separate *L* area, and *W* and *Z* in a separate $\bar{L}$ area, the excess *NB* is, as before, measured by the sum of the elements in what would then be the V^{12} submatrix. For this measures the excess over the *NB* of the C outcome from *X* and *Y* no longer having to compensate *Z* and *W*, these latter themselves being no worse off in a separate prohibited area than they were in a joint prohibited area. This new excess *NB* is therefore 31 as compared with 26 under the symmetric matrix. If, on the other hand, we follow our rule and place in the separate *L* area all individuals whose column totals are positive, in this case *X, Y* and *Z* all of whom secure exemption from the $\bar{L}$ law under the C procedure, we partition the matrix as shown. V^{12} now contains −6, −6, −5, a total of −17, indicating that, under the C procedure, 17 was the minimum compensation required by *W* to exempt *X, Y,* and *Z* from the $\bar{L}$ law while he, *W*, remained in this area. When *W* is placed in a separate $\bar{L}$ area these payments are not needed, and the excess *NB* compared with the

C outcome is 17. A formal treatment of the m-person case is provided in Appendix 2.

IV

We now remove the provisional assumption of no costs of change and consider total costs incurred in implementing any of these four decision rules, additional to whatever costs are incurred in maintaining unchanged the existing situation under the L law. The total of these costs in implementing the A rule is denoted by $G(\text{A})$, that in implementing the B rule, by $G(\text{B})$, and so on. We must, therefore, revise our requirement for the B outcome to be regarded as a Pareto improvement, compared with the initial situation, from $NB(\text{B}) > 0$ to $NB(\text{B}) - G(\text{B}) > 0$. Similarly, for the D outcome to be regarded as an improvement over the C outcome, it is required that $\{NB(\text{D}) - G(D)\} > \{NB(\text{C}) - G(\text{C})\}$.

We may divide these total costs, G, associated with implementing any one of the four decision rules into three main groups: G_1 are the costs of reaching agreement to move from the existing situation under L to the outcome associated with the decision rule in question. They include the costs of negotiation among members of a group having the same interest, and those arising from negotiations between groups having conflicting interests. G_2 are the costs of administration and supervision connected with maintaining the agreement reached. G_3 are the capital costs, if any, required to implement the outcome of the decision rule in question.

The G_3 costs may be important in the creation of separate facilities, though in the instances that come easily to mind—separate smoking and nonsmoking facilities in trains, cinemas, and restaurants, beaches where games, or radios, are prohibited, quiet study rooms in universities, pedestrian precincts—usually require little more than a revision of the law as it applies to existing facilities. However, there may be cases where the costs of partitioning areas, or of shifting equipment from one area to the other, may be substantial.[19]

[19] Moreover, possible economies of scale in a joint area may have to be forgone if the area is divided. Any such loss is to be subtracted from $\{NB(\text{D}) - NB(\text{C})\}$.

The G_2 costs may be significant in supervising separate facilities, or in enforcing optimal arrangements under the C procedure. The weaker the sense of civic responsibility the greater are these costs likely to be. It is possible, however, that any increase of effort entailed in administration and supervision of the new arrangements, as compared with the arrangements under the status quo, is only an addition to the existing duties of personnel drawing fixed salaries. Though in real terms this counts, no additional demands appear to register on the resources of the economy.

The G_1 costs are easily the most significant of the three groups, and are likely to vary greatly with the state of the law. Writing $G_1 = G_1(n, d, f)$, it is suggested that G_1 varies directly with *n*, the number of individuals, or families, affected adversely or otherwise under the *L* law, who might benefit under any of the alternative solutions. G_1 also varies directly with *d*, regarded as some index of geographical dispersion of the *n* people within the area. Other factors that are less tangible, but which may also increase these costs considerably—ignorance of the identity of the members of an adversely affected group, ignorance of the law, lack of worldly experience or organizing ability within such a group—are summarized in the symbol *f*.

Although no reliable studies have been made in this connection, it seems likely that the costs both of collecting information and reaching agreement among a group adversely affected by some activity under the *L* law—agreement both in respect of compensation to offer to the party creating the damage, and in respect of contribution to be made by each member (in the case of the C decision rule)—will rise exponentially with the magnitude of *n*. Whatever the values to be placed on the other factors, *d* and *f*, their effect on *G* will also be greater the larger the size of *n*. For the larger the number in any group that is adversely affected, the higher will be the costs incurred in overcoming geographical and other obstacles.

It is, of course, possible that the total of such *G* costs, so far as they can be estimated, are not so high as the potential gains from adopting the outcome of, say, the C or D decision rule, notwithstanding which such an arrangement is not undertaken. The obvious explanation is in terms of inertia, or lack of initiative. But it is tautological, as well as complacent, to infer from the observed fact, that mutual arrangements, apparently profitable, are not undertaken, that costs—including "costs of initiative"—are too high, and that potential Pareto improvements do not really exist.[20]

What makes such an inference tautological is, of course, the implicit valuation of the "costs of initiative" as being, in all pertinent instances, a sum which is more than enough to bridge the gap by which estimated costs *G* fall short of the potential net benefit associated with some decision rule, usually C. Such a tautology is unnecessary. For it is quite feasible for the government, say, to set up an agency for the specific purpose of organizing the interests of such adversely affected groups in cases where the group was large and dispersed and inexperienced, thus setting a cost for the required initiative. If it did so under the existing law, voluntary arrangements hitherto neglected would now appear and would yield net benefits above all *G* costs (when these are revised to include the costs of initiative) so effecting Pareto improvements.[21]

What makes such a proposal complacent in addition is the unquestioned acceptance of the existing costs of altering the status quo as a datum whereas the magnitude of these costs, particularly those in the G_1 category, vary with the state of the law. Thus, unless we choose to regard the existing *L* law, permissive in respect of a range of spillover effects on the community at large, as a constraint, one must admit the possibility of a wide range of voluntary agreements, tending to increase the community's net benefit, remaining unrealized.

The alterations in the outcomes that might follow a change from the *L* law to the $\bar{L}$ law are made explicit in the following

[20] See in particular arguments of Buchanan & Tullock [3], R. H. Coase [4].

[21] One cannot be much impressed by the argument of noninterventionists that if some new arrangement, say a separate facilities solution, could in fact yield net benefits to the otherwise afflicted group, then it must be possible, if not for the group itself to come together and organize it, for some entrepreneur to make a profit by promoting the arrangement. And the fact that such an arrangement has not come into being is, therefore, held to be prima facie evidence that it does not yield net benefits. If this argument were taken seriously one would infer that no new form of enterprise could possibly be discovered in the future; that no further social or managerial innovation remains to be discovered. The ever-vigilant and omniscient entrepreneur has foreseen every possible opportunity for making profits, the only forms of innovation remaining are purely technological.

section where we reexamine briefly the conventional conclusions of a variety of instances in the light of the above analysis.

V. Application of the Analysis to Particular Instances of Social Cost

1. We may begin with the simplest case of one individual inflicting damage on another.[22] For each state of the law we have a 2×1 matrix. We can suppose that individual *Y* wishes to site a house in the country, though in a location that obscures the view from *X*'s house. The decision rule obviously results in a tie. Therefore we consider the B decision rule, which in this simple two-person case, is the same as the C decision rule.

If the permissive *L* law prevailed then *X* is to be made worse off and *Y* better off by *Y*'s decision; therefore unless *X* approaches *Y* with an offer *Y* is certain to build on his chosen site. Above the cost of the house to *Y* the value he places on the site is such that he will not accept less than $28,000 to abandon the site. If *X* is willing to pay a sum larger than this, say $30,000, to induce *Y* to move elsewhere, the optimal outcome results in *Y*'s choosing some other site. A change to $\bar{L}$ law, which prohibits any new building without consent of those affected will confirm this outcome. For the assumption of normal welfare effects implies that *Y* would offer to pay less than $28,000 for the site while *X* would require more than $30,000, as a result of which, again *Y* must seek a site elsewhere.[23]

It is quite possible, however, to meet with cases in which the optimal outcome varies with the law. The figures in the Matrix (*i*) are such that agreement cannot be reached under either law. If the *L* law prevails, the $25,000 maximum that *X* is willing to pay is below the $28,000 minimum that would induce *Y* to change his mind. Under the *L* law, therefore, *Y* sites his house and ob-

[22] An example in which benefit is conferred by one individual upon the other is of small interest unless the individual who confers the benefit damages his interest in the process, in which case it is formally similar to the problem treated in the text.

[23] A separate areas solution cannot be proposed in such a case since the effect enjoyed by *Y* depends upon his new house being located in the particular area that obstructs *X*'s view.

scures X's view. On the other hand, if the $\bar{L}$ law prevailed instead, the maximum sum that Y could offer X for permission to site his new house would be $23,000 which sum, however, falls short of the $30,000 minimum that would be acceptable to X. Under the $\bar{L}$ law, therefore, Y cannot build his house to obscure X's view. It follows that under the L law the optimal outcome requires that Y build his house. Under the $\bar{L}$ law, the optimal outcome requires that Y does *not* build his house.

	L	$\bar{L}$
X	25,000	−30,000
Y	−28,000	23,000

MATRIX (*i*)

Finally, if some factor affecting the interest of both parties could be varied the magnitude of the variation would, in general, depend upon the prevailing law. Suppose that additions to the height of Y's new house would add to his satisfaction, though at a diminishing rate, while they would increase X's dissatisfaction at an increasing rate. It is now supposed that under the L law X would pay a maximum of $15,000 to dissuade Y from building the lowest-height house contemplated. Y, however, could not be persuaded from building this squat house for less than $30,000. These figures are marked on the vertical axis of Figure 1. By assuming continuity between height of house and compensation we construct the solid lines X_L and Y_L. The highest point on the Y_L curve indicates the height, H_Y, that would be chosen by Y under the L law and in the absence of any agreement with X. At this height, however, the maximum compensation to be offered by X for a height reduction of, say, one foot, exceeds the minimum sum acceptable to Y. While this condition is met agreement on successive height reductions can be reached until the optimal height H_L—that at which the marginal benefit to Y is equal to the marginal cost to X—is attained. The optimal height corresponds to the largest vertical distance between the Y_L and X_L curves and provides, therefore, the greatest surplus of benefit to Y above the loss to X. If now we change to $\bar{L}$ law, Y is prepared to pay a

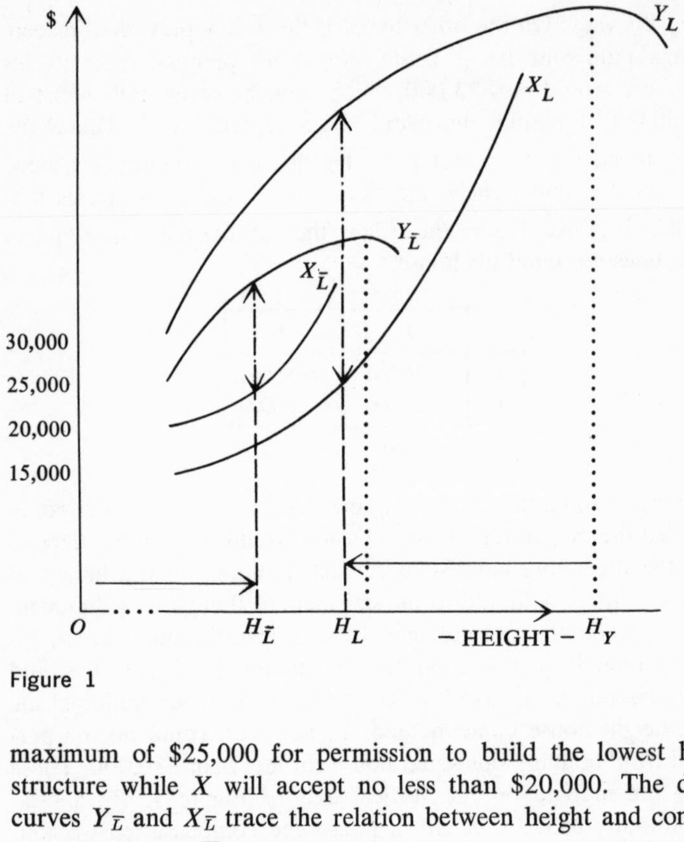

Figure 1

maximum of $25,000 for permission to build the lowest height structure while X will accept no less than $20,000. The dotted curves $Y_{\bar{L}}$ and $X_{\bar{L}}$ trace the relation between height and compensation under the $\bar{L}$ law. In the absence of any approach by Y, no building will take place on the site in question. Yet Y is able to bribe X to permit a building of increasing height until $H_{\bar{L}}$ is reached, where $H_{\bar{L}}$ is the optimal height under the $\bar{L}$ law and is below H_L, the optimal height under the L law.[24]

2. The topical example of aircraft noise differs from the above in two respects: first, in the obvious respect of the large numbers which, under the L law, suffer disturbance to their quiet, and secondly, in that the compensatory payments of the airline company are determined uniquely by reference to the market.[25] The

[24] This example is adapted from the one suggested by Buchanan and Stubblebine [2]. Their unique optimal is to be compared with the result above.

[25] This sum is equal to its rent, or excess profit, in using that particular air-

maximum sum it will offer to continue operating planes from its airfield and the minimum it will accept to move elsewhere are exactly equal. Once again, there are no reciprocal effects, and for the n residents or families affected an $(n + 1) \times 1$ matrix summarizes the position under either law if the airline company counts as one. Irrespective of the law, under the A decision rule, the voting would go against the company. The B and C decision rules are equivalent in this case because of the absence of reciprocal effects. Indeed if we group the compensatory payments of the n residents together, the problem can be collapsed to the two-party case having the possibilities already treated in the previous problem. As for the variable factor, in this instance it could be represented by variation in the number of planes operating from the airfield.[26]

Matrix (*ii*) can be taken to summarize the position. Under the permissive law L, the n residents represented as X are able to afford a maximum payment of $30 million, which sum exceeds by $10 million the minimum compensation of $20 million demanded by the airline company. The figures for the $\bar{L}$ law are $50 million required by X and, again, $20 million for the company.[27]

	L	$\bar{L}$
X	30m.	−50m.
Y	−20m.	20m.

MATRIX (*ii*)

field compared with the next most suitable airfield available to the airline company, plus the costs of movement.

[26] If represented on a diagram similar to the figure, with the company's compensation line as the Y line, there would be only one such Y line irrespective of the law, the difference in the optimal number of planes under the L law as compared with the $\bar{L}$ law arising only from differences in the X line.

The smoke nuisance case is treated in a similar manner. If the damaging effects from smoke can be completely offset by the purchase of soap, laundering services, and the like, the X line would be uniquely determined, and so also would be the optimal output—if we ignore all costs of implementation.

[27] On issues that make a significant difference to the individual's welfare the difference between the maximum sum he would pay to avoid a certain fate (his view being permanently obscured, or his peace being shattered over a long period) and the minimum sum he would accept for submitting to that fate is likely to be far greater than is habitually suggested by our notions of differences in welfare effect, so frequently assumed negligible in order to reach elegant theoretical results. The current and prospective income and assets of a person form a limit to the maximum he can afford to pay and remain alive, while no such limit

Under the existing L law, the company could not be induced to move to another airfield if the total G costs exceeded \$10 million. If such costs are accepted as unavoidable, the existing situation has to be accepted as the optimal outcome. But the unavoidability of such costs does not arise from the economic facts of life but from the legal facts. For if the L law were changed to $\overline{L}$, and made prohibitive of aircraft noise, the company would be obliged to make the approach. The G_1 costs now associated with the airline's reaching agreement on maximum compensation, would be slight compared with G_1 costs incurred by the n residents.

In this example, as it happens, the sum the company can afford to offer to bribe the residents into accepting the airfield in their midst would not suffice, and the company, therefore, would be obliged to move elsewhere.

Once again, the outcome varies with the law, but not, as in the previous example, because of the welfare effects on compensatory payments. Indeed we could have supposed zero welfare effects for the residents, and substituted -30 instead of -50 in the (*ii*) matrix, without altering the results. The excessive costs, especially the G_1 costs, associated with a large number of residents, implies $NB(\mathrm{C}) - G(\mathrm{C})$ is negative: since everyone cannot be made better off under the L law by a voluntary approach by residents to bribe the company, the existing outcome is accepted as optimal. Under the $\overline{L}$ law, on the other hand, the prohibition of aircraft from the residential area would be the optimal outcome: for the company could not operate the planes while making everyone better off.

3. We may now turn to a mixed case in which some individuals of the population regard themselves as victims of the activities of others while the remainder regard themselves as beneficiaries of these activities, or less extreme but more realistic, one in which some people mind very little and others mind a great deal. We could think, in this connection, of a spacious residential area in

restricts the minimum sum he would consent to receive. A man dying of thirst in the middle of the Sahara could offer, for a bucket of water that would save his life, no more than his prospective earnings (above some subsistence level). And this sum would be infinitesimal compared with the sum of money needed to induce him to forgo the bucket of water and fatally reduce his chance of survival.

which some X-type inhabitants were sensitive to automobile noise of others and/or attached little value to their own use of this form of transport. The Y-type inhabitants, on the other hand, are not unduly disturbed by such noises and/or attach great store by their automobiles. Under the permissive L law, the matrix would be like the V matrix, with all the $v_{ii} \leqq 0$ and all the $v_{ij} \geqq 0$ $(j \neq i)$.[28] For the X-type, the v_{ii} will be (absolutely) smaller compared with their v_{ij}, the reverse being true for the Y-type. The row totals for the X-type are therefore positive, for the Y-type they may be negative, zero, or positive. The A outcome is determined by the number of X-types compared with Y-types, and the B outcome by the algebraic sum of the matrix elements. What makes this case interesting are two things: (a) as in the preceding case, the influence of the law on the G costs, and (b) the superiority of the separate facilities solution is particularly marked.

We illustrate with specific matrices $(iii)L$ and $(iii)\overline{L}$ in which there are two persons of each type. Since in a reversal of law from L to $\overline{L}$ X-types gain heavily, and Y-types lose heavily, the absolute values of the elements must be revised upward for the X rows in $(iii)\overline{L}$ and downward for the Y rows. The A and B decision rules give the same outcome under either law—a tie, and prohibition of motoring, respectively. Applying the C rule Y_1 and Y_2 will be left driving under the L law, while no one secures consent to drive under the $\overline{L}$ law.

[28] The determination of an optimal number of cars on a given stretch of road can, incidentally, be illuminated by this matrix scheme. In such problems, it is often supposed that only the individuals who actually use the road for driving suffer damages as a result of growing congestion. Provisionally accepting this assumption, we build up the matrix under an $\overline{L}$ law by introducing one car at a time in descending order of the value they set on driving over this stretch of road. As the number of cars increase from 1, 2, 3, to m, we represent the position by a 1×1, a 2×2, a 3×3, and eventually an $m \times m$ matrix. The mth car also has a positive v_{mm}. It inflicts damage on the $(m-1)$ other cars, hence the negative elements in the rest of the m column. However, it suffers damage from each of the $(m-1)$ other cars, hence the negative elements in the rest of the m row. In the conventional case, where it is assumed that the additional driver inflicts on each of the others the total congestion cost experienced by introducing his own car, each negative element in the rth column is equal to the sum of the negative elements in the $(r-1)^{\text{th}}$ row. In deciding whether to use the road, the individual driver consults only his row total; if positive he drives. The optimal solution, however, will admit all those cars having positive column totals.

	X_1	X_2	Y_1	Y_2	
X_1	−10	18	30	35	73
X_2	25	−12	20	30	63
Y_1	4	6	−62	10	−42
Y_2	4	6	10	−80	−60
	23	18	−2	−5	34

→

MATRIX $(iii)L$

	X_1	X_2	Y_1	Y_2	
X_1	12	−20	−35	−40	−83
X_2	−30	15	−25	−30	−70
Y_1	−2	−4	55	−8	41
Y_2	−3	−5	−8	60	44
	−23	−14	−13	−18	−68

MATRIX $(iii)\bar{L}$

Once we recognize the magnitude of the G costs, in particular the G_1 costs, which are likely to rise rapidly with the numbers involved, incurred in a movement to the C outcome, the advantage lies predominantly with the group, or type, enjoying the status quo. In the absence of initiative by a government agency seeking to promote optimal outcomes under the existing law, the initial situation under the L law is likely to perpetuate itself notwithstanding the large potential NB of a C solution.

Finally, if we place individuals in separate areas according to their *row* totals in either matrix, the D outcome under either law captures a much greater NB than does the C outcome. Under the L law for instance, X_1 and X_2 would have paid row totals 73 and 63 respectively, a total of 136, to have the whole area converted into a nonmotoring zone, as between which and dwelling in a nonmotoring separate area they are deemed indifferent. Y_1 and Y_2 also gain. They would require under the L law minimum payments of 102 to consent to having the area made into a nonmotoring zone. Now they can be lodged in a separate permissive area which is superior to the existing permissive area inasmuch as they are not disturbed there by X_1 and X_2. Once in the separate area the minimum acceptable sum for each will rise by 10, a total of 20 (equal to the sum of the elements in the submatrix V^{21}). Compared with the initial situation, then, the D outcome provides an NB of 156 compared with 41 from the C outcome.

In general, the greater the population, and the larger are the absolute v_{ij} of the X-type of individual relative to the Y-type, the larger become the elements in V^{12} compared with those in V^{21}, and the greater the superiority of the D outcome compared with the C. The excess $NB(D)$ over $NB(C)$ is, however, equal to the sum of the elements in V^{12}.

Moreover, granted the initiative was there, the capital costs of providing separate facilities may not be heavy. The existing area, if large, may be partitioned into two separate and viable areas, and the costs of movement for either type may not be great relative to the expected advantage over a long period. There would be no, or practically no, additional costs of supervision and administration, as compared with a C outcome. Nor need there be heavy costs incurred in estimating the actual compensatory sums of the individuals. A simple question asked of each individual or family would suffice: if a separate area were created would you, if necessary, be prepared to move into it (with, or without, financial aid)? [29]

VI

The general belief, attacked in this paper, is that an optimal solution in a partial setting is uniquely determined [**3,** pp. 61–62; **4,** p. 3; **15,** p. 55], or that it may reasonably be treated as uniquely determined [**2,** p. 385], a belief that may appear justified if the treatment is confined to spillover effects as between firms or industries [as, for instance, in **8,** and **5**] or if the estimate of damages inflicted on the public may be costed by reference to market prices. Even in such cases, however, the belief is unwarranted. Resorting once more to Pigou's smoky chimney example, the supposition that a given amount of soap is alone sufficient to undo the damage caused will still not determine an optimal output irrespective of the law. For the soap used by the victims of smoke damage may well be produced by an industry that disposes of its waste products by

[29] If, on the other hand, the specific instance in mind was the disturbance caused within a residential area by motorized lawn mowers, an outcome with a higher *NB* than either the C or the D outcome may be reached by agreement on the pattern of activity within the period. The initial matrix, we could suppose, had reference to compensatory payments per week for exemptions under the *L* law from any lawn mowing during the week. Any optimal C solution would leave a certain number of individuals free to mow their lawns any time they wished, while prohibiting the remainder from any motorized lawn mowing at all. It is now entirely possible that a consensus on confining lawn mowing activity to limited periods, say Wednesdays from two to four and/or Fridays from four to six, would confer a larger *NB* than the C outcome.

contaminating the air or polluting a river, so reducing the welfare of other sections of the public which, under the existing law, are unable—because of exorbitant G costs—to bribe the soap industry either to reduce its output or to install effective safeguards. Inasmuch as a change of law that puts the burden of compensation on the soap industry would raise its long-run costs (whether compensatory payments cause it to reduce its output, or whether in operating antipollution devices, it increases its running costs and/or overheads) reference to the market price of soap under this new law entails higher costs and, consequently, a smaller optimal output in the smoky chimney industry. Nor need we stop here. In so far as any of the inputs of the original smoky chimney industry, or any of the inputs of the soap industry, or any of the inputs of these inputs, would be produced at higher costs under a law that places the onus of compensation on those generating the external diseconomies, the level of costs and outputs of the final and contributory industries are all affected. Thus, if we begin with what appears to be a set of optimal outputs and prices in the economy, a change of law in the respect indicated changes in general the whole set of optimal prices and outputs. The implication may be put otherwise: no output or set of outputs in the economy can be justified by the Pareto criterion without implicit support of the existing law bearing on the question of compensation.

There are, moreover, several reasons for expecting that the difference to the patterns of costs and outputs following such a change of law would be substantial. Significant external diseconomies involving the effects on the amenity of the public at large both of the operation of modern industry and the use of new commercial products are on the increase. Moreover, inasmuch as the external effects wrought on the environment enter heavily into a man's welfare they entail a significant differential between the maximum amount which (under the L law) he is willing to pay to rid himself of the unpleasantness in question and the minimum sum which (under an $\bar{L}$ law) he is willing to accept to bear it. Finally, according as the ratio of the number of people affected by noxious by-products to the number of enterprises generating them increases so do the G_1 costs under the L law as compared with the G_1 costs under an $\bar{L}$ law.

Granted the general conclusion that the pattern of costs and outputs varies with the state of the law, is there a case for the economist's supporting one kind of law as against the other? If we regard the existing law as being predominantly *L* law, that is, predominantly permissive with respect to incidental disamenities generated, then a case for a switch-over to $\bar{L}$ law can be made on grounds (1) of efficiency, and (2) of equity.

1. There are three reasons why a change to the $\bar{L}$ law may be expected to promote allocative efficiency.

(i) We have shown that, by provisionally ignoring all *G* costs, the pattern of "optimal" outputs under an $\bar{L}$ law is, in general, different from that under the *L* law. What is relevant, with respect to allocative efficiency alone, however, is our proposition that the *G* costs (in particular, the G_1 costs) to be incurred in arranging to bring into effect an optimal output are small under $\bar{L}$ law compared with those incurred under *L* law. If, therefore, we begin, under either law, with a number of sectors in which outputs are uncorrected for net external diseconomies, there will be some of these sectors that yield a positive *NB* under an $\bar{L}$ law—the potential gain in moving to optimal outputs exceeding their corresponding *G* costs—but not under the *L* law. Thus, under an $\bar{L}$ law it becomes cheaper for the economy to approach its pattern of potential optimum outputs than to do so under the *L* law.

(ii) Once the burden of full compensation for disamenities generated either in the production or use of the commodity or service is borne by the manufacturer, on a legal par with the costs incurred in compensating people for the use of their factors, he has an immediate and often powerful incentive to direct resources into discovering low-cost devices—low enough on balance, that is, to reduce total costs *including* compensation under an $\bar{L}$ law—that enable him to increase his profits and extend his outputs. Under the *L* law, in contrast, there is no such incentive to switch part of his resources from current research into raising quality or reducing costs of existing goods to reducing, instead, the costs of eliminating the negative goods he inadvertently produces. For either he totally ignores these negative goods or, if it is forthcoming, accepts full compensation for curtailing his output or for installing known methods of combating them.

(iii) Finally, in those cases where it remains costly, in the state of current technology, to remove or appreciably reduce those spillover effects over which people's reactions are divided, establishment of the $\bar{L}$ law, putting the burden ultimately on the manufacturers, provides the greater incentive to promote separate facilities solutions which, as we have seen, can be productive of greater *NB* than optimal solutions constrained within single areas. The larger the proportion of the population in any given area that can be divided roughly into "sensitive" and "insensitive" types with respect to some given by-product, the larger the potential *NB* to be found in a separate facilities solution compared with a constrained optimum solution.[30]

These three considerations merit some attention by economists, above all at a time like the present when the products of advancing technology in a growing economy tend swiftly to reduce environmental areas and city centers to a common and depressing pattern. So long as economists implicitly accepted the existing state of the law as being neutral in respect of allocation, the economic case against resisting the spread of subtopia could not be made with the necessary cogency. Recognition of the role played by the law, both in determining the pattern of the optimal output set and in determining the magnitude of the costs necessary to implement that pattern, plus the recognition also of the superiority of a separate facilities solution[31] to some externality problems, should

[30] If the world were otherwise than that described here, in particular if, on balance, (a) it were more costly to bring about optimal arrangements under an $\bar{L}$ law and (b) optimal arrangements under the $\bar{L}$ law resulted in a less satisfactory distribution of welfare, then clearly the case for a change from L to $\bar{L}$ law would be weakened. The case for such a change would rest more heavily on the ethical considerations which considerations should in any case, I believe, predominate.

I do not find it easy, however, to think of instances in which the facts, in respect of G costs at least, are other than those assumed in the text. Widespread disamenity resulting from mass usage of the recent products of industry are no exception. Under an $\bar{L}$ law the initiative towards improved economic arrangements would come from the large firms or from trade associations which, being highly organized decision-making bodies, could promote the new economic arrangements at much lower G costs than can the unorganized members of the affected public under the existing L law. Indeed, in many cases the cheapest method of correcting the externality, that of redesigning the product so as to remove the offending features, would involve practically no G costs under an $\bar{L}$ law while being almost impossible to bring about under the existing L law.

[31] It is perhaps an unnecessary precaution to remark that there is no affinity whatever between my separate-facilities proposal and the doctrine of "separate but equal facilities." If anything, my proposal implies the reverse of that doctrine:

enable economists to justify proposals for more radical social choices—the choice, for instance, of viable residential areas undisturbed by engine noises of any sort—than those which can be expected to emerge through the operation of the market under the existing laws. It follows, therefore, that legislation recognizing the citizen's rights to amenity—the right to such once free goods as quiet, fresh air, natural beauty—and putting the burden of compensation squarely on the incidental destroyers of amenity without exception, would not only be equitable in itself, it would promote a wider range of choices than is offered under the present dispensation.

[A final word is needed. In any assessment of the likely consequences of substituting $\overline{L}$ law for the existing L law one must bear in mind the inertia inevitably imparted to the status quo as a result of the magnitude of decision costs which act to prevent realization of potential Pareto improvements—confirming ourselves to cases in which separate areas solutions are inapplicable.

As indicated earlier, whatever the state of the law the existence of a potential Pareto improvement arising from some uncorrected spillover, $NB(\text{C}) > 0$, does not of itself imply that the potential improvement will, or should, be effected. It is necessary also that the decision costs be smaller than the value of the potential improvement; it is required, that is, that $NB(\text{C}) - G(\text{C}) > 0$. Clearly, such decision costs, $G(\text{C})$, act as a cost barrier to a number of potential Pareto improvements irrespective of the state of the law—although, as indicated, the cost barrier for the L law is likely to be much wider than that for the $\overline{L}$ law and likely, therefore, to be less productive of actual Pareto improvements than the $\overline{L}$ law.

Nonetheless, if we restrict ourselves to that number of spillover activities with potential Pareto improvements that would, because of their associated decision costs, be excluded under *either* law, the status quo resulting from the existence of the L law will be markedly different from that resulting from the existence of the $\overline{L}$

---

facilities in the two (or more) areas are designed to be different, while the choice of area in which to reside is entirely up to each individual family.

law. And since there will be this marked difference it goes without saying that the law should be chosen so that the status to be perpetuated is the less intolerable of the two.

Suppose, for example, a particular type of air pollution by industry was one of such spillover effects. If the decision costs were zero, the pollution would be reduced, we can imagine, to 1/4 of its unprohibited extent under the *L* law, and to 1/5 of this extent under the $\overline{L}$ law. But because of the magnitude of the decision costs, whatever the state of the law the appropriate Pareto optimal pollution will not be realized. Over time, of course, changes in technology and changes in taste may well reduce decision costs relative to potential Pareto gains under either law so as to eventually make a Pareto solution possible. But in the meantime, and so long as decision costs are prohibitive under either law, the Pareto improvement is in abeyance. The prevalence of the *L* law would, in the meantime, therefore, prevent any pollution control whatsoever. In contrast, the prevalence of the $\overline{L}$ law would entail total prohibition of this type of pollution.

Certainly with such spillovers in mind as those that create irrevocable damage, the interests of posterity are better served by the inertia of the status quo under the $\overline{L}$ law (issued in total prohibition) than by that under the *L* law (issued in uninhibited license). On the grounds of equity and welfare distribution the outcome of the inertia under the $\overline{L}$ law is to be preferred to that under the *L* law.] *

VII

2. As a contribution to equity, the establishment of the $\overline{L}$ law would tend to produce a greater equality in the distribution of welfare in so far as the commodities and services that generate the outstanding diseconomies—air and water pollution, noise, visual disturbance, destruction of natural beauty—are purchased by and earn incomes for the wealthier groups in the community. More important than distributional considerations perhaps is the inequity *per se* of a law that countenances the inflicting of a wide

* This bracketed passage did not appear in the original paper.

range of damages on others without effective means of redress. In the absence of comprehensive sanctions against trespass on the citizen's amenity, existing institutions lend themselves inadvertently to a process of blackmail in so far as they place the burden of reaching agreement on the person or group whose interests have been damaged. Although the disabilities inflicted on innocent parties may be judged with less severity when they are generated as a by-product of the pursuit of gain under the existing laws than when, instead, they are produced for the sole purpose of exacting payment, the Pareto principle is met in either case by the "voluntary" agreement of the party whose rights, liberties, or interests are under threat. Indeed, the virtue of the Pareto principle resides in its alleged neutrality: if *A* habitually amuses himself by throwing smoke bombs through *B*'s window, but agrees to desist on payment of $25 a week, both are made better off if *B* chooses to pay it rather than continue to suffer these depredations.[32] Though all existing law acts to prevent calculated blackmail and victimization, there is still this hiatus in the law that enables incidental damage—though frequently severe and lasting damage—to be inflicted on people unless they can find the means to bribe the perpetrators. Indeed, the law as it stands, tends to encourage an extension of social damage beyond that which appears incidental in the first instance. For there is an incentive where it is possible to add, surreptitiously, to the incidental damage with the aim of "optimizing" the size of the bribe.

Such a depressing fact makes it all the more imperative to perceive a distinction within the notion of ethical neutrality, conceived, on the one hand, as a *disregard* of ethical implication—which is the sense in which the Pareto principle is, in fact, neutral—and, on the other hand, as *impartiality* between the alternative ways of

[32] Stigler in his 1943 Note [**14**] protests that the compensating principle is repugnant to our moral code inasmuch as it would apparently sanction compensation of successful thieves for the amounts they would otherwise steal. I pointed out in a footnote in my *Survey* paper [**9**, p. 39] that this criticism did not apply to *hypothetical* compensation tests, which left the question of *actual* compensation to be determined on other grounds, generally by reference to the distributional implications—though, of course, one might bring in other ethical considerations.

Nonetheless, in so far as the working of the market is sanctioned ultimately by this Pareto principle and, indeed, the working of the market under the existing laws *does* place the burden of payment on the victims of the incidental damage caused by industry, the core of Stigler's criticism can be justified.

giving effect to the principle, which is, albeit mistakenly, the sense usually attributed to it.[33] Thus the fact that whether *A* successfully compensates *B*, or whether *B* successfully compensates *A*, a Pareto improvement is effected, is all too frequently believed illustrative of the cardinal virtue of an economic principle that is above and independent of the law.[34] If the nonsmoker's enjoyment is reduced by the smoker's freedom to smoke, so, it is argued, the smoker's enjoyment is reduced by abstaining for the sake of the nonsmoker. Each interferes with the enjoyment of the other. The conflict of interest, it is concluded, is symmetric in all relevant respects, and the determination of which of the parties ought, if possible, to compensate the other is either held to be of no interest to economists, or else may be settled by reference to the distributional implications (as, for instance in [**9**]). But this apparent ethical dilemma, at least, does not stand up to scrutiny. In accordance with the liberal maxim, the freedom of any man to smoke what he chooses and when he chooses would, indeed, be conceded

[33] Paradoxically, perhaps, this interpretation is borne out by the familiar misgivings about the neglect of the distributional implications of applying hypothetical compensation tests. (For particular instances the reader is referred to the articles by Hotelling [**6**], Scitovsky [**13**], Radomysler [**12**], and Baumol [**1**].) A distributional proviso may be attached to the compensation tests, as has been suggested by Scitovsky [**13**], Little [**7**], and many others. What the distributional proviso should state, however, is not always clear, but it is generally conceded that the statement, to command general assent, must have reference to the ethics of society.

While this explicit concern with distribution rather than the uncertain implications for distribution of the marginal utility approach may be seen as one of the redeeming features of the New Welfare Economics, the question of who, under the circumstances, ought to pay compensation, must also be referred to ethical considerations, distinct from and possibly in conflict with those invoked in discussing the distribution of welfare. If my neighbor's weeding machine is eccentric enough to blow his weeds into my garden, I should not like to think that the question of who compensates whom is to be decided by reference to our relative incomes.

[34] Coase [**4**, p. 2] writes: "The question is commonly thought of as one in which *A* inflicts harm on *B* and what has to be decided is: how should we restrain *A*? But this is wrong. We are dealing with a problem of a reciprocal nature. To avoid the harm to *B* would inflict harm on *A*. The real question that has to be decided is: should *A* be allowed to harm *B* or should *B* be allowed to harm *A*?" A conflict of interest does not *per se*, however, imply reciprocal damage. Thus, in one of the instances adduced, that of a confectioner *A* the vibration from whose machinery disturbed a doctor *B* at his work, reciprocity would require that the doctor, in his turn, damage the production of confectionery, which was not alleged. It follows that *B* has an incentive to approach *A* for the terms on which he, *B*, may obtain relief while *A* has no such incentive. The only incentive *A* has is to add gratuitously to the noise in order to expedite and increase the bribe offered by *B*.

—but with the crucial proviso that his smoking take place in circumstances which do not reduce the freedom of others. In so far as it does, the freedom of the smoker is not symmetric with that desired by the nonsmoker who merely wishes to breathe unpolluted air and, in the pursuit thereof, and unlike the smoker, does not reduce the amenity of others. The nonsmoker, who suffers damage to his enjoyment, has an incentive to approach the smoker in the hope of reaching an agreement to limit the damage. The smoker, who suffers nothing from the nonsmoking activity, has no such incentive. Similarly, the benefits enjoyed by any person as a result of his operation of noisy vehicles, lawn mowers, or airplanes, do incidentally damage the amenity of others; the person who lives quietly does not. The conflict of interest does not arise, therefore, from *reciprocal* effects and does not imply equal culpability. The conflict arises from the damage inflicted only by one of the parties on the other. It follows that unless the law is altered to provide comprehensive safeguards for the citizen's rights to certain fundamental amenities, the range of voluntary agreements that are, or might be, entered into within the existing legal framework cannot be vindicated, at least not on ethical grounds, by reference to invisible-hand arguments.[35]

In the current obsession with economic growth, little heed is paid to these critical features of the existing pricing system. Economists busy contriving yet more sophisticated growth models are already sufficiently occupied experimenting with a variety of production functions, with saving and investment coefficients and time responses. As for those engaged in empirical studies aimed at discovering the sources of economic growth, they are sure to invoke demarcation arguments: their concern with the growth of wealth, in some aggregative sense, as measured by indices of national out-

[35] Throughout the paper we have deliberately evaded the difficulties associated with checking the accuracy of subjective estimates of compensatory payments. It might reasonably be suspected that many people suffering from the existing disamenities, inflicted on them by industrial expansion, would make exaggerated claims. But, even if we assume that such difficulties are not likely to be satisfactorily resolved, exaggerated claims would tend to provide greater incentives for those generating external diseconomies to take the initiative in promoting a separate facilities solution. If, for instance, enthusiastic motorists were called upon to satisfy the claims of those sensitive to their disamenity-creating potential, the purchase of large motorized residential areas by the automobile interest is likely to prove a far more economical solution than a mixed Pareto outcome within each of the existing residential areas.

put, being regarded as separable both from familiar distributional problems and from the ethical implications under the existing law that have been raised in this paper. However, whether or not they accept the arguments for a change in the existing legal framework, in so far as they justify their study of economic growth as evidence of concern with the real growth of wealth, they can hardly ignore the effects of those alterations in the legal framework that would promote Pareto improvements unattainable under the existing system. For the effect is surely to expand the range of society's choices in a significant way: not merely in the provision of more gadgetry, at least in affluent societies, but in ways that are vitally important to the individual's well-being, in the choice of environment.

Of course the growth economist may choose to ignore this implication also. But he cannot, with any pretense at consistency, claim to be concerned with ways of increasing real income, under any acceptable definition, and yet to be unconcerned with an existing legal framework that acts to inhibit socially significant choices from being brought into effect.

REFERENCES

1. Baumol, W. J., "Community Indifference," *Review of Economic Studies*, Vol. 14 (1947).
2. Buchanan, J., and W. C. Stubblebine. "Externality," *Economica* (November 1962).
3. Buchanan, J., and G. Tullock. *The Calculus of Consent*. Ann Arbor: University of Michigan, 1962 (especially pp. 47–48, pp. 61–62, and Chapter 7).
4. Coase, R. H. "The Problem of Social Cost," *Journal of Law and Economics* (October 1960).
5. Davis, O. A., and A. Whinston. "Externalities, Welfare and the Theory of Games," *Journal of Political Economy* (June 1962).
6. Hotelling, H. "The General Welfare in Relation to the Problems of Taxation and of Railway and Utility Rates," *Econometrica* (1938).
7. Little, I. M. D. *A Critique of Welfare Economics*. 2nd ed. Oxford: Oxford, 1957.
8. Meade, J. E. "External Economies and Diseconomies in a Competitive Situation," *Economic Journal* (March 1952).
9. Mishan, E. J. "A Survey of Welfare Economics, 1939–1959," *Economic Journal* (June 1960). Reprinted in this volume. See pp. 11–86.

10. Mishan, E. J. "Welfare Criteria for External Effects," *American Economic Review* (September 1961).

11. Pigou, A. C. *The Economics of Welfare*. 4th ed. London: Macmillan, 1932.

12. Radomysler, A. "Welfare Economics and Economic Policy," *Economica* (1946).

13. Scitovsky, T. "A Note on Welfare Propositions in Economics," *Review of Economic Studies* Vol. 9.

14. Stigler, G. J. "The New Welfare Economics, A Communication," *American Economic Review* (1943).

15. Turvey, R. "Side Effects of Resource Use," *Environmental Quality in a Growing Economy*. Baltimore: Johns Hopkins, 1966.

APPENDIX 1

Under the L law which, in Section 2, permits radio playing, consider the "perverse" case—each individual being faced with an *increasing* marginal utility of the good (the good being, in this example, the elimination of others' radio noise). Since the sum of payments offered by the remainder to bribe each additional person from playing his radio grows with the size of the population in consequence of the larger payment each is willing to offer to prevent the playing of the nth radio as compared with the payment of the $(n-1)^{th}$, it should be clear that one can always choose a population large enough to ensure that the *NB* of the C outcome is positive. Thus, even if the order in which the radios were prohibited from playing were such as to yield negative figures for the first r column totals, a large enough population n will ensure that the remaining $(n-r)$ column totals add up to a positive sum that is larger, absolutely, than the sum of r negative column totals. The significant implication for the increasing marginal utility case is, therefore, that a population can always be chosen which yields a positive *NB* from exempting each member of the population from the L law. As a corollary the C arrangement is, in effect, an alteration of the L law and produces the same positive *NB* as the B arrangement.

However, in such cases it is a sufficient condition for the D arrangement to yield a larger *NB* than the C or B arrangement, that not all the *row* totals are positive. For if all the $(n-h)$ persons having positive row totals are placed in a separate $\overline{L}$ area they become better off in not having to compensate the *h* individuals having negative row totals (as required in the C arrangement). And this is not all. The *h* individuals left in a separate *L* area may now enjoy their radios the more in the absence of the $(n - h)$ radios, the additional enjoyment being represented by the sum of the payments each was willing to pay to turn off the $(n - h)$ radios which have now been removed to the separate $\overline{L}$ area. And though it is possible that a different division of the population between the separate areas could be found to yield a still larger *NB*, the selection rule that allocates to the $\overline{L}$ area only those with positive row totals (those who, on balance, prefer a quiet area) will always produce a positive *NB* larger than that arising from the C or B outcomes, both of which result in total prohibition.

Although the result that a sufficient increase in population can always justify a change of law for the area as a whole makes the case of increasing marginal utility rather less interesting than the "normal" case of diminishing marginal utility, the implications for the C outcome of populations below this crucial size may be briefly indicated.

If it is possible to arrange the order of individual prohibition as to begin with positive column totals, we should, as in the "normal" case, begin with the highest positive totals. In that event it is possible, by prohibiting the radios of the first *r* persons having positive column totals, to secure a positive *NB* greater than that emerging from the B arrangement. As an instance, the Matrix *I*(*L*) is reproduced below except that the row-wise directions of the positive figures are reversed in order to accord with the notion of increasing marginal utility.

	W	*Z*	*X*	*Y*	
W	−14	4	5	6	1
Z	8	−25	9	10	2
X	3	7	−33	9	−14
Y	10	15	16	−35	6
	7	1	−3	−10	−5

It is manifest that in this case also the C solution prohibits *W* and *Z*, although now yielding a positive *NB* of no more than 8.

By the method discussed in the text, the D solution, placing W and Z in the $\bar{L}$ area produces an excess NB of 35. This instance serves also to introduce the possibility of column totals being initially positive, then negative, and eventually positive again. For if we continue to add population to this group of four, the greater magnitude of the positive figures in each additional column would eventually produce positive column totals. If, at some such population, the sum of *all* the column totals were positive but less than 8, the C outcome that would prohibit only W and Z is obviously to be preferred. If, on the other hand, this sum were greater than 8, the C outcome with the higher NB would require complete prohibition. The C outcome in such a case would be then the same as the B outcome both in respect of arrangement and NB.

Finally, there may be instances for which it is not possible to arrange columns so as to provide an initial positive column total. Nonetheless, if the population is large enough, the column totals eventually become positive and, as in the B outcome, we are faced with all-or-nothing decisions according as the sum of the column totals is positive or negative. In the example below, the NB of the C outcome is the same as that of the B outcome and equal to 2.

	W	*X*	*Y*	*Z*	
W	−14	4	5	6	1
X	5	−14	8	10	9
Y	3	5	−14	7	1
Z	0	2	4	−15	−9
	−6	−3	3	8	2

If, according to our selection rule, we now allow W, X, and Y to move into a separate area under the $\bar{L}$ law they would be better off there than they were in the common area subject to the L law by 11—the payments they would jointly make to be in a quiet area. Z, being placed in a separate L area, would be better off by 6. Thus $NB(D) - NB(C)$ is equal to 15.

The reader may satisfy himself that, for the zero welfare case, if the same population were subjected instead to the $\bar{L}$ law, the corresponding "perverse" assumption of decreasing marginal disutility (of radio noise) produces symmetrical results.

APPENDIX 2

A general n-person model may be briefly outlined by identifying the $n \times n$ Matrix V with the L law, and the $n \times n$ Matrix $\overline{V}$ with the $\overline{L}$ law. The element v_{ij} ($\overline{v}_{ij}$) is individual i's compensation to exempt individual j from the existing L ($\overline{L}$) law. If the exemption of individual j from the L ($\overline{L}$) law confers an advantage on individual i, v_{ij} ($\overline{v}_{ij}$) is positive and is interpreted as individual i's maximum payment to individual j for j's exemption. If, on the other hand, j's exemption from the $L(\overline{L})$ law inflicts some liability on individual i then v_{ij} ($\overline{v}_{ij}$) is negative, and is interpreted as the minimum sum acceptable to individual i as compensation for j's exemption. In particular v_{ii} ($\overline{v}_{ii}$) is the individual i's compensation for his own exemption from the $L(\overline{L})$ law, positive if it is an advantage to be exempt from the existing law, negative if it is a disadvantage. We need not in general impose any restrictions on the signs, but if all elements had all the same signs, whether positive or negative, the outcome of each of the decision rules would be the same. In order for the analysis to have any interest the matrix must have elements with positive and negative signs, and for an optimal or separate facilities outcome, at least one column total must have an opposite sign to the others.

From the relevant data the V matrix is arranged so that the sum of the first m column totals ($m < n$) yield a maximum positive value. The small v in the bottom right hand corner is the algebraic sum of the $m \times n$ elements of the V matrix.

$$
\begin{array}{cccccccc}
v^{11} & v^{12} & \cdot & \cdot & v^{1m} & \cdot & v^{1n} & v^{1\cdot} \\
v^{21} & \cdot & \cdot & \cdot & v^{2m} & \cdot & v^{2n} & v^{2\cdot} \\
\cdot & \cdot & \cdot & \cdot & \cdot & \cdot & \cdot & \cdot \\
\cdot & \cdot & \cdot & \cdot & \cdot & \cdot & \cdot & \cdot \\
v^{m1} & \cdot & \cdot & \cdot & v^{mm} & \cdot & v^{mn} & v^{m\cdot} \\
\cdot & \cdot & \cdot & \cdot & \cdot & \cdot & \cdot & \cdot \\
v^{n1} & \cdot & \cdot & \cdot & \cdot & \cdot & v^{nn} & v^{n\cdot} \\
v^{\cdot 1} & v^{\cdot 2} & \cdot & \cdot & v^{\cdot m} & \cdot & v^{\cdot n} & v^{\cdot\cdot} \\
\rightarrow & & & & & & &
\end{array}
$$

MATRIX V

Each of our decision rules may result in some change from the initial (uncorrected) position in which all are subject to the L law. A change resulting from the A decision rule may, or may not, be a Pareto improvement as compared with the initial situation. Changes resulting from the B, C, or D, decision rules are always Pareto improvements compared with the initial situation.

A. SINGLE OUTCOME VOTING Designate the algebraic sum of any i^{th} row as $v_{i.}$, and attribute a value of plus one to each row having a positive total and minus one to each row having a negative total.[a] If so valued $\sum_{i=1}^{n} v_{i.} > 0$, then the L law is changed to $\overline{L}$.

B. PARETO SINGLE OUTCOME We now require that each row total assume its actual algebraic value. Again, if $\sum^{n} v_{i.} > 0$, the L law is reversed.

It is clear that, owing to the different systems of weighting the row totals in A and B, the outcome from applying the B rule may differ from that of applying the A rule. If under the B rule, however, $\sum^{n} v_{i.} > 0$, and, accordingly, the law is changed from L to $\overline{L}$, there is a Pareto improvement compared with the initial situation, an NB which is equal to $\sum^{n} v_{i.}$.

C. PARETO MIXED OUTCOME Designate the algebraic sum of the elements in any j^{th} column as v_j and exempt all those individuals having positive column totals. As mentioned above, we have

[a] We ignore the rows whose algebraic totals are equal to zero. Such individuals are indifferent to being subjected, along with the others, either to the L law or to the $\overline{L}$ law.

already arranged the matrix so that the first m columns have positive totals and together yield a positive value as great or greater than any other arrangement of the data. The remaining $(n - m)$ individuals will all have negative column totals and will remain subject to the L law. Compared with the initial situation, the net benefit of this outcome, $NB(\mathrm{C})$ is equal to $\sum_{j=1}^{m} v_{.j}$.

The superiority of the C outcome over the B outcome is easily demonstrated:

$$NB(\mathrm{B}) = \sum^{n} v_{i.} = v, \text{ and where } v > 0 \quad NB(\mathrm{B}) > 0$$

By arrangement of the matrix, however,

$$NB(\mathrm{C}) = \sum^{m} v_{.j} \geqq \sum^{n} v_{.j} = v = NB(\mathrm{B})$$

For the relevant case, $m < n$, however,

$$\sum^{m} v_{.j} > \sum^{n} v_{.j}$$

and therefore

$$NB(\mathrm{C}) > NB(\mathrm{B})$$

D. SEPARATE FACILITIES OUTCOME We can partition the V matrix as shown, placing the first m individuals in a separate $\bar{L}$ area, the remaining $(n - m)$ individuals being placed in a separate L area. Partitioning results in the four submatrices V^{11}, V^{12}, V^{21}, and V^{22}. First consider the case in which $V^{11}I \leqq 0$. The D outcome yields an excess NB over the C outcome equal to (a) the negative of the algebraic sum of the elements in V^{11}, plus (b) $\sum^{m} v_{i.}$. This is explained as follows:

(a) If, in the C outcome, the algebraic sum of the V^{11} elements were negative, a net payment was required to compensate the first m individuals for their exemptions from the L law. This net sum—equals $-(V^{11}I)$—has to be met, in the C outcome, by the $(n - m)$ unexempted group from their net positive payments, equal to $V^{21}I$, to exempt the m group. Once the exempted m group is placed in a separate exempted area, the unexempted $(n - m)$ group is therefore able to dispose of a greater surplus, compared with the C outcome, to an amount exactly equal to $-(V^{11}I)$.

(b) The individuals of the exempted m group, however, are not in general indifferent as between (i) being exactly compensated for their exemption in an area in which the remaining $(n - m)$ individuals are unexempted, as under the C outcome,[b] and (ii) being exempted in a separate $\bar{L}$ area. If we continue to make the assumption that they are indifferent between being in a larger or smaller area in either of which there is total exemption, their net gain from changing from an L area (or its equivalence—complete compensation under a C outcome) to an $\bar{L}$ area can be calculated as the algebraic sum of their row totals. If this is positive, it represents the amount of money they would offer, on balance, to have the whole area under $\bar{L}$ law. The effect being the same when they are placed in a separate $\bar{L}$ area, this sum can be regarded as a positive surplus. If, on the other hand, the algebraic sum of the m row totals is negative, there is a negative surplus to be added to (a) above.

Thus $\{NB(\text{D}) - NB(\text{C})\} = \{(\text{b}) + (\text{a})\} = \overset{m}{\Sigma}\, v_{i.} - V^{11}I$, or $V^{11}I + V^{12}I - V^{11}I = V^{12}I$. Or, more generally, for the case in which $V^{11}I \leqq 0$, $NB(\text{D}) \gtreqless NB(\text{C})$ according as $V^{12}I \gtreqless 0$.

In the case for which $V^{11}I > 0$, we set the (a) component equal to zero, as the unexempted group does not dispose of a greater surplus, compared with the C outcome, when it remains in a separate L area. Thus $\{NB(\text{D}) - \text{NB}(\text{C})\} = \{(\text{b}) + (\text{a})\} = \overset{m}{\Sigma}\, v_{i.}$ only, $(= V^{11}I + V^{12}I)$. Or, more generally, in the special case, $NB(\text{D}) \gtreqless NB(\text{C})$ according as $\overset{m}{\Sigma}\, v_{i.} \gtreqless 0$.[c]

[b] The m group is, of course, indifferent to being exactly compensated for its exemption under the C outcome and remaining in the initial situation under the L law.

[c] An alternative method of reaching the same result is to compare the row totals for each group under separate areas with their row totals in the initial situation. From the NB(D) so calculated we can subtract NB(C).

Compared with the initial situation the net benefit for the m exempted members when placed in a separate $\bar{L}$ area is, as explained in the text, equal to $\overset{m}{\Sigma}\, v_{i.}$.

As for the remaining $(n - m)$ group, remaining in a separate L area their net benefit in each row is increased by removal therefrom the algebraic sum of the first m elements, this sum being the net amount of all compensatory payments for exempting each member of the m group from the L law—no longer necessary when the m group is placed in a separate $\bar{L}$ area. The net benefit of this $(n - m)$ group, compared with the initial situation is, therefore, equal to $V^{21}I$.

Thus $NB(\text{D}) - NB(\text{C}) = (\overset{m}{\Sigma}\, v_{i.} + V^{21}I) - \overset{m}{\Sigma}\, v_{.j}$

The simplest plausible situation in which $NB(\text{D}) > NB(\text{C})$ under the L law is that in which (i), for each individual the activity is advantageous to himself but disadvantageous to others, and (ii) each member of the m group attaches greater value to resisting his own exemption than he does to exempting the remaining members of the m group, conditions that were exemplified in the Matrix $I(L)$.

A change to the $\overline{L}$ law is to be associated with a $\overline{V}$ matrix having elements $\overline{v}_{ij}$. In the special case of zero welfare effects with respect to the activity in question, the $\overline{V}$ matrix is equal to a $-V$ matrix, with $\overline{v}_{ij}$ equal to $-v_{ij}$. With all signs reversed, the results are symmetrical and the outcomes the same.

A. If the voting under L was a majority for $\overline{L}$, under the $\overline{L}$ law the voting will be a minority for L. In both cases the voting outcome would be for $\overline{L}$. The converse is obviously true.

B. If, under L, $\sum^{n} v_{i.} > 0$, under $\overline{L}$ it will be $\sum^{n} \overline{v}_{i.} < 0$. The outcome in both cases is the adoption of the $\overline{L}$ law. Again, the converse is obviously true.

C. If the V matrix was so arranged as to have the first m column totals sum to a maximum, the remaining $(n - m)$ column totals must sum to a maximum (absolute) negative value. In the $\overline{V}$ matrix, with all signs reversed, the first m column totals now have the maximum (absolute) negative value, and the remaining $(n - m)$ columns the maximum positive value. These $(n - m)$ individuals, each having positive column totals, will now be exempted from the $\overline{L}$ law while the m members remain subject to it. This is effectively the same result as that reached with the V matrix; $(n - m)$ members being there subject to the L law, and m being exempted. Thus if V is associated with the permissive law, the C outcome under both laws is that the $(n - m)$ group engages in the activity and the m group does not.

---

or $$\sum^{m} v_{i.} + V^{21}I - V^{11}I - V^{21}I$$

or $$\left(\sum^{m} v_{i.} - V^{11}I\right) = V^{12}I,$$

as above, for the first case in which $V^{11}I \leq 0$.

For the special case of $V^{11}I > 0$, however, it is $\sum^{m} v_{i.}$ alone.

Though the optimal outcome is the same for both laws, the NB(C) under the $\bar{L}$ law will not in general be equal to the NB(C) under the L law. Under the $\bar{L}$ law NB(C) is equal to $\sum_{j=m+1}^{n} \bar{v}_{.j} \gtreqless \sum_{j=1}^{m} v_{.j}$, which is NB(C) under the L law.

D. Again, under the $\bar{L}$ law we are guided by the C outcome in leaving the m group in a separate $\bar{L}$ area and the remaining $(n - m)$ members moving to a separate L area. The excess NB compared with the C outcome of this arrangement is equal to $-\bar{V}^{12}I$. For if the algebraic sum of the elements in $\bar{V}^{12}$ is negative, this represents, under the C outcome, a net compensatory requirement by the members of the m group for their agreement to exempt the $(n - m)$ members from the $\bar{L}$ law. Once the m group is placed in a separate $\bar{L}$ area then provided $\bar{V}^{12}I \leqq 0$,[d] it is no worse off than being in the initial situation under the $\bar{L}$ law (which situation is also exactly equivalent to being compensated for the $(n - m)$ exemptions in the C outcome). The $(n - m)$ group, however, no longer has to make this payment, equal to $-\bar{V}^{12}I$. Hence, $\{NB(\text{D}) - NB(\text{C})\} = -\bar{V}^{12}I$.[e] Or, in general, $NB(\text{D}) \gtreqless NB(\text{C})$ according as $\bar{V}^{12}I \gtreqless 0$.[f]

[d] If, on the other hand, $\bar{V}^{-12}I > 0$, this indicates that, on balance, the m group derives net positive benefit from the $(n-m)$ group's exemption from the $\bar{L}$ law under the C outcome. Therefore placing this m group in a separate $\bar{L}$ area—without the presence of the exempted $(n-m)$ members—must make it worse off.

The $(n-m)$ group in the separate L area, on the other hand, is no worse off (unless, of course, we have it compensating the m group in the separate $\bar{L}$ area —in which case the m group is no worse off, having shifted the burden to the other group). However, if $V^{12}I > 0$ the n members as a whole are worse off by $-V^{12}I$ when placed in separate areas than they were under the C outcome.

[e] This apparent asymmetry in calculating $NB(\text{D}) - NB(\text{C})$ under the $\bar{L}$ law as compared with the L law springs from the two different ways in which the C outcome is reached. What we might call the prevailing group, $(n-m)$, in the C procedure paying to exempt the others—the m group—under the L law, but paying to exempt themselves under the $\bar{L}$ law.

[f] Again, an alternative method of reaching the same result is to compare the row totals for each group in the separate areas with their row totals in the initial situation. From the NB(D) so calculated we subtract NB(C).

Assuming the m group is no better or worse off in a separate $\bar{L}$ area than in the initial situation under a joint $\bar{L}$ area, we need consider only the $(n-m)$ group. Recall that the n row elements in the initial situation are the individual's compensatory payments to exempt each of the n members from the $\bar{L}$ law. Thus

The simplest plausible situation in which $NB(\mathrm{D}) > NB(\mathrm{C})$ under the $\bar{L}$ law is that in which, again, the individual's activity though advantageous to himself is disadvantageous to others. Under the prohibitive law $\bar{L}$ each of the elements in $\bar{V}^{12}$ is negative and therefore $\{NB(\mathrm{D}) - NB(\mathrm{C})\}$, equals $-\bar{V}^{12}I$, is positive.

If now, when L is reversed, we allow that welfare effects alter the absolute size of the compensatory payments—so that $\bar{v}_{ij} \gtreqless -v_{ij}$, and therefore $\bar{V} \neq -V$—the outcomes of applying the decision rules A, B, C, and D are no longer uniquely determined irrespective of the law. In particular, the optimal outcomes under the C rule will, in general, differ according as the law is L or $\bar{L}$.

---

a negative algebraic sum of the first m elements in any of the $(n-m)$ rows entails a net compensatory sum required by that individual for consenting to exempt from the $\bar{L}$ law the m group as a whole. Once such an individual is placed in a separate area without the m group, *though without for the moment changing the existing $\bar{L}$ law,* these m row elements are omitted for each of the $(n-m)$ individuals. The remaining elements for this $(n-m)$ group comprise those in the submatrix $\bar{V}^{22}$. The sum of these elements is the net amount which the $(n-m)$ group is willing to pay to change this now separate $\bar{L}$ area into a separate L area. If, now, the area is put under the L law, these $(n-m)$ individuals do not in fact have to pay the sum $\bar{V}^{22}I$ which, consequently, measures $NB(\mathrm{D})$.

Since $NB(C)$ is equal to

$$\sum_{j=m+1}^{n} \bar{v}_{.j}$$

$$\begin{aligned} NB(\mathrm{D}) - NB(\mathrm{C}) &= \bar{V}^{22}I - \sum_{j=m+1}^{n} \bar{v}_{.j} \\ &= \bar{V}^{22}I - \bar{V}^{12}I - \bar{V}^{22}I \\ &= -\bar{V}^{12}I, \text{ as above.} \end{aligned}$$

PART 4

APPLICATIONS OF WELFARE ECONOMICS

CHAPTER 9

Interpretation of the Benefits of Private Transport*

I

In this article I construct a hypothetical situation to reveal some of the circumstances under which consumer's surplus, when used as an index of the benefits to be derived from private automobile travel, may give perverse results—a rise in the index being accompanied by a reduction in the benefit experienced by motorists. Less surprisingly, it will also be shown that the use of consumer's surplus in determining optimal traffic flows, in benefit-cost studies, and in estimating rates of return in road investment results in solutions leading to overinvestment in road construction unless the alternatives to private automobile travel are properly priced.

Although not essential, it will simplify the analysis to assume (1) that in all sections of a fully employed economy, except those under examination, price is already equal to social marginal cost,

* From *Journal of Transport Economics and Policy,* Vol. 1 (May 1967). Reprinted with the permission of the London School of Economics and Political Science (University of London).

and (2) provisionally at least, that there are no neighborhood effects external to the transport industry that affect the amenity of the public. We estimate the consumer's surplus for each individual in terms of present discounted value of expected surpluses over the future, using as discount rate whatever rate is deemed appropriate. A measure of this consumer's surplus, represented by the compensating variation[1] on the purchase of a new automobile, requires the individual to anticipate at the time of purchase the total number of miles for which the car will be used, valuing each mile at its maximum present worth to him (net of all variable costs, including fuel and maintenance) and arranging these sums in descending order to the point of zero maximum worth. This arrangement produces a function $V(m)$ of total expected mileage. After completing M miles the automobile is to be sold for a sum having a present value of £T. If the car when bought costs £B, including tax,[2] the present discounted value of the compensating-variation measure of consumer's surplus, CS, is equal to $\int_0^M V(m)\,dm$ —$(B - T)$, this sum being the maximum the individual would be prepared to pay in order to secure a permit to buy the car at the price £B, given his expectation of reselling for the sum mentioned after motoring M miles.

Phase I of the situation is one in which there is no private traffic. An efficient system of public transport, say a bus service, links all parts of the city. Individual A, typical of others, uses the bus daily to take him to the center of the city in about ten minutes. Public transport is also used for his occasional outings.

Phase II is the transitional one in which A buys a new car which in the circumstances prevailing (which he, short-sightedly, projects into the future) is expected to take him to the center in five minutes. On his anticipations of the future he makes a CS of, say, £800. Provided that only A buys a car, and nothing else

[1] In this context, the compensating variation is the maximum sum an individual will offer for the privilege of buying a good at a given price. See J. R. Hicks, "The Four Consumer's Surpluses," *Review of Economic Studies,* Vol. 9 (1944).

[2] This tax may be an underestimate or overestimate of the costs of road maintenance and administration incurred by the community (exclusive of the costs of mutual congestion) in keeping the traffic moving on the existing system of roads. The analysis assumes that the tax is exactly equal to the costs incurred.

changes, *A* is to that extent better off in phase II than in phase I.

Phase III occurs after a large enough number of others follow *A*'s example. Within two or three years, we may suppose, the increase in the number of private cars is such that it takes *A* 15 minutes to drive to work. He realizes now that he was better off in phase I, but that opportunity is now closed to him. For, owing to the build-up of private traffic, the congestion is such that it would now take him 25 minutes to reach his office by bus. Moreover, since bus drivers have had to be compensated for the increased difficulties and risk of driving, the bus fare has risen.

Phase III′ is the situation after public transport has been withdrawn altogether, as may happen if commercial considerations alone prevail. Analytically, it differs from III only in being a more extreme case of it.

II

By assumption, *A* is now worse off in phase III than he was in I. He would, of course, prefer II to either III or I. But II is a transitional phase only: it is no longer open to him, and could be reserved for him only if he were granted special privileges.

Since *A* is typical of other individuals who have changed from being passengers to being motorists, we can assume that I is *socially* preferred to III: dealers in motor cars and accessories may, themselves, be on balance better off, but we suppose that they could not compensate the rest of the community and remain as well off as they were in I.

There are two points to notice. First, under existing institutions there are no self-generating forces that can restore to the community the socially preferred phase I. Only a collective decision could return the community from the existing III or III′ phase to the original I situation. Second, *A*'s *CS* on his automobile in phase III will exceed that in phase II notwithstanding that he gets less benefit from it in phase III. It was, in fact, just because public transport was so cheap and efficient in phase I that the maximum amount he was prepared to pay for successive miles of private driving was lower then than it is now in phase III, in which the public transport alternative is less attractive. If now, for example, we move to phase III′, in which the public transport alternative is completely withdrawn, a loss of welfare will certainly be experienced by the remaining passengers. Some of these ex-passengers will have little choice but to purchase automobiles. Nevertheless, compared with their new alternatives—those of walking to work and of not working in the city—the *CS* on their purchase will be positive, and may even be large. Since we may assume that the cars used by the displaced passengers in phase III′ take up more road space than did the displaced buses, the motorists in phase III′, of whom *A* was a typical example, will also be worse off than they were in III.

If the benefit conferred by the private automobile on its owner is measured by his *CS,* or any proxy measure, the chronological change through II, and III, and III′ will appear to register a continuously increasing benefit, notwithstanding the continuous deterioration in his welfare in this respect.

A similar development could, of course, arise in other situations, for instance in a suburb linked by rail to the city. At the given rail fare n commuters are required for the railway to "break even." If, therefore, owing to an initial change from rail to road, only m commuters remain ($m < n$), the railway service must close down. The closure clearly makes the m commuters worse off. But it also makes worse off those who before the closure were travelling by private automobiles, because: (a) m commuters now have to travel by road and increase the congestion there, and (b) even though automobile travellers made no use of the railway, or used it infrequently, it did provide a form of insurance in case the car was out of service—or for any occasions when, for one reason or another, the motorist did not feel up to driving.

Again, however, despite the fact that everyone going into the city is adversely affected by the railway closure, the community's demand for road travel will be seen to have expanded and the individual and, therefore, the collective consumer's surplus of automobile owners will reveal a gain. Each ex-train-commuter who has now perforce to purchase an automobile must reveal a positive *CS*. As for the remainder, once the railway service has been removed the only alternative, we may suppose, is walking to the city. The maximum amount any individual would be willing to pay for the ith journey by car is consequently greater.

These simple illustrations may serve to remind us that there are difficulties other than those of statistical measurement. Not only can the index of consumers' benefit rise over time without any actual experience of benefit—simply because "real" income is increasing, and therefore people are prepared to pay more for the ith unit of any good, or service, whose actual utility to them in fact remains unchanged—but such an index can rise concurrently with an actual reduction of benefit. The more significant parts of the other factors which may affect any consumer's surplus (and rent) analysis relate to the constancy of the prices, and/or availabilities, of the close substitutes, and complements, for the good or service in question. The more effective is the good y as, say, a substitute for x, the smaller will be the consumer's surplus on purchase of x at the given prices. Raise the price of y, and ultimately withdraw it from the market, and this simultaneously *reduces* the welfare of the consumer and *increases* his measure of consumer's surplus on purchases of x.

III

We may now use the same two illustrations to show that any road engineering recommendations flowing from such estimates of the demand curve for automobile travel are invalid in the absence of optimal outputs in all the alternative services. In the first illustration, as the community moves into phase III the transport engineer will continue to revise upward his estimate of the "optimal traffic flow," [3] which appears to expand, therefore, along with the fall in motorists' welfare.[4]

The transport engineer may also use the data in III and III′ to justify investment in road widening, flyovers, freeways, and bridges in the attempt to accommodate the expanding number of private automobiles.

[3] By calculating the marginal congestion cost of traffic $dC/dN = dC/dT.dT/dS.dS/dN$, where C is total congestion cost, N the number of vehicles, T the total time taken by the traffic over the given route ($= tN$, where t is the average time taken per automobile) and S is the average speed of traffic over that route. The optimal traffic flow is that which equates marginal congestion costs dC/dN to the demand *price* $P(N)$ for that route.

[4] Of course, in the event of phase III′ being reached, there remaining no alternative but to walk to work, the elasticity of demand may be so low as to make little difference, if any, between the actual traffic flow and the optimal traffic flow.

Now, if there were effective methods for imputing congestion costs in the first place, other recommendations would follow which, under our assumption that in all other sectors price was equal to social marginal cost, could be justified. Beginning with a satisfactory public transport in phase I, such a mechanism would require that full compensation for any inconvenience caused to every passenger and bus driver by the marginal private car be imputed to the marginal private car. Such a scheme would ensure that no additional car be allowed on the route(s) in question unless it were able to effect a Pareto improvement: the owner of the car being better off after compensating everyone else using the roads—but passengers, bus drivers, and intra-marginal automobiles—than he would be without the use of his car. Such a requirement, which would ensure growing benefits from traffic, might well entail an optimal flow with very few private automobiles.

Be that as it may, it is only *after* this optimal flow is established that one may proceed to estimate correctly the returns to investment in road widening, freeways, and other traffic-accommodating projects. A traffic flow that has not been corrected implies that marginal congestion costs already exceed marginal benefit for some part of the existing traffic flow. Total congestion costs incurred being, then, greater than the optimally determined congestion costs, the saving by traffic investment will appear correspondingly greater. It is possible, therefore, that an initial optimal traffic flow might reveal no economic case for traffic investment, whereas failure to establish this optimal flow would allow traffic to pile up congestion costs and would consequently enable investment to appear profitable, in effect, by reducing excess traffic costs that were not warranted in the first place.

Similar remarks apply to our second illustration. If, as a consequence of rail closure, congestion occurs on the roads connecting the suburb to the center of the city, the establishment of an optimal flow of motorized traffic must precede any estimate of the benefits of road investment. More important, the rationale of the proposed rail closure itself should be scrutinized before this requirement. A fall in the number of fare-paying passengers below some critical number n is generally irrelevant in this connection. The line should be kept running for the time being if, at any number of passengers for which price is equal to marginal operating costs, total benefit exceeds total operating costs.[5] Benefits may be reckoned as the sum of three items: (a) the fares that could be collected from all those willing to pay the marginal cost price (as determined by the existing demand schedule) *plus* the consumer's surplus of every such individual, (b) the insurance value of the railway service to those who do not anticipate any particular railway journeys, and (c) the sum total of any (additional) congestion costs that would be inflicted on all motorists having to use the suburb-to-city road after the railway closure.[6] It would not be surprising if many of the railway services closed or due for closure could prove economic viability by meeting these conditions.[7] At all events, closing a railway service which on this criterion ought not to be closed brings about a misallocation of scarce resources, including those released by closing the railway. After resources have been misallocated by closing the railway service, investment in roads that would otherwise (if the railway services were available) be clearly seen as wasteful might well appear profitable.

Before concluding, it is worth emphasizing that the application of the consumer's surplus concept in transport economics goes far beyond its direct application in the analysis of optimal flows. Its use is implicit in cost-benefit analysis and in other transport investment criteria. Inasmuch as the estimated benefits of a bridge or new road will include savings in running costs and savings in motorists' time *as compared with existing alternatives,* the value of these benefits entails an upward revision of the individual's schedule of marginal valuation, roughly equal to his demand curve, with respect to motoring mileage. This being so, the withdrawal of any

[5] Largely the earnings of *necessary* personnel, fuel, and maintenance charges.

[6] To be more exact, (c) should be included in so far as this contingent addition to congestion has not been anticipated. If it were wholly anticipated it would have raised the consumer's surpluses of existing, and potential, railway users, and would also have raised the value of the railway to motorists who make no regular use of the railway.

[7] Professor George Clayton, in private correspondence with me, points out that there is no common pattern of decision about rail closures, and that many lines have been closed or are threatened with closure even though they carried, or currently carry, heavy local traffic. In particular he cites the proposed closures of (1) the Liverpool–Southport electric line, carrying over 100,000 passengers a week, mainly during rush hours—but this proposal has been dropped pending further study; and (2) the Cardiff–Coryton line, which offers only a peak hour service—permission to close the line has been refused, owing to the heavy commuter traffic, but eventual closure is still possible.

existing substitutes for private motoring raises all such marginal valuation schedules and shifts to the right the aggregate demand curve for motoring—the number of motoring journeys increasing as a result both of the induced rise in the motoring population and the induced rise in the average number of journeys per motorist. Thus, as public transport is withdrawn or rendered less efficient, *benefit-cost ratio* calculation is increased, since estimated "benefits" of constructing a road or bridge begin to appear which would not have appeared under an optimally controlled traffic flow. Moreover, inasmuch as the expected returns from any capital investment in roads or bridges are derived from just such benefits, the resulting *internal rate of return* calculation also becomes inflated whenever the existing traffic flow exceeds the optimal flow. And though it is possible that, in some cases, this spurious rise in the estimated benefit-cost ratio or internal rate of return is not large, it may be enough to raise the estimates beyond the crucial figure at which the investment decision becomes operative.

IV

We have confined ourselves in this note to external diseconomies that are internal to private motoring, *i.e.*, to the mutual congestion costs of motorized traffic, following the popular custom of relegating to a parenthetical remark the unmeasurable, though probably much more important, effects on the physical environment. The private car carries along with it, however, another much neglected disamenity potential as the chief agent of urban sprawl and ribbon building. As "developers" set up estates farther and yet farther from city centers, in the assurance that wherever they site their buildings families with private cars will be prepared to make the longer journey in order to live in country areas, the advantages of those families already settled in these areas are diminished.[8]

[8] Again, however, if some institutional mechanism could be established whereby each additional home buyer (who adds to the existing number in or near the area and so contributes to its transformation into a suburb) were obliged to compensate existing householders for the loss of amenity endured by his settling there, the criterion for a Pareto improvement could be met. Such external diseconomies would then be automatically corrected and urban sprawl be subject to a built-in check.

Even if we restrict the analysis to a given area (say the city and its dormitory areas), the continual visual disturbance, the pollution of the air by exhaust fumes, and the incessant engine noise and vibration generated by any *n* travelers using private transport are very many times greater than would be generated by the same number, using public transport, especially if public transport were electrically powered. Hence, although an optimal flow of traffic calculated with respect only to mutual traffic frustration already favors public transport at the expense of private transport (comparing this optimal flow with the usual free-for-all that makes road investment appear so profitable), an optimal flow that also takes into consideration these other environment-damaging consequences—no less relevant or significant for being statistically elusive—would further reduce the warrantable flow of private traffic. If the number of private car journeys consistent with this more comprehensive measure of the optimal flow were believed to be few, the costs involved in their regulation might well suggest prohibition of all private traffic within a given area as the most economical solution—allowing, perhaps, for a given number of private taxis within the area for emergency purposes.

It may, of course, happen that, contrary to our initial assumption, an existing public transport system is already inefficient in coverage, speed, and frequency. However, an analysis yielding a Pareto optimal solution requiring the provision of an efficient public transport service does not depend for its validity upon the chronological sequence posited.[9]

[9] In general, if all vehicles differed in size and other relevant characteristics, and if the value attached by their occupants to travelling the distance in question differed for any i^{th} journey, we should determine the optimal traffic flow and its composition by maximizing the social surplus. This is got by ranking the individual journeys by the excess of *CV* over the marginal congestion cost until the excess is zero. In the absence of welfare effects on the *CV* measure (these would be brought into operation by compensatory payments), the optimal flow and composition of the traffic is uniquely determined. For any flow having a social surplus smaller than this maximum indicates a potential Pareto improvement. Thus some journey(s) currently excluded by the composition of the existing traffic could replace some journey(s) currently included, and thereby increase the social surplus. The additional gain from such exchange operations could, of course, be distributed among the participants so as to make each of them better off.

CHAPTER 10

A Proposed Normalization Procedure for Public Investment Criteria*

The development of criteria for public investment, over the years, seems to have found favor in admitting and ranking public projects by comparing the present discounted values of their streams of returns and against comparisons based on the internal rate of return.[1] This gathering weight of opinion has been influ-

* From *Economic Journal* (December 1967). Reprinted with the permission of the Royal Economic Society. I am indebted to Professor D. McFadden, Dr. L. Needleman, and Mr. R. Turvey for critical comments on an earlier draft of this paper.

[1] To choose a few instances out of many, Hirschleifer, in an excellent paper elaborating Fisher's dual approach to the investment decision [**9**], draws a "main positive conclusion," that the present-value rule is universally correct "in a limited sense" given a perfect capital market, and a "main negative conclusion," that the internal-rate-of-return rule for the multiperiod case (under the usual definition) is not generally correct. P. Steiner [**21**, p. 897] compares investment projects by discounting their expected future returns using the social rate of time preference as the appropriate discount rate. O. Eckstein [**4**] argues that the general use of the internal rate of return method does not give optimal results, and that normative significance in ranking is obtained only by discounting future receipts by a subjective time preference. More recent papers like those of S. Marglin [**12**] and M. Feldstein [**6**] have taken the present discounted value method for granted and concentrated chiefly on the elaboration of the present value of a social opportunity cost. R. McKean [**16**] might be quoted as an earlier exception

enced by two considerations. First, that the present discounted value and the internal rate of return methods lead, in general, to different rankings of a set of investment streams and, since the logic of the present discounted value method appears unassailable, in cases of discrepancy the internal rate of return method is rejected. Second, and strongly reinforcing the first consideration, is the fact that the present discounted value method yields a unique magnitude with respect to the discount rate adopted, whereas more than one positive internal rates of return may be found to correspond to a given investment stream.[2]

The aim of this paper is to make explicit a normalization procedure setting forth the conditions under which, alone, comparisons of investment streams by either criterion have economic significance. The resulting normalized investment criteria, whether based on internal rate of return or on present discounted value (and whether, with this latter, benefit *less* cost or benefit-cost ratio is used [3]), invariably produce the same ranking for any given set of investment projects. One implication of this normalization procedure is of particular interest: notwithstanding that future negative returns of an investment stream may produce more than one

---

to the consensus, but the exception is more apparent than real. In the problem of choosing among a given number of investment projects subject to a capital budget he suggests using the highest rate of discount that yields a net present value greater than or equal to zero for each of the investment outlays that together add up to the amount of the capital constraint. This highest discount rate is equal to the marginal internal rate of return and gives a net present value of zero to the marginal project. This resulting marginal internal rate of return that is used as a discount rate depends upon the budget constraint and is not necessarily related to the social rate of time preference or to the return on private investment.

[2] J. Lorie and L. J. Savage [**11**] use a simple example to show how the present value of an investment stream varies from negative to positive and negative again as the rate of interest increases, thus providing two positive internal rates of return. Because of this ambiguity in the internal rate of return method they propose the present-value method. Ezra Solomon [**20**], in comparing the two methods, points out correctly that the usual present-value method implies reinvestment of future receipts at the discount rate adopted while the internal-rate-of-return method implies reinvestment at the resulting internal rate. Yet if the ambiguity of the latter method is acknowledged no solution is offered. The reader is left to infer that only the use of the present discounted value method avoids ambiguity. J. Hirschleifer [**9**] also recognizes that such a method does not give unique answers and turns to the present discounted value method for correct decisions.

[3] S. Marglin [**12**] and others, concerned as they are with a criterion for introducing a public investment project, adopt the benefit-less-cost form. The "Green Book" [**22**], on the other hand, rejects the benefit-less-cost form on grounds that it may favor large projects over small ones.

positive internal rate of return as ordinarily defined, the economics of the normalization procedure entails a definition more apt to the concept of an internal rate and one yielding a unique value.[4]

I

The assumptions which are to be maintained in this paper are common to recent contributions on the subject of public investment criteria; (i) full employment of resources, implying that public expenditure of any kind can be increased only at the expense of private expenditure, (ii) certain foreknowledge of the returns to any investment project, (iii) the existence of a single rate of interest, r, to represent society's rate of time preference,[5] (iv) a certain rate in perpetuity, ρ, to all investment in the private sector of the economy, and (v) r less than ρ, which implies that the volume of investment for the economy is below the optimal volume.[6]

The steps to be taken in order to ensure identical ranking of investment streams irrespective of which criterion is used, and which comprise the process of normalization, are four in number:

1. All benefits and outlays of any investment stream are to be compounded forward to yield a *terminal value, TV,* at some future date.

[4] If the ranking resulting from the normalized internal rate of return is always the same as that resulting from the normalized present-value criterion it might seem to follow that the present-value method ranking is invariant to the rate of discount used. Once the normalization procedure is understood, however, it will be seen that this implication is incorrect.

[5] Steiner [**21**] identifies this rate r as the opportunity cost of deferred consumption, and lists in his footnote 8 (page 897) a number of actual rates of interest in the U.S. economy with which it should not be confused. Marglin [**12**] calls r a social rate of interest, one that reflects the weighting of consumption at different periods. Feldstein [**6**] talks of a social-time-preference discount rate, a normative interest rate that represents government policy. Margolis [**14**], in reviewing Eckstein [**4**], McKean [**16**], and others, discusses their proposals for determining this ideal rate in the American economy. This present paper does not contribute to this discussion. It is concerned with what ought to be done about public investment when a proxy to such an ideal rate is available.

[6] This is assumed in the recent papers by Marglin [**12**] and Feldstein [**6**]. Marglin [**13**] invokes an external effects argument, further formalized by Lindt [**10**] and challenged by Usher [**23**], to provide reasons why, even in a perfect capital market, the rate of interest may be above some optimal rate and, therefore, the existing volume of investment below the optimal. The assumption of an *unchanged* r and ρ in the analysis is valid for a period during which the additional volume of investment is small. But the assumption of a *discrepancy* between r and ρ is valid for a nonoptimal volume of investment.

2. The maximum reinvestment potential is to be realized for each investment stream.
3. A capital outlay common to all the alternative streams under comparison is to be established.
4. The investment streams under comparison must be brought to a common period.

A word about each of these:

1. Once the *TV* of each investment stream is computed under the above rules, they may be ranked either directly, or first reduced to *present discounted values,* PV_i, at any rate of interest, *i*. Alternatively the internal rate of return may be calculated for each of the *TV*'s. These transformations do not affect the ranking.

2. By assumptions (iv) and (v) no reinvestment of revenues at a rate below ρ is undertaken, but opportunities for yields greater than this must be considered.[7] The stream of primary benefits[8] attributable to a public investment may exceed the stream of primary revenues that are actually collected. Though governments have the powers necessary to raise, by taxes, revenues equal to the estimated value of the benefits and to make these revenues available for reinvestment, the analysis will have a wider range of applications if we recognize existing political limitations as a part of the given institutional constraints. This means that if, owing to such constraints, a part or all of any benefit does not accrue as cash receipts during the period in question then that part, or all, of the benefit is not available for reinvestment and may, therefore, be regarded as consumption which is constrained to take place within the period.[9] It follows that the policy maker

[7] In his seminal paper **[20]** Ezra Solomon argued that the ultimate criterion is total wealth arising from investment by some terminal date and, therefore, some assumption about the reinvestment of receipts before that date is necessary. The concept is crucial though it was not at the time formally elaborated. In order to do this satisfactorily, it would be necessary to solve the internal rate of return paradox and to explain the implications of the unique ranking apparently without recourse to a discount rate. Neither of these problems was broached in that paper, however. If they had been, this article would have been unnecessary.

[8] *Primary* benefits (and primary receipts) from any investment are those which would exist in the absence of all opportunities for reinvestment. *Secondary* benefits (and secondary receipts) are those which arise from the reinvestment of primary receipts, or from the further reinvestment of secondary receipts or, generally, from the reinvestment of the receipts of any subsequent reinvestment.

[9] Alternatively, one may assume that, since noncash benefits received by the citizen augments his real income, some fraction of this real increment will be

may choose an investment project, A, having a somewhat smaller primary return within each period than an alternative project, B, simply because the reinvestment potential of the latter is known to be restricted.

All collectible revenues, however, will be able to earn ρ in the last resort, but again, owing to institutional constraints, there may be specific opportunities open to the receipts (primary and/or secondary) of a public project A that are not available to an alternative project B. Whatever the specific reinvestment opportunities, if any, the normalization procedure requires that a choice be made for each project among the alternative reinvestment paths as to secure for it the largest *TV* possible. Any uncollectible benefit, b_t, conferred on the community during period t, and deemed to be consumed in that period, is, however, to be compounded forward to the terminal date n at the appropriate *social rate of time preference, STP,* to yield an equivalent *TV* of $b_t(1 + r)^{n-t}$, when r is the appropriate *STP*.[10]

3. All initial and subsequent outlays on any project must be brought to a common point of time: either to the terminal period n in order to be subtracted from the terminal value of benefits

---

reinvested in the private sector at ρ, and that of consequent increments of income accruing the same fraction is reinvested. The government, we assume, has no control over the reinvestment of indirect benefits—the resulting streams of consumption and secondary reinvestments generated from the indirect benefit being regarded as a constraint.

If the fraction saved, Θ, were the same as the marginal propensity to save, then Θb_t would be saved, and invested at ρ in the initial period, the remainder, $(1-\Theta)b_t$ being consumed. Of the subsequent returns from this secondary investment we again assume a fraction Θ to be reinvested and the remainder consumed, and so on. The value of b_t in the terminal period becomes

$$\frac{b_t}{P\Theta - r}[\Theta(1 + P\Theta)^{n-t}(\rho - r) - r(1 - \Theta)(1 + r)^{n-t}]$$

However, the normalization rules—in particular the rule of compounding forward each part of any period's benefit up to the terminal period n at the appropriate rate—are the same whichever assumption about the treatment of indirect benefits is deemed appropriate. For simplicity of exposition we have adopted the assumption in the text, that indirect benefits are wholly consumed as they accrue.

[10] It is true that if any individual is certain of being able to collect ρ in perpetuity for every pound of forgone consumption, simply by investing it in the private investment sector, the marginal time preference of each individual is also equated to ρ. This means only that each *individual's* time preference is equated to ρ, and therefore above the *STP*, r. For the economy, however, intertemporal comparisons of consumption are, by definition, to be made with the *STP*.

and to yield, therefore, the *net terminal value, NTV,* of the stream, or else to be discounted to the present so that, with reference to the *TV* generated, a normalized internal rate of return may be calculated. All such costs must therefore be either compounded forward to the terminal date, or discounted backward to the present, at the common opportunity yield ρ, since all such outlays could have earned ρ in the private sector if they were not otherwise tied up with the realization of a particular investment stream.[11] Where the capital sums of the investment projects to be compared are different we choose as the common outlay[12] the largest costing project subject to the budget constraint. The other projects must then employ the additional funds as advantageously as they can. If, for example, the cost of an A project were £10 million and that of an alternative project B were £8 million, the additional £2 million placed at B's disposal for the purpose of the comparison would be regarded as invested in the private sector at ρ.[13]

4. Without a common period the investment stream having a longer period adds to its terminal value through reinvestment. It is a matter of convenience that the terminal date common to the alternative investment projects be chosen as the date after which no further primary benefits and no further *specific* reinvestment

[11] Though one could, of course, regard the benefits of some specific investment project as the opportunity cost of some alternative specific investment project, such pair-wise comparisons are cumbersome, even where the alternative specific projects are few. If, therefore, we wish to rank a number of specific projects and, at the same time, exclude from admission those having a normalized internal rate below ρ, much the simplest way is to adopt ρ as the common opportunity yield. In effect, this method enables us to rank all investment projects by their excess (normalized) yield above ρ.

[12] Operational costs are, strictly speaking, to be entered as outlays and not to be thought of as a "revolving fund" from which payments for productive services and materials are repeatedly met over a period. The logic of the above procedure would therefore require that we split up the common period to the extent necessary to enter all such payments over the year, say, as outlays, and such profits from the sale of products or services as benefits.

[13] It might seem that this step could be avoided by employing a benefit-cost ratio. Indeed, Ezra Solomon [**20**] suggested that if two investment projects require different outlays one should compare the *PV* of their benefits *per dollar* of outlay. This ratio is useful when choosing a number of projects together up to the limit of a capital budget, as described in the Appendix. For comparing *alternative* projects, however, we have to settle on a common total outlay. The benefit-cost ratio for a B project may well be higher than that for an A project, but the total benefit to the £10 million available for *either* one *or* the other could be higher for A if the £2 million "left over" in the specific B project has no opportunity other than ρ in the private investment sector.

opportunities are due for any of the projects under comparison.[14] Any investment streams whose primary or secondary stream of receipts come to an end before the common terminal date n are made comparable simply by reinvesting the value of those benefits at the prior date up to the terminal date, and reinvesting the collectible part compounded at the rate ρ, otherwise at r.[15]

II

The implications of this normalization procedure should be apparent. It enables us to transform the stream of benefits and outlays of any investment project A; $(b_0 - c_0)$, $(b_1 - c_1)$, . . . , $(b_m - c_m)$, where b_t is the primary benefit and c_t the outlay in period t, into a stream 0, 0, . . . , 0, . . . , $(b^n - c^n)$, where b^n is the *normalized terminal value of the benefits of the A stream,* $TV^n(\text{A})$, and c^n is the normalized terminal value of the outlays. Alternatively, if $\text{B}_t \equiv (b_t - c_t)$, we transform the streams B_0, B_1, . . . , B_m into the stream 0, 0, . . . , 0, . . . , B^n, where B^n is the normalized terminal value of the *net* benefits of the A stream, $NTV^n(\text{A})$, defined as $(b^n - c^n)$. It will be convenient, from now on, to denote the normalized terminal value of the outlays, c^n, as K, and therefore (1) to define $NTV^n(\text{A})$ as $TV^n(\text{A}) - K$. Having defined $TV^n(\text{A})$ and $NTV^n(\text{A})$, we are now in a position to define (2) $PV_i^n(\text{A})$, (3) $NPV_i^n(\text{A})$, and (4) $\lambda_A{}^n$, these expressions corresponding to: (2) the normalized present value of the benefits of the A stream discounted at any

[14] In practice, the common period chosen may be shorter for two reasons: The additions to the TV made by extending the common period in accordance with the above rule may be negligible in terms of PV. The higher is the discount rate the more rapidly does PV converge to a constant. Secondly, once we remove the assumption of certain returns one tends to discount more heavily the more distant returns.

[15] The common period is not, therefore, the least common multiple of the benefit streams under comparison, an impression conveyed by the oversimplified example provided by R. Robinson [**18**]. If, for example, the last specific benefit on the A investment stream occurs in the twelfth year and the A project is not renewable, while B's last benefit falls due eight years from the initial outlay, though with some part of this last benefit having a specific reinvestment opportunity for a further three years, the common period is twelve years. If the three year specific opportunity on B's last return could be extended a further three years the common period would be fourteen years. In that case the normalized terminal value of A's benefits and outlays in the twelfth year would be compounded forward for an additional two years at ρ so as to render its NTV comparable with that of B.

rate of interest i, (3) the normalized present value of the *net* benefits of the A stream, again discounted at any rate of interest i, and (4) the normalized internal rate of return.

$$PV_i^n(\text{A}) \text{ is defined as } \frac{TV^n(\text{A})}{(1+i)^n} \tag{1}$$

$$NPV_i^n(\text{A}) \text{ is defined as } \frac{NTV^n(\text{A})}{(1+i)^n} \tag{2}$$

$$\lambda_A{}^n \text{ is defined as } \sqrt[n]{\frac{TV^n(\text{A})}{K^*}} - 1, \quad \text{where } K^* \equiv \frac{K}{(1+\rho)^n} \tag{3}$$

In other words, $\lambda_A{}^n$ is defined as the discount rate which makes TV^n(A), the normalized *terminal* value of the benefits of the A stream, equal to K,* the normalized *present* value of the A outlays. Inasmuch as TV^n(A) and K^* are positive, $\lambda_A{}^n$ is single-valued and positive.

Recalling that normalization requires, for each of the alternative investment projects, the same normalized terminal capital K, it is simple to prove that each of these three expressions, regarded as normalized criteria, will produce the same ordering for a group of projects as that resulting from the employment of TV^n(A) and NTV^n(A).

Given $TV^n(\text{A}) > TV^n(\text{B})$, we may infer each of the following:

$$TV^n(\text{A}) - K > TV^n(\text{B}) - K \tag{i}$$

hence, by definition (1), $NTV^n(\text{A}) > NTV^n(\text{B})$

$$\frac{TV^n(\text{A})}{(1+i)^n} > \frac{TV^n(\text{B})}{(1+i)^n} \tag{ii}$$

hence, by definition (2), $PV_i^n(\text{A}) > PV_i^n(\text{B})$

$$\frac{TV^n(\text{A}) - K}{(1+i)^n} > \frac{TV^n(\text{B}) - K}{(1+i)^n} \tag{iii}$$

hence, by definition (3), $NPV_i^n(\text{A}) > NPV_i^n(\text{B})$

$$(1 + \lambda_A{}^n)^n \cdot K^* > (1 + \lambda_B{}^n)^n \cdot K^* \tag{iv}$$

and, therefore

$$\lambda_A{}^n > \lambda_B{}^n$$ [16]

[16] Put otherwise, $\lambda_A{}^n$ and $\lambda_B{}^n$ are defined such that $\frac{TV^n(\text{A})}{(1+\lambda_A{}^n)^n} = \frac{TV^n(\text{B})}{(1 = \lambda_A{}^n)^n} = K^*$. If $TV^n(\text{A}) > TV^n(\text{B})$, the equation requires that $\lambda_A{}^n > \lambda_B{}^n$.

Finally, since normalization requires that the alternative investment projects have the same K, or K^*, it is evident that the benefit-less-cost criterion gives the same ranking as the benefit-cost ratio criterion, whether benefit is measured as TV^n or, more commonly, as PV^n, and also whether benefit is measured net of capital outlay or not.[17]

III

So far we have been concerned chiefly with a normalized ranking of the alternative investment projects. A criterion for the admissibility of any single investment project A, $NTV^n(\text{A}) > 0$, must also be met. The $TV^n(\text{A})$ discounted to the present at r—that is, $PV_r^n(\text{A})$—may well yield an *equivalent present value, EPV,* in excess of the initial capital outlay.[18] But this shows only that the community's equivalent present welfare may be increased by maximizing the potential benefit over time of the A project as compared with the alternative of using this capital outlay for *current consumption,* whereas the relevant alternative to the A benefit stream is the investment of its capital outlay in the private sector at the perpetuity ρ. Indeed, when this capital outlay is compounded forward at ρ to the terminal period to yield the sum K, such a sum may be larger than the $TV^n(\text{A})$ if, for any reason, some parts of the primary benefits cannot be reinvested at a yield as high as ρ.[19] Clearly, if both these terminal sums are discounted to the present at r, the resulting equivalent present value of the outlays, $K/(1 + r)^n$, may then be larger than that of the benefits, PV_r^n (A), in which case the adoption of the specific project A serves only to reduce the potential *EPV*. The criterion $NTV^n(\text{A}) > 0$ guards against this possibility. Indeed, it ensures that the A project yields a greater *EPV* for the community than does the capital outlay when

[17] Thus, if $\frac{PV_i^n(\text{A})}{K^*} > \frac{PV_i^n(\text{B})}{K^*}$ then $PV_i^n(\text{A}) - K^* > PV_i^n(\text{B}) - K^*$. Moreover, the second inequality follows from the first (a) whether we substitute K for K^* throughout, and (b) whether we substitute throughout either TV^n, NTV^n, or NPV_i^n, for PV_i^n.

[18] Or an equivalent initial outlay which, as has been argued, is arrived at by discounting future outlays at the opportunity cost ρ in the private sector.

[19] This is true, for instance, if parts of the stream of benefits of the A stream were indirect and could, therefore, be assumed to be wholly consumed as they accrued.

the latter is invested at ρ in the private sector. For $NTV^n(\mathrm{A}) > 0$ implies $TV^n(\mathrm{A}) > K$, which is to say that the normalized terminal value of the benefit stream is required to exceed the normalized terminal value of the outlays. It should be noted, moreover, that from $NTV^n(\mathrm{A}) > 0$ we may infer $NPV_i^n(\mathrm{A}) > 0$, and also $\lambda_A^n > \rho$,[20] both of which are alternative forms of the admissibility criterion for a specific investment project.

IV

Before comparing the results of a set of investment projects using ordinary criteria with those of normalized criteria, a puzzling feature of the latter demands an explanation. Bearing in mind Fisher's rate of return over cost—the rate of discount at which, as between two alternative investment streams,[21] preference-reversal (on a present-value basis) takes place—one is accustomed to thinking of the present-value ranking of projects as depending crucially upon the rate of discount adopted. Yet once we have evaluated the normalized terminal net benefits of any set of investment streams, and remarked the ranking, we may discount them to present value using *any* rate of interest without affecting the ranking. This may seem to suggest that the *STP*, *r* in this paper, has nothing to contribute in the ranking, or admissibility, of investment projects. Under the assumptions used in this paper, however, the *STP* is placed in a new perspective. First, and turning for a moment from the ranking-invariance puzzle, the use of the *STP* as the discount rate has normative significance inasmuch as it reduces the TV^n of any benefit stream to its *EPV*, this being the value in the present as between which and the potential terminal value of the benefit stream the community is deemed to be indifferent. Secondly, and more important, the *STP* provides a lower limit to the opportunity rate at which compounding forward may take

[20] If $NTV(\mathrm{A}) > 0$, then $\frac{NTV(\mathrm{A})}{(1+i)^n} > 0$ and, therefore, by definition $NPV_i^n(\mathrm{A}) > 0$.

Again, $NTV(\mathrm{A}) > 0$, or $TV^n(\mathrm{A}) - K > 0$, implies $TV^n(\mathrm{A}) > \mathrm{K}^*(1+\rho)^n$. Since λ_A^n is such that $TV^n(\mathrm{A}) = K(1+\lambda_A^n)^n$ substituting the latter term for $TV^n(\mathrm{A})$ in previous inequality gives $K(1+\lambda_A^n)^n > K^*(1+\rho)^n$, or $\lambda_A^n > \rho$.

[21] An appraisal of the economic significance of Irving Fisher's rate of return over cost can be found in Alchian [**1**].

place. Primary and secondary benefits are under no circumstances to be reinvested at a rate below the *STP*. Indeed, in our model, the private reinvestment opportunity yield ρ being greater than r, the *STP*, no reinvestment of any revenues below ρ is to be undertaken. Only in so far as some parts of the social benefits of a specific project do not accrue as revenues, and are regarded wholly as consumption within the periods they fall due, are they to be compounded forward at the *STP* to their equivalent value in the terminal period.[22]

V

Table 2 shows three investment streams, A, B, C, each over a period of five years, $t_0, \ldots . t_4$. In the right hand half of the

	t_0	t_1	t_2	t_3	t_4	(1) B	(2) K	(3) $(B - K)$	(4) $\frac{(B - K)}{K}$	(5) λ
A	−20	15	16	·	·	27.5	20	7.5	0.375	0.34
B	−100	·	·	160	·	120.2	100	20.2	0.202	0.17
C	−45	351	−402	·	·	315	374	−59	−0.63	0.46 4.56

TABLE 2

table the B in column 1 stands for conventional (nonnormalized) present value of the benefits when discounted at an *STP* of 10 percent. The *K* in column 2 represents the single initial capital outlay involved in projects A and B. It represents the outlays of project C when discounted to the present at 10 percent. The (B – *K*) in column 3 is therefore the *net* benefit of the investment streams, positive for A and B, negative for C. Column 4 shows the net benefit-cost ratio, (B – *K*)/*K*, again positive for A and B, and negative for C. Finally, the conventional internal rate of return, ρ, is shown in column 5, C having two (positive) internal rates of return.[23]

[22] If, on the other hand, we used a model in which $\rho < r$, no reinvestment opportunities at ρ would be undertaken, and all specific reinvestment opportunities would have to yield an average return greater than r over the reinvestment period in question.

[23] In general, since solving for the internal rate of return *on the conventional*

Columns 3, 4, and 5, may be used as alternative ranking criteria. The benefit-less-cost criterion would rank the projects in the order B, A, C, with C being inadmissible, its discounted cost exceeding its discounted benefit. The net benefit-cost ratio would rank the streams in the order, A, B, C, with C again being inadmissible. On the other hand, whichever of C's internal rates of return we adopt, the final column shows a ranking of C, A, B. Such are the rankings using nonnormalized criteria.

We now require additional information in order to take the steps necessary to obtain normalized criteria. Provisionally we shall restrict our attention to projects A and B. Since we must know the investment opportunities in the private investment sector, we assume a ρ of 20 percent per annum. Allowing that the capital available in the choice of these investment streams is not less than 100, we can multiply the A stream by 5 only if in fact it is possible to increase the scale by 5. If this is not possible, if, say, no more than a scale factor of 3 were possible, we should have a "surplus" capital outlay of 40 in the A project which surplus would be compounded at 20 percent to the terminal date. For convenience, however, let us suppose that the A stream can be increased five-fold, the figures now reading -100, 75, 80.

If there are no specific reinvestment opportunities open to A's primary returns but the return of 160 in the B stream can be reinvested in a specific project of one year's duration to yield 210 in t_4, the common terminal period to be adopted is t_4. Compounding forward, if the whole of the primary benefit of 75 in t_1 is an indirect benefit it may be regarded as wholly consumed within the t_1 period. Its terminal value of 99.8 in t_4 is calculated by compounding 75 for three years at the *STP* of 10 percent. If, on the other hand, the primary benefit of 80 in t_2 were in revenue, it could be reinvested in the private sector for two years at 20 percent to appear as 115.2 in t_4. The total terminal value of the A benefits is

---

definition involves the roots of a polynomial, an investment stream of n periods provides a maximum of $n-1$ different internal rates. Only those that are positive are of interest. Negative rates make sense, but are usually of slight interest. Complex roots do not appear to make economic sense.

Incidentally, in order to contrive more than one positive rate of return, it is not necessary that the first and the last return of the investment stream be negative. A small enough positive return, placed one or more periods both before and after the above C stream, would still allow us to produce two positive internal rates of return.

therefore 215.0. In the normalized Table 2, the TV^n's of A and B, 215 and 210 respectively, appear under B′ in column 1. In column 2, K' now represents the terminal value of the outlays, 207, for both A and B—the initial capital sum of 100 being compounded at 20 percent for four years. In column 3, (B′ − K') indicates the NTV^n of the investment streams. The normalized benefit-cost ratios of column 4—derived from dividing the NTV^n's of column 3 by their common terminal value of capital, 207.4—is obviously again positive for A and B, both of which are therefore admissible.

The normalized internal rates of return in column 5 of Table 3 are very different from those in Table 2. As a result of compounding A's primary benefit of 75 forward for three years at only 10 percent per annum compared with an outlay that is being compounded forward at 20 percent per annum, the resulting normalized internal rate of return becomes 20.7 percent. This is above the private opportunity rate of 20 percent and confirms the inclusion of the A project as a worthwhile specific investment. Stream B, on the other hand, has its normalized internal rate of return raised to 20.3 percent as a result of transforming 160 in t_3 to 210 in t_4, and therefore qualifies by a smaller margin using each of the normalized criteria in columns 3, 4, and 5.

	t_0	t_1	t_2	t_3	t_4	(1) B′	(2) K'	(3) $(B' - K')$	(4) $\frac{(B' - K')}{K'}$	(5) λ'
A	−100	75	80	·	·	215	207.4	+7.6	$\frac{+7.6}{207.4}$	0.207
B	−100	·	·	160	·	210	207.4	+2.6	$+\frac{2.6}{207.4}$	0.203
C	−15	117	−134	·	·	202	207.4	−5.4	$\frac{-5.4}{207.4}$	0.192

TABLE 3

Turn now to investment stream C which, we assume, has no special reinvestment opportunities open to its single collectible benefit of 351 in t_1. Since normalization requires a common magnitude for the capital outlays, stream C provides an alternative only if it can be scaled down to the available finance. If this is 100, it must be scaled to one-third, the value of its discounted, or compounded, outlays being then the same as that for A and B. We assume this possible, and enter C in Table 3 as the stream −15, 117, −134, having therefore a compounded outlay in the terminal period of 207.4, equal to that for A and B. Since the receipt of 117 in t_1 can be reinvested in the private sector at 20 percent for the three more years necessary to render it comparable with projects A and B, we enter 202 under B′ in column 1. The derived entries for columns 3, 4, and 5 place C consistently below B by a small margin, which, however, renders C inadmissible. The normalized internal rate of return of 19.2 percent, it will be noticed, is unique and compares with the two nonnormalized internal rates in Table 1 of 46 percent and 456 percent.

VI

This contrast between the results of the conventional internal rate of return and the uniquely determined normalized version requires a word of explanation. The ordinary definition of the internal rate of return—the discount rate which brings the net present value of an investment stream to zero—realizes the conventional *conception* of the internal rate, as an average of growth of an investment, only in the particular case of but a single capital outlay in period zero. Wherever there are subsequent outlays, the ordinary definition departs from the underlying conception. In such cases, the subsequent outlays are, in effect, reduced to a present value by employing as discount rate the resulting internal rate or rates of return, which rate or rates of return are applied also to the benefits, whereas the present value of the subsequent outlays can be determined only by recourse to the investment opportunities provided by the investment market. For only through such a market can a present payment be traded against a future payment. At the market rate ρ, therefore, an investor is financially indifferent between a payment of c_m in period t_m and a payment of $c_m/(1 + \rho)^m$ in the present. Consequently any internal rate of return (on the ordinary definition) greater than ρ will effectively understate the discounted present value of the later outlays, and vice versa.

This argument may be illustrated with reference to the C stream in Table 3. An investor comparing the growth potential of an investment in the C stream as compared with, say, one in the B stream, must transform the outlay of 134 in t_2 into a present outlay by recourse to the market yield, 20 percent in this example. He will, then, be financially indifferent as between a payment of 134 at t_2 and $134/(1 + .2)^2$ or 93, at t_0. (This is the best he can do: the liability of 134 at t_2 can *not* be settled for a current payment of about 65, or a current payment of about 6, which are the present values implied by reducing subsequent outlays using an internal rate of return of 46 percent or of 456 percent respectively.) The existing investment opportunities provided by the market therefore enable him to transform the C stream into $-(15 + 93)$, or -108, at t_0 and 117 at t_1, which stream yields an annual growth rate of about 8 percent.[24] Though there are no further positive returns, reinvesting the 117 for another period at 20 percent raises this average rate of growth. Extending the period to t_4 raises it further to give an average growth rate over the four periods of 19.2 percent—the longer the terminal date chosen the closer to 20 percent will the normalized internal rate-of-return approach.

The inadequacy of the ordinary definition of the internal rate of return in such instances may be further appreciated by slightly recasting the argument. Thus, if an investor were told that an opportunity existed of earning an internal rate of return of 46 percent per annum over a two-year period by investing 15 now, he would conceive of the opportunity in terms of a stream equivalent to -15, 0, $15(1 + .46)^2$. He would certainly feel cheated if, on paying 15 now, he was told to expect a receipt of 117 in the following year and a liability of 134 the year after. Of course, if he could lend at 46 percent, he would be able to put down 65 now in order to meet the payment of 134 at t_2, thus converting the C stream into -80, 117, which stream *does* give him a 46 percent return over the year.[25] But in fact he can lend only at 20 percent and is, therefore, indifferent, as stated, between a payment of 134 at t_2 and of 93 at t_0. By availing himself fully of the market, he realizes, as mentioned above, a return on this specific project of only 8

[24] If, contrary to the normalization procedure, the 134 in t_2 were exchanged for a payment of 112 in t_1 (instead of 93 in t_0), thereby converting the C stream to -15, 5, the annual growth rate would be negative.

[25] Alternatively, if he *could* lend at 456 percent, he would be able to put down 6 now to meet the payment of 134 in t_2, thereby converting the C stream into -21, 117, which would in fact give him a rate of return of 456 percent over the year.

percent over the one year. Needless to remark, he would feel even more cheated if he were told of an internal rate of return of 456 percent and anticipated a stream equivalent to -15, 0, $15(1 + 4.56)^2$.

The normalized internal rate of return both accords with the popular conception of an internal rate, as an average rate of growth over the relevant period, and necessarily ensures the same result as the other normalized investment criteria, whether they are used for ranking alternative projects or for determining the admissibility of specific projects. Thus, in Table 3, C is ranked last by all three criteria, and by all three fails the test of admission by a small margin—$B' - K' < 0$, $B'/K' < 0$, and $\lambda' = \lambda_c^n < \rho$. Both in respect of consistency of criteria[26] and rationale, the significance of normalization is brought out by a comparison of the two tables.

VII

In the special case where (a) all benefits are regarded as collectible revenues and (b) there are no special reinvestment opportunities exclusive to the investment projects under comparison, the normalized procedure for ranking and for admissibility becomes simpler. The (a) feature implies that all primary benefits have reinvestment opportunities yielding not less than ρ, while the (b) feature implies that such reinvestment opportunities do not yield more than ρ. With an *STP* $r < \rho$, a pound of any primary or secondary benefit will have a smaller terminal value if any part of it is consumed before the terminal date than if it is continually reinvested to the terminal date. Thus, the terminal value for any investment stream is made largest by reinvesting at ρ the full amount of all receipts, both primary and secondary, until the common terminal date.

But if all the revenues of any investment project have to be reinvested to the terminal date at exactly ρ, it makes no difference to its present value if the returns are each discounted back to the present in the ordinary way, using ρ as the discount rate than if,

[26] Since $NPV_i^n\ (A) = \dfrac{NTV^n(A)}{(1 + {}_i)^n}$ the ranking in Table 3 is unaltered by using the normalized *present* value of net benefits, instead of the normalized *terminal* value of net benefits as in Table 3.

instead, they are all first compounded forward at ρ to the terminal date and this sum then discounted back to the present at ρ. Under these special conditions, therefore, there will be no difference in the resulting figures as between (i) the net *normalized* present value of the investment projects when discounted at ρ, and (ii) the net *nonnormalized* present value of the investment streams when discounted at ρ. For a pound received at time t is now worth $1/(1 + \rho)^t$ at times zero without normalization. And it is worth the same when, as with the normalized procedure, it is first compounded at ρ to the nth period, there to be rediscounted back to time zero at ρ. It follows also that a nonnormalized admissibility criterion—that the net present value of a stream A discounted at ρ be positive, or NPV_ρ (A) > 0—is not different from the corresponding normalized criterion $NPV_\rho^n(A) > 0$.

These propositions are easily proved. In this special case, the normalized *terminal* net benefits of an investment stream A, having a stream of net receipts, positive or negative, $a_0, a_1, \ldots, a_m$, is

$$NTV^n(A) = \sum_{t=0}^{m} a_t(1 + \rho)^{n-t}$$

Therefore, the net normalized *present* value of the A stream when discounted at any interest rate i,

$$NPV_i^n(A) = \frac{1}{(1 + i)^n} \sum_{t=0}^{m} a_t(1 + \rho)^{n-t}$$

If we let $i = \rho$

$$NPV_\rho^n(A) = \sum_{t=0}^{m} a_t \frac{(1 + \rho)^{n-t}}{(1 + \rho)^n} = \sum_{t=0}^{m} \frac{a_t}{(1 + \rho)^t} = NPV_\rho(A)$$

and this latter expression is the *ordinary* (nonnormalized) present value of the A stream, using ρ as discount rate.[26]

What about common capital outlay and common terminal period? With regard to the first, since a specific investment project having a smaller capital outlay can employ additional funds only in the private sector—which investment yields an NPV_ρ of zero—any normalizing in this respect leaves the NPV_ρ^n of the set of specific

[26] Since $NPV_i^n(A) = \frac{NTV^n(A)}{(1 + _i)^n}$ the ranking in Table 3 is unaltered by using the normalized *present* value of net benefits, instead of the normalized *terminal* value of net benefits as in Table 3.

projects completely unchanged. Finally, although a common terminal period could be set to embrace the specific investment having the longest stream of primary returns nothing is added to the NPV_ρ of any shorter investment stream by having its primary returns reinvested at ρ to this terminal date. This last feature of the normalization procedure then also proves otiose under these conditions.

Under special conditions (a) and (b) therefore, the employment of ρ as the relevant discount rate, *not* $STP = r$, enables one to use an ordinary present value criterion, NPV_ρ, both for admissibility and for ranking of alternative investment projects.[27]

REFERENCES

1. Alchian, A. "The Rate of Interest, Fisher's Rate of Return over Costs, and Keynes' Internal Rate of Return," *American Economic Review* (December 1955).
2. Bailey, M. J. "Formal Criteria for Investment Decisions," *Journal of Political Economy* (October 1959).
3. Eckstein, O. "Investment Criteria for Economic Development," *Quarterly Journal of Economics* (February 1957).

[27] These special conditions are apparently those assumed by Marglin [**12**] in his model III. The more complex expression for a public investment criterion reached in that paper is the result: (1) of making a distinction between that part of the capital outlay financed by borrowing in the capital market—a part which was made to carry an opportunity rate of ρ—and the remainder which was raised by taxation and to which was attributed an opportunity rate of only r. However, as has been made clear in the text, the opportunities for funds raised by the government alternative to a specific project are (a) returning them to the public earmarked for consumption, in which case an expenditure of £1 today is worth £$(1+r)$ tomorrow, or (b) investing them in the private sector where a £1 today is worth £$(1+\rho)$ tomorrow. Inasmuch as $\rho > r$, the relevant opportunity cost of £1 invested in any specific project is ρ irrespective of how the £1 was raised. (2) On assuming that, of the primary and secondary returns to any investment, only a fraction—equal to the community's propensity to save—is reinvested at ρ. However, ρ being greater than r, the *whole* of the primary and secondary revenues ought to be reinvested for maximum terminal value.

If these errors are corrected we could, after calculating the terminal value of the specific investment stream A, discount it back to the present. Discounting it thus at r yields the *EPV* of the A stream. The Marglin procedure would then be to compare this *EPV* with its *social opportunity cost,* SOC: the terminal value of an equal outlay invested in the private sector when discounted back to the present at r. The use of the market opportunity rate ρ, instead of r, as the discount or compounding factor, makes calculation of the SOC unnecessary. We can apply the criterion $NTV(\mathrm{A}) > 0$, or $NPV_\rho(\mathrm{A}) > 0$ directly, under these special conditions, as indicated in the text.

These remarks are applicable also to the elaboration of the Marglin model by M. Feldstein [**6**].

4. Eckstein, O. *Public Finances, Needs, Sources and Utilization.* New York: National Bureau of Economic Research, 1961.
5. Eckstein, O. *Water Resource Development—the Economics of Project Evaluation.* Cambridge, Mass.: Harvard, 1958.
6. Feldstein, M. "Net Social Benefit Calculation and the Public Investment Decision," *Oxford Economic Papers* (March 1964).
7. Feldstein, M. "Opportunity Costs Calculation in Cost-Benefit Analysis," *Public Finance,* Vol. 19 (1964).
8. Galenson, W., and H. Liebenstein. "Investment Criteria, Productivity and Economic Development," *Quarterly Journal of Economics* (August 1955).
9. Hirschliefer, J. "Theory of Optimal Investment Decision," *Journal of Political Economy* (August 1958).
10. Lind, R. C. "The Social Rate of Discount and the Optimal Rate of Investment: Further Comment," *Quarterly Journal of Economics* (May 1964).
11. Lorie, J., and L. J. Savage. "Three Problems in Rationing Capital," *Journal of Business* (October 1955).
12. Marglin, S. "The Social Rate of Discount and the Optimal Rate of Investment," *Quarterly Journal of Economics* (May 1963).
13. Marglin, S. "The Opportunity Costs of Public Investment," *Quarterly Journal of Economics* (February 1963).
14. Margolis, J. "The Economic Evaluation of Federal Water Resource Development," *American Economic Review* (March 1959).
15. Massé, P. *Optimal Investment Decisions: Rules for Action and Criteria for Choice.* Englewood Cliffs, N.J.: Prentice-Hall, 1962.
16. McKean, R. N. *Efficiency of Government through Systems Analysis.* New York: Wiley, 1958.
17. Nichols, A. "The Opportunity Costs of Public Investment: Comment," *Quarterly Journal of Economics* (August 1964).
18. Robinson, R. "The Rate of Interest, Fisher's Rate of Return over Costs, and Keynes' Internal Rate of Return: Comment," *American Economic Review* (December 1956).
19. Sen, A. K. "Capital-Intensity in Development Planning," *Quarterly Journal of Economics* (November 1957).
20. Solomon, E. "The Arithmetic of Capital-Budgeting Decisions," *Journal of Business* (April 1956).
21. Steiner, P. O. "Choosing among Alternative Public Investments in the Water Resource Field," *American Economic Review* (December 1959).
22. U.S. Subcommittee on Benefits and Costs, Federal Inter-Agency River Basin Committee. *Proposed Practices for Economic Analysis of River Basin Projects.* Washington, D.C.: 1950.
23. Usher, Dan. "The Social Rate of Discount and the Optimal Rate of Investment: Comment," *Quarterly Journal of Economics* (November 1964).

APPENDIX
Choosing a Set of Investment Projects Subject to a Budget Constraint

The normalization procedure puts us in a position to carry a stage further the technique proposed by P. O. Steiner [**21**] for selecting a number of investment projects, both public and private, to serve specific purposes. The main departures from the methods laid out in that paper are: (1) the substitution of *normalized* terminal values for Steiner's nonnormalized present values, (2) whereas in his treatment *each* public investment project chosen is permitted to raise just so much of its capital by nonrenewal of existing public enterprises, the method used here is to put aside a fraction α of the total available capital to be met by government expenditure, the remaining fraction $(1 - \alpha)$ being financed by displacing existing public enterprises, (3) we remove certain restrictions adopted in the Steiner model, in particular (i) that the returns on all existing public enterprises are the same, and (ii) that there exists, at the most, one specific private project (alternative to public projects) suitable for each specific purpose.

To encompass both public and private investment options we construct an array, along each row of which are elements T_{iv} to indicate the NTV^n of the vth alternative investment option that can provide the ith service out of a total of q services under consideration. Of these elements in any i^{th} row, a number arise from *public* investment options alone, the typical one being T_{ij}, with j running from 1 to any number not exceeding m. The remainder arise from *private* investment options, the typical one being T_{is}, with s running from $m + 1$ to any number not exceeding n.[1]

Since we are no longer comparing alternative single investment projects, we no longer require that their capital outlays be equal: each of the several projects chosen from any number of investment options may have quite different capital outlays, the sum of which, however, must be within the budget restraint. In order to choose that combination of investment options yielding a higher terminal value than any other combination, we are first required to calculate, for each investment option, its corresponding *per pound* terminal value. Thus, dividing each T_{iv} by its corresponding total terminal capital requirement, $\overline{K}_{iv} = K_{iv}(1 + \rho)^n$, where K_{iv} is the initial capital sum or the normalized present value of the outlays, yields us τ_{iv}, the per pound normalized net terminal value of the iv^{th} investment option. An array of the τ's may be formed corresponding to the array of the T's.

(A) First we consider the more common case in which no private investment competes with public investment. Also, we confine ourselves, for the present, to the simpler constraint (1), $\alpha = 1$, which implies that any amount of capital up to a total of K may be raised by the government, but only by reducing private expenditure to the same amount. The choice of public investment projects is determined by maximizing

$$\sum_{i=1}^{q} \sum_{j=1}^{m} \tau_{ij} w_{ij} \overline{K}_{ij} \tag{1a}$$

(1a)[2]

subject to:

$$\left.\begin{array}{l} w_{ij} = 1, 0 \\ \tau_{ij} > 0 \end{array}\right\} \tag{2a}$$

[1] The same type of service required in a different locality is to be regarded as a different service. If, within a locality, two or more services under consideration may be combined and served by a single investment project, each possible combination of services counts as a distinct service. As for investment options, if two or more projects can be combined to provide a distinct service, each of such combinations of projects is to be treated as a separate investment option. If there are scale effects in any given investment option, each scale of project worth distinguishing (in the light of the expected demand for the service in question) is treated as a separate investment option for that service.

[2] Since j runs from 1 to any number not exceeding m, each of the i services having fewer than m investment options will have one or more τ's equal to zero in order to complete the $m \times q$ matrix of τ's.

$$\sum_{i=1}^{q} \sum_{j=1}^{m} w_{ij}\overline{K}_{ij} \leqq \overline{K} \tag{3a}$$

$$\sum_{j=1}^{m} w_{ij} \leqq 1 \quad \text{(for all } i\text{)} \tag{4a}$$

The first part of condition (2a), $w_{ij} = 1, 0$, indicates that the weight w_{ij}, attached to the ij^{th} option, is equal to unity if that option is selected as part of the public investment program, and is equal to zero if it is excluded from the program. The second part of condition (2a), $\tau_{ij} > 0$, indicates that no public investment option is to be admitted unless its normalized internal rate of return exceeds the opportunity yield ρ in the private investment sector. Condition (3a) states that the sum of the terminal capital requirements of the chosen investment options shall not exceed $\overline{K} \equiv K(1 + \rho)^n$, the value of the budget constraint compounded forward at ρ to the terminal period.[3]

If for some i^{th} service $\sum_{j=1}^{m} w_{ij} \neq 1$ then, from condition (2a), it must equal zero, in which case the ith service is not provided.[4]

A sufficient condition for employing a simple algorithm is that

[3] Where the final list of the investment projects in the program are few, we may have a choice of using a good deal less than $\overline{K}$, or more. There may, however, be political constraints to prevent our exceeding $\overline{K}$ by more than a specified margin.

[4] Two further departures from Steiner's treatment may be observed: (1) whereas Steiner would require $\Sigma w_{ij} = 1$, implying that *each* of the listed services is to be provided by some investment option, in the above treatment a service is provided only if it qualifies subject to yield constraints—whether public investment, as above, or private also. (2) Steiner [**21,** p. 903] defines an investment "facility" (option) with respect to a given *locality* (e.g. a particular dam site). Consequently, if it is used for any one "purpose" (service) it obviously cannot also be used for another—hence his "incompatibility restraint" (d). If this restraint were adopted here it would imply that in any one column of the array of options no more than one could be chosen. Since in the above treatment, however, the same service in a different locality defines a different service, there is no such restriction. The investment options appropriate to any one service can be arranged in any order and, consequently, there is nothing to preclude the choice of any number of investment options in the same column.

Finally, with conditions (5a), (6a), and (7a) below, we may allow for differences in the yields on existing public enterprises when we remove the constraint, $\alpha = 1$, and instead allow funds to be raised by abandoning some of the existing public enterprises.

The simpler alternative, proposed by Steiner, of assuming the same yield p on all existing public enterprise would require, instead of these conditions, only that each new public project in the final program have a positive NTV^n when its outlays are compounded forward at p $(p \geq \rho)$ to terminal date n.

along any one row the terminal capital sums $\overline{K}_{ij}$ corresponding to each of the alternative options are all the same. Where it is met we choose the highest τ for each row and list them in descending order starting with the highest. We go down the list, multiplying the highest τ for each row by its corresponding capital requirement, and summing as we go down until $\overline{K}$ is used up. The condition may seem stringent, but it will probably give the correct solution even where it is only approximately met.

In order to make provision for the more general constraint (2), $\alpha \leqq 1$, we suppose $\alpha \leqq 1$, and therefore $(1 - \alpha)K$ of the required capital sum is to be raised by abandoning, within the decision period, a number of public enterprises that otherwise would be renewed. We can be sure of some social gain, when using the funds thereby made available by displacing $(1 - \alpha)K$ of existing public enterprise, if the aggregate terminal value of the new investment projects which are substituted exceeds that of the displaced enterprises. But if we are to maximize social gain under these conditions, we should choose to abandon those among the existing renewable public enterprises which together requiring an initial capital sum $(1 - \alpha)K$, show the least possible aggregate terminal value. We select them by minimizing

$$\sum_{h=1}^{H} \tau_h w_h \overline{K}_h \tag{5a}$$

where $h = 1, 2, 3, \ldots\ldots H$, is the subscript for renewable public enterprises subject to

$$w_h = 1, 0 \tag{6a}$$

and

$$\sum_{h=1}^{H} w_h \overline{K}_h \geqq (1 - \alpha)\overline{K} \tag{7a}$$[5]

(Consistency requires, of course, that $\overline{K}_h$ be defined as $K_h(1 + \rho)^n$,

[5] In minimizing aggregate NTV^n the capital sum involved must be written as $\geqq (1 - \alpha)\overline{K}$. If it were set $\leqq (1 - \alpha)\overline{K}$ a routine solution of the linear programming problem would yield a minimum NTV^n by discarding all existing renewable public investment. If, owing to indivisibilities, this operation requires displacing renewable public investment in excess of $(1 - \alpha)\overline{K}$ we may be constrained to return the surplus funds, thereby reducing, to that extent, the public works budget. Otherwise we may be permitted to borrow a bit extra to renew the otherwise marginally discarded new public project.

T_h as the NTV^n of the hth existing public project if renewed, and τ_h as $T_h/\overline{K}_h$.)

Set within the A(2) constraint, additional expressions (5a), (6a), (7a) ensure maximum net gain only if it so happens that the smallest τ of the chosen set of new public investment is no smaller than the largest τ of the outgoing renewable public enterprises. For to the extent this requirement is *not* met we might increase aggregate NTV^n by withdrawing new investment projects with the lowest τ's in order to restore the displaced (potentially renewable) public enterprise(s) with higher τ's. This procedure, *if necessary,* subtracts from the total terminal capital available for new public projects, $\overline{K}$, a sum equal to, say, M $(M \geqq 0)$. Since the sum M represents the terminal capital value of the otherwise outgoing public enterprises that are to be restored, the capital sum $(1 - \alpha)\overline{K}$ released by abandoning such existing public enterprises is to be reduced by this amount M.

It is therefore required that we revise some of these conditions, in both the maximizing and the minimizing formulae.

For (3a) we write $\sum_{i}^{q} \sum_{j}^{m} w_{ij}\overline{K}_{ij} \leqq \overline{K} - M \quad (M \geqq 0)$ (3′a)

For (7a) we write $\sum_{h=1}^{H} w_h\overline{K}_h \geqq (1 - \alpha)\overline{K} - M$ (7′a)

And in order to determine the sum M we add condition:

$$\tau_i{}^* \geqq \tau_h{}^* \tag{8a}$$

$\tau_i{}^*$ are the τ's of the new public projects finally selected, and $\tau_h{}^*$ is the highest τ of the outgoing public services. Therefore condition (8a) requires that all new public projects adopted have a τ at least as high as the highest τ of the outgoing public enterprise.[6]

(B) We turn to the case in which specific private investments are to compete with alternative public projects in a number of

[6] If several public enterprises had to be restored in order that condition (8a) be met, indivisibilities may produce a situation in which the aggregate value of the restored enterprises falls short of, or exceeds, the capital value of the displaced public investment project. In such a case, provided there is sufficient latitude in the budget, we should choose to restore an additional public enterprise and, if necessary, exceed the capital value of the thereby rejected new public investment project, only if the former had a τ no smaller than that of the latter.

services, again (1) assuming first that $\alpha = 1$. We are not, however, to subject the whole array that includes both public and private enterprises to a capital constraint, as no political constraint is imposed on the amount of private capital contributed. It is not impossible that private capital could meet all the required services more efficiently than any of the public investment alternatives, in which case no part of the new public funds would be employed. At all events, the simplest method to employ in this more complex case, in which for each of the required services there are in general several alternative private projects, is to do the best we can with only private investments after which we introduce public alternatives wherever doing so increases aggregate terminal value.

In maximizing NTV^n with specific private investment alone, capital requirements need not be taken into account. For example, suppose that in providing the jth service we could choose either project X requiring a capital of 1,000 and yielding a NTV^n of 200, or Y requiring only 100 of capital and yielding a NTV^n of 180, we choose X simply on the grounds that 200 exceeds 180. For nothing is lost in transferring 900 more from the general private sector in order to construct the X project rather than the Y project. True, this extra 900 could have earned ρ if left in the general private sector. But it also earns at least ρ in the specific private project X; indeed, when transferred, and because X is chosen rather than Y, it yields an extra 20 to our aggregate NTV^n.

The first step is therefore to select the set of specific private projects by maximizing

$$\sum_{i=1}^{q} \sum_{s=m+1}^{n} w_{is} T_{is} \tag{1b}$$[7]

subject to

$$\left.\begin{aligned} w_{is} &= 1, 0 \\ T_{is} &> 0 \end{aligned}\right\} \tag{2b}$$

$$\sum_{s} w_{is} \leqq 1 \quad \text{(for all } i\text{)} \tag{4b}$$

There is no problem in maximizing under these conditions. Once

[7] We could as well have maximized $\Sigma\Sigma\tau_{is}\, w_{is}\, \overline{K}_{is}$ for greater uniformity of treatment. But since there is no budget constraint K we may use T_{is} directly (instead of $\tau_{is}\, \overline{K}_{is}$).

we have the array of T_{is} for private specific investment projects we merely choose the largest positive T in each row.

In order to determine next how to employ the available public funds, K, to maximum advantage, we draw up for all public projects an array of τ'_{ij}, where $\tau'_{ij} \equiv (T_{ij} - T_{is}{}^*)/\overline{K}_{ij}$ using T_{is} to indicate the largest private T_{is} chosen for the ith service. Thus τ'_{ij} is a measure of the *excess* terminal value per pound of any public investment over the chosen private investment providing the ith service. It goes without saying that we need consider only positive values of the τ'_{ij}: if for any service there is no positive τ'_{ij}, that service has to be provided by the private project in question. Thus, we use public funds K to maximize the excess of aggregate terminal value over that given by the provisional selection of a set of private investment projects by maximizing

$$\sum_{i=1}^{q} \sum_{j=1}^{m} \tau'_{ij} w_{ij} \overline{K}_{ij} \tag{5b}$$

subject to

$$\left.\begin{matrix} w_{ij} = 1, 0 \\ \tau'_{ij} > 0 \end{matrix}\right\} \tag{6b}$$

$$\sum_{i=1}^{q} \sum_{j=1}^{m} w_{ij} \overline{K}_{ij} \leqq \overline{K} \tag{7b}$$

$$\sum_{j=1}^{m} w_{ij} \leqq 1 \quad \text{(for all } i\text{)} \tag{8b}$$

As in case A, a sufficient condition for using the same sort of algorithm to solve the above is that along any one row the terminal capital sums $\overline{K}_{ij}$ corresponding to each of the alternative public investment options be the same. If it is met we choose the largest τ' for each row and list them in descending order starting with the highest. We move down the list, multiplying each such τ' by its corresponding capital requirements, summing as we go down until $\overline{K}$ is entirely used up.

(2) For the more general case where $\alpha \leqq 1$, with $(1 - \alpha)K$ of the initial capital sum to be raised by relinquishing existing public enterprise, we proceed much as we did in case A. If $(1 - \alpha)K$ of the existing public enterprises that come up for renewal within the decision period are to be removed, we must

choose to remove those yielding the least aggregate NTV^n. Therefore conditions (5a), (6a), and (7a) apply here also.

As in A(2), we shall not have maximized aggregate NTV^n if any of the outgoing public enterprises has a τ larger than any of the incoming new public investment projects. For if this happened aggregate NTV^n might be increased by withdrawing some of the newly chosen public projects in favor of otherwise outgoing public enterprises having a higher τ. Consequently we are again required to work out the $\tau_i{}^*$ of all the incoming new public investment, and, as in case A(2), to make the following amendments:

In the maximizing procedure above, substitute (3′a) for (7b).

In the minimizing procedure to be applied—(5a), (6a), and (7a)—substitute (7′a) for (7a), and, finally, add condition (8a), viz. $\tau_i{}^* \geqq \tau_h{}^*$.

BIBLIOGRAPHY
On Welfare Economics, 1939-1959

Abbreviations

A.E.A.	American Economic Association
O.E.P.	*Oxford Economic Papers*
E.J.	*Economic Journal*
J.P.E.	*Journal of Political Economy*
Q.J.E.	*Quarterly Journal of Economics*
S.E.J.	*Southern Economic Journal*
S.A.J.E.	*South African Journal of Economics*
C.J.E. & Political Science	*Canadian Journal of Economics and Political Science*
A.E.R.	*American Economic Review*
R.E.S.	*Review of Economic Studies*

1. Abramovitz, et al. *Allocation of Economic Resources*. Stanford, Calif.: Stanford, 1959.
2. Allais, M. "Rendement Social et Productivité Sociale," *Econometrica,* Supplement to Vol. 17. Section: Theory of Choice and Utilization of Resources (1949), p. 129.
3. Allen, C. L. "Modern Welfare Economics and Public Policy," *S.E.J.,* Vol. 19 (1952–1953), p. 28.
4. Allen, J. E. "A Fairer Income Tax," *E.J.* (1940), p. 475.
5. Archibald, G. C. "Saving and the Welfare Theory of Taxation," *Economic Record* (1955), p. 90.
6. Archibald, G. C. "Welfare Economics, Ethics and Essentialism," *Economica,* N.S., Vol. 26 (November 1959), p. 104.
7. Armstrong, W. E. "Utility and the Theory of Welfare," *O.E.P.,* N.S., Vol. 3, No. 3 (1951), p. 259.
8. Armstrong, W. E. "A Reply," *O.E.P.,* N.S., Vol. 5, No. 3 (1953), p. 264.
9. Arrow, K. J. "The Possibility of a Universal Social Welfare Function." Project Rand Rad (L)–289 (October 26, 1948). Lectographed.
10. Arrow, K. J. "A Difficulty in the Concept of Social Welfare," *J.P.E.,* Vol. 58, No. 4 (1950), p. 328.
11. Arrow, K. J. "Little's Critique of Welfare Economics," *A.E.R.* (1951), p. 923.
12. Arrow, K. J. "The Allocation of Risk Bearing" [Abstracts], *Econometrica* (1955), p. 342.

13. Arrow, K. J. "An Extension of the Basic Theories of Classical Welfare Economics," *Proceedings of the 2nd Berkeley Symposium on Mathematical Statistics & Probability*. Berkeley: University of California Press, 1951.
14. Arrow, K. J. *Social Choice and Individual Values*. New York: Wiley, 1951.
15. Arrow, K. J., and L. Hurwicz. "Dynamic Aspects of Achieving Optimal Allocation of Resources" [Abstracts], *Econometrica* (1952), p. 86.
16. Atkinson, F. J. "Saving and Investment in a Socialist State," *R.E.S.*, Vol. 15 (2) (1947–1948), p. 78.
17. Bailey, M. J. "The Interpretation and Application of the Compensation Principle," *E.J.* (1954), p. 39.
18. Bailey, M. J. "The Welfare Cost of Inflationary Finance," *J.P.E.*, Vol. 64, No. 2 (1956), p. 93.
19. Baldwin, R. E. "A Comparison of Welfare Criteria," *R.E.S.*, Vol. 21 (2), No. 55, p. 154.
20. Baldwin, R. E. "The New Economics and Gains in International Trade," *Q.J.E.* (1952), p. 91.
21. Balogh, T. "Welfare and Freer Trade—A Reply," *E.J.* (1951). p. 72.
22. Bator, F. M. "The Simple Analytics of Welfare Maximization." *A.E.R.* (1957), p. 22.
23. Baumol, W. J. "Community Indifference," *R.E.S.*, Vol. 14 (1), No. 35, p. 44.
24. Baumol, W. J. "The Community Indifference Map: A Construction," *R.E.S.*, Vol. 17 (3), No. 44, p. 189.
25. Baumol, W. J. Review of K. J. Arrow, *Social Choice and Individual Values*, *Econometrica* (1952), p. 110.
26. Baumol, W. J. *Welfare Economics and the Theory of the State*. London: Longmans, 1952.
27. Benham, F. "The Terms of Trade," *Economica* (1940), p. 360.
28. Benham, F. "What Is the Best Tax System?" *Economica* (1942), p. 115.
29. Bergson, A. "Socialist Economics," in H. S. Ellis (ed.), *A Survey of Contemporary Economics*, Vol. 1. A.E.A., 1948.
30. Bergson, A. "On the Concept of Social Welfare," *Q.J.E.* (1954), p. 233.
31. Blau, J. H. "The Existence of Social Welfare Functions," *Econometrica* (1957), p. 302.
32. Blaug, M. "Welfare Indices in 'The Wealth of Nations,'" *S.E.J.*, Vol. 26 (October 1959), p. 150.
33. Boulding, K. E. "Income or Welfare," *R.E.S.*, Vol. 17 (2), No. 43, p. 77.
34. Boulding, K. E. "The Concept of Economic Surplus," *A.E.R.* (1945), p. 851.

35. Boulding, K. E. "The Concept of Economic Surplus—Corrections," *A.E.R.* (1946), p. 393.
36. Boulding, K. E. "Welfare Economics," in B. F. Haley (ed.), *Survey of Contemporary Economics,* Vol. 2. A.E.A., 1952.
37. Boulding, K. E. Review of W. J. Baumol, *Welfare Economics and the Theory of the State, Econometrica* (1953), p. 210.
38. Bowen, H. R. "The Interpretation of Voting in the Allocation of Economic Resources," *Q.J.E.* (1943–1944), p. 27.
39. Braybrooke, D. "Farewell to the New Welfare Economics," *R.E.S.*, Vol. 22 (3), No. 59, p. 180.
40. Break, G. F. "Excise Tax Burdens and Benefits," *A.E.R.* (1954), p. 577.
41. Break, G. E., and E. R. Rolf. "The Welfare Aspects of Excise Taxes," *J.P.E.*, Vol. 57, No. 1 (1949), p. 46.
42. Brown, E. C. "Mr. Kaldor on Taxation and Risk Bearing," *R.E.S.*, Vol. 25 (1), No. 66, p. 49.
43. Buchanan, J. M. "Knut Wicksell on Marginal Cost Pricing," *S.E.J.*, Vol. 18 (1951–1952), p. 173.
44. Buchanan, J. M. "Individual Choice in Voting and the Market," *J.P.E.*, Vol. 62, No. 4 (1954), p. 334.
45. Buchanan, J. M. "Social Choice, Democracy and Free Markets," *J.P.E.*, Vol. 62, No. 2 (1954), p. 114.
46. Bye, R. T. "Welfare Considerations in Economics: A Reply" [Communications], *A.E.R.* (1952), p. 384.
47. Checkland, S. G. "The Prescriptions of the Classical Economists," *Economica* (1953), p. 61.
48. Coase, R. H. "The Marginal Cost Controversy," *Economica* (1946), p. 169.
49. Coase, R. H. "The Marginal Cost Controversy. Some Further Comments," *Economica* (1947), p. 150.
50. Coen, E. "Decreasing Costs and the Gains from Trade," *Economica* (1951), p. 285.
51. Corlett, W. J., and D. C. Hague. "Complementarity and the Excess Burden of Taxation," *R.E.S.*, Vol. 21, No. 54, p. 21.
52. Crutchfield, J. A. "Common Property Resources and Factor Allocation," *C.J.E. & Political Science,* Vol. 22 (1956), p. 292.
53. Davis, R. G. "Comment on Arrow and the 'New Welfare' Economics," *E.J.* (1958), p. 834.
54. Debreu, G. "The Co-efficient of Resource Utilization," *Econometrica* (July 1951), p. 273.
55. Dehem, R. "Welfare Losses" [Abstracts], *Econometrica* (1950), p. 297.
56. Denis, H. "A Note on the Theory of Tariffs," *R.E.S.*, Vol. 12 (2), No. 32, p. 110.
57. Dessus, G. *The General Principles of Rate Fixing in Public Utilities*. Report presented to the Congress of the Union Internationale des Producteurs et Distributeurs d'Energie Electrique,

1949. Translated in *International Economic Papers,* No. 1 (1951), p. 5.
58. Dobb, M. H. "A Note on Index Numbers and Compensation Criteria," *O.E.P.*, Vol. 8, No. 1 (1956), p. 78.
59. Dorfman, R., P. A. Samuelson, and R. M. Solow. *Linear Programming and Economic Analysis.* New York: McGraw-Hill, 1958, Chapter 14.
60. Duesenberry, J. S. *Income, Saving and the Theory of Consumer Behaviour*. Cambridge, Mass.: Harvard, 1949.
61. Eckstein, O. "Investment Criteria for Economic Development and the Theory of Intertemporal Welfare Economics," *Q.J.E.* (1957), p. 56.
62. Ellis, H. S. "Competition and Welfare," *C.J.E. & Political Science,* Vol. 11 (1945), p. 554.
63. Ellis, H. S., and W. Fellner. "External Economies and Diseconomies," *A.E.R.* (1943), p. 493.
64. Farrell, M. J. "Mr. Lancaster on Welfare and Choice," *E.J.* (1959), p. 588.
65. Farrell, M. J. "In Defence of Public-Utility Price Theory," *O.E.P.,* Vol. 10 (1958), p. 109.
66. Fisher, F. M. "Income Distribution, Value Judgments and Welfare," *Q.J.E.* (1956), p. 380.
67. Fisher, F. M., and P. B. Kenan. "Income Distribution, Value Judgments and Welfare: A Correction," *Q.J.E.* (1957), p. 322.
68. Fleming, J. M. "On Making the Best of Balance of Payments Restrictions on Imports," *E.J.* (1951), p. 48.
69. Fleming, J. M. "A Cardinal Concept of Welfare," *Q.J.E.* (1952), p. 366.
70. Fleming, J. M. "Cardinal Welfare and Individualistic Ethics, a Comment," *J.P.E.*, Vol. 65, No. 11 (1957), p. 355.
71. Frankel, S. H. " 'Psychic' and 'Accounting' Concepts of Income and Welfare," *O.E.P.,* N.S., Vol. 4, No. 1 (1952), p. 1.
72. Friedman, M. "Lerner on the Economics of Control," *J.P.E.*, Vol. 55, No. 5 (1947) p. 405.
73. Friedman, M. "A Reply," *J.P.E.,* Vol. 60, No. 4 (1952), p. 334.
74. Friedman, M. "The Welfare Effects of an Income Tax and Excise Tax," *J.P.E.*, Vol. 60, No. 1 (1952), p. 25.
75. Friedman, M. "What All Is Utility?" *E.J.* (1955), p. 405.
76. Frisch, R. "The Dupuit Taxation Theorem," *Econometrica* (1939), p. 145.
77. Frisch, R. "A Further Note on the Dupuit Taxation Theorem," *Econometrica* (1939), p. 156.
78. Gorman, W. M. "Tariffs, Retaliation and the Elasticity of Demand for Imports," *R.E.S.,* Vol. 25 (3), p. 133.
79. Gorman, W. M. "The Intransitivity of Certain Criteria Used in Welfare Economics," *O.E.P.,* N.S., Vol. 7 (1955), p. 36.

80. Gorman, W. M. "Are Social Indifference Curves Convex?" *Q.J.E.* (1959), p. 485.
81. de V. Graaff, J. "On Optimum Tariff Structures," *R.E.S.*, Vol. 17 (1), No. 42, p. 47.
82. de V. Graaff, J. "A Note on the Relative Merit of Taxes and Subsidies," *S.A.J.E.*, Vol. 15, No. 2 (1947), p. 149.
83. de V. Graaff, J. "Towards an Austerity Theory of Value," *S.A.J.E.*, Vol. 16 (1948), p. 35.
84. de V. Graaff, J. *Theoretical Welfare Economics*. Cambridge, England: Cambridge, 1957.
85. Haberler, G. "Some Problems in the Pure Theory of International Trade," *E.J.* (1950), p. 223.
86. Haberler, G. "Welfare and Freer Trade," *E.J.* (1951), p. 777.
87. Hare, A. E. C. "The Theory of Effort and Welfare Economics," *Economica* (1951), p. 69.
88. Haroldson, W. C. "A Note on Welfare Economics and Rationing," *Q.J.E.* (1943–1944), p. 146.
89. Harsanyi, J. C. "Welfare Economics of Varying Tastes," *R.E.S.*, Vol. 21 (3), No. 56, p. 204.
90. Harsanyi, J. C. "Cardinal Utility in Welfare Economics and in the Theory of Risk-Taking," *J.P.E.*, Vol. 61, No. 5 (1953), p. 434.
91. Harsanyi, J. C. "Cardinal Welfare, Individualistic Ethics and Comparisons of Utility," *J.P.E.*, Vol. 62 (1955), p. 309.
92. Henderson, A. "Consumer's Surplus and the Compensating Variation," *R.E.S.*, Vol. 8, No. 2, p. 117.
93. Henderson, A. "The Case for Indirect Taxation," *E.J.* (1948), p. 538.
94. Henderson, A. "Discussion of Social Choice Functions" [Abstracts], *Econometrica* (1953), p. 481.
95. Henderson, J. M., and R. E. Quandt. *Microeconomic Theory—A Mathematical Approach*. New York, McGraw-Hill, 1958.
96. Hicks, J. R. "The Foundations of Welfare Economics," *E.J.* (1939), p. 696.
97. Hicks, J. R. "The Valuation of the Social Income," *Economica* (1940), p. 105.
98. Hicks, J. R. "The Valuation of the Social Income. A Comment on Professor Kuznets' Reflections," *Economica* (1948), p. 163.
99. Hicks, J. R. *A Revision of Demand Theory*. Oxford: Clarendon Press, 1956.
100. Hicks, J. R. "The Rehabilitation of Consumer's Surplus," *R.E.S.*, Vol. 8, No. 2, p. 108.
101. Hicks, J. R. "The Generalized Theory of Consumers' Surplus," *R.E.S.*, Vol. 13 (2), No. 34, p. 68.
102. Hicks, J. R. "The Four Consumer's Surpluses," *R.E.S.*, Vol. 11, No. 1, p. 31.

103. Hicks, J. R. "Consumers' Surplus and Index Numbers," *R.E.S.*, Vol. 9, No. 2, p. 126.
104. Hicks, J. R. *Value and Capital, an Enquiry into Some Fundamental Principles of Economic Theory*. Oxford: Clarendon Press, 1939.
105. Hicks, J. R. "The Measurement of Real Income," *O.E.P.*, Vol. 10, No. 2 (1959), p. 125.
106. Hildreth, C. "Alternative Conditions for Social Orderings," *Econometrica* (1953), p. 81.
107. Hotelling, H. "The Relation of Prices to Marginal Costs in an Optimum System," *Econometrica* (1939), p. 151.
108. Hotelling, H. "A Final Note," *Econometrica* (1939), p. 158.
109. Houghton, R. "Consumer's Surplus and Discriminating Monopoly," *R.E.S.*, Vol. 26 (1), No. 69 (1958), p. 72.
110. Hunter, A. "The Monopolies Commission and Economic Welfare," *Manchester School* (January 1955), p. 22.
111. Hunter, A. "Product Differentiation and Welfare Economics," *Q.J.E.* (1955), p. 533.
112. Hurwicz, L. "Decentralized Resource Allocation" [Abstracts], *Econometrica* (1955), p. 342.
113. Inada, K. "Alternative Incompatible Conditions for a Social Welfare Function," *Econometrica* (1955), p. 396.
114. James, S. F., and W. Beckerman. "Interdependence of Consumers' Preferences in the Theory of Income Distribution," *E.J.* (1953), p. 70.
115. Johnson, H. G. "Optimum Welfare and the Maximum Revenue Tariffs," *R.E.S.*, Vol. 19 (1), No. 48, p. 28.
116. Johnson, H. G. "Optimum Tariffs and Retaliation," *R.E.S.*, Vol. 21 (2), No. 55, p. 142.
117. Johnson, H. G. Review of J. E. Meade, *The Theory of International Economic Policy, Vol. 1, The Balance of Payments, E.J.* (1951), p. 812.
118. Joseph, M. F. W. "The Excess Burden of Indirect Taxation," *R.E.S.*, Vol. 6, No. 3, p. 226.
119. Kahn, R. F. "Tariffs and Terms of Trade," *R.E.S.*, Vol. 15 (1), No. 37, p. 14.
120. Kaldor, N. "Income Burden of Capital Taxes," *R.E.S.*, Vol. 9, No. 2, p. 138.
121. Kaldor, N. "Community Indifference, a Comment," *R.E.S.*, Vol. 14 (1), No. 35, p. 44.
122. Kaldor, N. "A Note on Tariffs and the Terms of Trade," *Economica* (1940), p. 377.
123. Kaldor, N. "Welfare Propositions in Economics," *E.J.* (1939), p. 549.
124. Kaldor, N. "Risk Bearing and Income Taxation," *R.E.S.*, Vol. 25 (3), No. 68, p. 206.

125. Kemp, M. C. "Arrow's General Possibility Theorem," *R.E.S.*, Vol. 21 (3), No. 56, p. 240.
126. Kemp, M. C. "Welfare Economics: A Stocktaking," *Economic Record* (1954), p. 245.
127. Kemp, M. C. "The Efficiency of Competition as an Allocator of Resources," *C.J.E. & Political Science,* Vol. 21 (1955), I. External Economies of Production, p. 30; II. External Economies of Consumption, p. 217.
128. Kemp, M. C. "Technological Change, the Terms of Trade and Welfare," *E.J.* (1955), p. 457.
129. Kemp, M. C., and A. Asimakopulos. "A Note on Social Welfare Functions and Cardinal Utility," *C.J.E. & Political Science,* Vol. 18 (1952), p. 195.
130. Kenan, P. B., and F. M. Fisher. "Income Distribution, Value Judgments and Welfare: A Correction," *Q.J.E.* (1957), p. 322.
131. Kenan, P. B. "On the Geometry of Welfare Economics," *Q.J.E.* (1957), p. 426.
132. Kendrick, M. S. "Ability-to-Pay Theory of Taxation," *A.E.R.* (1939), p. 92.
133. Kennedy, C. M. "The Economic Welfare Function and Dr. Little's Criterion," *R.E.S.*, Vol. 20 (2), No. 52, p. 137.
134. Kennedy, C. M. "An Alternative Proof of a Theorem in Welfare Economics," *O.P.E.*, N.S., Vol. 6, No. 1 (1954), p. 98.
135. Klawe, K. W. Review of A. L. Macfie, *Economic Efficiency and Social Welfare, C.J.E. & Political Science,* Vol. 12, p. 105.
136. Konüs, A. A. "The Problem of the True Index of the Cost of Living," *Econometrica* (1939), p. 10.
137. Koo, A. Y. C. "Welfare and Direct Taxation," *C.J.E. & Political Science,* Vol. 21 (1955), p. 43.
138. Kozlik, A. "Conditions for Demand Curves whose Curves of Total Revenue, Consumers' Surplus, Total Benefit and Compromise Benefit Are Convex," *Econometrica* (1940), p. 263.
139. Kozlik, A. "Note on Consumer's Surplus," *J.P.E.*, No. 5 (1941), p. 754.
140. Kuznets, S. "On the Valuation of Social Income. Reflections on Professor Hicks' Article," *Economica* (1948), Part I, p. 1; Part II, p. 116.
141. Lancaster, K., and R. G. Lipsey. "The General Theory of Second Best," *R.E.S.*, Vol. 24 (1), No. 63, p. 11.
142. Lancaster, K. "Welfare Propositions in Terms of Consistency and Expanded Choice," *E.J.* (1958), p. 464.
143. Lancaster, K., and R. G. Lipsey. "McManus on Second Best," *R.E.S.,* Vol. 26 (3), No. 71 (1959), p. 225.
144. Lange, O. "The Foundations of Welfare Economics," *Econometrica* (1942), p. 215.
145. Lange, O. *The Practice of Economic Planning and the Optimal*

Allocation of Resources. Supplement to *Econometrica,* Vol. 17 (1949), p. 166.

146. Lazere, M. "Welfare Economics, A Misnomer" [A Communication], *A.E.R.* (1940), p. 346.
147. Lerner, A. P. "Theory and Practice in Socialist Economies," *R.E.S.*, Vol. 6, No. 1, p. 71.
148. Lerner, A. P. *The Economics of Control.* New York: Macmillan, 1946.
149. Lerner, A. P. "Discussions of Social Choice Functions" [Abstracts], *Econometrica* (1953), p. 482.
150. Levin, H. J. "Standards of Welfare in Economic Thought," *Q.J.E.* (1956), p. 117.
151. Lewis, W. A. "The Two-Part Tariff," *Economica* (1941), p. 249.
152. Lewis, W. A. "The Two-Part Tariff (A Reply to Mr. Rowson's Notes)," *Economica* (1941), p. 399.
153. Lipsey, R. G. "The Theory of Customs Unions, Trade Diversion and Welfare," *Economica* (1957), p. 40.
154. Little, I. M. D. "The Foundations of Welfare Economics," *O.E.P.*, N.S., Vol. 1, No. 2 (1949), p. 227.
155. Little, I. M. D. "Direct Versus Indirect Taxes," *E.J.* (1951), p. 577.
156. Little, I. M. D. "The Valuation of the Social Income," *Economica* (1949), p. 11.
157. Little, I. M. D. "Welfare and Tariffs," *R.E.S.*, Vol. 16 (2), No. 40, p. 65.
158. Little, I. M. D. Review of T. Scitovsky, "Welfare and Competition," *Econometrica* (1952), p. 703.
159. Little, I. M. D. "A Note on the Interpretation of Index Numbers," *Economica* (1949), p. 369.
160. Little, I. M. D. *A Critique of Welfare Economics.* 1st ed. Oxford: Oxford, 1950.
161. Little, I. M. D. *A Critique of Welfare Economics.* 2nd ed. Oxford: Oxford, 1957.
162. Little, I. M. D. "Social Choice and Individual Values," *J.P.E.*, Vol. 60, No. 5 (1952), p. 422.
163. McGarvey, D. C. "A Theorem in the Construction of Voting Paradoxes," *Econometrica* (1953), p. 608.
164. McKenzie, L. W. "Ideal Output and the Interdependence of Firms," *E.J.* (1951), p. 785.
165. McManus, M. "Comments on the General Theory of Second Best," *R.E.S.*, Vol. 26 (3), No. 71 (1959), p. 209.
166. Majumdar, T. "Armstrong and the Utility Measurement Controversy," *O.E.P.*, Vol. 9, No. 1 (1957), p. 30.
167. Malinvaud, E. "Capital Accumulation and Efficient Allocation of Resources," *Econometrica* (1953), p. 233.
168. Manne, A. S. "Multiple Purposes Public Enterprises—Criteria for Pricing," *Economica* (1952), p. 322.

169. Margolis, J. "Welfare Criteria, Pricing and Decentralization of a Public Service," *Q.J.E.* (1957), p. 448.
170. Marris, R. L. "Professor Hicks' Index Number Theorem," *R.E.S.*, Vol. 25 (1), No. 66, p. 25.
171. Meade, J. E. "Mr. Lerner on 'The Economics of Control,'" *E.J.* (1945), p. 47.
172. Meade, J. E. *The Theory of International Economic Policy*. Vol. 2, *Trade and Welfare*. Oxford: Oxford, 1955.
173. Meade, J. E., and J. M. Fleming. "Price and Output Policy of State Enterprise. A Symposium," *E.J.* (1944), p. 321.
174. Meade, J. E. *The Theory of Customs Unions*. Amsterdam: North-Holland, 1955.
175. Melville, L. G. "Economic Welfare," *E.J.* (1939), p. 549.
176. Metzler, L. A. "Tariffs, the Terms of Trade, and the Distribution of National Income," *J.P.E.*, Vol. 57, No. 1 (1949), p. 1.
177. Mishan, E. J. "The Principle of Compensation Reconsidered," *J.P.E.*, Vol. 60, No. 4 (1952), p. 312.
178. Mishan, E. J. "An Investigation into Some Alleged Contradictions in Welfare Economics," *E.J.* (1957), p. 445.
179. Mishan, E. J. "Realism and Relevance in the Theory of Consumer's Surplus," *R.E.S.*, Vol. 15 (1), No. 37, p. 27.
180. Mishan, E. J. "A Reappraisal of the Principles of Resource Allocation," *Economica* (1957), p. 324.
181. Mishan, E. J. "Arrow and the 'New Welfare' Economics, a Restatement," *E.J.* (1958), p. 595.
182. Mishan, E. J. "Rent as a Measure of Welfare Change," *A.E.R.*, Vol. 49, No. 3 (1959), p. 386.
183. Mishan, E. J. "Mr. Lancaster's Welfare Definitions. A Comment," *E.J.* (1959), p. 395.
184. Moore, D. A., and E. Schwartz. "Distorting Effects of Direct Taxation: A Re-Evaluation," *A.E.R.* (1951), p. 139.
185. Mulcahy (S.J.), R. E. "The Welfare Economics of Heinrich Pesch," *Q.J.E.* (1949), p. 342.
186. Musgrave, R. A. "Proportional Income Taxation and Risk-Taking," *Q.J.E.* (1943–1944), p. 388.
187. Myint, H. "The Classical View of the Economic Problem," *Economica* (1946), p. 119.
188. Myint, H. "The Welfare Significance of Productive Labour," *R.E.S.*, Vol. 11, No. 1, p. 20.
189. Myint, H. *Theories of Welfare Economics*. London: Longmans, 1948.
190. Myrdal, G. *The Political Element in the Development of Economic Theory*. London: Routledge & Kegan Paul, 1953.
191. Newman, P. "Mr. Lancaster on Welfare and Choice," *E.J.* (1959), p. 588.
192. Nordin, J. A. "The Marginal Cost Controversy: A Reply," *Economica* (1947), p. 134.

193. Norris, H. "State Enterprise, Price and Output Policy and the Problem of Cost Imputation," *Economica* (1947), p. 54.
194. Oort, C. J. *Decreasing Costs as a Problem of Welfare Economics.* Amsterdam: North-Holland, 1958.
195. Phipps, C. G. "Friedman's 'Welfare' Effects," *J.P.E.,* Vol. 60, No. 4 (1952), p. 332.
196. Pigou, A. C. "Comparisons of Real Income," *Economica* (1943), p. 93.
197. Pigou, A. C. "Real Income and Economic Welfare," *O.E.P.,* N.S., Vol. 3, No. 1 (1951), p. 16.
198. Pigou, A. C. "Some Aspects of Welfare Economics," *A.E.R.* (1951), p. 287.
199. Polak, J. J. " 'Optimum Tariff' and the Cost of Exports," *R.E.S.,* Vol. 19 (1), No. 48, p. 36.
200. Pole, D. "Pareto on the Compensating Principle," *E.J.* (1955), p. 156.
201. Poole, K. E. "Spending Tax, Problems of Administration and Equity," *A.E.R.* (1943), p. 63.
202. Radomysler, A. "Welfare Economics and Economic Policy," *Economica* (1946), p. 190.
203. Ramaswami, V. K. "Trade Imbalance, Gains from Trade and National Income Change," *E.J.* (1955), p. 450.
204. Reder, M. W. "Welfare Economics and Rationing," *Q.J.E.* (1942–1943), p. 153.
205. Reder, M. W. "Theories of Welfare Economics," *J.P.E.,* Vol. 58, No. 2 (1950), p. 158.
206. Reder, M. W. "Welfare Economics," in B. F. Haley (ed.), *Survey of Contemporary Economics,* Vol. 2. A.E.A., 1952.
207. Reder, M. W. *Studies in the Theory of Welfare Economics.* Oxford: Oxford, 1947.
208. Robbins, L. C. *The Theory of Economic Policy in English Classical Political Economy.* London: Macmillan, 1952.
209. Robertson, Sir Dennis. "Utility and All What? Part III," *E.J.* (1954), p. 675.
210. Robertson, Sir Dennis. "Utility, A Rejoinder," *E.J.* (1955), p. 410.
211. Robinson, H. W. "Consumer's Surplus and Taxation ex Ante or ex Post?" *S.A.J.E.,* Vol. 7 (1939), p. 270.
212. Rothenberg, J. "Marginal Preferences and the Theory of Welfare," *O.E.P.,* N.S., Vol. 5, No. 3 (1953), p. 248.
213. Rothenberg, J. "Conditions for a Social Welfare Function," *J.P.E.,* Vol. 61, No. 5 (1953), p. 389.
214. Rothenberg, J. "Welfare Comparisons and Changes in Taste" [Communications], *A.E.R.* (1953), p. 885.
215. Rothenberg, J. "Reconsideration of a Group Welfare Index. A Rejoinder on Marginal Preference," *O.E.P.,* N.S., Vol. 6, No. 2 (1954), p. 164.

216. Rothschild, K. W. "Monopsony, Buying Costs and Welfare Expenditure," *R.E.S.*, Vol. 10, No. 1, p. 62.
217. Ruggles, N. "The Welfare Basis of the Marginal Cost Pricing Principle," *R.E.S.*, Vol. 17 (1), No. 42, p. 29.
218. Ruggles, N. "Recent Developments in the Theory of Marginal Cost Pricing," *R.E.S.*, Vol. 2, No. 43, p. 107.
219. Ruggles, N. Review of B. P. Beckwith, *Marginal Cost Price Output Control, Econometrica* (1956), p. 501.
220. Samuelson, P. A. "Further Commentary on Welfare Economics, A Communication," *A.E.R.* (1943), p. 604.
221. Samuelson, P. A. "Evaluation of Real National Income," *O.E.P.*, N.S., Vol. 2, No. 1 (1950), p. 1.
222. Samuelson, P. A. *Foundations of Economic Analysis*. Cambridge, Mass.: Harvard, 1955, Chapter 8.
223. Samuelson, P. A. "Social Indifference Curves," *Q.J.E.* (1956), p. 1.
224. Sandee, J., and C. J. Van Eijk. "Quantitative Determination of an Optimum Economic Policy," *Econometrica* (1959), p. 1.
225. Schoeffler, S. "Note on Modern Welfare Economics" [Communications], *A.E.R.* (1952), p. 880.
226. Schultz, H. "A Misunderstanding in Index-Number Theory: The True Konus Condition on Cost of Living Index Numbers and Its Limitations," *Econometrica* (1939), p. 1.
227. Scitovsky, T. "A Note on Welfare Propositions in Economics," *R.E.S.*, Vol. 9, No. 1, p. 77.
228. Scitovsky, T. "Reconsideration of the Theory of Tariffs," *R.E.S.*, Vol. 9, No. 2, p. 89.
229. Scitovsky, T. "The State of Welfare Economics," *A.E.R.* (1951), p. 303.
230. Scitovsky, T. *Welfare and Competition, The Economics of a Fully Employed Economy*. London: Allen & Unwin, 1952.
231. Staehle, H. "Elasticity of Demand and Social Welfare," *Q.J.E.* (1939–1940), p. 217.
232. Stafford, J. "The Optimum Utilization of National Resources," *Econometrica*, Supplement to Vol. 17 (1949), p. 157.
233. Stigler, G. J. "The New Welfare Economics, A Communication," *A.E.R.* (1943), p. 359.
234. Strotz, R. H. "How Income Ought to Be Distributed: A Paradox in Distributive Ethics," *J.P.E.*, Vol. 66, No. 3 (1958), p. 189.
235. Theil, H. "Econometric Models and Welfare Maximization" [Abstracts], *Econometrica* (1954), p. 121.
236. Thirlby, G. F. "The Marginal Cost Controversy," *Economica* (1947).
237. Threlfell, R. L. "The Relative Merits of Taxes and Subsidies," *S.A.J.E.*, Vol. 15, No. 2 (1947), p. 149.

238. Timlin, M. F. Review of A. P. Lerner, *The Economics of Control, C.J.E. & Political Science,* Vol. 11 (1945), p. 285.
239. Timlin, M. F. Review of H. Myint, *Theories of Welfare Economics, C.J.E. & Political Science,* Vol. 15 (1949), p. 551.
240. Tinbergen, J. "The Influence of Productivity on Economic Welfare," *E.J.* (1952), p. 68.
241. Tintner, G. "A Note on Welfare Economics," *Econometrica* (1946), p. 69.
242. Tyszynski, H. "Economic Theory as a Guide to Policy: Some Suggestions for Reappraisal," *E.J.* (1955), p. 195.
243. Vickrey, W. "Some Objections to Marginal Cost Pricing," *J.P.E.*, Vol. 56, No. 3 (1948), p. 218.
244. Viner, J. *The Customs Union Issue*. New York: Anderson Kramer, 1950.
245. Wald, H. P. "The Classical Indictment of Indirect Taxation," *Q.J.E.,* Vol. 59 (1945), p. 587.
246. Weldon, J. C. "On the Problem of Social Welfare Functions," *C.J.E. & Political Science,* Vol. 18 (1952), p. 452.
247. Whittaker, E. "Wealth and Welfare, A Communication," *A.E.R.* (1940), p. 580.
248. Wilson, T. "The Inadequacy of the Theory of the Firm as a Branch of Welfare Economics," *O.E.P.,* Vol. 4, No. 1 (1952), p. 18.
249. Wiseman, J. "The Theory of Public Utility Price—An Empty Box," *O.E.P.*, Vol. 9, No. 1 (1957), p. 56.
250. Wiseman, J. "The Theory of Public Utility Price: A Further Note," *O.E.P.*, Vol. 11, No. 1 (1959), p. 88.

INDEX

INDEX

Allocation, *see* Resource allocation
Allocative rule, 23–28
Arrow, K. J., 20, 37, 47, 48, 50, 59–62, 78
Automobiles, consumer's surplus as index to benefits of, 275–283

Baldwin, R. E., 48
Bergson, A., 20–22, 59
Bickerdike, C. F., 33
Boulding, Kenneth, 102
Buchanan, James M., 191, 212, 223

Coase, R. H., 190, 191, 218–223
Community indifference curve, 33–35
  in resource allocation analysis, 121–127 *passim*
Community indifference map, 41–45, 82
Comparable welfare distributions
  defined, 126
Compensating variation, in consumer's surplus, 89–100 *passim*
Compensation tests, 38–45, 81
  role of, 62–63
Consumer's choice theory, 103–104
Consumers' surplus, 63–71, 81
  compensating variation and, 89–100 *passim*
  definitions of, 63–67, 110, 111

Consumers' surplus (*continued*)
equivalent variation and, 94–100 *passim*
as index to private transport benefits, 275–283
marginalism and, 63–64
Marshallian definition of, 110, 111
money measures of, 88–101
and rent, relationship between, 112–113
and transport economics, 275–283
See also Rent
Criteria, welfare, *see* Welfare criteria
Crusoe economy, 13, 17

Davis, R. G., 190, 214–218
Distribution
efficiency and, dichotomy between, 39–46
in Little's criteria, 166–168
Duesenberry, J. S., 73–74, 83, 197–199
Dynamic welfare analysis, 76–79, 83

Economic organization, 181
Economic rent, *see* Rent
Efficiency, distribution and, dichotomy between, 39–46
Ellis, H. S., 200–204
Envy, social, 74–75, 82, 84, 187–188, 197–200
Equilibrium theory, in external effects analysis, 184, 193–197
Equivalent variation, in consumer's surplus, 94–100 *passim*
Exchange optimum, 23–24
in resource allocation, 135–138
External effects, 180–224, 227–229
allocatively significant, 223
ambiguity of term, 182–183
area under study, establishment of, 188–189
correction for, 181–182
cost of optimal output realization, 190–191, 218–223
damages inflicted by output variations, 191–192, 218–223
distributional aspects of, 184–186, 193–197 *passim*
envy, 187–188, 197–200
equilibrium theory and, 184, 193–197
external to industry, 185–186, 190, 193–197 *passim*, 204–211, 214–218
classification of, 190, 204–214 *passim*, 223
infra-marginal, 223
interdependent-utilities as, 187–188, 197–199
internal to industry, 185–186, 189, 193–197 *passim*, 200–204
mutuality of, 217
nature of, 180–181

External effects (*continued*)
Pareto relevant, 223
partial analysis of, 188
pecuniary, 186, 193–197 *passim*
of production, 184–186
social value, loss of, 192–193, 218–223
technological, 186

Fellner, W., 200–204
Fisher, F. M., 293

Galbraith, J. K., 79
General equilibrium theory, 50–62, 195
Gorman, W. M., 52
Graaff, J. de V., 20, 33, 36–38, 77–80, 173, 196

Harrod, R. F., 38
Henderson, A., 32, 65, 89–91, 138–139
Hicks, J. R., 37, 39, 40, 45–53, 63–69, 71, 89–91, 94, 106, 107, 111, 122, 143, 144, 159, 160, 163, 169–172, 176
Hypothetical compensation
compensation tests, 38–45
contradictions in, 37–38

Incentive good, definition of, 104
Indifference curve, *see* Community indifference curve
Interdependent utilities, 73–76, 82
as external effects, 187–188, 197–199
Investment, and external effects, 194–197
Investment criteria, normalized, 284–310
assumptions of study, 286
with benefits regarded as collectible revenues, 299
choosing projects subject to budget constraint, 303–310
capital outlays, 304
Steiner's technique, departures from, 303
private competitive with public, 307–310
private noncompetitive with public, 304–307
private and public, method for encompassing both, 303–304
common capital outlay, 300–301
common terminal period, 300–301
conventional criteria compared with, 294–299
discounted value method, 284–286
identical ranking of investment streams, 286–290
implications of, 290–292
interest rate and, 293–294
internal rate of return method, 284–286
conventional compared

Investment criteria (*continued*)
with normalized, 294–299
reinvestment, 299–300
for single investment project, 292–293
without special reinvestment opportunities, 299
terminal value, 286–290

Johnson, H. G., 33

Kahn, R. F., 18, 25, 30–31, 33, 35
Kaldor, N., 33, 37–40, 45–53, 63, 71, 122, 143, 144, 159, 160, 163, 169–172, 176
Kennedy, C. M., 164, 172, 173
Knight, F. H., 90–94, 189, 201–204

Lancaster, Kelvin, 13, 72, 142, 144
Land, Ricardian concept of, 112
Lange, O., 20
Law
distribution of welfare and revision of, 229–230
external effects, 227–229
Pareto mixed outcome
in *n*-person model, 266–267
under permissive (L) law, 233–237
under prohibitive ($\overline{L}$) law, 238–241
and social costs, 244–251
total costs in implementing, 241–244, 255–256
Pareto single outcome, in *n*-person model, 266
period studied, length of, 227
permissive (L), 230–237
prohibitive ($\overline{L}$), 230–237
as starting point, 237–241
prohibitive ($\overline{L}$), switch to, 253–271
blackmail and, 257–260
compensation and, 253, 257–260
decision rules, cost of implementing, 255–256
equality in distribution of welfare and, 256
growth economist, implications for, 259–260
marginal utility and, 262–264
n-person model, 265–271
optimal outputs and, 253
redress for damages and, 256–260
separate facilities outcome and, 253–254
radical social change and, 254–255
separate facilities outcome, 253–254
in *n*-person model, 267–268

Law (*continued*)
under permissive (L) law, 235–237
under prohibitive ($\bar{L}$) law, 238–241
and social costs, 244–251
total costs in implementing, 241–244, 255–256
single-outcome bargaining
under permissive (L) law, 233
under prohibitive ($\bar{L}$) law, 238–241
and social costs, 244–251
total costs in implementing, 241–244, 255–256
single-outcome voting
in *n*-person model, 266
under permissive (L) law, 232–233
under prohibitive ($\bar{L}$) law, 237–241
and social costs, 244–251
total costs in implementing, 241–244, 255–256
social-costs applications of study, 244–251
total costs in implementing decision rules, 241–244
Lerner, A. P., 18, 30
Lipsey, R. G., 72, 142, 144
Little, I. M. D., 30, 32–37, 46–52, 69–71, 79, 81, 139, 140, 144, 158–161

Marshall, Alfred, 19, 33, 64–68, 109–112, 194
Meade, J. E., 33, 169, 204–211
Metzler, L. A., 77
Monopoly, 138
in allocative economies, 30–32
Myint, H., 63

Nationalization of industry, 81
New Welfare Economics, 37, 120–121, 158
welfare criteria in, 121–127 *passim*

Offer curve, 33–35
Optimality
allocative rule, 23–28
comparison between optimum plans, 129–135
exchange optimum, 23–24
factor-product adjustment, 26–27
free trade, 33–37
law and, 225–261
lower-level, 151
monopoly, 30–32
movement to, 143–144, 176–178
nonoptimality compared with, 130–135
occupational preference and, 26
perfect competition, 27–29
price equals marginal cost, 31–32
production optimum, 23–24
proportionality thesis, 25
tariffs, 33–37
taxation, 32–33

Optimality (*continued*)
theory of, survey, 17–38 *passim*
top-level, 24, 146–148, 151–152
uniquely determined in partial setting, 251–255
See also Pareto optimality; Second-best theory

Pareto optimality, 22–38 *passim,* 57, 62, 143, 157–179 *passim*
Pigou, A. C., 18–20, 31, 47, 63, 181, 187, 189, 190, 200–202, 211, 217, 219, 224, 251
Price, marginal cost rule for, 31–32
Pricing, discriminatory, 148–151
Private investment, *see* Investment
Private marginal products, value of (*VMP*), 181–182, 204–211
Private ownership, 189, 200–204
Private transport, benefits of, 275–283
Private value, 85
social value distinguished from, 20
Producer's surplus, Marshallian, 111
Production
external effects of, 184–186
optimum, 23–24
resource allocation and, 128–135
optimum, 135–138
Proportionality thesis, 25
Public investment, *see* Investment

Rationing, 148–151
Reder, M. W., 30, 76, 79–80
Rent, 200–204
consumer's surplus related to, 112–113
definitions of, 102–103
as economic surplus, 103–109
consumer's choice theory and, 103–104
individual indifference map, 105–107
Marshallian concept, 109–112
productive service of individual, 108–109
welfare increase, 107
in second-best theory, 148
See also Consumers' surplus
Resource allocation
allocative rule, 23–28
comparable welfare distributions, defined, 126
complete optimum, 128–129
community indifference curves, 121–127 *passim*
criteria, framework of, 119–120
criticisms of, 118–119
comprehensive criterion, 123
contradiction, possibility of, in, 123–127

Resource allocation (*continued*)
exchange optimum, value of, 135–138
fundamental role of, 118–119
"ideal," nature of, 128–129
interpersonal comparisons and, 133–135
Little's criteria and, 176–178
monopoly and, 138
optimum
complete, 135
lower levels of, 135–138
movement to, 176–178
nonoptimum plans compared with, 130–135
plans compared, 129–135
value of plans, 120
principles reappraised, 117–140
production conditions and, 128–135
production optimum, value of, 135–138
taxation and, 138–140
value judgments about distribution, 133–135
welfare criteria and, 118
Ricardo, David, 112
Robbins, L. C., 38, 46
Robertson, Sir Dennis, 164–165

Samuelson, Paul, 20, 37, 41, 50–59, 62, 70, 102–103
Scitovsky, T., 33, 37, 40, 41, 45–53, 122, 127, 143, 144, 160–161, 169, 176, 189, 193–197
"Scitovsky criterion," 47–49, 160
Second-best theory, 72–73, 81, 141–156
broad sectors, optimizing in, 155–156
community utility maximization, 146, 147
constrained sectors, free sectors and, 153–156
constraints, effects of, 147–148
discriminatory pricing, 148–151
exchange optimum, 146–148
first-best compared with, 144
individual utility maximization, 146
and lower-level optima, 151
optimizing and, 156
price-marginal cost ratio in, 152–155
production constraint, 151
production optimum, 146–148
quantities purchasable, constraints on, 148–151
rent, 148
role of, 156
taxation, 144
three-tier optimum scheme, 146–147
and top-level optima, 146–148, 151–152
utility and, 142–144, 146–147
See also Optimality
Social cost, 244–251

Social marginal products, value of (*SVMP*'s), 181, 188, 206–211
Social value, private distinguished from, 20
Social-welfare function, 59–63
  utility-possibility curve and, 50–59
Static welfare analysis, dynamic versus, 76–79
Steiner, P. O., 303
Stigler, George, 103
Stubblebine, William Craig, 191, 212, 223

Tariffs, incipient, 33–37
Taxation, 32–33, 208
  progressive income, 74, 83–84, 187–188
  and resource allocation, 138–140
  in second-best theory, 144
Top-level optimum, 24, 146–148, 151–152
Transport economics, consumer's surplus concept and, 275–283

Utilities, interdependent, 73–76, 82
Utility
  interpersonal comparisons of, 38
  in second-best theory, 142–144
Utility-possibility curve, 41, 50–59
Utopianism, piecemeal approach to, 46–50, 81

Welfare criteria, 37–63
  community indifference map, 41–45
  compensation tests, 38–45
  efficiency and distribution, dichotomy between, 39–46
  general equilibrium welfare, 50–62
  Little's, 46–50
    consistency, 169–173
    distribution, 166–168
    intransitivity, 173–175
    points Q_1, Q_2, and *H, J,* 159–166, 169–178 *passim*
    recent debate on, 157–178
    and resource allocation, 176–178
  in New Welfare Economics, 121–127 *passim*
  Paretian, 39, 43–44, 50, 57
  potential improvement, 121, 122
  resource allocation and, 118
  Samuelson's, 50–59, 62
  Scitovsky's, 40–46, 51–53
    "Scitovsky criterion," 47–49, 160
  social welfare function, 50–63
  transitivity, 169–173
  utility-possibility curve, 41, 50–59
  See also authors' names

Welfare economics
areas of development in, 157–159
criticisms of, 279–284
defined, 13
distribution of welfare, 14–15
economic egalitarianism facilitates, 83
empiricism, need for, in, 80
ethical judgments in, 14
future of, 84–86
lack of specialization, 11
lack of theory, 4
methodology, 15–17
propositions, testing of, 15–17
resource allocation, importance of, 117–118
survey method, 11–17
theoretical, 12
defined, 13
See also New Welfare Economics; specific entries
Whinston, A., 190, 214–218

Zero welfare elasticity, 112